Terry Tales 2

More stories of Litchfield, Minnesota

with

The History of Downtown Litchfield: The Next Thirty Years

By Terry R. Shaw

TERANDLO PUBLISHING

Cover design by Terry R. Shaw

Published by
Terandlo Publishing
1601 15th Avenue Southwest
Willmar, Minnesota 56201

Printed in the United States of America
Library of Congress Control Number: 2004097573
International Standard Book Number: 0-9744109-5-0

Copyright © 2004 by Terry R. Shaw, Willmar, Minnesota. All rights reserved.

Author's Note: As the information in *The History of Downtown Litchfield: The Next Thirty Years* deals with a historical subject, specific items of information are necessarily derived from many other sources, most notably old newspaper articles. I have attempted to give those sources the credit due them. However, the combination, layout and presentation of this information is original, copyrighted and may not be copied or reproduced in any form or medium without the express permission of the author. Anyone who feels that any item in these pages may have inadvertently breached their own copyright should advise the author at the email address torshaw@hotmail.com so that appropriate remedial action can be taken.

Table of Contents

	Dedications		
	Forward		
Chapter One	Up To Speed	Page	1
Lyric	Dreamers	Page	5
Chapter Two	Manannah Masquerader	Page	6
Chapter Three	Stories Of The Sioux Uprising – Part One	Page	9
Chapter Four	Stories Of The Sioux Uprising – Part Two	Page	16
Chapter Five	Stories Of The Sioux Uprising – Part Three	Page	23
Lyric	Ahead Of Me	Page	29
Chapter Six	I Read It In The Paper – Part One	Page	31
Chapter Seven	I Read It In The Paper – Part Two	Page	39
Chapter Eight	I Read It In The Paper – Part Three	Page	47
Lyric	Elmer McCurdy	Page	55
Chapter Nine	Brightwood Beach Memoirs – Part One	Page	58
Chapter Ten	Brightwood Beach Memoirs – Part Two	Page	64
Chapter Eleven	Mrs. Howard's Monument	Page	70
Lyric	Because Of You	Page	76
Chapter Twelve	The Great Willmar, Minnesota Raid – Part One	Page	77
Chapter Thirteen	The Great Willmar, Minnesota Raid – Part Two	Page	82
Chapter Fourteen	The Great Willmar, Minnesota Raid – Part Two	Page	87
Chapter Fifteen	Other Banks, Other Robberies – Part One	Page	91
Chapter Sixteen	Other Banks, Other Robberies – Part Two	Page	96
Lyric	Come And Get It	Page	101
Chapter Seventeen	Bald Headed Girls	Page	102
Chapter Eighteen	More Railroad Tragedies	Page	105
Chapter Nineteen	Do You Have A Stencil?	Page	109
Poem	A Toast	Page	114

Chapter Twenty	The Rosemary Home	Page	115
Chapter Twenty-One	Baseball and Litchfield – Part One	Page	120
Chapter Twenty-Two	Baseball and Litchfield – Part Two	Page	125
Lyric	Don't Complain	Page	130
Chapter Twenty-Three	I Remember	Page	131
Chapter Twenty-Four	The Baby Boomers	Page	137
Chapter Twenty-Five	Baby Boomer Toys	Page	140
Lyric	I Like To Sing	Page	147
Chapter Twenty-Six	The Bernatson Boys – Part One	Page	149
Chapter Twenty-Seven	The Bernatson Boys – Part Two	Page	154
Chapter Twenty-Eight	Prospecting For Babbit	Page	159
Lyric	It's Getting Late	Page	163
Chapter Twenty-Nine	Mosquito Days	Page	164
Chapter Thirty	Our First TV and Winky Dink	Page	167
Chapter Thirty-One	Bikes	Page	174
Lyric	Chicken Pluckers Jingle	Page	179
Chapter Thirty-Two	Letter Stories: Herbert	Page	180
Chapter Thirty-Three	Letter Stories: Dickey	Page	187
Chapter Thirty-Four	Letter Stories: Two Guys	Page	193
Chapter Thirty-Five	Letter Stories: The Askeroths	Page	201
Lyric	A Simple "I Love You"	Page	204
Chapter Thirty-Six	Art Krout – Part One	Page	205
Chapter Thirty-Seven	Art Krout – Part Two	Page	211
Chapter Thirty-Eight	Dennie's Chapter: The Missing Ingredient – Part One	Page	216
Chapter Thirty-Nine	Dennie's Chapter: The Missing Ingredient – Part Two	Page	222
Lyric	He Is The Key	Page	228
Chapter Forty	The Rockin' Shaws – Part One	Page	229
Chapter Forty-One	The Rockin' Shaws – Part Two	Page	237
Chapter Forty-Two	The Rockin' Shaws – Part Three	Page	245
Chapter Forty-Three	The Rockin' Shaws – Part Four	Page	253
Lyric	The Song Goes On	Page	260
Chapter Forty-Four	Lenora's Disappearance	Page	266
Chapter Forty-Five	Jerry and Edgerton	Page	270
Chapter Forty-Six	The Hoochy Coochy Show	Page	278
Lyric	Donna Sure Is Actin' Strange	Page	285
Chapter Forty-Seven	Moving The Bank	Page	286
Chapter Forty-Eight	Keep Litchfield From Dying - Part One	Page	292

Chapter Forty-Nine	Keep Litchfield From Dying - Part Two	Page	298
Lyric	The Sleep Song	Page	304
Chapter Fifty	The Highway Shooting	Page	305
Lyric	Excuses	Page	310
Chapter Fifty-One	The Night An Angel Was Born	Page	311
Chapter Fifty-Two	Bernie – Part One	Page	317
Chapter Fifty-Three	Bernie – Part Two	Page	322
Chapter Fifty-Four	Bernie – Part Three	Page	328
Lyric	The Child's Name Is Peace	Page	334
Chapter Fifty-Five	The Perfect Christmas Gift	Page	335
Poem	Her Hands	Page	344
Lyric	It Wouldn't Be Christmas (Without You)	Page	346
Poem	A Christmas Tradition Explained	Page	347
Chapter Fifty-Six	The Proposal	Page	349
Lyric	There's Always Someone Else	Page	352
Chapter Fifty-Seven	Three Wedding Songs – Part One	Page	353
Chapter Fifty-Eight	Three Wedding Songs – Part Two	Page	361
Lyric	Thank My Lucky Stars	Page	366
Chapter Fifty-Nine	Some Unattached Thoughts	Page	367
Chapter Sixty	Pete Hughes	Page	373
Lyric	Myself	Page	379
Chapter Sixty-One	The End	Page	380
Appendix	The History of Downtown Litchfield: The Next 30 Years	Page	383
	Orphans	Page	447
	Acknowledgements	Page	449
	About The Author	Page	451
Index		Page	453

Dedications

I dedicated my first book to my wife Lois, my brother Pat Shaw, and my grandson Ethan Ryan Peterson. All the reasons I gave in *Terry Tales* for dedicating that book to them still stand and I dedicate this book to them too. But I must add a few more people.

My brother Mick, the hero of the *Terry Tales* chapter called "Heart Heroes" and on whose coattails I rode into rock and roll history, is deserving of a dedication also.

My oldest brother Dennie, who led Mick and I into rock and roll[1], deserves a dedication. After all, he was a *Terry Tales* collaborator and contributed to this book also by writing another excellent chapter for me. Dennie drove me to excellence in my songwriting. He and I would collaborate on many songs long distance, he in Montana and I in Minnesota. We also had a healthy competition going in our individual songs. He'd write a song, mail it to me and I'd sit down and try to write a better one to mail back to him. We were honest critics of each other's work, making the work better.

Dennis, Terry, Mike and Pat Shaw

I dedicated *Terry Tales* to my grandson Ethan because his birth inspired me to write the book in the first place. I didn't want to leave this earth with my stories locked away in me. I wanted Ethan to know about his Rockin' and Rollin' Gramps.

Now I have a granddaughter. Ethan's little sister Karra Bree Peterson needs a dedication. I want her to remember Gramps as well.

---

[1] See Chapters Thirty-Seven through Forty, parts one, two, three and four of "The Rockin' Shaws".

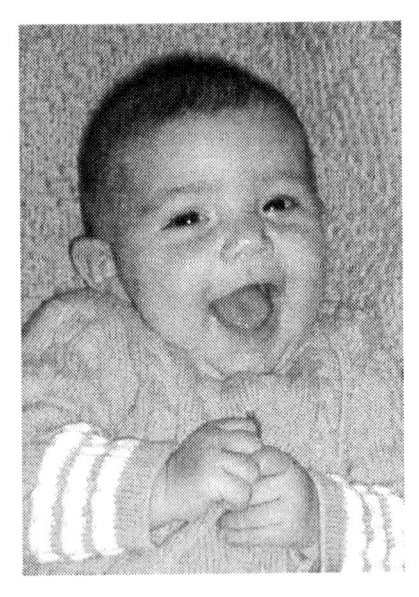

Karra Bree Peterson at three months and at five months below.

There's one more person I want to include in my dedications. This time it isn't a family member. I wrote a long piece about this person for this dedication page and then I decided that he needed to be told about in his own chapter. So I ask you to please read Chapter Fifty-Seven and learn why I want to dedicate this book to my good friend, the late Peter Allen Hughes.

Forward

It was suggested, in an anonymous letter I received after the publication of *Terry Tales*, that the book should have been called *Tattle Tales* instead. The letter reminded me that no one likes a tattletale. I felt bad about that. Everyone wants to be liked and I didn't set out to be a "snitch". I just wanted to entertain people with interesting stories.

Dona Brown, head of the Meeker County Historical Society at the GAR Hall in Litchfield, Minnesota at the time of the writing of the book, warned me that once my book came out I was going to cause a lot of arguments about the accuracy of stores' locations and so forth. Actually I only got a couple of letters correcting me or disputing something. The type of letters, besides the many I received offering me praise, that I received the most of, (a half dozen or so), were of the "bringing up things my family has been trying to live down for forty years" type.

I agonized over putting certain things in *Terry Tales*. As someone told me, "If you hadn't put the good stuff in, it would've been a dull book." I didn't just put things in the book to liven it up, though. I simply put things in as a reporter. I reported everything I could find about the town, its characters, individuals and the families I knew. Except in the case of newspaper accounts, I tried to use the journalists' "two source" policy, unless, of course, I was an actual witness or participant in an event. In my defense, the newspaper articles I got information from weren't always 100% accurate, I later found out.

However, some things did bother some people and if I hurt anyone in any way, that was never my intent. Some stories touched people, especially the ones about my mother and for that I am glad. That was my intent in writing the book. I also wanted to get stories down so they wouldn't be lost to future generations.

Why write a "sequel" to *Terry Tales*? Well, it turns out I didn't get every single story told. So many people came up to me and said, "I loved your stories about so and so, but did you know...or... you didn't tell the story about...or... you didn't even have so and so in your book at all." So, another book was almost thrust upon me. And, I only did the first one hundred years of Litchfield's existence as far as the buildings' histories were concerned, so I thought I should do the next thirty years, bringing the book up to date.

When I decided to write the "sequel", it was suggested that I expand on and include some of the best stories of *Terry Tales* in it. I've done that, so if you've read *Terry Tales* you might recognize a couple of the stories. I had already rewritten some of them for inclusion in some magazines such as *Good Old Days* and *Reminisce*.

Not all of the stories are just about Litchfield this time, but somehow they had a Litchfield connection, and all of the stories are again true. This time I don't think I've stepped on any toes. I hope that doesn't mean this book is dull. In *Terry Tales* I took the reader on a walk around town and let the stories unfold that way. They weren't necessarily in chronological order. In this book, I've decided to try to keep my stories in order, working my way from the days of the Sioux Uprising in 1862 to the present day.

I've written a lot of songs over the years. The lyrics to songs are actually poems. I decided to include some of that "poetry" in this book. There are several different ways to write poetry or lyrics. The most common format is one that you'll see I used quite a bit. It's called the "A A B A" format. The A is a verse and the B is a bridge or chorus. What's the difference between a bridge and a chorus? (Once a teacher, always a teacher...) A chorus is repeated throughout the song. It sometimes has the same melody as the verse. A bridge does what the name suggests. It forms a bridge between verses. It generally isn't repeated and ideally is a different song in it's own right, with a different melody. John Lennon and Paul McCartney were known to write bridges for each other's songs as in the song *A Hard Day's Night*. John wrote the body of the song, "It's been a hard day's night...", while Paul wrote the bridge, "When I'm home, everything seems to be right...".

I hope you enjoy my lyrics (without the music). I'll make a deal with you, however. If you'd like to hear the music with the lyrics, send me $3 to cover the expense of making the CD and for the postage, and I'll mail a home-recorded version of my songs to you. The address is the publisher address on the copyright page.

Terry R. Shaw

Terry Tales 2

More stories of Litchfield, Minnesota

By Terry R. Shaw

Chapter One
Up To Speed

If you haven't read *Terry Tales* (the first), I imagine I should bring you up to speed. I grew up in the fifties, a fact that'll be driven into your head by other chapters in this book about my being a Baby Boomer and such. The fifties and sixties were wonderful times, at least for me. People didn't make a lot of money back then, the average salary was under $3000 a year, but you didn't need a lot of money when you could buy a new car for $1000 and fill it up with gas for 30¢ a gallon. People saved money at the bank for a rainy day and repaired things themselves. In the fifties, you would rather fix something than buy a new one, what ever it was.

I grew up in a one-parent home. I came home from school to an empty house every day because my mother worked to raise her four boys on her own. When I watched *Ozzie and Harriet, Father Knows Best, Leave It To Beaver,* and *The Donna Reed Show*, I was jealous and I felt cheated. I thought to myself, "This is how life should be."

TV's *Father Knows Best*

On those TV shows, the mother stayed at home, all dressed up with her hair done and she had pearls around her neck. So, years later, when I started a family, I "asked" that my wife be a "stay at home mother" while I worked at two jobs. I guess, in the long run, that was a mistake and I was living in a dream world. But it wasn't totally my fault, you see.

There was something called "small town trust" back in the fifties. Mom never locked our house, except when we slept. And then, in the summer, the windows were left open all night. Very few people had air-conditioning. So the locked doors served no purpose.

1

People didn't lock cars back then and some, while they were in church or shopping, would even leave their keys in the ignition.

My oldest brother, Dennie, lived near Chicago in the seventies, and once when he visited me at my home in Glencoe, Minnesota, we decided to go out for pizza. As my kids were jumping into the car and Dennie and I were walking down my driveway, he turned to me and said, "Aren't you going to lock up?" referring to my house.

"What for?" I said, climbing into my car. "We'll be back in an hour." Who would bother my house? My neighbors would surely watch it for me and tell me if anything went wrong.

That's the way it was in the fifties and sixties too. Parents didn't worry so much about their kids because they knew if the kids were up to any mischief they would hear about it from some other adult, who probably would yell at the imps, "You kids knock that off and get home. I'm calling your mother." I never heard of a kid being abducted by some stranger back then either. I'm sure it happened somewhere, but not in my hometown, Litchfield, Minnesota.

If you fell off your bike or hurt yourself somehow, a couple of mothers would run out of their houses to see if you were all right. There were block parties and people lived in the same neighborhood for generations. We knew all of our neighbors and their families. The women in the neighborhood were our surrogate mothers or grandmothers. If my brother Pat and I were screwing around with friends at our house while Mom worked, we could be sure that Mrs. Alma Colman, to our south, Mrs. Mary Jensen, north of us, Mrs. Pat McCormick, to our east, or Kate Pierce or Grandma Ericson, west across the street, would tell Mom as soon as she got home. They would say, "I'm sure you're mother wouldn't want you kids doing that." And if we needed an adult for help, we'd run to them instead of bothering Mom at work.

Terry Tales was a tribute to my mother and Litchfield. Whenever I was asked to sign a copy of the book, I signed it "For the honor and glory of my mother and my hometown." I wanted people to know how my mother raised four little boys all by herself after our father had left us when I was three. Not getting any child support, Mom worked every day of the week, including Sundays, refusing to go on welfare. And I wanted people to know that. Although I told secrets and scandals about Litchfield, I really loved my hometown and thought it was the best place in the whole world to grow up in.

Terry Tales: Growing up in the fifties in Litchfield, Minnesota

with The History of Downtown Litchfield: The First 100 Years

By Terry R. Shaw

My hometown was full of characters whose stories I told about in the book, sometimes to the chagrin of their descendants. They couldn't see the forest for the trees, maybe? Finally, the book gave a history of Litchfield from its inception up to 1970. I researched that part mostly through the pages of the newspapers at the Meeker County Historical Society museum. There, now you are up to speed.

All my life, I've always been fascinated with the idea of time travel. When I was immersed in the pages of those old newspapers, reading every little story and looking at every business ad, there were times when I felt like I was back in the times I was reading about. It was a neat feeling. And knowing what I now know about the people in town, it was a little scary to read of beginning marriages I knew would end in heartbreak or the birth of a child I personally knew would one day get killed in an accident.

Gee, I would love to go walking down Sibley Avenue again in the fifties on a warm summer afternoon and slip into a booth at Fransein's Café for a Coke or onto a stool at Johnson's Drug for a Suicide phosphate or into a booth at the Traveler's Inn for a Mudball or onto Roscoe Keller's barber chair in his basement barbershop underneath the New Bakery, where the combined smells of fresh bread and Bay Rum just drove me crazy, or onto another stool at

Janousek's Eat 15¢ café for the cheapest and best hamburgers in all of Minnesota or buy a nickel bag of popcorn or a dime homemade Neapolitan ice cream sandwich at the corner popcorn wagon, where we'd ask for the "old maids" to chew on before they were thrown away, and listen to the city band give a concert in the bandstand[1] in the park or pay 20¢ to sit in the first seven rows at the Schnee brothers' Unique Theater and hold Jeanette Oliver's hand and watch a hokey monster movie or lay on the wooden loading platform in front of the Quonset hut at the Swift Avenue railroad crossing with my brother Pat and watch the trains switch boxcars. I can still smell the coal smoke, see the cinders in the air, hear the distinct sounds of empty boxcar couplings slamming into each other as the Great Northern steam engine pulled cars out of sidings at the Land O Lakes Powder Milk Plant, Cargill elevator and the lumber yard.

But I can't do any of those things again unless I slip back in time with my memories. Come along with me.

---

[1] The bandstand was torn down in May of 2001 and then rebuilt to look exactly as it had when it was first built. Today it doesn't have the green painted floor or side rails that it had when I was a kid.

Dreamers

 Dreams are a favorite subject for songwriters and poets. But, not wanting to be like everyone else, I tried to stay away from the subject. However, I found myself pulled to it. After all, I would say that I'm a dreamer, imagining "what if" many times in my life. If it weren't for dreamers like Edison, Ford and Einstein, we'd be living in a much different and darker world. My marriage to Lois and my retirement years have brought me to a time in my life when most my dreams and wishes are coming true. So, be a dreamer too. Yours might also come true.

Dreamers

Sometimes dreams come true.
If you want them to.
And dreams of love
are worthy of your time.

'Cause dreamers make things grow.
They reach for life's rainbows
and make a wish
that love they miss will shine.

Dreamers take the dark away.
They turn the night into the day.

So be a dreamer too.
And make your dreams come true.
In dreams of love,
to stars above you'll climb,
with other dreamers.

Chapter Two
The Manannah Masquerader

In the summer of 1858, eleven years before Litchfield became a town, a man named La-Roi Lobdell showed up in old Manannah.[2] He was "a hale fellow, well-met" who was not only a pleasant man especially liked by the youngsters, but La-Roi was a marksman and superb hunter. Add to the list his ability to play the violin and you can see that La-Roi was easily able to find work and a place to stay, boarding with one of the locals.

La-Roi didn't talk much about his past. He just said that he came from the state of New York and was looking for a better place to make a living as a hunter. He didn't tell that he had worked his way west by giving singing lessons along his way. He did reveal that he had spent some time in St. Paul in 1856, where he had met a fellow named Edwin Gribbel. The two hit it off and Gribbel hired La-Roi to guard his claim on the shore of Lake Minnetonka near what is now Minnetrista. A claim jumper had moved in nearby and Gribbel wasn't taking any chances. The two men "tramped together through the woods in pursuit of game."

Tiring of the poor hunting in the area, La-Roi told Gribbel he wanted to move on and settled for a payment of Gribbel's seventy-five dollar rifle. Lobdell headed west to the Kandiyohi Lake area and was again hired to guard a claim while living with another hired guard in a cabin on the old Kandiyohi townsite north of Kasota Lake. The men were hired by Minneapolis investors who were going to start building what they thought would become the Minnesota state capital. That winter their provisions ran out and the two lived on squirrel that La-Roi shot. When summer came, La-Roi Lobdell moved on to Manannah.

One day La-Roi's "secret" got out. Secret? Yes, La-Roi Lobdell was secretly Lucy Ann Lobdell. If they would've had electric fans back then, something brown would've hit it at that point, if you know what I mean. The local citizens were outraged that a woman had been fooling them and earning a man's wages. Meeker County Attorney William Richards filed charges of "one Lobdell, being a woman, falsely impersonates a man, to the great scandal of the

---

[2] The townsite was moved to its present location in 1871.

community and against the peace and dignity of the State of Minnesota." Lucy was acquitted, however, as there wasn't and still isn't a law against a woman wearing a man's clothing. But Lucy was politely, yet forcefully told to leave the county and "go home". Except for her rifle, she had nothing to her name, so she was made a ward of the county and given money for transportation back to Long Eddy, New York where her parents lived. That was the last Manannah saw of its "Wild Woman" as Lucy had become to be known.

Lucy had grown up among lumberjacks and hunters, who had taught her how to shoot and track animals. One day, she wandered off and returned a couple of days later dragging a panther behind her. Before long, Lucy added 150 deer, 11 bears, and a few wildcats and foxes. She told of "hand-to-paw" combats with wounded bear. A legend was born.

A raftsman named Henry Slater (also given as George Washington Slater) came along one day and made twenty-six year old Lucy a proposition.
"I'll take you on in a shootin' match and if I win, you become my wife."
Unable to back down from a man's challenge, Lucy accepted and then proceeded to lose to the filthy, unkempt man. But, true to her word, she married Henry, who moved her to Pennsylvania, impregnated her and then left her. While she was pregnant, Lucy wrote her autobiography in which she told of her plan to abandon the baby and dress as a man in order to get better wages. "As a man, I can travel freely though unprotected and find work," she wrote. Being capable of "doing men's work, and getting men's wages, I resolved to try...to get work among strangers." Lucy also wrote of the inequality of pay for woman. The book was published in 1855 under the title of *Narrative of Lucy Ann Lobdell, The Female Hunter of Delaware County.*
After a baby girl was born, Lucy named her Helen, put her in the Almshouse in Delhi, New York and then set out for the bountiful west she had heard stories about.

Back in New York, disgraced and humiliated, Lucy was surprised to find Slater back wanting to "try it again". Lucy turned him down and wandered around, continuing to dress as a man. She met and fell in love with another "Wild Woman" named Marina Perry. Lucy changed her name to Reverend Joseph Lobdell and called herself a minister. She and Marina married themselves to each other and lived together in a cave in the woods for about twelve years, eating roots and berries. When the "marriage" broke up, Lucy starting losing her sanity and she once again wandered the streets. She was arrested several times as a vagrant and a nuisance, eventually being placed in the Ovid Asylum after having a "maniacal attack".

The *New York Times* mistakenly published Lucy's obituary in October of 1879. Some reports said that she had faked her own death to be left alone. She died in the Binghamton Psychiatric Hospital in May of 1912 and was buried in a potter's field.

In 1883, the British medical journal *Alienist and Neurologist* published an article about Lucy and used the term "Lesbian" for the first time ever. Maybe that is the Manannah masquerading "Wild Woman's" legacy. Her great-great-great granddaughter is also named Lucy and today is an Air-Traffic Controller in the military in Hawaii.

Chapter Three
Stories of the Sioux Uprising – Part One

My hometown of Litchfield didn't officially come into being until 1869. But people were settling in the area long before that. The first settler was Benjamin Dorman. Patrick Joseph Casey, Sr. came to Meeker County in 1856 and settled near Darwin on a piece of land next to a lake. Of course, the lake was named Casey Lake. There Patrick started a farm and a family; his son Daniel being the first white male born in Darwin Township. Patrick was friendly with the Indians. His friendship began when he caught a couple of braves stealing some rutabagas from his garden. The braves had been camped out on the shores of the lake.

"There's no need to take them from me," Patrick told them. "You can have all that you want. Come to my house. Let's see if my wife (Mary Hughes) can find you something better to eat."

The Indians took an immediate liking to Casey and on one visit they sat in his kitchen and offered him and Mary their peace pipe. One day Patrick's Indian friends came hurriedly to him. They appeared agitated and tense.

"You must leave your home," they told Patrick. "Soon our brothers will come here and they will kill you and your family if you are still here. They say the white man must leave our land."

Patrick believed his friends. He took his family to the county seat of Forest City, six miles northeast of Litchfield. Four-year-old Daniel was instructed to care for the milk cow. The stockade at Forest City was only in the beginning stages, not quite built, so after three days, Casey and his family continued on to St. Anthony[3].

Nels Danielson, who came to the area by covered wagon in the spring of 1857, had almost daily visits from the local Indians and they got along fine also. The braves had a camp by Hope Lake near where Hans Jensen lived. Chief Cut Nose[4] used to come to Nels' farm to sharpen his hunting knife[5] on the Danielson grindstone and whetstone. Chief Cut Nose was the local chief and he had acquired

---

[3] Minneapolis, Minnesota.

[4] Marpiya Okinajin was his Indian name.

[5] Dr. Donald Dille, father of my classmate Senator Steve Dille, was known to have possession of the knife. I'm sure Steve has it today

the name because one of his nostrils had been bitten or cut off in one of his numerous fights with other tribes.

Nels would sharpen knives for the Indians and give them food, whenever he could spare any. It was understood that Chief Cut Nose should not steal from Danielson and he didn't.

Chief Cut Nose

William Worral Mayo

Chief Cut Nose had an encounter with a man whose name will live on forever in Minnesota. Dr. William Worral Mayo, who together with his sons William James and Charles Horace Mayo founded the Mayo Clinic in Rochester, Minnesota, was living in Le Sueur at the time. While making a sick call on horseback, Dr. Mayo was crossing one of the tributaries of the Minnesota River when three drunken braves waded out from the brush on the bank and demanded his horse. The doctor refused to give the horse up, telling the braves that he was on a mission of mercy. Surprised by his stubbornness and bravery, the Indians let him ride away. One of the braves, of course, was Cut Nose.

On Sunday, August 17, 1862 in nearby Acton Township, which is by Grove City, four Sioux from Rice Creek were out hunting for food. They stopped near Robinson Jones' cabin, which doubled as a store, and saw some eggs in a hen's nest by Jones' fence. One of the Indians bent over and picked up one egg.

"No," said another brave, "Don't take that. It belongs to the white man."

"I don't care. I'm hungry," replied the Indian with the egg.

"Put it down, quickly."

The other Indian threw it onto the ground, breaking it. "There," he said, "Now no one eats it. You are a coward. You are starving and you are afraid to take one egg from the white man because you fear him."

"I do not fear the white man," spat back the Indian. "Come with me. I will show you. I will kill the white man."

With that, he climbed over the fence and marched towards the cabin, followed by the other three. When they got to the cabin, they asked for liquor. Jones, the local postmaster, had a barrel of whiskey on hand but he refused the young Indians. After all, it was Sunday and besides he didn't think it was a good idea to give alcohol to some young armed Indian braves. Words were exchanged but Robinson held his ground, the Indians turned and left, and nothing came of the incident.

"Why didn't you kill the white man?" the young brave was asked by his companions.

"I have a plan..." came back the answer.

Meanwhile, Jones and his wife, the widow Ann Baker, left their adopted daughter Clara Davis Wilson, who was also their niece, to watch her little baby brother while they went to Ann's son Howard Baker's cabin, which was less than half a mile away on the same piece of land. It was their normal Sunday afternoon visit.

On the way to Baker's cabin, Ann and Robinson noticed the Indians, who had demanded the liquor, following them. But they seemed friendly enough. In fact, when they all reached Baker's place, the entire group entered into a discussion about hunting and marksmanship. Another neighbor named Viranus Webster joined the group along with his wife and two children. It was decided to have a contest to prove who could shoot better, the whites or the Indians. A large white oak tree was selected as the target. The Indians shot first and then reloaded their rifles as the white men were shooting.

Suddenly, as if the whole thing had been planned, the Indians turned on the settlers, who now had empty rifles, killing Baker, Webster, and Robinson Jones and his wife Ann. In fact, a story was told that previous to the whole event, the young Indian men had been arguing about who was the bravest and they had decided to do the shooting to show each other their daring. No doubt they had wanted the liquor to bolster their bravery. Howard's wife, Mrs. Webster and the children ran and hid. The Indians didn't pursue them. Instead they retraced their steps to the Jones' cabin where they saw Clara standing at the window. She was wondering what all the shooting was all about. The Indians shot Clara but not her baby brother, who they didn't see inside the cabin.

Mrs. Webster and Ann Baker ran to the Nels Olson home and told of the shooting. Then they continued on to Forest City. Olson alerted his neighbor Nels Danielson who was four miles to the west of the Baker place. Danielson got some other settlers, they armed themselves, and they went to investigate. At the Baker farm, eighteen-year-old Hans Evenson[6] was the first to discover the bodies. The men buried the dead in one grave at the Ness Lutheran Church cemetery and then they went to get their families to go to Forest City for protection.

While at his house, Nels heard shots being fired at his neighbor Anders or Andreas Olson's place. It was just fifty rods away. Sensing what was taking place and that the Indians were close by, Nels gathered his family and grabbed a few possessions including a single feather mattress with ticking, which was a luxury in the days of straw beds. He rolled the mattress up, strapped it to his back and he and his family took off into the woods, heading for Forest City. They ran and ran for their lives, never really seeing Indians but knowing they were close by. When they stopped to rest, Nels took the mattress off his back and only then discovered that there was an arrow sticking out of it. The mattress had saved his life.

It was later discovered that Olson and his family had been killed at their farm.

Swedish immigrant Peter J. Lund, who had recently been inducted into the Union Army, was walking with a couple of other men when they came across a small group of Indians. The Indians weren't hostile but were acting quite nervous. They were armed but said that they were hunting deer. The two groups parted company with no incident.

Lund had also been friendly with the Indians. He had even bought an Indian pony from them. The pony didn't like the Indians because they had been cruel to it. So, the horse was always running away. The Indians decided to sell or trade him and they approached

---

[6] He later did sentry duty at the Forest City stockade.

Lund about the horse. Peter didn't have any problems with the horse, so he bought it.

Peter had come to America and started out in Moline, Illinois. He and others decided to "go west" and they ended up in St. Anthony, which is present day Minneapolis. The group went further west to stake a claim of land and, in the spring of 1857, they finally settled in an area by a lake that is today called Lund Lake, close to Acton Township. Peter's daughter Sarah was born there in 1858, becoming the first white girl born in the township.

Upon arrival in Acton, Lund's group heard of the massacre and wondered if they hadn't come across the Indians involved and narrowly escaped with their lives. Lund decided to take his family to Forest City where the stockade was near completion[7].

The same day as the attack at Acton, a meeting of some of the settlers was being held in the morning at Nels Elofson's[8] house. The purpose of the meeting was to find three men to go off into service in the Union Army. Swede Grove Township was required to fill the draft quota made on it by the government. Nels Elofson was the grandfather of Gladys Elofson, who married Litchfield baker Wayne Rayppy[9]. Nels was the second white man in Meeker County. At about ten o'clock in the morning, Nel's neighbor's children came to the house and informed their father, Mr. Monson, and the other settlers there that Indians were about in the area. They were frightened and wanted to stay. Monson and Swan Nelson went to see what the trouble was. Along the way, they met some Indians on horseback. One of the Indians reached down from his horse and grabbed Nelson by the whiskers. Then he pointed to the east. Swan

---

[7] It was completed on September 3, 1862 under the direction of Ole Halvorson Ness, a veteran of the Norwegian Army.

[8] Born in 1834, Nels came to America from Sweden in 1857. In January of 1870, he returned to Sweden and brought three hundred emigrants back to Minnesota with him. Nels was the first postmaster of Swede Grove Township and he held that office for seven years. From 1872 to 1876 he was in the agricultural implement business at 23 Second Street East. It was the site of Dick Baldwin's TV repair shop and is a parking lot today behind Mutt's. Nels was also a Justice of the Peace at one time.

[9] Rayppy had bakeries in Litchfield from November of 1933 to April of 1964. All of them were called the "New Bakery". The first was where Nicola's is today and the last was where Re-Max is today. At one time Wayne Rayppy owned two bakeries in town.

13

didn't understand what the Indian was trying to tell him. They parted company peacefully.

The Indians stopped at Elofson's, who knew several of them. They told Nels that they were on their way to the "Big Woods" for the purpose of killing some Chippewas who, they said, had been killing the whites. They then rode off. Before long news of the murders of the Jones and Baker families got to Nels and in the evening he and Nels Hanson went to the scene of the murders where others had gathered before their arrival. There they learned the details of the attack and were told to come back the next morning to help bury the dead, which they did. While they were there, nine Indians came in sight and several shots were exchanged, but no one was hurt. Elofson returned to his home and helped to start his own and all neighboring families for Ripley (now Litchfield).

When the settlers returned to their homes later, they found that the Sioux had burned down most of the houses, except for a couple. They were the homes of men who had been friendly with the Indians and even had bothered to learn their language. Their homes had been "protected" by a yellow feather on a stake in the ground out front. The Sioux had placed it there meaning "friend to Indian, leave alone."

The four young Indians, who had done the shooting, stole four horses and went south to their village forty miles away in the Lower Agency on the Minnesota River. They told their chief what they had done. The crowd, which had gathered around them, insisted on going to Little Crow's village and asking him to lead them into war against the whites.

When Chief Little Crow[10] heard what they had done, he told them "No!"

"Then we will fight anyway, even if you are afraid to," Little Crow was told.

"You are fools," Little Crow told them. "You will be hunted down like rabbits in the winter." Finally, he decided that it was "kill or be killed".

---

[10] Little Crow was born in about 1810 with the name Tayoyateduta, "Ta-Oyate-Duta" or (His Red Nation or People). He was born in the Mdewakanton Dakota village of Kaposia (near the "Dayton's Bluff" area of St. Paul). He was the eldest son of Cetanwakuwa (Charging Hawk). It was on account of his father's name, mistranslated Crow, that he was called "Little Crow" by the whites. Both his father and grandfather had been leaders of the Kaposia band of the Dakota or Sioux tribe.

"You are fools, but I am not a coward. I will die with you." With those words, the Sioux Uprising of 1862 officially started. Little Crow gathered all the chiefs together and they decided the time was right to rid their land of the invading white men.

Chief Little Crow

Chapter Four
Stories of the Sioux Uprising – Part Two

Peter Lund and his family arrived at Forest City with the Indian pony and corralled it with the other horses just outside the stockade in a fenced area. There were now two hundred and forty settlers assembled inside the stockade. They knew they needed more help and they decided someone should ride to the State Capitol in St. Paul with a letter to the Governor asking for help.

The Capitol was about a hundred miles or more on horseback through Indian country. Fifty-nine year old Jesse Branham, Sr. was the only person to volunteer to go. Looking like an Amish Santa Claus, Branham, Sr. didn't look the part of a "pony express" rider or hero. But his stern face showed that he wasn't one to be messed with. At 6am on Wednesday, August 20th, 1862, he took off on his famous ride.

Jesse V. Branham, Sr.

Nils Axel Viren had a homestead near Eagle Lake in Kandiyohi County. His last name was really Werin, but he changed it to Viren when he came to America from Sweden in 1855. He was on his way to Forest City with his wife Hedvig and children, which included young Frank, baby Josephine, and Nils' widowed mother-in-law Stina Greta Sandstrom and her children. They were all packed onto a cart pulled by two oxen. They had forty slow miles to cover and no roads to follow, only Indian trails.

When the group arrived at a crossing over the Crow River, a lone Indian approached them and demanded an ox. He said he would kill it and take it anyway if they attempted to cross the Crow River. Nils didn't want to give up the ox and he wanted to get his family to the safety of Forest City, so he crossed the river anyway, thinking the brave' wouldn't do anything as he was outnumbered, even if it was mostly women and children.

The Indian, true to his word, shot and killed one of the oxen. When some of his comrades arrived, they started butchering the ox. Nils and his family were surprisingly allowed to continue on. A little further on they came upon a neighbor lying wounded outside of his burned cabin. They loaded him on their cart and continued on.

Nils had gotten along with the Indians previously. Many times they had come to his cabin hungry and he had allowed them to help themselves to his food. They didn't like his salt pork, however, and threw it on his dirt floor, thinking it had gone bad. The Indian women were fascinated with baby Josephine. On two occasions, they took her away to show her off at their village and then returned her to Hedvig unharmed.

The Virens moved to Litchfield in the early 1800s and lived at 308 Marshall Avenue South. When Nils' son Frank finished Business College in Minneapolis, he came back to Litchfield, married Rose Lenhardt, and managed the Lenhardt Hotel. In June of 1908, Frank joined up with Nathan Johnson and started a clothing store next door to the hotel. They originally called their store Frank and Nate's, but later changed it to Viren-Johnson.

After Nate died, Frank Viren had the store by himself. In August of 1945, Frank, despondent over slipping sales because of his inability to get clothing items because of the war, left the store, went home, walked into his bathroom with his shotgun and blew a hole in his chest. His widow Rose sold the store to Frank's friend and fellow worker Arthur L. "Art" Tostenrud in September of 1945. Art left the store name Viren-Johnson, as did Don Larson, who bought Tostenrud out in 1962 and Jerry Tierney, a classmate of my older brother Dennis, who owned it next. Jerry Tierney closed the doors for the last time in February of 1989. The store had been called Viren-Johnson under different owners for eighty-one years, even though Johnson had died early on and Frank's widow had sold it in 1945.

News of the Indian Uprising spread like wildfire from Meeker County all across our young state. Everyone was in a panic. On Wednesday, August 20th, 1862, while Jesse Branham, Sr. was riding to St. Paul for help, a boatload of soldiers was on its way up the Minnesota River from St. Paul to New Ulm. Bored or in a effort to frighten off any Indians who might think of ambushing them from the

17

shore, the soldiers began discharging their muskets over and over into the shore's brush and trees. The boat was just past Henderson and heading for Le Sueur. Shooting blindly into the dense green growth along the shore, the soldiers wounded a little boy, Cyrus McEwen, in the leg. Cyrus had rushed to the shore from his father's farm to see what all the shooting was about.

On the Ottawa township farm of young Edward Gleek along the river, Gleek's hired man Jean LaRue, who had recently come to the area from France, panicked on hearing the approaching gunfire. He was in fear for his life after hearing all of the stories of what the dreaded savage Indians would do to him if they caught him. He ran back to the farmhouse where he grabbed his rifle, bullet pouch and powder horn, and some of his belongings. Especially important to him were his daily journal and his life savings of $783.50. He had been saving his earnings in hopes of one day buying his own piece of land to settle on.

Jean remembered a gigantic white oak tree in the nearby woods. It was partially dead and Jean had discovered that the bottom part of the tree was hollow. The hollow part started several feet above the ground and went on for about fifteen feet straight up until the hollow part ended at a large opening. The branches of the tree hid the opening, which Jean had surmised could accommodate the size of an adult man. It would make the perfect hiding spot. The savages would never discover him there.

LaRue ran to the tree and scrambled up to the opening. There he carefully lowered himself and his rifle into the hollow tree. What Jean hadn't counted on was how wet and slick the dead wood inside the tree was. He slid all the way down to the bottom of the hollow part. Realizing his mistake, he tried to pull himself back up to the opening. But, with only enough room inside so that he could just bring his hands up to his face, it was impossible. Afraid to yell for fear of alerting the Indians, he resigned to himself that he would have to at least wait out the day and then hope that his boss Mr. Gleek would come looking for him.

Fifty-seven years later, a very old Edward Gleek, still living on the same farm in the summer of 1919, decided to finally clear the small woods by his farm for the added acreage. He hired some men to do it. When the men cut down the gigantic white oak, which crashed to the ground with a thud, a hollow part broke open. To their horror, they saw the mummified body of a man. He wasn't decayed at all, just dried and shriveled like an Egyptian mummy. The men summoned Mr. Gleek.

Edward immediately recognized his former hired man by his clothing and hair. Inside his pockets were the $783.50 and the journal. Gleek opened the book carefully to the last entry, which was undated, but it followed the Friday, August 29, 1862 entry.

"Can not get out," the entry read. "Surely must die. If ever found send me and all my money to my mother, Madam Suzanne LaRue, near Tarascon, in the province of Bouches, Du Phone, France."

Jean had survived at least nine days in his slimy tomb of wood, which had preserved his body, not allowing it to decay. To add to Jean's misery, his body, not aware of Jean's predicament, must have caused Jean to urinate and defecate on himself, adding to his discomfort. Being claustrophobic myself, I can't imagine the horror he went through in his last nine plus days on this earth. At least being buried alive, you would eventually suffocate and pass out to a peaceful death. At some point, Jean must have thought about suicide. But, in his tight quarters, he couldn't raise his musket, let alone try to load it with powder and a shot. All he was able to do was carefully pull his journal out of his pocket, raise it up to his face, pull out his pencil, tucked away in the binding, and slowly record his thoughts and wishes in the last agonizing week of his life.

Back to the Forest City Stockade. It had been Jesse Branham, Sr.'s son Jesse, Jr.'s idea to build the stockade for protection against the Indians. The stockade had been begun before the uprising but it wasn't quite finished when the Indians had begun attacking the settlers. The majority of the stockade went up in one day, on September 3rd. Luckily there were logs close by that were going to be used to build a church and a road. The settlers hurriedly put the stockade up with about 1200 logs. While his father rode to St. Paul, Jesse, Jr. rode around the county like Paul Revere alerting settlers that the Indians were attacking. Like his father, Jesse, Jr. didn't look the part of a hero. Meek looking, he could pass for a scholarly professor or a banker.

Jesse V. Branham, Jr.

The following day, Jesse, Sr. arrived in St. Paul at 1am, and he delivered his message to Governor Ramsey. Ramsey gave Captain George C. Whitcomb the responsibility along with seventy-five muskets and ammunition. Thirty-one muskets were dropped off in Hutchinson on the 22nd, because the town pleaded for help.

Whitcomb arrived in Forest City on the 23rd. He knew the Indians were preparing to ambush Captain Strout's troops, so on September 2nd, he asked for volunteer scouts to warn Strout. Three men, Jesse V. Branham, Jr., Thomas G. Holmes, and Albert H. Sperry, stepped forward. The volunteers encountered Indians the next day. A fight started. Jesse, Jr. stopped to reload his rifle and was shot in the chest. The bullet passed through his lungs, and came out his back. He never fell and he was able to walk instead to his team of horses and go for help. A doctor was summoned after Jesse collapsed at a farmhouse.

"I can do nothing for this man," the doctor said, after taking one look at Jesse. "Make him as comfortable as you can. He'll be dead in three hours."

Obviously, he was wrong. Jesse, Jr. lived long enough to become Litchfield's first mayor[11] and also see his son, Hiram S. Branham, become the mayor of Litchfield in 1889. Hiram, a founder of the Brightwood Beach resort, then committed suicide because he was involved in a bank scandal. He has since been left off Litchfield's list of mayors.

---

[11] The position was first called the President of the Village Council.

Not everyone went to Forest City for protection. Some settlers only heard rumors of the Indian Uprising and stayed put on their land. Charles McCune had built a small house on a hill overlooking the Crow River in Union Grove Township. Charles did something unusual for the times when he built his house. He put in a back door. Doors and windows were used sparingly in the pioneer days as they were costly and were places to lose much needed heat in our cold winters. Charles was out working in his field and his wife was in the house cooking his noon dinner. She had the back door open as it was a warm morning and her cooking made her kitchen warmer.

Mrs. McCune glanced up from her work and noticed a small group of Indians approaching the house on the back door's side. They had war paint on their faces. Her immediate thoughts were to get her small baby in the other room and run for it, but she realized she would only make the Indians pursue her. Instead she went to the rear door and greeted the Indians with some food.

"Please come into my house and share my food," she said to the braves, smiling and holding out some great smelling fresh bread. The Indians grabbed the food and devoured it, following her into the house. No doubt they were very hungry.

"Please sit," she said, pulling out a chair. The Indians understood and sat down while Mrs. McCune hustled around the kitchen serving them everything she could find. The baby in the next room gave out a muffled cry and the Indians hardly looked up from their eating as the white woman went into the next room. There she picked up her baby and quietly slipped out the front door. The Indians were used to white men's houses with only one door so they never thought to check on the lady.

The terrified lady ran down the hill to where her husband and some other men were mowing hay.

"There's a war party of Indians in our house Charles," she yelled, running up to her husband. Wiping his brow, it took only a few seconds for Charles to grasp the situation. He ran over to the other men, talked briefly and then grabbed his wife and baby and they took off running on the trail to Manannah, five miles to their east. Along the way, they warned all the settlers they could find. David Hoar and Jeremiah Leaming were two of them. Fortunately most were in their homes at the time eating their noon meal. They all grabbed their guns, hitched up their wagons, threw in some possessions and started a wagon train to Manannah.

Back at the McCune house, a brave went to check on the missing white woman and found the front door open. He alerted the others and they took off to find the escaping woman. The settlers had only gone about a mile towards Manannah when they saw the Indians who had stopped at McCune's approaching from their rear. By this time, however, the settlers outnumbered the braves, who stopped in their tracks, talked amongst themselves and then turned and left. Mrs. McCune's quick thinking no doubt saved many lives that day.

Chapter Five
Stories of the Sioux Uprising – Part Three

On September 4th, in the darkness just after midnight and prior to their attack that day, the Sioux snuck up on the Forest City stockade corral to take the horses so that the settlers would be trapped inside the fort. They had no problem accomplishing their task except for Peter Lund's Indian pony, which shied away from the Indians and started making noise. Finally it bolted out of the corral and headed for the gate of the stockade where an aroused sentry let the horse inside. Thus, Lund's pony was the only horse the settlers had during the attack until help later arrived.

The Forest City Stockade drawn from descriptions.

About two hundred Indians attacked around 3am and were driven off in a couple of hours. There were four dead braves[12] and only two wounded whites in the stockade. They were Aslog Olson and William Branham. A state of siege existed at the stockade for ten days following. No one could come or go and the provisions inside were meek. A young man risked his life running through the Indian camp to return to his home for a sack of flour. Surprisingly, he made it back to the stockade. Finally, on September 15th, Company B of the 8th Minnesota Volunteer Regiment came and the Indians scattered.

On September 28th, the Battle of Wood Lake, the turning point of the war against the Indians, took place. From that point on, the Indians were the pursued, not the pursuers, and they were quickly overwhelmed by the Minnesota troops. Little Crow escaped to Winnipeg, Canada where he tried to get the British to give him help.

To punish the four Minnesota Sioux tribes for the uprising, the Indians were banished from their homes in Minnesota. Some ran north and west to escape punishment, but three hundred and three

---

[12] Different figures have been given, ranging from three to eleven.

were tried for their involvement. They were convicted and sentenced to death by hanging. President Abraham Lincoln reduced the death penalty to only forty of the Indians. Eventually only thirty-eight of the forty were hanged at Mankato, Minnesota on December 26th, 1862.

The mass execution was performed for all to see from a single scaffold platform. It was and still is the largest execution in the history of the United States. Nels Danielson's friend Chief Cut Nose was convicted of being involved in the attack on New Ulm, Minnesota and he was one of the thirty-eight hanged.

The bodies of the Indians were pronounced dead by the regimental surgeons and then they were buried in a long trench, which was dug in the sand of the riverbank. Before they were buried, however, a "Dr. Sheardown" supposedly removed some of the Indians' skin. Little boxes containing the skin were sold in Mankato after the hangings. Over the years, many "souvenir" pieces of skin have continued to be sold, some on ebay. Of course, most are hoaxes and are just hunks of pigskin.

At that time, bodies used for dissection by medical men were hard to come by, so some of the many medical men attending the hanging asked for the bodies. That's why they had come to the public hanging in the first place. One of those men was Doctor William Worral Mayo, who you read about in the previous chapter. The mass grave was re-opened and the bodies were removed and distributed. As fate would have it, Dr. Mayo received Cut Nose, the brave he had encountered earlier. Dr. Mayo brought Cut Nose's body back to Le Sueur. There, Mayo dissected it in the presence of some medical colleagues. Afterwards, the skeleton was cleaned, dried and varnished so other students could benefit from it.

The remaining convicted Indians stayed in prison that winter. The following spring, they were transferred to Rock Island near Davenport, Iowa where they were held in a prison for almost four years. By the time of their release, one third of the Indians had died of disease. The survivors were sent with their families to Nebraska. Almost five hundred white men, women and children were killed in the uprising in Minnesota. Some figures go as high as nine hundred.

In June of 1863, Little Crow returned to Minnesota with his son One Who Appears (Wowinapa) and about nine other braves. Their mission was to steal horses to start to rebuild their tribe. In accomplishing the mission, they happened to kill a few people. One of them was James A. McGannon, who lived near Fairhaven. Little Crow took McGannon's coat as a trophy.

Little Crow's son Wowinapa or One Who Appears.

Nathan Lamson and his son, Chauncey, were leaving Hutchinson, Minnesota on July 3, 1862 to return to their farm. After they had traveled six miles, Nathan saw two Indians, a young one and an older one, picking raspberries. Without provocation, Nathan started firing at the Indians, hitting the older brave in the groin area. Although gravely wounded, the brave returned fire and hit Nathan in the shoulder. Then he turned his rifle in the direction of Chauncey and fired just as Chauncey was firing at him. Chauncey was missed but was his shot hit the brave in the chest.

Thinking his father was dead, or scared for his life, Chauncey ran off, leaving Nathan on the ground in the bushes. Nathan wasn't dead and, lying as still as he could, he heard a noise in the bushes. He saw the young Indian boy kneeling beside the older man. The older brave asked for water, which the boy gave him, and then he died. The teenaged Indian put a new pair of moccasins on his father's feet, covered his body with a coat, which was later found to be that of McGannon, and he ran off into the brush.

Chauncey and Nathan Lamson

The older Indian was found to be Chief Little Crow, identified by two of his most known peculuarities...extra teeth and hands that turned in from Little Crow being shot in both wrists long before. The Hutchinson people, who came with Chauncey and Nathan's youngest son Birney to recover Nathan's body the next morning, were surprised to find he was gone. Nathan had got up and left the area, leaving behind his bloodied shirt, after the young Indian had left. The Hutchinson citizens dragged Little Crow's body back to their town where they left it lying on Main Street. A bunch of boys put firecrackers in the Chief's ears and nostrils and lit them, blowing off pieces of the Indian's face. Chauncey scalped the head, which he later turned in for the $75 bounty. Finally Dr. John Benjamin came up to the desecrated body. He begged the citizens to help him move Little Crow out of town where there was a pit. There, the doctor covered the body with dirt and left.

Later a cavalry officer dug the body back up, took his sword and severed the head. Dr. Benjamin found out about it and he was able to retrieve the head. But when the good doctor returned it to the grave, he found that the rest of the body had disappeared.

Nathan was given the $500 reward for shooting Little Crow, which he accepted, even though his son had actually fired the fatal shot. Little Crow's son was tried by the military and found guilty of participating in the uprising, attempted murder and horse stealing. He was sentenced to be hanged. But eventually he was released. He became a Christian and took the name of Thomas Wakeman and was the founder of the YMCA among the Sioux Indians. Little Crow's bones eventually ended up in the hands of many people who kept them as souvenirs. A man named Frank Powell donated the skull to the Minnesota Historical Society in 1896. It was put on display there along with the scalp and some bones. In 1971, Little Crow's grandson asked to have his grandfather's remains. He was given them and he took them to South Dakota where they were buried in a private family cemetery lot.

In 1865, Patrick Casey returned to his land with his family along with the $200 per family the government gave the settlers to help cover their losses. Patrick's grandson, P. J. Casey, went on to be a lawyer in Litchfield and write a history of Meeker County.

In 1889, the Frank Daggett Post of the G.A.R. in Litchfield was given an oak log from the actual cabin of the Jones family. The log was taken to a sawmill in Forest City and made into lumber from which an altar or podium and a gavel were made. They were both used during meetings at the Hall and I gave a speech from the "altar" at my book signing for *Terry Tales*. The altar is thirty-two and a half inches square and thirty-six inches high. It has a cushioned top covered with heavy leather.

My grandson Ethan on the "altar" in the G.A.R. meeting room.

27

In the northwest corner of the meeting room at the G.A.R. Hall is a miniature model of the Jones' cabin. It was also made from wood from that log.

The Jones cabin model in the G. A. R. Hall.

Over time, the stockade disappeared from a combination of the elements and the desire for building logs or fire wood for surrounding settlers. On September 12, 1976, a restored Forest City stockade was dedicated in a grand ceremony and it is now open to the public.

You might have read in *Terry Tales* how the ghosts of the Indians killed near the stockade still linger on their nearby sacred hunting ground, now called Indian Ghost Hill[13], where they will push your car, while it is in neutral, UP a hill and away from their land, having the last say on the matter of whose land it is.

---

[13] Take County Road 2 north out of Forest City, going over a bridge. Go 1.5 miles from bridge to 330th Street, turn right and go .5 mile to 660th Street, turn right again and drive up the small hill. The hill is just before the curve to the left. Turn around to face north and observe that it's downhill behind you and in front of you. Drive about half way down the hill and stop. Put your car in neutral and take your foot off the brake. The farther you go down the hill the faster you will be pulled back up the hill.

Ahead Of Me

I've always been fascinated with our obsession for being first and/or first in line. I'm guilty of it too, but not to the point where I will ever sleep out in the cold to be first person to purchase a concert or a movie ticket. My obsession has to do with my impatience. I don't want to stand around at dinnertime waiting for my turn to go through a buffet line. I did that for two hours once at a casino in Biloxi, Mississippi, while I was visiting my son, Adrian, who was stationed there in the Air Force. I'll make a beeline for that potluck table at every family reunion. I'm sure I wear my "trophy" on my belly showing everyone that I was first and often at the buffet

Ahead Of Me

Take a look around you.
What do you see?
People pushing people.
People pushing me.
Everybody's scrambling
trying to get ahead of me.

Better not ever
step from the line.
When you return,
I'm sure you will find
your place is gone and
"Don't stand ahead of me!"

Hey, do you find you're
always on the run?
Reachin' and a-graspin'
for the Number One?
Take a look behind you,
maybe you're ahead of me.

Everybody's striving
for the front row seats.
Standing at the table
grabbing for the eats.

"I got here first.
How come you're ahead of me?"

What is this fear
we have of being last?
Why do we grind our teeth
when we're passed?
"There you go now;
you're ahead of me!"

You're a special person.
Go and "buck" the line.
If there's only ten,
don't be with the nine.
They've already
pushed in ahead of me.

If you think it's wrong
then listen to this song
and take a look at you.
Maybe you will find
in searching through your mind
that you're a-pushin' too.

Chapter Six
I Read It In The Paper – Part One

Digging through all those old newspapers in the Meeker County Historical Society museum, I came across several stories that I didn't think added anything to the stories of my first book, but were interesting nevertheless. They were interesting for various reasons; they told of odd events, strange things that people did, weird things that happened to people, or funny ways of writing about things in the newspaper, usually by Litchfield's *News-Ledger* editor W. D. Joubert, who had a wonderful way with words. I hope they fascinate you as much as they did me the first time I came across them.

We Minnesotans like to feel superior to our neighbors. I love telling Iowa jokes to my sister-in-law, Shirley Shaw, who was originally from Iowa. What's the best thing to come out of Iowa? I-35. What do they call duct tape in Iowa? Chrome. What do you call a bunch of tractors parked at a McDonald's in Iowa on a Saturday night? Prom. Anyway, you get the idea. It seems that neighbor jokes and slams aren't a twentieth century thing. The following article came out of the May 22, 1873 *News-Ledger* newspaper:

"A gentleman from abroad has been located in this village for some days…maybe two weeks…engaged in purchasing beef cattle for to drive onto the wide and barren prairies of Dakota, there to slaughter for food that the deluded and mistaken men who wander out there may not die of hunger. He purchased many fine looking cattle and it makes us mad to think that such good beef should be wasted on men who have no better taste than to live in that undesirable territory of Dakota."

Our idea of settlers from the east heading out west in wagon trains, (which we got from movies and television shows, such as *Wagon Train*), isn't that far from the truth. Our local newspapers seemed to be obsessed with the settlers. The July 17, 1873 *News-Ledger* read, "And still they come, emigrants with their household goods in covered wagons and their cattle driven by barefoot maidens, sometimes of uncertain age. Hardly a day passes but several of these pilgrims to the 'shrine of homestead' pass through our village. Let 'em come, the more the merrier."

So many kept coming through Litchfield that the local newspaper referred to them as being as thick in 1877 as the grasshoppers were during the locust plaque. I get the feeling that the "welcome mat" started getting worn out. A May of 1879 *News-Ledger* read, "Emigrants! Emigrants! Emigrants! Emigrant wagons are passing through the city, west, in unusual numbers."

A slow moving team of oxen sometimes pulled the "prairie schooners". The newspaper noted that one such a wagon came through with "Oregon or Bust; J. T. M., St. Peters" painted on the side canvas. The newspaper also noted that the schooner was moving at a speed of about a half a mile an hour. The reporter/editor wondered how long it would take to get to Oregon at that pace. Over two hundred days, I calculate.

Although the Uprising was eleven years in the past, the people in this area still hated and feared the Indians in 1873. The Indians had been either sent out of the state or put on reservations, but their plight of hunger, which had partially driven them to start the war against the white man in the first place, had not been solved. The reservations were not the best of land, certainly not flush with wildlife for eating, so the Indians started sneaking off to get deer elsewhere. That prompted the following article in the April 3, 1873 *News-Ledger*: "The Chippewa Indians are killing deer off the reservation (by St. Cloud). They don't want to come down this way killing deer or there will be trouble."

The local newspaper reported about love also. And it was reported in a straight forward manner...no beating around the bush. The November 6, 1873 *News-Ledger* reported, "A chap came in from the country a few days ago and wanted a permit to get married. Clerk Leavett[14] inquired the age of the fair creature about to be made so blessed by becoming the conjugal partner of a man so brave and noble as he who stood before him. The reply was: 'Oh, the damn thing's 'bout thirty or forty, I s'pose.' The blunt honesty in the answer was more appreciated by the outsiders than by the lady herself, we could presume."

Maybe Editor Joubert picked up on the anti-woman attitude, but I think he was reporting, "tongue-in-cheek" when he wrote, "Mrs. Miller is an unreasonable woman. She had her husband arrested on charges of habitual drunkenness and failure to provide for her. She should know that in these difficult times, it is difficult for a man to have enough money to drink heavily and still support a wife."

Minnesota was considered part of the west back in those days. And little Litchfield, with it's many saloons, was considered the Wild West. In 1889 and 1890, they were eight saloons in Litchfield and most of them were on the east side of Sibley Avenue. Fights spilled out into the street, bodies actually did fly threw glass windows, and sometimes there were gunfights.

An August 7, 1879 Litchfield newspaper had this little blurb: "Last Monday night, about 9 or 10 o'clock, parties living in the east part of town were startled by the shrieks of a woman, and then a revolver shot, after which all was quiet. Can't somebody get up and explain?"

In that same paper was a story of a Friday night of that same week, when a lot of farm hands came to town to celebrate the end of the harvest work. They all got "beautifully drunk," as the Litchfield newspaper reported, "and being beautifully drunk, of course, (they) had to get into a fight." One young farm hand "put an eyebrow on another fellow's cheek" and then he took off. Deputy Myers took after him on foot.

When the two got south of the railroad depot, Myers yelled, "Stop! Stop or I'll shoot, blast you."

The young man kept running, so the deputy pulled out his pistol and "undertook to let daylight enough through him so that he would

---

[14] Silas Wright Leavett had a lumberyard at 100-124 Commercial Street East in 1871 and he sold it to John Esbjornsson in September of 1876. He built a couple of buildings downtown also.

see the error of his way." He fired once, missing the runner. Marshall Jim Hooser caught up to Deputy Myers who handed over the revolver, all cocked and primed.

"Go git the cuss, Jim," Myers said.

Marshall Jim took the gun and shoved it into his hip pocket, taking off after the farm hand. He only took a few steps when he heard a gunshot behind him. Was somebody shooting at him from the rear?

"What the hell?", the Marshall said. "Who the hell's shooting at me?" The deputy stood there stunned, frightened and laughing, all at the same time, while he pointed at the hole in the Marshall's hip pocket. The cocked revolver had discharged and the lucky Marshall had been...well, lucky.

Storeowners John and Dick Hayford[15] rode up with two more horses and the posse took off in pursuit. They headed the desperado off just in front of pioneer lawyer Charles H. Strobeck's house where the Marshall collared him. The young man was brought before Justice Virgil Homer Harris where he was fined the huge sum of $12.05. He paid it gratefully thanking God that the deputy's aim was so bad.

Even the "wild west" town of Litchfield got a little too tame at times for the newspaper's liking. This article ran in an 1879 edition of the *Review*: "Why don't somebody pass the herring, step on an orange peel, call somebody a liar, or get up a dog fight for a little excitement? It's awful dull in these parts nowadays."

There was an old custom that has pretty much died out since WWII. It was called a charivari[16] and was brought to America by way of Louisiana by the Creoles and Acadians. The custom is Latin in origin, and had been practiced in France. Originally, it was a superstitious ceremony in which noise was made by beating drums, or beating on pots or other objects to make a loud racket outside the home of newlyweds. The purpose? Frighten away evil spirits so that the couple could have a blessed life together ahead of them.

---

[15] Their father, M.T. Hayford, owned the Litchfield House hotel in the early 1870's. It used to be located just to the east of the old library building. I don't know what kind of store John and Dick had at this time, but Dick went on to own a flour and feed store behind what is today the Sparboe office on Sibley Avenue.

[16] Pronounced shivaree. It is a French word meaning "headache".

In the form we got to know it, a newlywed couple was loudly woke up, preferably on their first night together, and they were expected to entertain their surprise guests by providing drink and food. Sometimes the combination of drink and a "ruined" honeymoon night caused tempers to be short or craziness to follow, so most cities outlawed the practice.

In July of 1884, Michael Shaughnessey, who lived five miles out of Manannah, lost his wife in childbirth. He had six little kids to care for so Nellie Branner, his dead wife's niece, came to stay at his house, to help raise the children and housekeep for Michael. Less than two years later, in March of 1886, Michael and Nellie were married. They honeymooned in Minneapolis for a couple of days and then came back to their home on a Friday.

On the previous Tuesday night, a group of masked men had visited the Shaughnessey home to charivari the couple. Because the newlyweds were gone, all that the group accomplished was to scare the hell out of the little kids, who were being watched by the oldest, a fifteen year old. The mob came back the next night and this time, not believing that the newlyweds still weren't home, searched the house, overturning furniture and again frightening the children.

When Michael returned with his bride on the Friday of the week, he was told what had happened. He was upset that his kids had been scared so badly and his "castle" entered. That night he heard the mob approaching again. He went out on his porch to meet them, taking his rifle with him to show that he meant business.

"I don't like what's been goin' on," he yelled to the masked mob of men. "You've been scarin' the hell out of my kids and if you don't leave now, someone's gonna get hurt." More angry words were said back and forth, even though the group was primarily made up of Michael's friends.

"Now, I'm warnin' you fools. Get off my property and leave us alone," Michael repeated. "I've got my gun and I'm not afraid to use it, if I have to."

Angered by being treated so rudely by the man the group had just come to have a good time with, one of the men in the group stepped forward.

"It's your game," he said to Michael, "and we can play at the same." With that, he raised his gun at Michael and fired.

Shaughnessey got hit in the arm. The surprised and stunned group scattered.

Michael's arm was so badly damaged that it had to be amputated. A man named Clement "Dig" Woods, who led the mob, was arrested and charged with assault, but the man who did the shooting, Thomas Welch, couldn't be found. The other members of the group[17] were charged with unlawful assembly. Meanwhile, Shaughnessey had complications from the amputation and he died. Now it was murder...all over a silly custom.

The group was indicted in November, while the hunt went on for Welch. A jury acquitted the group in December, believing the defendant's attorney who said the boys were just out to have some innocent fun with their friend. Welch was never found.

A couple of years ago, one of the ladies at the Meeker County Historical Society got a phone call from a lady in Canada asking for some genealogical help. This is a very common occurrence at the Historical Society. Most of the ladies' time at the Historical Society is spent doing research for people and helping people find information on old relatives. Finished with her inquiries, the lady who called asked if the Historical Society worker had ever heard of something called the "Manannah Charivari".

"Yes, we have," she was told.

"Is it true that someone was killed?" the Canadian lady inquired.

"Yes. That's true also."

"We've always heard rumors that someone in our family was involved in a shooting in Manannah a long time ago."

"Well, the rumors are probably true. Are you related to the person involved?"

"Er...yes...I guess I am," the caller replied. Then she hung up. The family she was researching was, of course, the Welch family. An old mystery was solved. Thomas Welch had run off to Canada and started a new life and family there, and he hadn't changed his name.

Another crazy post-wedding practice was "stealing the bride". When I came home on leave from the Army to get married to my first

---

[17] James Gibney, William Stewart, David Stewart, Charles Snell, Finley Snell, Michael Ryan, James McGowan, Michael Foley and John McCann.

wife, I was told that her male cousins had stolen the bride at a previous wedding and had kept the bride out all night. I was only home for a little while, so the thought of losing any time at all with my new bride frightened me. Sure enough, during the reception in the Lake Lillian Lutheran church basement, I suddenly noticed that my new wife was missing. Fearing the worst, I grabbed my brothers Mick and Pat and sister-in-law Karen Shaw and off we went in pursuit. We found the rascals in Bird Island parked in front of the liquor store. I rescued my bride and angrily took her back to the reception.

Several years later, while teaching in Glencoe, Minnesota, I opened my newspaper one Sunday morning and read about another bride theft after a wedding in the neighboring twin towns of Norwood-Young America. Once again the thieves decided to get liquored up before speeding off to another town to bar hop with the bride. They never got to the next town. They had a car accident; killing the bride they had stolen.

A March of 1888 local newspaper clipping read, "Belle Boyd, the ex-rebel spy, lectured to a rather small audience in Town Hall Monday evening. It was announced that the proceeds would go for the benefit of Company H. When the bills were paid, just five cents was left, which sum was duly turned over to the treasurer of the Company." I thought that was funny and it reminded me of some of our early Rock and Roll dances that my brother Mick and I put on. The name Belle Boyd intrigued me, however, and I decided to find out what I could about her.

Belle Boyd

Belle was considered one of the most famous of Confederate spies. She served the Confederate forces in the Shenandoah Valley starting at the young age of seventeen. She operated her spying operations from her father's hotel providing valuable information to Generals Turner Ashby and "Stonewall" Jackson during the spring of 1862 campaign of the war. Jackson made Belle a captain and honorary aide-de-camp on his staff. Betrayed by her lover, she was arrested on July 29, 1862, and held for a month in the Old Capitol Prison in Washington. Exchanged a month later, she was in exile with relatives for a time, but was again arrested in June 1863 while on a visit to Martinsburg. On December 1, 1863, she was released, suffering from typhoid, and was then sent to Europe to regain her health. The blockade-runner (ship) she attempted to return on was captured and she fell in love with the prize master, who later married her in England. While in England, Belle had a stage career and published *Belle Boyd in Camp and Prison.* She died while touring the western United States twelve years after she was in Litchfield. Her tombstone proudly proclaims "Confederate Spy".

Chapter Seven
I Read It In The Paper – Part Two

Apparently in 1888, we were still the "Wild West" in Litchfield and the surrounding towns. An August article in our local paper told of an episode that sounded like a scene out of an old-time western movie.

"There was a row in one of the saloons in Dassel one day this week, in which a stranger drew a revolver on two of our citizens and, under its protection, backed from the saloon and ran. The citizens followed with guns...but he escaped in the brush south of town."

Sometimes, as in the case of this September 2, 1889 Litchfield newspaper clipping, the stories don't need a set-up. Just read and enjoy. "Mr. L. L. Wakefield's[18] bull dog attempted to cross the track in front of Monday evening's passenger train. He wasn't quick enough, however, and when the train passed, his head was on one side of the rail and his tail on the other. Moral: Dogs have no rights that railroads are bound to respect."

Rival town Willmar, Minnesota had a newspaper called the *Willmar Argus*. An article ran in an *Argus* from early July 1890, which confirmed what we Litchfield-ites already knew: "Litchfield will have a large delegation from Willmar on the Fourth (of July). The boys of Willmar are kind of stuck on the good looking girls in Litchfield and the good looking Willmar girls are way up on the **good looking boys** in Litchfield."

Ah yes, finally we were recognized for what we were. You might find it interesting that two good-looking Willmar High grads found this Litchfield boy good looking enough to marry me. The grass, apparently, is always greener...or the women are blinder.

Indians tribes were still feared in the late 1800s, but a new "tribe" came into the area about that time. This tribe caused fears and fascination, at the same time. Bands of Gypsies were roaming the area, stealing whatever wasn't nailed down and conning people out of their money. Some appeared to be earning a legit living by entertaining, when given permission to set up their tents near town.

---

[18] Leander L. Wakefield, who came to Meeker County in the fall of 1856, leased the Exchange Hotel on Marshall Avenue in June of 1889.

They were no doubt the forerunners of the "carnies", whom we were fascinated with and feared at the same time in the 50s and 60s.

In the same August of 1890 Litchfield paper, two articles ran which showed this conflict of feelings towards the Gypsies. A group came to town and because their big tent had been ruined in a previous show, they asked to do their major show in the town hall and then set up their games of chance, fortune telling booths, etc. in Howard Park, where Burger King is today. The article reported "They (the Gypsies) were unable to furnish us with a full program but they promise something good in the way of entertainment. Music, both vocal and instrumental, dancing and a Gypsy wedding." Elsewhere in the paper, parents were put on alert to "take care of their little boys and girls (and it might be well to watch the older ones, too) next week for some of the Gypsies may kidnap them." I remember my grandpa telling me about Gypsy kidnappings in the 1920s and 1930s. Hard to believe, isn't it?

Oh, the trials and tribulations of being a gentleman in the 1800s. All the extra things gentlemen had to do, especially concerning their dealings with the fairer sex. It must have worn the poor souls down. I mean with all the opening of doors, pulling back and pushing in of chairs, the bowing from the waist, the kissing of gloved hands, and the tipping of hats when meeting women on the street. Well, the gentlemen of Litchfield finally said, "Enough is enough!" in a Litchfield newspaper of September in 1890.

"Gentlemen are not supposed to lift their hats when they meet ladies hereafter, but should give a courteous military salute with their hand," the article read. "It is stated that many bald-headed men have caught severe colds by lifting their hats to ladies...hence, the change is necessary." Well, if it concerns a poor gentlemen's health...

That same month, in that same 1890 Litchfield newspaper, there was a story about an afternoon passenger train coming through town and stopping at our depot. On board were a dozen old gray haired Sioux Indians from the Sisseton reservation. They were on their way to Duluth to attend the U. S. Court there as witnesses in some trial. The conductor, named Goran, told the newspaper that the Indians had asked him to let them know when the train got to Litchfield.

The newspaper reporter wrote, "These Indians were no doubt some of the fellows that took part in the terrible massacre in the county, and they probably wanted to see the country where they had committed some of their terrible deeds." Twenty-eight years after the Uprising, hatred of the Indians and bad feelings still were evident.

I was surprised to find, while researching my first book, that Litchfield had a chapter of the KKK and that crosses had been burned on lawns. So when I read the following from the *Cokato Enterprise* newspaper, I wasn't surprised at all.

"Last Thursday night, (August 29, 1901), about twenty women, wives, and daughters, of the most prominent men of Smith Lake, went to the home of John Williams about midnight and seized Miss May Porter, who was making her home at the place, and treated her to a coat of tar and feathers. Miss Porter had carried on a disgraceful career at that place for a long time and has had repeated warnings to leave." My, my, what had Miss Porter been up to?

Litchfield's police force has always been up to date, I've always believed. During my researching, I read about the day the police cars finally got two-way radios and a dispatcher, replacing the light suspended between the hotel and Greep's which the telephone operator turned on to alert the patrolman he was being sought. I'm sure there was an article in the 1980s or 1990s about the day the force got its first stun gun. How about this bit from an August 7, 1909 Litchfield newspaper?

"The Village Council had its regular session on Monday evening and among the business items approved was the purchase of four sets of **ball and chain**." Way to go, Litchfield. That'll make the criminals think twice before entering our little town.

New fangled inventions intrigued the local population and sometimes were written up about in the local newspaper. In *Terry Tales,* I told a couple of stories about this. In one, a local businessman was selling televisions and he got a TV in his home and invited people to come over, by appointment, to view this marvelous invention. He predicted it would someday be as common in homes as radios. In the old days, even the first electric clippers at a local barbershop in town deserved newspaper space.

In April of 1910, an article ran in the newspaper announcing that the village of Litchfield had received its first vacuum cleaner. The cleaner and connections could be leased by a housekeeper for house cleaning purposes at a "moderate rental per day". The wonderful machine could be connected to any electric light socket. And "full directions for using accompany the machine (so) that those who use it may not be left in doubt as to what connection is required for any particular work."

Sometimes the smallest blurb in the newspaper would catch my eye and get me to thinking. Such was the case of this September 10, 1910 article: "A carload of Indians, west bound, attracted some attention at the depot." Nothing more was said of the moving of Indians to a reservation in the Dakotas. Forty-eight years after the Uprising, the Indians were still hated, feared and looked at in wonderment.

An out of town friend once told me that what he liked about my hometown was the drive in from the lake. He loved all of the beautiful homes on Sibley Avenue, which was lined with great big beautiful shade trees. After my friend told me that, I looked at my hometown a little different as I drove in from my home in Glencoe. Yes, we do tend to take our own backyard for granted sometimes.

Did you know that those trees continued down Sibley Avenue right into the main downtown area at one time? Well, it's true, but of course progress, the widening street, and the need for sidewalks meant that the trees had to go. A couple of big trees were left for a while in front of a couple of establishments on the east side of our main street. One tree was in front of Fred Hankey's saloon and the other was in front of George H. Beach's repair shop. (The True Valu Hardware part of town.) The buildings' occupants loved the trees because the west setting sun beating on the storefronts was intense and the trees provided a free awning.

Progress and the pleading of the neighboring storeowners, though, meant that the last trees of downtown had to go. Len T. "Buck Buck" Inselman was hired to do the job and he chopped them down flush with the sidewalk early one morning in June of 1911. A. N. Werner then used his team of horses to pull away the logs of the last trees of downtown Litchfield.

Ironically, in March of 1974, the city purchased forty planters to put on the sidewalks downtown. What did they put in the planters? Trees, of course. Eight trees to each side of each block of downtown Sibley Avenue. The planters would soon go however. Why? Nobody had thought ahead that for many months in Minnesota, it snows a lot. The storeowners had one devil of a time shoveling their sidewalks because of the round concrete nuisances, so, in November of 1976, the planters were put into "storage", never to return.

Kids called Len T. Inselman "Buck Buck" because of something he continually said that rhymed with "buck". Len would stand by the rear of his car downtown and yell, "Melons, fresh melons, f**k, f**k..." Then he'd let fly with a bunch more expletives usually dominated by that "f-word", along with some facial and neck tics or twitches, before yelling "Melons..." again. We had heard that Len's father had caught him saying the "f-word" once and had beaten him so severely that the word stuck permanently into his daily vocabulary. That was just one of the several rumored reasons for his behavior. Another was that he had fallen while painting the water tower and banged his head. Years later, while watching a television show, I learned of something called Tourette syndrome that caused the same behavior. No doubt, that's what poor old Len had, but we didn't know the real reason and it was fun to speculate.

The summer of 1925 Litchfield newspaper headline read: "Man, 93, Arrested as Still Tender, Stands on Rights. Nels Elefson (Elofson was the correct spelling) of Meeker County Held as State's Oldest Moonshiner." Other than the fact that the paper got his name and age wrong, the old settler, who died a couple of months later in July at the correct age of 91, was going to go out with a bang. Nels, who I wrote about in Chapter Three concerning his involvement in the Sioux Uprising, was still the oldest man ever accused of bootlegging in Minnesota And he was the grandfather-in-law of Litchfield baker Wayne Rayppy, owner of the New Bakery. Prohibition agent Ole Olson brought Nels into custody. According to the newspaper article, Nels was "said to have been caught red-handed in the act of tending a still cooker in Grove City, Meeker County. Elefson was born in 1831 (1834) and used to be a justice of the peace in his county."

"It's my constitutional right to make moonshine if I want to," Nels stated.

The article went on that "the still, said to have been operated there by the aged man, was in a tiny teapot and that it took him (Nels) three weeks to make a quart of alcoholic liquor which he used in his coffee in the morning, the habit of 80 years. Elefson was the second white man in Meeker County and is known as a pioneer and Indian fighter of the early days. He was released on his own recognizance." Oh, the crimes reported in Meeker County.

Back to the downtown trees. There were trees in the alleys also at one time. A huge old cottonwood tree was in the alley behind the Red Owl store, where Cliff Schaefer's Studio and Cameras is today. The old tree, three feet in diameter, was considered a downtown landmark. It had been standing since before Litchfield's birth. One cold morning in February of 1929, it too fell to the woodchopper's ax. The newspaper article said of it that "No longer will it make its annual contribution to cotton litter on the streets and downtown stores."

When I was growing up in the fifties in Litchfield, the entire basketball, football or baseball seasons seemed to hinge on one thing. Not the record, not how far we got in the Districts, but it hinged on whether or not we beat our hated rivals...the Willmar High School Cardinals. Reading through the old newspapers dating back to the late 1800s, I found that the rivalry was ageless, and it didn't just apply to sports. An April 18, 1882 Litchfield newspaper had this short but spiteful article about Willmar: "Willmar editors have got a chance to crow, and are making the most of it. The basis for their exultation is the fact that at their recent village election that town polled 248 votes while at the Litchfield city election, only 240 votes were brought out. On this slim foundation they base their assertion that the population of the village exceeds that of this place. We will allow them the pleasure of indulging in the delusion, but investigation would quickly show that Willmar will have to grow a little before she is able to discount Litchfield, which is the prettiest town in Minnesota, and the largest place on this line of road between Minneapolis and Moorhead."

But in sports, a victory over Willmar deserved front-page headlines for as far back as I wanted to dig. And there was a football trophy passed back and forth between the rival cities over the decades. It was a "Little Brown Jug". If it's not in a trophy case in either school, it's sitting in a storage room or closet and future generations will not know of its significance.

Probably the greatest victory of all for Litch over its rival was witnessed by the largest crowd ever to see a basketball game in town, up to that time, on a Thursday night in February of 1929. In that game, our Litchfield Dragons held the hated Cardinals to one field goal (two points) and two free throws for a total of four points. Yes, you read that correctly. Of course Litchfield only scored fourteen points that night but that's beside the point. The game was held in the old Noreen Pavilion, a dance hall Litchfield once had where the old produce stood for years. Why was the game held in such an odd place? The high school and gymnasium had burned down and the pavilion was substituting. Contributing to the low score was the pavilion's low ceiling. The shooter couldn't put much of an arch on the ball.

Jack A. Hunter owned a livery stable in Litchfield at 25 Depot Street East in the early 1900s. Dwight B. Lounsbury consolidated with Hunter because of the decreased business caused by the rise of the number of automobiles. The livery building got into disrepair and, in October of 1915, the owners were told by the city to tear it down, as it was a fire hazard. Guess what? It mysteriously caught fire and burned down in November. Mr. Hunter was looked at suspiciously but nothing could be proven. The livery was rebuilt and owned by Lounsbury and Son in 1916. It just missed getting burned down again when the Wells[19] store on the west corner had their big fire in the late fall of 1916.

On February 16, 1929, Kandiyohi County Sheriff Paul E. Anderson and Litchfield Chief of Police Frank T. Nelson, acting on a tip, raided Hunter's house. Jack was under suspicion of making moonshine and bootlegging it. He had been arrested and convicted once before for the crime. The house search turned up one bottle of "moon" and a big brown jug containing three gallons of the stuff. That was all the law needed. Walking out of the house with the jug and Jack, the lawmen suddenly felt Jack break free. But instead of running for it, Jack grabbed his wood-chopping axe. He swung it at the brown jug, hoping to break it and destroy the evidence. No evidence, no arrest. Either Jack's strength wasn't enough or the jug was too well made, because it didn't break. It just cracked a little. Jack smiled and shrugged his shoulders. What the heck, he had tried.

Jack was fined $250 and spent six months in the county jail. He got released in October and went to live with his daughter in Willmar. Even though he was only fifty-seven, his health had gone downhill in the jail. Immediately, he worsened and his daughter took him to the

---

[19] Wells became Greep's and today is Sibley Antiques.

General Hospital in Willmar. There, Jack died...from kidney failure. Possibly he had drunk too much of his own moon?

I'm not sure how unusual the next thing I'm going to write about was during the years of World War II, but I thought it was remarkable. In January of 1945, after Werner Allen had enlisted in the service, Mr. and Mrs. John Algot Allen of Litchfield had six of their nine sons in the military. They displayed a banner outside of their home with six stars on it. There was Werner, Lloyd, Archie, Willard, Arnold and Andy. How do you suppose the Allens spent their evenings? They must have written a letter to each son one day per week.

Archie was the first son to go into the service. In fact, he was the first of Litchfield's men to get drafted when the war broke out in 1941. The other three boys would've gone into the service also but they were "frozen" in their jobs. All six of the Allen boys came home from the war. One of the sons who didn't go was Raynold Algot Allen, who you'll read about in connection with the Brightwood Beach resort. His son, Richard, was a good friend of my brother Mick.

John Allen's story was also interesting. After giving John nine boys and one girl, his wife Wilhelmina, known as Minnie, died in July of 1928. What could John do? Give away the children? He couldn't afford a nanny to come to his small farm. He asked the older children to help with the cooking and cleaning and he took the younger ones out in the field with him. He managed that way for over seven years until he met and married a woman named Blanche in December of 1935 and had another daughter with her. Besides farming, John did some hauling with his wagon and team of horses. He hauled all the telephone poles around the area for Meeker County's first telephone system. John died in 1959.

Chapter Eight
I Read It In The Paper – Part Three

I wrote in *Terry Tales* about an interesting family called the Esbjornssons. The male heads of each generation of the family were characters, to say the least. Old Hugo Esbjornsson was a real character. He was an avid outdoorsman; so avid that he disregarded the hunting season laws and limits. Hugo came to America from Sweden with his adopted parents, the John Esbjornssons, in 1910, when he was thirteen. John and his wife Ericka had gone back to Sweden to visit John's sister, Mrs. Swanson. Being childless, the Esbjornssons offered to take one of the sister's boys back to the States and raise him. They were given Hugo Swanson as a foster child. They never adopted him, but Hugo took their last name and eventually took over the family lumberyard.

Hugo couldn't speak a word of English, so, even though he was thirteen, he was put into the fourth grade in school to learn the language. Hugo didn't like that and he got himself out of there and into the high school in six months. But he was a problem in and out of school so John sent him to the Shattuck Military Academy for two years to get straightened out. Hugo came home and graduated from the Litchfield High School.

Hugo had a pet Dalmatian hound named King. He usually took King everywhere he went. I wrote about King also in the first book. I'll refresh your memory about the dog. Hugo Esbjornsson would walk into Fransein's restaurant with King. He would plop down on a stool by the lunch counter and the dog would jump up and sit on the stool next to him. No one dared to say a word about it to Hugo. The Esbjornssons were one of the pioneer families of Litchfield, they owned one of the lumberyards and they were one of the town's elite. They were known for their great dinner parties and eccentric men. Anyway, the dog never messed with anyone's food. It just sat there at attention while Hugo finished his coffee and sweet roll.

Hugo and King were sitting in Fransein's one day and Hugo was swearing up a blue streak. Behind him, sitting in a booth, happened to be a minister, who got up and walked over to Hugo.

"Excuse me, sir, but I'm a minister of God and I don't appreciate you taking the Lord's name in vain like that," he said to Hugo's back.

Hugo didn't turn around. Instead he looked down at King and said, "Tell that preacher to go to hell, King." King started barking at the stunned minister, who turned and left.

Hugo would go into a liquor store out of town with King and then he'd touch a bottle on a display, making sure the clerk didn't see him do it. When the clerk would ask Hugo if he could help him, Hugo would say, "Oh well, I think I'll have a bottle of brandy." Turning to King, he'd continue, "Get me a bottle of brandy, King." The dog would rush over to the bottle Hugo had touched, grab it with his mouth and bring it back to him. Hugo would deposit it on the counter in front of the stunned clerk. Sometimes he'd make a bet with the clerk and get the bottle for free.

King's head was a little lopsided from the time a car ran over it, crushing a few bones. On the other side of his head, he had a huge scar where Hugo had accidentally shot him once. They were out hunting and King had scared up a badger. The badger decided to take King on. Poor old Hugo was trying to defend his dog, but his aim wasn't as good as he thought it was. Maybe King's name should have been Lucky?

Albert Blosser was a neighbor of Hugo's farm, a mile east of Litchfield. In March of 1952, Albert kept thinking he was hearing a dog barking. It was getting to the point of distraction. He thought it was coming from the farm across the road from him. After two weeks of the barking, the Blossers were ready to go looking for the dog and put him out of his misery. After a warm early spring weekend, when much of the snow had melted, the barking was weaker but more distinct and clearer sounding.

"I think it sounds like some dog is caught in a fence," said Ed Blosser. "I'm gonna go looking for it." He started walking out behind their own farm buildings and passed an old eight-foot deep pit that the Blossers had abandoned and boarded up. Suddenly he heard the barking again. It was coming from the pit. He pulled the few remaining boards aside, brushing off the remaining snow and looked down to see an emaciated King staring up at him.

There wasn't much work pulling the wonder dog out of the pit. King normally had weighed sixty pounds but now weighed a mere thirty. Hugo and his wife had left on a trip to Texas and asked Hugo's son John to look after King. But when John went out to the farm to feed him, King was nowhere to be found. King had wandered off to the Blosser's looking for his master, who often visited the farm. King had walked on and broken through the boards covering the pit. He couldn't get out and had lived for thirteen days on the snow, which had fallen in with him. King, the wonder dog, certainly lived a charmed life.

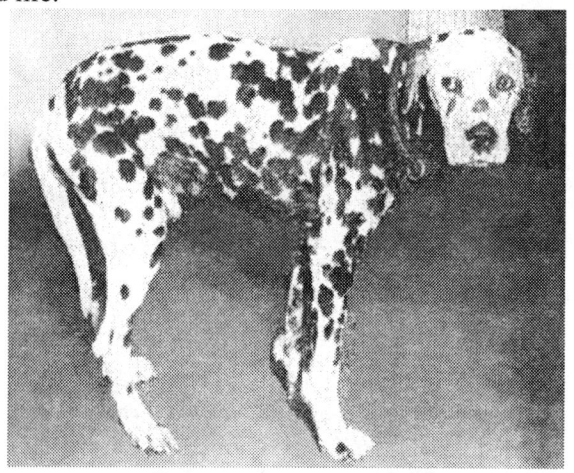

King, the "wonder dog" after his "fast".

Hugo Esbjornsson died in an Alexandria nursing home in October of 1993. He was ninety-five years old. Maybe he led a charmed life too?

One of Litchfield's dentists, Bob Farrish, had something unusual happen to him. Bob had his office right over the First State Bank at the corner of Sibley Avenue and Second Street. I related the story in my first book of how Bob had ended up on an island in the South Pacific during WWII. There he found another hometown boy, sailor Ray Nelson, who was Bob's barber back home in Litchfield. Bob worked on Ray Nelson's teeth, but didn't get the job finished because the war suddenly ended and the troops were all dispersed. The two soldiers returned home to Litchfield, where Bob finished the job he had started over 3000 miles away.

But that's not the unusual story I want to tell you. Bob was out golfing with his buddies Dr. Cecil Wilmot, Maurie Johnson and John Norbloom on a Saturday afternoon in mid-September of 1958. Bob had just stepped up to deposit his ball on his tee on the second hole tee and was just starting his swing.

The second tee was just west of the first green, where another friend of Farrish's, Bob Johnson, was hitting an approach shot just off the green. Johnson overshot the green and his ball bounced and bounded toward the second tee. Unbelievably, it bounced right in front of Farrish's ball on the tee just as Farrish was coming around in his swing. You guessed it. Farrish somehow hit both balls at the same time. Not knowing what he did, but looking up to follow the flight of his ball, Bob Farrish saw it travel 240 yards straight down the fairway and another mystery ball traveling along with it. The mystery ball only went 190 yards though. Wouldn't it have been great if Bob would've gotten a hole in one with at least one of the balls?

John Rogers has been in law enforcement for as long as I can remember, either as a patrolman under Chief George Fenner or as a deputy Sheriff under Eldon Hardy or as the Sheriff himself. He obviously was well respected enough to get elected to that last office, but he wasn't well liked by every one. When he was younger, he had a swagger about himself that rubbed some people wrong, especially teenagers. We thought he sort of picked on us and went out of his way to make life miserable for us. One who would agree would be my friend Skeeter Anderson. One day we heard a rumor that Rogers had pushed Johnny McAloon once too many times and big Johnny had met Rogers in an alley downtown and "cleaned his clock".

I never heard if that was true or not, but John did set himself up for retaliation and occasionally it happened. John worked hard and had a side business of digging with machinery. Esther Williams, not the movie star, bought a piece of land on the northwest side of Lake Ripley in 1936. In the spring of 1970, she almost fell through her garden. She had Rogers come out to investigate. Using his earth moving equipment, he uncovered two huge underground caverns or cellars. Both were brick lined with ceilings fourteen to sixteen feet high. The cellars were twelve feet wide and about fifty feet long. They had little tracks and carts that beer kegs were moved in and out with. Esther's piece of land had been the site of the old Lenhardt brewery and they had uncovered some of the original five cellars used for storing the brew.

When John Rogers was off duty and not working with his machinery, he liked to go dancing with his wife and friends. He preferred old-time music and would often go to the ballroom in Kimball, Minnesota. One night in the early fall of 1972, he came out after the dance to see that someone had let the air out of all of his car tires. That was a nuisance but no where near the nuisance he encountered several weeks later, as reported in the October 11, 1972 *Independent Review*. This time he came out of the ballroom and discovered that someone had removed the drive shaft from his car.

The drive shaft was later found in a ditch near Forest City. A twenty-year-old Forest City youth was arrested for the deed and, even though it was obvious that he couldn't have done the job alone, he wouldn't give up his four or five helpers.

It was the afternoon of October 24, 1987, and the Minnesota Twins were down three games to two in the World Series against the St. Louis Cardinals. This was the first World Series ever to be played indoors. It was at the Metrodome in Minneapolis and the fans had been lifting the roof off the place waving a sea of white "Homer Hankies". But today, the Twins were behind 5 to 2 as they were coming to bat in the bottom of the fifth inning. If they lost this game, the Series would be over and Minnesota would once again be the runner-up, as they were in the 1965 Series against the Dodgers.

The 55, 293 Dome fans were on their collective feet as the Twins came to life in the bottom of the fifth and pulled ahead 6 to 5. Then in the sixth, they loaded up the bases off reliever Bob Forsch. Greg Gagne had a single, Kirby Puckett walked and an intentional pass was given to Don Baylor. But there were two outs. "If we don't score there," manager Tom Kelly said later, "I saw them (St. Louis) taking the lead again."

The next batter was Kent Hrbek, Minnesota's homegrown hero, who had grown up just a few blocks from the old Met Stadium. During Kent's rookie year, he and two other Twins rented the house across the alley from my brother Pat in Richfield. Pat's neighbor's son mowed his lawn, and was compensated rather nicely, along with tickets as a tip. Kent was named runner-up rookie of the year to Cal Ripken, Jr. that year.

As a kid, Kent had played this World Series scenario over in his mind a thousand times in his backyard. The World Series, the bases loaded and little Kent was coming to bat. Crack! Little Kent saves the day and hits a grand slam home run! Only this time, the game was for real and it wasn't little Kent, but grown up Kent who stood in the on deck circle watching as the Cardinals manager, Whitey Herzog, called time and walked to the mound to take the ball from

Forsch and hand it over to ace relief pitcher Ken Dayley. Dayley hadn't allowed a run in seven Series appearances and Hrbek was 1 for 13 against the Cardinal lefties.

The Cardinal's scouting report had called for fastballs inside on Hrbek, but for some reason their catcher Tony Pena set up on the outside part of the plate, which is where Dayley threw his first pitch. Kent swung, and the ball took off into the Dome's air-conditioned air, landing 439 feet away, amid delirious fans. Kent rounded the bases with both arms raised in triumph and his mouth held open in a constant yell. "I wanted to circle the bases twice," he said later.

Kent Hrbek

As Kent rounded third, the third base coach raised his hand, which Kent slapped in a "high five". Nearing home plate, where the three Twins ahead of him were standing, waiting to greet him, and with the crowd standing and screaming in a deafening roar, the batboy also raised his hand for a "high five". Kent, high on adrenaline, slapped it and broke the poor kid's wrist.

Minnesota wound up winning easily, 11 to 5, forcing a decisive Game 7 to be played the next night, Sunday. An emotionally spent Kent Hrbek went home to his house on Lake Minnetonka to find his porch, his lawn and his driveway covered with reporters and TV cameras. At four o'clock Sunday morning, Kent got up and drove with a friend from his darkened house to do some relaxing duck hunting in, of all places, Litchfield, Minnesota. The reason? Kent grew up near his friend who was a nephew of Willard Piepenburg, who had a farm just south of Litchfield.

Arriving around 5:30am, Kent, Willard and Willard's nephew went out to sit in a chilly duck blind and take Kent's mind off the most important game he was ever going to play. But that was easier said than done.

"I'd say he was a bit preoccupied," Willard said. "When the first flock came over, he didn't shoot. He had forgotten to put shells in his gun."

Later that morning, the hunters returned to Willard's house for breakfast. Kent took his shoes off at the door and wolfed down his food, commenting during the meal that he thought the Twins would not only win that night, but would be a force for years to come. He left for his home about 11am. Kent had been coming out to Litchfield to hunt long before he became the Twins' star first baseman. He had even invited the Piepenburg family to his high school graduation.

"He was out here two or three weeks ago," Willard said. "We went to the Country Kitchen (Swan's Café). He wore dark glasses and only one person recognized him."

Do I really need to tell you what happened that Sunday night at the Metrodome? The game was almost anti-climatic. You knew the Twins were going to win. The Cardinals took a 2 to 0 lead in the second inning and that was it for them. Frank Viola, the Series MVP, allowed just two more hits through the eighth inning. Meanwhile, the Twins scored single runs in four different innings on their way to a 4 to 2, Series-clinching triumph.

The final out was a grounder that went to third basemen Gary Gaetti, who threw it across the infield to his buddy Kent, who caught the throw, toed the bag and leaped up in the air, again with his arms raised in triumph. Then he ran to the huge pileup of Twins that began to build between first base and the pitcher's mound.

During their previous year as the American League bottom dweller, our team was called a derogative name.

"We are no longer the Twinkies," said second baseman Steve Lombardozzi. "We're the World Champion Minnesota Twins."

It was with great sadness that I read about the razing of the Unique Theater building in a May of 1996 *Independent Review*. The "event" happened on Thursday, May 23, to be exact. I wasn't there. I couldn't have watched. I had so many great Friday nights and Saturday afternoons in the Unique, (we called it the "Uni-Q"), sitting next to my brother Pat watching *The Creature From The Black Lagoon* or The Bowery Boys in *Spook Chasers*.

I'm sure that many young men, like me, also had their very first date there. Mine was with Jeanette Oliver, thirty-nine years and seven months earlier. Somehow, at twelve and a half years old, I had convinced Jeanette's mother that she could trust me to take Jeanette to a movie unchaperoned on Friday, December 20, 1957.

I was surprised to learn that Don "Donnie" Wheeler didn't go watch the building being torn down either. He couldn't bear the sight of it. Donnie, the father of my drumming idol Jerry Wheeler, had spent a good part of his life in that theater running the projector.

The American Amusement Company leased the building at that location in December of 1910 and by February of 1911 they had started the Unique Theater. Donnie, at that time the twelve year old son of Litchfield pioneer barber Ray Wheeler, went to work for the Schnee brothers, who owned the theater, in 1927 helping his cousin Floyd Wheeler, who was the projectionist. Donnie hand cranked the projector, as it wasn't automated in those days. He made 10¢ a night. That was okay. He got to see every single movie...more than once. His all-time record for movie viewing? He saw *Gone With The Wind* thirty-four times. At one time or another, the entire Wheeler family, Donnie, his wife Lucille, and his children Jerry and Yvonne worked for the Schnees.

Elmer McCurdy

One day, back in 1977, I picked up my daily newspaper and read a story about an unfortunate man named Elmer McCurdy. Elmer was an outlaw from Oklahoma at the end of the old "Wild West" days. He had been shot and killed while robbing a train near Okessa, Oklahoma on October 7, 1911. It was the wrong train, not the one he thought had cases of champagne and a huge railroad payroll on it.

Because Elmer had no family, no one would claim his body or pay for a burial. So the Pawhuska, Oklahoma undertaker embalmed McCurdy in arsenic, wrapped him up, shipped him off to his Arizona establishment for some reason and let him lay around there. In the desert climate, Elmer mummified. Eventually, to recoup his losses, the undertaker started selling tickets to see the old outlaw. One day two men came into the establishment and claimed to be McCurdy's relatives. They wanted to give him a proper burial, they said. For some reason, the undertaker believed them and gave old Elmer up. The two con men sold McCurdy to an amusement park in Long Beach, California claiming he was a real mummy.

When an episode of The Six Million Dollar Man *was being filmed at the amusement park on December 7, 1976, the director wasn't happy with the dummy hanging from a rope in one part of the fun house. He asked a crewmember to move it. When the man grabbed the dummy, its arm broke off exposing the bone of a real mummy. Investigators were brought in and one medical examiner opened the mummy's mouth for clues to his age and where he came from. He was surprised to find a 1924-penny and a ticket from the Museum of Crime in Los Angeles inside. That ticket and newspaper accounts helped police identify the mummy as an old robber, our old friend Elmer McCurdy. A collection was taken up and Elmer finally got his burial on April 22, 1977 complete with a horse drawn hearse.*

Elmer McCurdy

Elmer McCurdy, no more "Hurdy Gurdy".
They finally dug a hole for you.
They thought you were a dummy,
all wrinkled like a mummy,
but now you're gonna get your due.

You picked the wrong profession.
I'm sure you learned that lesson
when they shot the holes in you.
There's ways of earning your pay,
but robbing trains is no way
to try to build your revenue.

Elmer's
U.S. Army
photographs.

They sent you up to heaven
in nineteen-eleven.
The posse's aim was sure and true.
You held up the wrong train.
There wasn't any champagne,
just two jugs of whiskey brew.

Because of your offences,
no one would pay expenses
when the funeral bill was due.
So they sold you to a Side Show,
"See the mummy!" they'd crow.
And there you made your stage debut.

Now sixty-six years later,
while filming a third-rater
for TV cameras and a crew,
the truth was discovered.
Your body was uncovered and
now your waiting's finally through.

They took you up to Boot Hill.
Your funeral was a real thrill
with two white horses pulling you.
Your circus days are over,
you Oklahoma rover.
They finally dug a hole for you.

ELMER McCURDY
SHOT BY SHERIFF'S POSSE
IN OSAGE HILLS,
ON OCT. 7, 1911
RETURNED TO GUTHRIE, OKLA.
FROM LOS ANGELES COUNTY,
CALIF.
FOR BURIAL APR. 22, 1977

Chapter Nine
Brightwood Beach Memoirs – Part One

The recent interest in cleaning up Lake Ripley and restoring the beach to its glory years, made me think of the wonderful resort, Brightwood Beach, which once graced Ripley's southern shore. For a brief period, it was one of the resort "jewels" of Minnesota. It took a long time to get a resort built here and it was gone much too quickly. I mentioned it briefly in *Terry Tales*.

A small article in a June 27, 1878 Litchfield newspaper asked the question, "Why don't some fellow, who has got more wealth than he knows what to do with, build a handsome summer resort hotel on the banks of Lake Ripley? We believe he would realize a handsome interest on his investment."

It took ten years for somebody to heed the newspaper's advice. In 1888, two young enterprising Litchfield businessmen got together and made plans to make the "good ole days" a little better. They knew they were living in an ideal place in Litchfield, unless you wanted to count the terrible winters, oppressively hot and humid, bug-infested summers, and wild west atmosphere of their multi-salooned (there were eight) infant town, and they wanted to turn the area into a Minnesota resort haven.

Litchfield was growing rapidly with a population of two thousand, the railroad's passenger trains serviced the town and just a mile away from downtown Litchfield was beautiful Lake Ripley. The industrial revolution was freeing up people to enjoy the fruits of their labors. The five hotels in town were flourishing.

"Why not," the two men asked themselves, "build a summer hotel on the south shore of the lake and invite people from all over the country to come to the relatively cooler Minnesota and enjoy one of our 10,000 lakes?" Ripley was said to "abound in the finest Black Bass, Silver Bass and Crappies". Why not indeed.

Charles A. Greenleaf and Hiram S. Branham were the two men who stepped up to the call. Charles, a stockbroker, was the son of lumberyard owner, businessman and realtor William H. Greenleaf, who would have a town just south of Litchfield named after him. Hiram was the son of Litchfield's first mayor and Sioux Uprising hero Jesse V. Branham, Jr.[20] and Hiram had money at his disposal. He was co-owner, with Hamlet Stevens, of the Stevens and Branham bank in Litchfield. Hiram had just been elected mayor, although the history books don't show that fact, for a reason I'll get into later.

The two gentlemen finalized their plans over the winter and in February of 1889 they hired Architect G. B. Phelps to plan the main hotel for the resort. It was to be forty-two feet by fifty-six feet and two stories high. In addition to the main hotel, the resort would have a dozen cottages, a dance pavilion, tennis courts, croquet and softball grounds, curving drives, winding walks, and beautiful flower beds. Work on the buildings was started.

Brightwood hotel and guests.

A steamboat was ordered from Little Falls and it arrived in early May of 1889. Christened "LuLu", after Hiram's sister, it was thirty feet long. It was chugging across the lake on June 1. Israel Miller, a Civil War veteran who owned the Litchfield Feed Mill, operated the boat. Four years earlier, Israel had built another steamboat, which he took people around the lake on. During the off-season, he took out the steam engine and used it in his feed mill.

---

[20] See Chapter Four.

"LuLu" the steamboat

LuLu took guests to the resort across the lake from a landing at the site of today's Anderson Gardens[21]. In those days, a road came to the lake from downtown, but there wasn't a road around the lake. Tokens to ride LuLu could be purchased in downtown Litchfield and a long horse drawn carriage, named the "Brightwood Bus", took the patrons to the boat landing. Most of the guests were met and picked up at the train depot.

E. L. Danforth was hired to manage the hotel. Mr. Danforth also managed a hotel in Minneapolis for part of the winter and then he traveled around the country promoting the resort. I read one letter of his that he wrote to the editor of the *Litchfield Ledger* from Georgia in his promotional travels. He talked of the success of his trip and the interest of the southern people in our resort. Brightwood opened with a gala affair on the 4th of July.

A weekly program was set up for the first season and it was announced in the local newspapers. Lawn tennis clubs would meet on Mondays, there would be excursions on LuLu on Tuesday

---

[21] Started in 1994, the little park was dedicated in October of 1995 after a gazebo had been built in its center. A turret top was added to the gazebo in the fall of 1995. The top had been on the home of Dr. James W. Robertson, one of the eventual owners of the Brightwood Beach resort. The house had been built in 1892. Robertson had Litchfield's first hospital in the upstairs offices of his corner building across from the park at Sibley and Third. Three of his sons became doctors and were big athletes at the U. of M. Dr. Robertson's house was torn down in the fifties to make room for the Litchfield Clinic, which today has Sparboe's offices. Warren McQuay had the turret. He had helped tear down the house and he donated it to Litchfield.

evenings, a musicale would be held on Wednesdays, and every Friday evening there would be a ball and social. It was also announced that private dances, dinner parties, and steamboat excursions could be held "on short notice". The newspaper reported "Nothing can be more pleasant than a day, week or season at this charming resort. Every effort is made for the comfort and pleasure of guests. The table is excellent and charges are very reasonable." When September rolled around, the first season of Brightwood was hailed a success.

The next season was even better. The resort's 4th of July celebration was supposedly attended by 10,000 people. That figure is a little hard to believe. Tennis tournaments were held and there were baseball games played by two girls' teams. One was called the *Brightwood Belles* and the other was the *Invincibles*. The elite from town came out for parties at the resort. Everything seemed to be going wonderfully when suddenly, Branham sold his half interest to Greenleaf. Branham's bank was failing and he needed the capital.

One night in December of 1890, Delaney Ezra or "Abe" Branham, who owned the City Grocery in Litchfield where the Ed Olson Agency is today, visited his brother Hiram. Later that evening, Hiram excused himself, went into his bedroom and put a bullet in his chest just below his heart with a .32 revolver. He lingered until the next morning, when he died at the young age of thirty-four. One of the officers of the bank was subsequently arrested for embezzlement and many people lost their money. Hiram's name was permanently removed from Litchfield's list of mayors.

Brightwood had a fairly busy summer in 1891. Danforth had arranged for the Minnesota Editorial Association to hold their annual meeting at the resort. Over one hundred editors and their families were guests. The next summer in 1892 was the busiest summer so far, but not financially. Greenleaf decided to get out, or at least bring in more investors. That winter he put the resort up for sale. Eighty-six people from town, including Greenleaf, formed the Brightwood Association, Inc.[22] and bought the resort for $25,000. They fired Danforth and hired W. T. Hoopes for the summer of 1893.

On a Tuesday afternoon in May of 1893, two young ladies reported a story to the local newspaper. I don't know if the event they reported actually happened or if they made it up to help the struggling resort's business. The ladies and their male companions were out on

---

[22] The chief investors were druggist A. J. Revell, Dr. James W. Robertson, general store owner John T. Mullen, dry goods store owner Ed Benson, downtown buildings owner and investor Ortho H. Campbell, photographer Clark L. Angell, veterinary surgeon Dr. William Dickson and stockbroker Charles A. Greenleaf.

the Brightwood pier fishing one beautiful spring morning, when they suddenly heard a roaring, buzzing noise. "Terrified", they looked further out onto Lake Ripley and saw a large dark object, looking very much, they said, "like a sea serpent". Were the young couples familiar with the looks of a sea serpent?

A drawing of a typical sea serpent.

"The fishers", the newspaper reported, "were so frightened that they lost no time in getting back to town and it is doubtful if they have as yet recovered from the fright." Then came the "kicker" in the article: "The Brightwood managers can now advertise a sea serpent and will no doubt succeed in getting hundreds of people here to come out and see the monster of the deep." All I can say is that it's a good thing my brother Pat and I never knew about this sea serpent in the late fifties or we would've never set foot into the murky waters of Ripley's swimming beach again.

Chapter Ten
Brightwood Beach Memoirs – Part Two

Many employees of the Great Northern Railroad came to the resort the summer of 1893. A toboggan slide was added. A person could climb to the top of the slide, sit on a toboggan, much like an auto mechanic's "creeper", and zip down the slide, shooting out over the water several feet. Lake Ripley beach had a similar one in the thirties. Maybe it was the same one?

The water slide in the thirties.

It seems the owners were pulling out all the stops to make the 1893 season at Brightwood a success. For the upcoming Fourth of July celebration, an "aeronaut" named Professor T. I. Cash and his companion Miss Eva Daniels were hired to take a hot air balloon up to 3000 to 5000 feet and then have the young lady jump with a parachute.

Over five thousand people showed up for the celebration on the Fourth, which began with the customary speeches. Then there was singing by a girls' quartet, a shooting tourney, won by real estate broker Peter E. Hanson, a bicycle race, won by Willmar's W. T. Markus, running and hurdle races, both won by downtown restaurant owner Percy Vorys, and a baseball game pitting the Leans against the Fats. Yes, that's right. To play for the Fats, you had to weigh over two hundred pounds. Local lamplighter and courthouse custodian, and Litchfield's sole black man, Van Spence pitched for the Fats. The Leans won the game.

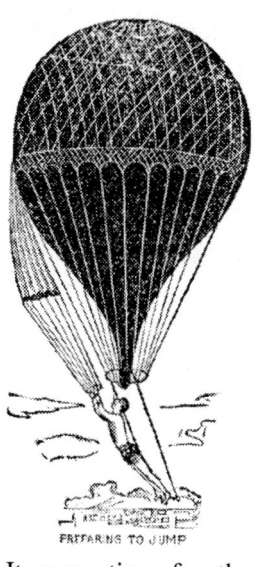

Drawings from the actual Litchfield newspaper advertisements.

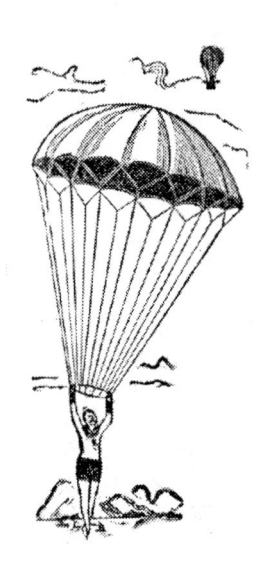

PREPARING TO JUMP

It came time for the grand finale...the balloon ascension and parachute drop. But, the wind was so strong that Professor Cash wisely insisted on waiting till late evening. Unfortunately, by then, the majority of the crowd assembled had gone home. Only 120 people remained. They had stayed for the grand ball complete with Griffin's Orchestra from Minneapolis. Nevertheless, the balloon started its ascent. It went up about one hundred feet and then suddenly fell to the ground. Shaken, Professor Cash climbed out, but Miss Daniels, still in the balloon, found herself tangled in the balloon's ropes. As soon as she got herself free, the balloon and she suddenly shot up to about two hundred feet and sailed away. She was able to bring the errant balloon down, however, in the area of today's R.V. camp.

Cash told the few people left that he would retrieve the balloon and make an ascent and jump on the next day. He went off with helpers to get the balloon and his companion. They found Miss Daniels standing next to the deflated balloon, which was ripped to shreds. She had brought the thing down on a wire fence.

Demoralized and embarrassed, Professor Cash came to town and telegraphed his partner in St. Paul, asking him to bring out their other balloon and have it here by the morning.

When the second balloon didn't arrive by noon the next day, Cash turned to Litchfield's excellent tailors, headed by Andrew O. Palmquist, for help. Andrew and a helper went to work feverishly on the balloon and by 5pm they had it sewn back together. A large crowd was assembled again at Brightwood and Cash fired up his burners to inflate the repaired balloon. The huge colored cloth balloon slowly rose up off the ground as it filled with heated air, slowly, slowly, getting rounder and rounder. Suddenly, just as the balloon was almost filled, it burst into flames. In seconds, the balloon's ashes snowed down onto the crowd. It was gone.

"No problem," red-faced Professor Cash announced to the assembly, "My other balloon is still on its way. We will ascend tomorrow. I assure you." A mumbling crowd of Litchfield's citizenry turned and left.

The second balloon did arrive and the following day the Professor and his partner actually got it up into the air, although they took off from a vacant lot by Israel Miller' feed mill, located where the Rainbow Body & Paint Shop is today, instead of from Brightwood. Miss Daniels climbed out of the balloon's basket and slid down to a trapeze when they reached about 2000 feet. The trapeze she sat on was attached to a parachute, which was attached to the side of the balloon. The young lady was supposed to set the chute free and fall for a bit before opening the chute, but instead, to the dismay of the crowd, she opened the chute first, inflating it, and then cut herself loose from the balloon, floating gently down to Waller's pasture north of Litchfield. I think she was thinking that this fiasco was doomed and she wasn't about to tempt fate any further.
Professor Cash was paid the $80 he had been promised, ($125 if he had gone up on the Fourth), and he went away knowing that he had lost his main balloon, which he said would cost $160 to replace. Not every businessman who comes to Litchfield is successful, you see.

A financial panic in the United States and the failure of both the sea serpent and the aeronaut to draw resort customers caused the 1893 season to be a failure. The resort shut down on August 28, never to open again. At various auctions, the Brightwood Association sold the nineteen acres of land, the ten cottages, the hotel, all the furniture, and the dock for LuLu and the other boats. The furniture auction was held on June 13, 1894. The cottages and hotel were auctioned off in February of 1896. Many of the cottages were moved into town for sheds or parts of homes. One large one stayed and it was the home of Christ Peterson in the sixties. The hotel was taken down in June of

1896 and the wood was moved to the farm of Patrick Joseph Casey, Sr. near Darwin where it was used to build a barn. The dance pavilion followed.

By July of 1996, only the steamboat LuLu, six cottages and twenty-five lots still remained. Slowly they were sold off. LuLu became part of a home in town at the corner of 4th Street and Ramsey Avenue where the J. C. Jacks family lived. When Northwestern Bell Telephone bought the lot for their new office[23] in 1959, the house was moved to the corner of South Street and Davis Avenue. For years, Lawrence and Helen Wisdorf occupied it at that location. One of the cottages was moved to 420 North Armstrong where it became a home. Today it has been replaced with a larger home. Part of one of the buildings became a barn on the Peter E. Hanson farm. The building became a machine shed on Hugh Benjamin's farm in the late seventies.

Back view of the octagonal cottage.

The octagonal cottage that was used as a steamboat waiting area and landing station remained on Lake Ripley. It was sold to Dr. Frank E. Bissell and later to T. F. McClure in 1907. The McClures rented it out after enclosing the south side with screens and making a kitchen and bedroom in the main part. Vern Sederstrom bought the

---

[23] Northwestern Bell closed the office in March of 1983.

house in 1950 and he sold it to Raynold and Myrtle Allen, whose son Richard was a close friend of my brother Mike. Raynold was the son of John Algot Allen[24]. For many years, the octagonal cottage was the Allen's summer home. The Allens had the cottage registered on the National Registry of Historical Places.

My Grandpa, Louis Rheaume, was driving my brother Dennie around Lake Ripley one day when Grandpa and Grandma were visiting us when my brothers and I were little. They were, no doubt, checking out the fishing, and they noticed the octagonal cottage. Dennie also remembered the "Merry-Go-Round" building by the community building in town that we never knew had actually housed a steam driven Merry-Go-Round at one time.

"Grandpa, why did people build round barns and round houses in the old days?" Dennie asked.

"So that the devil couldn't corner them," Grandpa answered. There was probably more truth and logic to that statement than not.

The rear view of the octagonal cabin with the refurbished porch.

In late September of 1991, carpenters Ralph Elj and his son Nate were using a large auger on the back of a tractor digging one foot wide holes into which they were going to pour concrete for supports for a refurbished wrap around porch for the odd shaped cabin, recently purchased by Don Hokanson and Don Wagoner. At that time, the cabin was 107 years old. They were drilling down four feet and Nate was standing by the auger pushing away the dirt and rocks that the auger was bringing up from the hole. On the last hole, a

---

[24] See Chapter Seven.

larger looking rock came up and Nate kicked it away from the pile of dirt. As it rolled away, he noticed that it looked shinier than the other rocks. He walked over to it and picked it up. Turning it in his hands, a chill went down his spine. In his hand was a human skull, minus the lower jawbone.

Nate called to his dad, who stopped drilling and came to see what the problem was. Nate showed him the skull and they discussed what to do with it. They decided to call Sheriff Mike Hirman. Mike told them would come out to the cabin early the next morning. When he saw what the men had, Mike took the skull and sent it off to the State Bureau of Criminal Apprehension, who, in turn, notified the state's archeological society. They quickly determined that the skull was Native American and surmised that it had been buried there before the cabin and Brightwood Beach resort was built and therefore well over 100 years old. The Eljs had stumbled onto a probable Indian burial site or at the least the site of an Indian village. Whatever it was, Brightwood had been built on top of it.

The Native Americans got involved and the skull was reburied where it had been found, complete with a burial ceremony including dancing and drums. The Eljs went back to the business of erecting the porch over the burial site. Apparently the Native Americans didn't mind as long as the skull was put back. What the heck...thousands of Brightwood Beach resort visitors had already trampled over the site in Lake Ripley's golden days of the 1890's.

Chapter Eleven
Mrs. Howard's Monument

Some of the characters I wrote about in *Terry Tales* were seen riding around town on their bicycles, something that added to their being thought of as "characters", I imagine. What if one of them had been clad in a widow's black outfit, complete with a black veil over her face? And what if it wasn't the fifties and sixties but 1900? Such was the case of Emma Pennoyer Howard. The determined lady in black was on a mission. To understand Emma and her mission, let me tell you about the man she was mourning, her deceased husband Jacob.

Emma and Col. Jacob M. Howard

Colonel Jacob M. Howard, Jr. was an important man in Litchfield's history. Col. Howard came to Meeker County in 1867. The Civil War veteran had bought a farm in Greenleaf. A native of Detroit, Michigan, Jacob was born to Michigan State Senator Jacob M. Howard, Sr. and Catherine Shaw[25] on July 16, 1842. At the age of twenty, young Jacob enlisted in the Union Army as a private just as the Civil War was beginning. He quickly rose in rank because of his "gallant and meritorious conduct". By the time the war ended, he was Lt. Col. Howard, his commission being signed by Abraham Lincoln. But Jacob's health was impaired.

---

[25] A far as I know, Catherine, from Massachusetts was no relation to me.

Col. Howard, as he preferred to be called, became a wholesale grocer in Chicago after the war but the climate there didn't suit his failing health. Jacob quit after two years and moved west. Arriving in St. Paul with money given to him by his father, Jacob had to be taken to Litchfield lying down in a wagon. After being here for a year, he met and married Emma Pennoyer in October of 1868. She had helped nurse the Colonel back to health.

Still keeping his farm in Greenleaf, Jacob moved to the three-year-old village of Litchfield in 1872. He then built the first independent elevator in town on the railroad line. He bought and shipped grain but wanted to do more. Jacob sold the farm in 1879 so he would have the $19,000 he needed to build the grand Howard House hotel, which we always knew as the Litchfield Hotel. Col. Howard never ran the hotel. He always leased it out, but he could be found "holding court" many a day in the basement tavern.

Col. Howard built a mansion[26] on the shores of Lake Ripley in 1886 for himself and his wife Emma. The house had a tower the size of a good-sized farm silo. One of the founding fathers of the G.A.R. Hall in Litchfield, Jacob was an industrious man. He was one of the principal organizers of the Woolen Mill Company, serving as the first

---

[26] Once owned by Mrs. J. R. Johnson, the address of the house is 1200 South Sibley.

president of the company's board of directors. He was also the vice-president of the Creamery Association and Litchfield's mayor in 1885. That was the year that most of the downtown buildings, including the G.A.R. Hall, were erected.

The Colonel was most involved with the G.A.R. Hall and his Civil War comrades. He was the first commander of the Frank Daggett Post, No. 35, of the G.A.R., which Jacob helped organize in 1883 with thirteen of his fellow Civil War soldiers.

The G.A.R. Hall in 1885.

Jacob and Emma couldn't have children, so in 1882 they adopted a baby boy and named him Guy Garfield Howard. Just after his eighth birthday in March of 1890, little Guy came down with "la grippe" or the flu. It didn't seem serious but on a Saturday he took a turn for the worse and he died from heart failure on Sunday morning. His class at the Garfield elementary school draped his desk with a black cloth and sang at his funeral. Six of his fellow little boy classmates were his pallbearers. Emma started her constant wearing of black at that time.

Jacob was known as a frugal man, tightening up more and more in his old age. Seldom did his treat his comrades to a drink in the hotel's basement saloon. One day a local farmer came into town reporting that he had seen a black bear north of town. A "bear hunt" was quickly organized, to the amusement of Col. Howard. He stood in front of his hotel as every horse in town, it seemed, marched by him with a "bear hunter" mounted atop or in a wagon behind.

"You men are fools," he yelled. "There are no black bears in the whole of Meeker County nor any neighboring counties."

"You'll see," one of the riders told Jacob. "We'll bring the bear back and you can mount him in your bar."

"Ha!" Jacob laughed, as the bear posse rode off down Sibley Avenue.

As luck would have it, however, one of the posse, carpenter Frank G. Simmons[27], ran across a honest to goodness black bear and he shot him with his rifle. The rest of the hunters were assembled and soon a plot was thought up to hoodwink Col. Howard out of some drinks. Two of the posse was sent back to Litchfield to lay the groundwork. Back in town, the two went to the hotel and roused the Colonel.

"Col. Howard," one of the two said, "those men that went after that bear are fixin' to cheat you out of some drinks."

"Now just how are they gonna do that?" the Colonel queried.

"They took an old black Newfoundland dog, cut off his tail, and they're gonna bring it in to you, telling you it's the bear."

"What good will that do, sir?" the Colonel wondered.

"Well, they're gonna bet you drinks around that they got the bear before you get to see the dog."

"Ha! Very well then, sir. We shall see if they can put one over on Col. Jacob Howard."

Soon the herd of horses pulled up in front of the hotel.

"Col. Howard!" a spokesman yelled. "Come out here and see the black bear you said didn't exist."

Jacob stepped out of the hotel lobby, onto the dusty road and faced the riders.

"Okay gentlemen, where's this black bear?'

"Back there, under the canvas in that wagon," replied the spokesman.

"If you have a real black bear there," said the Colonel, "I'll buy you all a round of drinks downstairs. If that's not a bear, you sir," the

---

[27] In 1899, Frank G. Simmons owned the lot where Parkview Lunch is today.

Colonel declared, pointing at the spokesman, "will buy everyone two rounds and give me an apology for wasting my time."

"Now," the Colonel added, pointing at the wagon and raising his voice, "produce your bear!"

The canvas was lifted by a couple of the hunters and the black bear was thrown at the Colonel's feet. The Colonel could see it was the real thing and he knew he'd been had. But in Litchfield, Minnesota, the Colonel's word was gold, even if his pockets now had less of it. The riders nearly broke the doors down getting their bellies up to the bar.

Jacob died on July 27, 1900. Emma thought there should be a monument to him somewhere in town, possibly in the park across the street from his beloved G.A.R. Hall. Knowing the Colonel was never one to blow his own horn, Emma changed her mind and decided the monument should be to all the soldiers who had fought to keep the Nation preserved and it should be in the cemetery, which was so close to their home on Lake Ripley. It would have a bronze statue of a Civil War soldier holding his rifle and he would be atop a grand double pedestal.

Emma set out to raise money for the monument. She started by kicking in some money of her own and then she visited the schools, talking about the War's heroes and begging the children for their extra pennies. Bicycles were vogue at the time, so Emma decided to ride hers around town to ask for money from businessmen, church groups, clubs and ordinary citizens. So the sixty year old widow, still dressed in her black mourning clothes, was easy to see coming, riding up and down Sibley Avenue and out into the country soliciting funds.

Before long, Emma seemed to have exhausted her sources and she wasn't such an oddity anymore riding around on her bicycle. People lost interest in her project and months turned into years. Finally the Colonel's beloved G.A.R. organization stepped in and raised the rest of the money for Emma. The "Soldiers and Sailors Monument", as it was called, was unveiled at the Memorial Day program on June 1, 1909. The "teachers and children of the public schools" who had given their pennies to Emma and the "citizens of Litchfield" were invited to the ceremony.

The monument.

Emma Pennoyer Howard gave a short speech and then she presented the statue to Litchfield Mayor Charles H. March, who was once considered as a possible candidate for President of the United States. Little Dorothy Miller pulled the cord attached to the drapery over the statue and the monument was revealed. The mayor spoke and then G.A.R. Commander August T. Koerner addressed the people.

A plaque at the six-foot high soldier's feet reads "Grand Army of the Republic Veteran 1861 – 1865". At the base of the eighteen-foot high pedestal at the bottom was another plaque. It has the words "To the Honor and Memory of the Loyal Soldiers and Sailors of the War of 1861 to 1865."

Emma died in January of 1927, but her monument showing her love for her husband and honoring the men of his beloved G.A.R. still stands and is the center of each Memorial Day's ceremony.

Sadly, the other monument to her husband, for many years THE most recognizable landmark of Litchfield, his grand hotel at the corner of Sibley Avenue and Depot Street, was torn down in 1979.

Because of You

The lyrics I've been sharing with you are here because I thought they worked well as poetry. The one I'm going to put here now doesn't fit into that category, I feel. You be the judge. It's hard to judge your own work. Many people have told me that this is my best song. I don't know if that's true or not, but here's the lyrics anyway.

I feel that for a marriage to work, each person needs to give a little more than 100%. I know that's impossible, but what I mean is that you need to bend over backwards sometimes and swallow your pride, etc. I was thinking about my marriage and I thought that sometimes, over the many years, I wasn't giving that extra percentage, even though I truly loved my wife. But, I always felt that she was giving me 110 % and our marriage was working, not because of me, but because of her. That's what these lyrics are about.

Because of You

If I could reach up to a star,
I'd grab it just for you.
Can you believe we've come this far?
It's all because of you.

Honeymoon keeps shining down.
Rainbows of love keep going around us
just because of things you do.
It's all because of you.

So long ago since we first met.
But, days seem short and few.
I've loved you true but I know yet,
it's all because of you.

Honeymoon keeps shining down.
Rainbows of love keep going around us
just because of things you do.
It's all because of you.
It's all because of you.

Chapter Twelve
The Great Willmar, Minnesota Raid - Part One

I hope it's not sacrilegious to tell a Willmar story in a book about Litchfield, given the rivalry between the two towns over the years. There is a Litchfield tie-in to the story, however, so I imagine I'll be forgiven. After all, I do live in Willmar now and even though my stepson plays for the Cardinals, I find it so hard to rout for the team. My heart is still Dragon green.

Each September, the city of Northfield, Minnesota celebrates the day that the Jesse James gang and the Younger Brothers botched a hold-up of the city's First National Bank. Several movies have been made about the event, most notably 1972's *The Great Northfield, Minnesota Raid*. And each September, when I'm reminded of that event, I can't help but think of a successful robbery of the Bank of Willmar supposedly by an equally notorious outlaw. Yet, few people know much about it, if anything at all. And Willmar doesn't celebrate the event or even talk about it. Why? Maybe because the bandits got away with their money?

"I can't remember a holdup in the history of the state since the raids of the Younger Brothers and Jesse James gangs," the head of Minnesota's Bureau of Criminal Activity stated, "which compares to the one at Willmar for daring and cold-blooded disregard of human life."

It looked to be another hot and muggy mid-summer Minnesota day the morning of Tuesday, July 15, 1930. People were trickling into their various places of employment, not looking forward to spending the day inside their respective buildings without air conditioning, as they had done the day before.

Myrtle Wilson went to work in an office on the second floor of the Red Owl store building across the street from the Bank of Willmar, one of Willmar's two banks. Myrtle immediately opened the window facing the bank anticipating the coming heat. Dr. C. E. Gerretson went into Willmar's other bank, the Security National Bank, which was kitty corner from the Bank of Willmar. The doctor started climbing the dark stairway to his office on the second floor.

Rudy S. Paffrath opened up his jewelry store on Fourth Street, more than a block away from the bank corner. Construction worker Sam Evans had already arrived an hour earlier for what looked to be a very uncomfortable day digging a basement for a new building on Litchfield Avenue. Fourteen Bank of Willmar employees[28] were either already at the bank or just arriving at the bank's location at the corner of Litchfield Avenue and Fifth Street. And, as usual, several people were in their homes planning shopping trips to downtown Willmar, some with a stop off at the bank.

Meanwhile, anywhere from five to eight nervous men were driving west on Highway 12 from the Twin Cities in two separate cars. It's doubtful the number was eight. More than likely, it was five or six. For various reasons, they each had decided that crime was their vocation and today they were on the job. The group might have been involved in the hold up of a bank in Lehr, North Dakota the day before, netting about $8000. The men had good information that a large amount of railroad payroll money sat daily in a small bank in a little town one hundred miles west of the Twin Cities. Taking the money from some Minnesota farmers should be an easy enough job, they must have thought, just as the James gang and the Younger brothers had thought sixty-four years before.

The bandits were nearing Cokato and anticipated meeting up in Kandiyohi to drop off one of their cars and, possibly, some of the riders. Collectively known as the "Sammy Stein Gang", they had, according to a well-researched book[29] by Paul Maccabe, brought a celebrity into their fold for this job. His name was George R. Kelly[30], but he didn't mind being called the nickname "Machine Gun Kelly" that some newspapers had given him. George had just been released from Leavenworth prison. He had rented a room in Minneapolis and was looking forward to his September wedding to his fiancée Kathryn Thorne. In the thirties, St. Paul and Kansas City were considered "safe cities" for underworld figures because of the corrupt city governments there.

---

[28] George Robbins, Howard Hong, Laila Nordstrom, her brother A. H. "Obbie" Nordstrom, Alice Heitmann (Hipp), June Fladeboe (Anderson), Arthur J. Swenson, Einar Brogren, Adeline Sunburg, Agnes Tommeraasen, Eleanor Gordhammer, C. F. Olson, Albert Struxness, Ed Selvig and E. L. Tommeraasen

[29] *John Dillinger Slept Here: A Crook's Tour of Crime and Corruption in St. Paul 1920-1936*

[30] His real name was George Barnes.

Above: Kelly's mug shots

Other gang members were thought to be at least four of this virtual "Who's Who" of bad men: Sammy "Jew" Stein (AKA Harry Silverman), Harvey Bailey, Verne Miller, Frank "Big Fritz" or "Weinie" Coleman, Mike Rusick, James Morrison, Francis "Jimmy" Keating and Thomas Holden.

Left: Francis "Jimmy" Keating

Right: Tommy Holden.

Keating and Holden had befriended "Machine Gun" Kelly in Leavenworth prison and, using forged trusty passes, they had simply walked out of the prison five months earlier. Prison officials accused Kelly of helping with the forgeries. He denied it and it couldn't be proven, but, supposedly, Keating and Holden showed their gratitude to Kelly by inviting him to participate in this pending bank robbery, his first job since his release.

Harvey John Bailey's criminal career was a long one, known to have begun in 1918 when he started running whiskey along the Missouri River. Bailey, commonly known as the "Dean of the American bank robbers", was "THE bank robber" in the twenties, "liberating" over one million dollars during that time. He tried going straight, opening up a couple of gas stations. But when he lost everything in the market crash of 1929, Bailey went back on the road robbing banks. He was actually more successful at it than John Dillinger, but much less known and is largely forgotten today.

Harvey Bailey's mug shot.

Verne Miller, a former South Dakota sheriff who switched sides of the law in the mid-twenties, was a gunman for Al Capone and was probably not with the gang. However, his name is mentioned often, probably because he associated with the known members of the robbery. Miller's most famous deed was the infamous Kansas City massacre on June 17, 1933, when he, Charles Arthur "Pretty Boy" Floyd, and Adam Richetti killed four law enforcement officers, including one FBI Special Agent, in an attempt to free their friend, Frank Nash, a Federal prisoner.

Vernon "Verne" Miller

I believe the gang arrived in Kandiyohi sometime after nine in the morning and left one of the cars and maybe one person there. Five of them continued on to Willmar in a new dark colored 1930 Buick Sedan with wire wheels. The gang had stolen the car in

Minneapolis from Carl Juul. The license plates had been stolen in St. Paul from A. H. Colvin.

A 1930 Buick Sedan.

Arriving in Willmar around 9:45am, they drove past the Bank of Willmar and around the block a couple of times getting their bearings and making sure they had picked the right bank of Willmar's two. Then they pulled over onto a side street to go over their assignments one more time. William Berg, a Standard Oil station attendant, remembered filling gas for a car full of men around 6am, but it's doubtful the gang would have come to town that early and waited around for four hours. Too many things could go wrong.

Chapter Thirteen
The Great Willmar, Minnesota Raid - Part Two

A little past ten, the gang pulled their car over to the curb on Litchfield Avenue, around the corner towards the rear of the Bank of Willmar. Three of the doors opened and four of the men, dressed in suits and Panama and straw hats, got out, leaving the driver in the car behind the wheel. The four men gathered on the sidewalk, calmly checked themselves over and, satisfied, they strolled up to the front of the bank on Fifth Street. There they deposited one of their members by the door. Looking dapper in a tan suit, Panama hat and brown and white Oxfords, he was thought to be Kelly because he hid a machine gun behind his back.

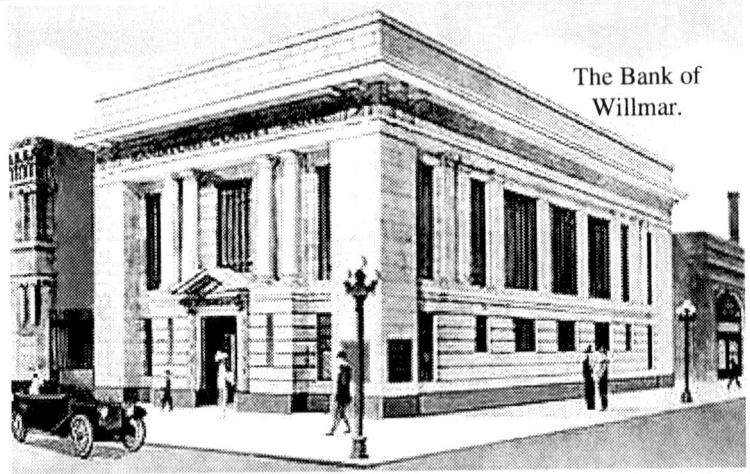

The Bank of Willmar.

At 10:15am, the seven customers already in the bank hardly noticed the three well-dressed men coming in the door and spreading themselves around the room. One of the newcomers, Mike Rusick, was in a white shirt with blue pants and another, Frank "Big Fritz" Coleman, wore a dark suit, straw hat and black shoes. Sammy Stein, a twenty-five year old Russian Jew immigrant, who was dressed in a tan suit with a straw hat, walked up to the first teller cage where cashier Norman H. Tallakson stood.

"Yes, sir," Tallakson said with a smile, looking across at the man who had approached his cage.

"Lie down," Stein said with a slight accent, pulling a pistol from his coat pocket, which he held on the counter pointed at the Tallakson.

Mulling the odd request over in his mind and then thinking he was being made the butt of a joke, Norman looked at Stein and replied, "My, that's a nice gun."

"Get down, quick!" Stein yelled back at him, realizing he hadn't made himself clear. "This is a holdup!"

Stein's loud voice got everyone's attention and they all stopped what they were doing to look over to where the yelling was coming from. Not noticing the other men pulling out guns too, the crowd saw Stein turn to face them and say, "Everyone, get down."

"Wha...?" someone muttered. At first they too thought it was a joke. A bank holdup in Willmar, Minnesota? You've got to be kidding. Ernest Person simply sat down on a sofa, annoyed at the interruption.

"Lie down there on the floor and keep quiet," Stein repeated, motioning to the floor with his pistol and thinking, "Are these people deaf or just plain stupid?" It appeared that Stein was going to do all the talking for the men.

"No fooling," a frustrated Stein added to emphasize his request. "We mean business." Finally, a swift kick to the stomach of one of the customers and a rap on the head of another convinced the people that this was no joke.

Still sitting on the sofa, Ernest Person figured he'd better do as he was told, so he slowly dropped to his knees to lie on the floor. Looking up at Stein, he asked, "Should I keep my face down too?"

"Damn you, yes," Stein yelled, "or I'll fill you with lead!" He must have thought, "What's with these stupid hicks?"

Then Arthur Swenson caught the eye of Stein, who saw him raise his head.

"Lie still there or I'll kill you," Stein yelled.

During the course of the hold up, kicks continued to be given to anyone who was dumb enough to raise his head.

Big Fritz herded the employees who were behind the counters towards the rear of the bank and told them to lie down also. Two of the women employees, eighteen-year old Alice Heitmann and June Fladeboe, quietly slipped down the stairs into the basement where they tried to get out the exit door. The door was locked and they didn't have a key, so they hid under the stairway.

Just then the door opened and Elmer Gardner, who worked for the Great Northern Railroad, walked into the bank. Somehow, he had walked right past the lookout at the door. Seeing what was going on, he turned to leave.

"No, you don't," said Rusick, finally speaking and sticking out his hand to stop Gardner. "Lie down on the floor and no one will hurt you."

Elmer quickly joined ex-Willmar policeman Frank Fransein[31], John and Arthur Swenson, Vance Nordstrom, Postmaster Earl A. Peterson, and Marie Wacker who were slowly dropping to the floor.

Young and pretty Miss Wacker was stopped on her way down by one of the bandits. "You needn't lie there," he said, smiling at the woman. "Stand up and rest on the counter."

Outside, Alderman Corbin approached the bank but, unlike Gardner, he was turned away by the lookout. "Bank's closed," the man standing by the door told him.

Inside the bank, bookkeeper L. Bedney stepped out of his office from another room to see what all the yelling was about. He looked around and muttered, "My God! It's a hold up!" Then he turned and walked back into his office.

Teller A. H. "Obbie" Nordstrom, whose birthday was today, and employee George M. Robbins took their time going down. On his way down, Obbie tripped the alarm, which immediately clanged outside the building. The bandits looked towards the door and were obviously annoyed but they didn't panic. Outside the bank though, people started scrambling. The gunman at the door nervously stood his ground, quickly glancing into the bank to see if something had gone wrong.

A. H. "Obbie" Nordstrom shows how he tripped the alarm.

---

[31] Frank will move to Litchfield and start Fransein's Café, which will be passed on to his son Wally.

"Who did that?" Stein yelled. No one moved but one of the gangsters mistakenly nodded towards Robbins and gave him a kick.

"We'll take you with if you're the guy that turned on that alarm," Stein said to Robbins.

Howard Hong, down on the floor behind a teller's cage, saw an opportunity and half ran-half crawled unseen to the posting room where he jumped out an open window.

Across the street from the bank, Myrtle Wilson dropped what she was doing and, looking out her office window, she grabbed her phone.

"A-number-pa-leese," she heard chief operator Barbara Williams say.

"There's a hold up at the bank!" Myrtle yelled into her phone. Barbara asked for more details and then said she would call the Sheriff's Office.

Over in the next block, Rudy Paffrath heard the alarm from his jewelry store. Figuring out what was going on, he grabbed the .22 revolver he kept under a counter and ran out the door. Sam Evans, who was working on the new Carlson building excavation, ran into the Ohsberg-Berquist hardware store just across Litchfield Avenue from the bank. There he asked for and got a new rifle and shells from a stunned clerk.

Rudy S. Paffrath

Sam Evans

The driver of the getaway car quickly drove up to the corner and stopped facing the car east down Litchfield Avenue. He peered around the corner and saw the machine gunner, who looked his way and shrugged his shoulders that he didn't know what was going on.

Inside the bank, one of the three men stepped behind the counter and quickly emptied the two tellers' cages. He and Mike Rusick then took C. F. Olson into the vault to open the safes.

"Open it up," one of the outlaws said.

"I don't know the combination," Olson replied.

"Open it up or we'll shoot you," a man yelled back.

"You'll have to shoot me then 'cause I don't know it," Olson replied.

He was shoved out of the vault and then Rusick ordered Obbie and either Robbins or Albert Struxness into the vault. The three safes were opened. One of the bandits produced a cloth sack and started loading it. The men knew what they were doing. Except for $5000 in gold, they left all the silver in the vault and took the lighter paper. In all, the heist's total was $45,213.75 in currency, $28,000 in negotiable bonds and an unknown amount in non-negotiable ones. This was like getting a half a million dollars today.

Outside, Rudy Paffrath had neared Fifth Street, but then he saw the lookout standing outside the bank. Rudy quickly crossed over Litchfield Avenue and ran up to the Security National Bank where he crouched down behind a parked car.

Telephone operator Williams had reached the Sheriff's Department, alerted them and then, as instructed, started calling neighboring county sheriffs. Claude Rasmussen started running down Litchfield Avenue yelling to the storeowners and customers, "There's a hold up at the bank. The bank's being held up."

Chapter Fourteen
The Great Willmar, Minnesota Raid - Part Three

Finished with their work inside the bank, the three bandits grabbed Marie Wacker and Robbins, who they still thought had set off the alarm, and, using them as human shields, began to leave the bank. As they emerged outside, a pistol shot "popped", barely audible over the clanging alarm, but a piece of the bank wall near the men exploded. Marie fainted and crumpled to the pavement in a heap. Paffrath had fired at them and missed, striking the façade of the bank building.

The man with the machine gun started spraying the street. Not firing anywhere in particular but in a sweeping left to right motion, the bullets, at first, just hit pavement and parked cars. One bullet, however, went through the windshield of Jacob H. Wilson's car, just missing him and his companion. A ricocheting bullet ended up in the leg of twenty-three year old Mrs. Donna Gildea[32] and another went through her sixty-year old mother's chest. They were in front of the Red Owl store across the street at the corner of Fifth and Litchfield. Mrs. Emil Johnson dropped to the sidewalk. Donna grabbed her arm and had just started to drag her to safety when another bullet struck Donna in the hip. She was still able to pick her mother up and carry her across the opposite street to the Security National Bank. They both later recovered.

Mrs. Donna Gildea and her mother, Mrs. Emil Johnson

The cars of Ole Barnstad and C. A. Oberg also took some bullets as did the front of the Tallman building and the Security National Bank. One bullet hit the wall in the Office of Deeds at the Court

---

[32] Her husband was Thomas.

House. Some bullets ended up in a living room wall of an apartment on Fifth Street. Kern Anderson came out of the Anderson Land Company building, heard a bullet whiz by his head and dove right back inside.

It's unbelievable how many people later confessed to having weapons on or near them that day and wisely, I think, doing nothing with them. Game Warden Johnny Hultgren had a sidearm and he came down Litchfield Avenue from City Hall, walking past the getaway car, reached the bank corner, saw the machine gun pointing his way and he wisely turned and ran. Dr. Gerretson, observing the scene from his office window, grabbed his shotgun, but thought better of firing it from that distance knowing the pellets would scatter all over the street and maybe hit a bystander. Arthur Johnson, owner of the Johnson Variety store, also had a rifle, but didn't shoot. "Jolly" Pearson said he had a gun but didn't fire. All of them, including Henry Stenson, William O'Neil and E. T. Sletten, who were all on the street unarmed, just watched as the bandit who had hold of Robbins struck him on the side of the head with his revolver, pushed him to the sidewalk and then ran to the getaway car at the corner.

Litchfield Avenue, facing east. The bank is on the right.

Across Litchfield Avenue, Sam Evans had already loaded the borrowed rifle. He went behind a weight scale that stood on the sidewalk, brought the rifle up to his shoulder and aimed at the driver of the getaway car. Sam fired once and saw the driver grab his neck and slump over in his seat. One of the bandits climbed into back seat of the car, pulled the driver into the back and then jumped over the front seat to take his place. In all the excitement, Henry Osmunds had the presence of mind to write down the license number: Minnesota plate B 45664.

With all the bandits inside, the car finally took off and sped east on Litchfield Avenue. Like an old gangster movie, the bandits roared down the street firing at anybody they saw moving while one of them scattered nails out a window of the car. Donald Gilman, who was standing on a street corner, caught a bullet in his heel. The desperadoes just missed service station attendant John Selin, whose oil company uniform they had mistaken for a policeman's. The bullet went through the "O" in the Pennzoil sign at the Bartles Scott filling station at the corner of Second Street and Litchfield Avenue.

Mrs. Hazel Dale was standing near the window of her parents' home when a bullet went through the window's glass and hit a picture frame on the living room wall. John Mickelson, visiting from Albert Lea, was seen by the bandits running across the street and he was fired at also. He quickly hit the dirt and then felt gravel kick up in his face as the bandits fired at him again.

By the time the criminals had left Willmar, a couple of cars loaded with high-spirited and armed citizens took pursuit but they were too far behind and had no idea in what direction the robbers had gone. The bandits drove to Kandiyohi where they had the other car waiting for them. From there, it's believed they took one of two different routes. One was to head to Annandale and Minneapolis, but more likely they drove south on County Road 8 and through Lake Lillian. Staying on the county roads as much as possible, it's believed they went through Stewart, Gibbon, Henderson, Lonsdale, and, ironically, Northfield on their circular route to St. Paul.

A couple of weeks later, on August 14th, three men, including gang leader Stein, were found executed gangland style in a lover's lane section of land near Wildwood Park by the Twin Cities. All were shot in the head. Two of the men were in a car and the other was found a distance away in the grass, as if he had tried to escape from his murderer. He had two bullet holes, maybe punishment for making the assailant run.

89

The Savings Bank of Ottumwa, Iowa was held up on September 30th. $40,000 was taken and Harvey Bailey, Tommy Holden, Francis Keating, Verne Miller and "Machine Gun" Kelly were believed to have participated in that robbery. The gang sounded a lot like the ones who held up the bank in Willmar.

During a prison interview in 1934, "Machine Gun" Kelly claimed Verne Miller had committed the murders after Stein/Silverman had "double-crossed him." Miller, at the time of Kelly's confession, was already dead and therefore couldn't confirm or deny the charge. Another man, probably the driver in the Willmar heist because of a wound in his neck, was found in a shallow grave near Owatonna, Minnesota. Frank "Big Fritz" Coleman and Mike Rusick were found shot to death on August 30th near White Bear Lake. They were hanging from the limbs of trees.

The money was never recovered although a thirty-seven year old man using the name James Morrison was arrested in Chicago in August of 1932 while trying to sell some of the bonds. Some Bank of Willmar employees identified him, but others weren't sure.

The bank robbery scared all the neighboring town banks enough that announcements were immediately put in all the local newspapers claiming that they had beefed up their security systems. They feared a potential run on the banks like they had witnessed a few years prior during the depression.

Although Rudy Paffrath was treated as a hero in the newspapers, let's not forget that his firing at the bandits accomplished nothing, endangered the lives of the hostages and actually made a bad situation worse. The bandits might have quietly left town. Paffrath could have caused the deaths of Marie Wacker, George Robbins, Mrs. Emil Johnson and Mrs. Donna Gildea, not to mention all the other people on the streets of Willmar who had narrow misses with bullets. In the very least, he caused a lot of damage to buildings and cars. One might argue that he prevented Wacker and Robbins from being taken hostage in the car. That's debatable.

But for a long time, at least the rest of that hot summer, Willmar citizens had something else to talk about besides how high the corn was getting or "Is it hot enough for you?"

Chapter Fifteen
Other Banks, Other Robberies – Part One

Bank robber Willie "The Actor" Sutton, from the thirties and the forties, was once asked why he robbed banks. His answer was simple, straight to the point and honest.

"Because that's where the money is," was Sutton's reply.

Researching other things in the newspapers, I couldn't help but come across the occasional "bank job" story. Other places were robbed; bars, stores and homes. But the bank heist has a certain flair about it that draws you to it, maybe because of the Jesse James-Bonnie and Clyde images. To my knowledge, Litchfield, Minnesota was spared the bank robbers' hand. But, I hope you share my interest as I tell you about a few more local "jobs".

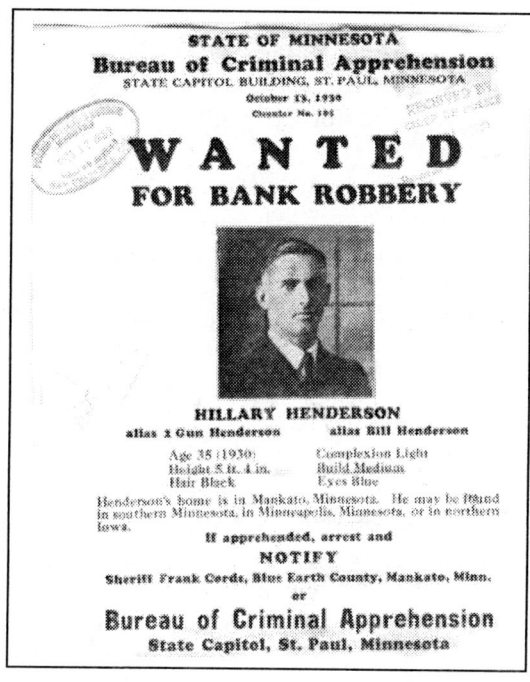

A typical Wanted Poster you might see in the Post Office.

Not all bank jobs were successful, and even the successful ones were not all that fruitful. And some of the jobs were "inside" jobs as in the case of the occasional embezzlement. Of course, there was some funny goings on in Litchfield's Stevens and Company Bank. Litchfield's mayor, Hiram S. Branham, son of Litchfield's first "mayor" Jesse V. Branham, Jr., was a co-owner of the Stevens and Company Bank, which failed due to some shady dealings. One night in December of 1890, while his brother D. E. "Abe" Branham was visiting him, Hiram went into his bedroom and put a bullet in his chest just below his heart with a .32 revolver. The next morning, he died at the age of thirty-four. One of the officers of the bank was arrested for embezzlement and many people lost their money.

In January of 1883, S. E. Thurston, another embezzler, was caught pilfering $2,500 from the Kandiyohi County Bank, where he worked as a bookkeeper.

William Matthews, an out of work locomotive fireman, decided he knew a way to get some money and an ideal way for a getaway. Around 9:30am or so, on a Thursday in February of 1902, William boarded the westbound train just out of Minneapolis. When the train got to Plato, Minnesota and stopped for a five-minute wait for passengers, William jumped off and ran the two blocks to the Plato bank. He ran in the door, drew a revolver out of his pocket and demanded all the cash.

The teller turned over $1500. Matthews ran back out the door and made the train just in time. When he got to Glencoe, the next town five miles away, policemen boarded the train and took William off. How did they know? The Plato bank had recently added one of those new fangled telephone things. The teller simply called ahead to Glencoe, who called the police. William, not so versed on new inventions, I suppose, handed over $1490. Somehow between Plato and Glencoe, William had lost or spent $10.

Most times, whether the hold-up was a success or not, bumps and bruises were all that happened to the tellers, bystanders, or robbers. The Willmar job was an exception. We had a tragedy a little closer to home, however, in November of 1914.

The patrons of the Citizen's Bank of Dassel were surprised to see the bank empty when they entered one by one during the day. Two or three came and went after shrugging their shoulders, but one patron thought it odd that the bank was wide open and no one was inside. So this one brilliant person out of so many...er...less intelligent ones, went to the police to report the oddity. When the police came to investigate, they went behind the teller cage by the vault where they found cashier O. M. Palmquist lying dead on the floor. He had been shot once in the back of the head at close range. Further investigation revealed nothing missing in the bank. Perhaps the robber(s) had been scared off before he could do anything. Or maybe it was a professional hit for some discretion committed by Palmquist. No one was ever arrested in the case.

Three men visited sleepy little Kingston, Minnesota, ten miles from Litchfield as the crow flies, one fall Wednesday morning in 1919. It was September 24th, to be exact. The men drove into town in a Buick-Six touring car. They were all dressed in hunting clothes, which wasn't unusual given the area and time of the year. But they didn't seem to be in any hurry to do any hunting.

Instead, they hung around town, walking the streets, standing next to their car smoking and talking. Finally, a little after noon, they ambled into the local café and had a bite to eat. Stretching their dinner out as long as they could, they paid their bills and walked back to their car. They got in and drove out of town.

About a mile out of town, they pulled over and got out and removed the car's license plates. Jumping back in, they turned around and headed back into town where two of them were deposited at 1:30pm in front of the Kingston State Bank, the only bank in town. The third man stayed in the car.

Then two men, still dressed in hunting clothes, walked into the bank and one of them walked up to cashier J. E. Matsen's counter. He started a conversation with Matsen about the weather, how the hunting was in the area, and just small talk, never once saying what he wanted in the bank. Matsen started to get suspicious. Suddenly the man pulled a revolver out of his pocket and pointed it in Matsen's face.

"This is a hold up," the man said.

Matsen looked at him and then just ducked down under his counter and pressed the alarm button. The robber fired his gun into the counter. Frightened by the alarm, the two gave up their quest and turned and ran out the door, where they jumped into the car and sped away.

Matsen ran out the door after the men, saw them head west out of town across the bridge. He ran to his own car, where J. A. Hannula joined him. The quickly formed posse took off after the outlaws. Just out of town they were met with some men moving a herd of cows across the road. Slowed down, they couldn't find their quarry again and gave up the pursuit. The men were never caught.

The Kingston Bridge about the time of the holdup.

Less than two weeks later, on Friday, October 3rd, somebody broke into the Danube State Bank and bored a hole into the three-foot thick wall of the bank's vault. They got away with some Liberty bonds and $70 in cash. Could that have been all the money that was in the little town's vault?

In November of 1923, some burglars entered the State Bank of Pennock, Minnesota in the wee hours of the morning and liberated the establishment of $3,000 to $5,000 worth of Liberty bonds. The bonds were in tin boxes on the floor of the vault, which had a simple combination lock on it. The liberators borrowed an acetylene gas tank for their torch from a nearby garage and melted the lock off. How did they get into the bank in the first place? They simply opened a rear window.

Three men made an attempt to rob the Cosmos First State Bank on Tuesday, April 21, 1924. The bandits parked out of town and walked into the sleepy little community where they got into the bank through a basement window. Before they came into town a little after one in the morning, they cut all the telephone and telegraph wires leading in and out of the town. One man was left to stand guard outside the bank.

Inside the bank, the other two packed the safe with explosives and set them off. The door opened, but the thieves were confronted with an upper and a lower compartment inside. Eeny meeny, miney moe...the duo opted for the lower one, which they blew open. Unfortunately, the bank's $5,000 in cash was in the upper compartment. The money had been received just the night before to pay the members of the local creamery. Do you suppose a creamery employee was involved in the attempted heist?

The noise from the first explosion aroused garage owner Emil Hackbarth from his sleep. He lived right across the street. Apparently Emil didn't like to be woken up. He reached for his revolver, which he conveniently had near his bed, and went to his window facing the bank and fired a shot off. I don't know if he saw the lookout there or not but J. H. Jerabek, who lived a couple of houses down the street did.

Jerabek, the bank cashier, lit a lamp and stepped out onto his porch where he ran into a shotgun.

"Get back in, or I'll blow your head off," is what Jerabek heard. He went back in and immediately grabbed his own shotgun, but he couldn't find any shells.

Alerted by the lookout that the town was waking up, the two men inside opened another window and climbed out. The three then ran to their car and sped off, never to be seen or heard of again.

Chapter Sixteen
Other Banks, Other Robberies – Part Two

It took six bandits armed with pickaxes, sawed off shotguns and a lot of nitroglycerin a little over two hours to terrorize the tiny town of Svea[33] and make off with a whopping $600. They left Svea's Farmer's State Bank[34], which was combined with the Farmer's Cooperative store and post office, in a $3,000 mess. This happened in August of 1924 and ironically, about sixty years later my wife Lois (before I married her) ran that Coop store and post office. The bank was gone by then.

The six bandits must have watched a few movies or read too many detective magazines, but they did have the thing planned out. Like the Cosmos bandits, they too cut all the wires leading in and out of the town before they came in a little after midnight. Myrtle Doran, the night telephone operator, heard a noise outside, went to the window, and watched as some men slashed the cable outside the office door. Four of the six men kept guard on the entire town, while the remaining two battered their way into the bank building and then set off four tremendous blasts with the nitro to get into the safe inside the vault, which they had broken into through its brick wall.

The explosions were so terrific that they totally wrecked the bank part of the building, hurling pieces of metal from the safe out onto the street. John Freed, who lived across the street from the bank building, lit a lamp to investigate. One of the "guards" ran to his door, pounded on it, and yelled, "Put out that light! Get back to bed." To make sure he was understood, he then fired two blasts from his sawed off shotgun into the air.

While the men worked for nearly two hours on the vault and safe, smashing the store's cash register also, frightened citizens carefully peeked out their windows. After the robbers left town with their booty, some volunteers drove to Willmar and alerted the law. William West, a convict from Iowa, was arrested a week later and got five years in Stillwater for his $100 cut of the booty. I don't know if any of the others were caught.

---

[33] The town is ten miles south of Willmar, Minnesota. In 1924 the population of the town was fifty people.

[34] My wife says that signs in the back of the store read "Svea State Bank".

Seven months later, a group of bad men tried to break into the vault in the bank in Good Thunder, Minnesota. But they were foiled by a homemade anti-burglary setup. When they got into the vault, a jar filled with ammonia and mustard gas fell to the floor and broke. The mixture immediately released acrid fumes into the entire bank and it drove the men to look elsewhere for their night's work. They drove all the way to Cold Spring, Minnesota where they too cut all the telephone and telegraph wires leading in and out of town. Maybe they also read the newspapers? This time they were successful in getting into the bank and they got $5,000 for their effort. Litchfield's Sheriff Paul E. Anderson and Chief of Police Frank T. Nelson were called at 5:00am and told to be on the alert for the bandits. I don't know if the men were caught or not.

Prinsburg and Cosmos had bank hits also and finally in March of 1925, the month of the Cold Spring job, the banks in Litchfield started improving their security systems. The local newspapers referred to the robbers, who blew the safes with nitroglycerine, as "yeggs" or "yeggmen". I had read this term before in the early days of Litchfield, always referring to bad men, so I finally looked it up. The dictionary said "safecrackers or robbers", so now I know a new "old" word.

A lot of people were depressed and down on their luck during this period and I started reading about weekly suicides in the newspapers of that time. The chosen method was hanging, usually in the barn or garage. Some leaned into their shotguns, while sitting in a chair. A man a block away from us did that, blowing off his face and wounding his brother, who was upstairs in the bedroom over the desperate man. Another man took no chances. He put a noose around his neck after climbing up on a chair and then shot himself in the head. The newspapers in the twenties gave all the gory details. A few took a horrific and odd passage to the other side by drinking acid and suffering, sometimes for days. One man simply laid his head on the railroad track. Do I dare wonder what was the last thing to run through his mind? (Did you get that crude joke?)

Mrs. Gottlieb Koerner, well-known butcher lady for years in Litchfield, had a son-in-law named T. E. Coleman, who was an assistant cashier at the First National Bank of Anoka, Minnesota. He and five other employees were in the bank at 10am with three customers in December of 1925, when four armed men entered and demanded money. A fifth man stood guard outside. After locking the employees and customers in the vault, the five bad men drove out of town with over $15,000. This had been the fourth bank holdup in Minnesota in nine weeks.

Fred LaBrie was down on his luck. He had come to Harrison, a few miles north of Atwater, Minnesota, and rented a farm. But farming didn't seem to be his thing. He wasn't making it. It was 1928 and desperate times called for desperate measures. Fred drove over to the small town of Kandiyohi in his green Essex Coach automobile and parked next to the city park. The park was across the street and south of the Home State Bank, which sat on the corner in the center of the town.

All around the country, it seemed, people had taken to robbing banks and most of them, again it seemed, were getting away with it. Why couldn't he? He wouldn't get greedy. He'd just hold up a small bank. Fred didn't even have a gun. He hadn't really planned this out, you see. He had just come to town to "case the bank out". Finally, at about 4pm, looking around the sleepy little town with virtually no pedestrians or traffic, Fred decided, "Why the hell not?" He got out of the car and opened his trunk. The only thing he had heavy to use was an auto spring leaf[35]. He reached in and picked it up.

Levi Lund had been in the bank getting change and saw Fred coming in just as he was leaving. He didn't recognize the man, but said, "Howdy" anyway as he left. Inside the bank, Fred looked around. Lady Luck was finally on his side. The bank was empty and the usual male cashier was even gone. He was out clerking an auction. The only person behind the bank counter was a little petite woman named Elsie Shosten. She was standing in front of the open vault door.

"This is a hold-up," Fred said to the little lady. "Do what I ask and I won't have to hurt you," he added, holding up the auto spring leaf. "Put all the money on the counter."

Elsie started turning to enter the vault.

"Just the money in the drawer," Fred said. Elsie turned back around, reached into her money drawer and pulled out a bunch of

---

[35] About eight inches long and three inches wide, it was a curved piece of metal. When about six were stacked on top of each other, they made the body spring for the old cars before shock absorbers.

bills. Spreading them out on the counter, she decided to leave the rest of the money in the drawer. This guy didn't seem too smart.

"Now get into the safe," he said, motioning towards the vault.

"No," Elsie replied. She was afraid of being locked in there. She might not be discovered until the next day. Who knew if there was air in there when the door was shut. "No," she repeated. "No, I won't."

"You're gettin' in there," Fred said, grabbing Elsie. She pushed him away and he grabbed her again. Now she really started struggling. Fred was afraid she would attract attention. He took his auto spring leaf, raised it up and brought it down hard on Elsie's head, knocking her out cold.

Scooping up a hand full of bills off the counter and leaving some, Fred ran out of the bank to his car. He didn't bother with the safe or the rest of the money in the drawer, but unbelievably what he got was about $1400.

Somebody must have recognized the green Essex or Fred because Sheriff Paul E. Anderson was at his place that night. Fred got into the Essex and took off down the road. The Sheriff caught up with him near Atwater. Before he got to him though, Fred had slit his throat and wrists with a pocketknife. He survived the suicide attempt and stood trial. Fred was given an odd sentence of five to forty years in the Stillwater State Prison. That's quite a spread.

The Kandiyohi Bankers Association, which owned the Home State Bank, gave Elsie a "gift" of $100 in gratitude for her "plunk" in standing up to the bank robber.

As I wrote earlier, to my knowledge none of the Litchfield banks were ever held up. I've gone through all the newspapers stored at the Meeker County Historical Society museum several times and I've never seen any mention of anything concerning the several banks Litchfield has had over the years.

One burglary was attempted, however. In the overall history of Litchfield, it happened fairly recently. Sunday morning, March 6, 1966, to be exact. I was in my third year of college and I no longer bothered to read the local paper, so I wasn't aware of the story. But it happened just a few blocks from our house, so my mother and stepfather must've mentioned it to me. I must have forgotten about it.

About ten in the morning that Sunday, a bank customer was dropping off some deposits into the night depository by the First State

Center bank's drive-in window on the west side of the bank. He noticed a 21-inch by 75-inch section of the ¼ inch thick plate glass in the bank's west door had been removed. He thought it odd enough that he immediately notified the police, who, in turn, notified the FBI.

The police did a walk through of the bank with the bank president and found nothing missing, except for the door glass. The opening was large enough for someone to crawl through, so they thought it odd that nothing had been touched. The bank's alarm system had been tampered with, however. Maybe it had scared the thief away? Chief of Police George Fenner recalled that the burglar alarm had sounded at 2:30am. "What?" I thought as I read the newspaper account. "And nobody investigated it?" Unfortunately the newspaper article was brief and gave no details on that odd fact.

A week later, night patrolman John Swanson was checking the alley entrances to stores when he noticed the glass to the rear door of Butterwick Drug had been broken with a block of concrete laying near by. He slipped quietly into the store where he found twenty-year old Gary Tollakson digging through some drawers. Upon seeing the policeman, Tollakson literally ran through the glass front door, while Swanson yelled, "Stop!" and fired his gun over the thief's head.

Tollakson, scratched and bleeding from the glass, didn't stop. A chase ensued with Swanson firing again in the air outside to stop his quarry. It still didn't work. The chase ended up by some bushes by the old Depot, where the burglar was found hiding. A search of his person turned up something odd. In his jacket pocket were several round chocolates wrapped in shiny foil so that they resembled a fifty-cent piece or a silver dollar. The First State Center bank had recently given them away in a promotion and a basket of them sat out on the counter in the bank. Apparently the bank robber of a week ago HAD gotten away with something.

Come And Get It

You can't stay away from the love theme when you write songs. 99% of the songs you hear on the radio must be about relationships. So, you always look for novel ways to approach the subject and write about it. Growing up, my brothers and I had an old novelty record called The Salesman Song. *The singer was selling himself, so to speak. I thought that was a novel approach so I tried it with these lyrics adding a little bit of a macho chauvinistic flavor to them. I was pleased with my rhyming.*

Come And Get It

If you want…lovin' that won't quit.
Come and get it. You won't regret it.
If you want…devotion with emotion.
Then I'm your man. Your biggest fan.

I'll be as faithful as a puppy dog.
Order anything in my catalog.
If you want…lovin' that won't quit. (I'll fit.)
Come and get it. You won't regret it.

Even if it's…only for a while. (I'll take it.)
You can fake it, 'til you wanna break it.
I just want…a moment of your time. (No crime!)
I won't stay any longer than you say.

I'll be as faithful as a puppy dog.
Order anything in my catalog.
Well, if you want…lovin' that won't quit (I'll fit).
Come and get it. You won't regret it.
Come and get it. You won't regret it.

Chapter Seventeen
Bald Headed Girls

I wrote in *Terry Tales* about a couple of sisters named Emma and Esther Swanson who owned the Silver Grill restaurant in town where Dueber's is today. The story told was that you could get more than food and drink at the Silver Grill, if you know what I mean. One oddity about the sisters, and there were many oddities, was that they were both completely bald. But no one ever knew it. They had beautiful black wigs that they always wore high atop their pretty heads. I never found out why the Swansons were bald. Researching this book, I found out that there were four other bald sisters in town, a little before the Swansons' time. They were Mathilda, Ann, Gertrude and Catheryn Post. Their baldness was work related.

When the railroad came to the area in 1869, a group of people started a town where Litchfield is today. It went through a couple of name changes before the people voted to call it Litchfield after a railroad investor, whose wife was a benefactor of the town's churches. Soon the population outnumbered the county seat of Forest City. The county seat was moved to Litchfield, literally. Many of the buildings in Forest City became buildings in Litchfield. One of those was F. G. Alvord's blacksmith shop. It became Dan Post's blacksmith shop in September of 1882 and then Nick Post's shop. Eventually during one of the Posts' reigns, it ended up near the corner of Third Street East and Marshall Avenue North. That would put it directly across the street from the present library.

Nick Post's house and blacksmith shop in the early 1910s.

Nick also had a house to the south of his shop, which was convenient because Nick needed all the help he could get in his shop. He'd pound out horseshoes, plowshares, disks, wagon rims, scythes and sickles and repair and sharper them too. Nick hated horseshoeing. It seems he was always getting bit or kick by a high-spirited horse. Nick repaired all kinds of farm machinery. Some days there'd be as many as eighteen disks lined up in front of the shop, waiting to be sharpened or repaired. Everyone in the family had to pitch in. Unfortunately, Nick had only four teen and pre-teenage daughters. His sons, Lloyd and John were too little to work in the shop. So the girls dutifully worked in the smithy, with soot and smoke in the air and under foot.

The four girls would come home every night blackened by the soot, smoke and dirt, as "black as little pickaninnies". In those days, a weekly bath was considered a luxury. You washed your face and hands in the washbasin and that was it. There wasn't extra water for washing four girls' soot blackened hair either. So Nick's wife simply shaved the girls' heads. Problem solved. I'm sure the girls loved getting teased about it in school and on the street. But in those days, you did what your parents told you and you didn't complain…to them.

Eventually Nick's boys grew old enough to work and they grew quite big and strong helping in the shop. Big and strong enough that Lloyd starred on the football field for Litchfield High and was named Captain. He also excelled on the basketball court. But, Nick lost his two boys. John drowned in a lake nearby when he was only fourteen and Lloyd was killed in January of 1930.

Lloyd and his friend Vernon Lindberg were on their way in a Ford automobile to Chicken Lake at eleven in the morning on a Sunday to do hunting. They brought along Lloyd's loyal companion, his hunting dog. They came to the railroad crossing three miles west of Litchfield and, for some reason, they didn't see the fast mail train. Lindberg, who was killed instantly, was thrown 110 feet. Lloyd's body was thrown in the air 120 feet, but he wasn't killed instantly. He ended up tangled in a wire fence. A witness called for help and rescuers spent a lot of time trying to extricate Lloyd from the fence. He died in his rescuers arms. A few feet from Lloyd lay his hunting dog, also dead.

Nick sold the shop to Ben Sandberg and Charles Osbeck in July of 1932. The days of blacksmithing was coming to an end. I don't know what other businesses followed, but the smithy was torn down, something replaced it and eventually, in September of 1959, Dr. Lowell Wilson put up a new office building at the corner for his chiropractic business.

Chapter Eighteen
More Railroad Tragedies

I wrote a chapter in *Terry Tales* about all the accidents that occurred over the years at the railroad crossings in Litchfield. Not all railroad accidents or tragedies happened at the crossings though. And some of the accidents bordered between tragedy and comedy. The following story could actually have been in the "I Read It In The Paper" chapters earlier in this book. It happened in March of 1890.

A Darwin man came to Litchfield with his horse-drawn sleigh to get some sacks of feed. While in town, he happened to drop in at one of the local saloons to have a sip or two of Rye. I think he had more than two sips of the stuff, because on the way out of town in the dark he slumped to the bottom of his sleigh, too loose to get back up on his seat. "No problem," he must've thought, snuggling in beside the thirteen sacks of feed. "My horses know the way home."

His horses did indeed know the way home, jingling through the snow, which was coming down pretty good by now. The team even knew enough to head for the right railroad crossing, but, for some reason, instead of turning on to the road just *after* the crossing, they turned left immediately and headed down the railroad tracks. An eastbound freight train came upon the horses, loaded sleigh and loaded driver about a half a mile west of Darwin. Sleigh and sacks went flying.

The horses were injured and the Darwin man ended up on his back far from the tracks. The railroad personnel found him and decided he was dead. They carried him to the Darwin depot. The Darwin section foreman and the boss of the tank house were summoned to the depot. The foreman laid his head on the dead man's chest and then looked up and said, "This man is still alive!" He grabbed a bottle of "la grippe" medicine and forced it down the injured man's throat. Nothing happened so the men commenced to rub the man's hands and feet and dump more medicine down his throat.

Suddenly the "dead man" came to life, sitting up and exclaiming, "Old woman, get the children up to do the chores." When he was fully conscious, the man claimed to be unaware that anything had happened to him. When asked how much he had to drink, he said, "Just a couple of sips of Rye. I must've been drugged." At least that's what he wanted his wife to believe.

105

There was a tragic "railroad involved" accident that happened to some Litchfield boys back in the winter of 1936. Older people in town keep bringing it up. Litchfield had an undefeated basketball team that year, some members of which were Bruce Anderson[36] and Karl Koerner[37] at guard, Orville "Orv" Pope[38], Wes Cassady and Joe Wegner at forward and Abe Johnson[39] at center.

Anderson, Pope, and Koerner wanted to go to the cities to scout Edison-Washburn High, whom they were sure they were going to meet in the upcoming regional tournament. So, they got a ride down to the cities on Saturday, January 25 with a friend of Koerner. They spent the night in Minneapolis and on Sunday morning they started hitchhiking home. The weather started turning colder and soon the senior boys were miserable.

By noon, they had gotten as far as the Dassel area where they ran into a filling station to warm up before going out to hitchhike again. The traffic on Highway 12 had been sparse, the rides had been few and the boys were freezing. They noticed a freight train rolling slowly through town on the nearby railroad tracks.

"Hey," one of the boys said. "Let's hop that freight!"

"Yeah," another said. "We'll get home in no time."

"I'm not gonna do that," Koerner said. "It's too dangerous. I'm gonna keep walking and hitching."

So, just Anderson and Pope jumped on the slow moving flatbed railroad car and off they went. It was a cold freezing ride, but they were finally getting somewhere.

When the train got to Litchfield, it didn't stop as the boys had thought it would. It sped right through the crossings, heading towards Willmar, twenty-five miles away. A few miles out of Litchfield, about a mile and a half east of Grove City, the boys made up their minds to jump off the moving train before they ended up in Willmar, compounding their problems.

Afraid of landing on top of each other, Anderson jumped off the left side of the train and Pope jumped off the right. Anderson landed in a snow bank. Pope didn't jump correctly and he got hit in the head

---

[36] Son of Alfred Anderson.
[37] Son of Albert Koerner.
[38] Son of Ray Pope.
[39] See Chapter Nineteen about the Johnson Brothers Construction Company.

by the next boxcar. Knocked out, he lay on the ground in the freezing temperature for a long time while Anderson first looked for him, saw what had happened and then ran looking for a farmhouse to ask for help.

He found the Alvin Eckberg farm but Eckberg told Bruce he had no phone.

"Go to the next farm," Eckberg said. "They've got a car. While you're doing that, I'll load up my team and go look for your friend."

Anderson got a ride to town and there he called his parents, Orv's dad Ray, and Dr. Macklin. They all went looking for Orv. Meanwhile Eckberg found Pope but a huge snowdrift prevented him from getting his team close enough to the unconscious boy. Eckberg couldn't lift and carry the big senior boy either. All he could do was cover him with a blanket. When he saw approaching headlights from Litchfield, he directed the rescuers as close as he could. They carried Orv back to the car and rushed the injured boy to the hospital.

Pope, who was unconscious until late Thursday afternoon, had a skull fracture, a deep head gash, and a broken jaw. He lost parts of his toes, two fingers and one thumb, and the tips of the rest of his fingers on his hands.

On February 10th, the team set up a benefit basketball game with Belgrade to raise money for Orville. Once again the weather caused problems. A blizzard came up and the Belgrade team couldn't get out of their town. So Litchfield called Howard Lake to help because Highway 12 was still open. Howard Lake came but the blocked roads and cold weather cut the crowd in half, at least. They only raised $100.

The team was drained emotionally over the loss of the core of their group and they never got to the regions, getting upset in the districts. Pope came back to play a little, shooting the ball with only parts of his fingers. It wasn't the same.

Most railroad tragedies did involve the crossings, however. And most of them, tragically, resulted in death. I was reminded of a crossing accident that went "a-fowl" in late 1973. This time it was at the crossing just up the street from the house I grew up in on Swift Avenue North.

On Thursday, October 11, 1973, my mother and stepfather, Helen and Floyd Young, walked up to the Swift Avenue railroad crossing a block away from their house to view the accident scene. It looked like it had snowed in Litchfield the previous night. White feathers were everywhere covering the ground like a blanket of new fallen snow. For a lot of local citizens, Thanksgiving had come early that October morning. Two hundred or so live turkeys were running loose all over town. Most of them never made it to their original destination, the Jennie-O plant a block away from the crossing.

Harold "Smokey" Schmidt, our neighbor and a retired dogcatcher and garbage collector, spent most of his Saturday plucking feathers off of about fifty of the big birds. His wife, Clara, hired herself out to clean and dress out game birds for hunters. For the last two days, Litchfield citizens had been dropping off the huge birds at the Schmidt house.

What had happened? Dennis Nygaard was driving his truck and trailer full of 1600 live turkeys across the railroad crossing at about a quarter past five that dark fall morning. Dennis was heading for the turkey plant a block east of the crossing. Suddenly there was a bump and a jerk and Dennis found himself driving away from the crossing without his trailer. Somehow, the trailer had come loose from his truck and stopped right on the tracks. Nygaard couldn't hook it back up without a tow truck's help. He knew that a morning passenger train always came through Litchfield about this time. Thinking quickly, Dennis drove to the turkey plant office where he attempted to call Amtrak and get them to stop the train. Unfortunately, time wasn't on his side.

At 5:32 am, the Amtrak passenger train slammed into the trailer at 78 mph. Feathers, turkey parts and trailer parts flew east down the tracks all the way through town to Schwartzwald's car dealership[40] three quarters of a mile away. The impact ripped away part of the crossing's signal system and disabled the locomotive, so another one had to be sent out to Litchfield from Minneapolis. The Amtrak passengers had to sit and look out their railroad car windows for over two hours as the morning sun came up to shine on a sea of white feathers and mangled turkey body parts.

---

[40] Once Ferguson's, today the Litchfield Chrysler Center is at that location.

Chapter Nineteen
Do You Have A Stencil?

One of the most successful businesses to operate out of the Litchfield area has been the Johnson Bros. Corporation, also known as the Johnson Brothers Highway and Heavy Construction, Inc. Run exclusively by a family from the company's meager start, its story is as American as apple pie.

The family-run business, which got its first highway[41] job in 1947 and its first million dollar contract in 1955, has operated for over seventy years, successfully doing jobs in all of the forty-eight contiguous states, Canada, Saudi Arabia and Kuwait. An interesting piece of trivia about working in those desert countries, which consist mostly of sand, is that Johnson Bros. has had to ship in sand for projects there. The desert sand is just too fine for cement mixing and the like.

The history of the company goes back four generations to a man named James M. "Jim" Johnson who did road construction in the Des Moines, Iowa area around 1900. His son Walter D. actually founded the company. Walter dropped out of school after the eighth grade to work with his dad. In the early 1900's, he met and married a woman named Rosalind.

Walter, Jim, and Walter's first son George[42] worked on road construction in Iowa in the early 1900s. But in the fall of 1918, Walter decided he needed a better way to support his growing family, which had expanded to five sons[43] at that time. He decided to buy a 160-acre farm up north in Minnesota near Long Prairie. He had heard about the terribly cold Minnesota winters so the family left one-year-old Abe with Grandpa Jim. The family was afraid a tiny baby would freeze to death in Minnesota. But eventually they found out they were wrong and sent for the baby, who went on to be the driving force in the company.

Thirteen-year-old George was asked to ride in the railroad boxcar with the horses and family possessions that the family loaded in Des Moines, Iowa, while the rest to the family came up in an old Ford touring car. The boxcar was unheated, of course, and, with the

---

[41] Highway 22 between Glencoe and Hutchinson, Minnesota.
[42] Born in 1906, George died at the age of ninety-two in June of 1998.
[43] They were George, Jim, J. R., Paul and Abe.

temperatures nearing zero, George kept from freezing by snuggling into the horses. Maybe Rosalind wouldn't have minded trading places with George driving hundreds of miles with three little boys in an unheated Ford.

To supplement his farm income, Walter went to work for the Todd County road department in construction. In 1926, he bought into a road construction company with Henry M. Nelson. Nelson's spending practices and poor management resulted in Walter buying him out and bringing his sons into the firm in 1929. The family had grown to eight sons[44] and they all pitched in with the work. Walter organized the Johnson Construction Company with his sons in 1931.

Having been awarded a big contract in Meeker County, the family moved to Grove City from Long Prairie in 1934. There, Walter befriended a well-to-do man named Louis "Louie" Johnson from Swede Grove Township. Louie happened to be the president of the Grove City Bank. When the government closed the banks in 1933, Louie kept his bank open, sometimes using his own money from home, which he brought to the bank in suitcases. (What? Didn't he trust banks?) Because of this, the multi-million dollar firm has done business with that little bank over the years.

In the early years of the company, the heavy work was done with a combination of primitive machinery, horses and the strength of the nine Johnson men and boys and a couple of additional employees. The strong athletic boys, the ones still of school age, were sort of "recruited" to go to Litchfield High School.

Walter decided that one of his boys should go on to college. He picked Abe because he thought Abe could get a scholarship because of his grades and athletic prowess. Walter said, "I don't wanna have to go and shake hands and talk to those bankers all the time. We need someone educated who can talk on their level." Abe did get an athletic scholarship to Hamline University.

On a Sunday morning in November of 1940, 56 year old Walter, his wife and eighteen year old Walter, Jr. were hit by the west bound Great Northern Empire Builder at the Armstrong Avenue crossing in Litchfield on their way to church. Eight-foot high snow banks had

---

[44] To the previous five were added Ray, Walter, Jr. and Robert.

blocked their view and Walter's car got stuck in the deep ice filled ruts of the crossing's approach.

Walter's son Bob was walking home from an earlier church service and had stopped at the Traveler's Inn to warm up. He heard the train's whistle blow and turned to look from the café's doorway just in time to see his dad's car being tossed into the air. He ran to the Sibley Avenue crossing, where the car had ended up, and saw his father dead in the car and his brother and mother laying on the gravel. Help came and Rosalind and Junior were taken to the hospital.

Bob ran back to the church and came in during the middle of the sermon. He found his other brothers, ran to their pew and he told them the news. They all ran out of the church. Others in the church had overheard what Bob had told his brothers and they stood and told the preacher who stopped the service.

Walter's wife survived but Junior died later that day at the hospital. Rosalind spent five months in the hospital. George, who had a house of his own, moved back home to help raise the other kids. The sons got together and decided to not let the tragedy stop the company's growth. Abe dropped out of college and came home to pick up the slack in the company. Walter's son Jim, who had taken over as the manager of the company, told Abe, "Dad had a plan about you goin' to college and we're gonna keep with Dad's plans. You're goin' back to school." Abe finished up at Harvard majoring in business.

World War II started and Abe, Ray and Robert went into the service. George, Jim, J. R. and Paul worked on defense construction projects, such as building an airport in Sioux Falls, South Dakota. They also worked on the Alcan[45] Highway up in Canada.

The road construction up there was very difficult because of the weather, of course, the frozen soil, but also because of the threat of wildlife such as the bears and wildcats. The men couldn't survey through the dense tree covered land so they aimed at a "target" and built towards it. Only once did they have to go back and rebuild a road using that method.

When the highway was done, George didn't want to leave the equipment up there to freeze up over the winter so he stayed to watch it and take care of it while his other brothers went home. All of the

---

[45] Alaskan/Canadian

equipment, the Johnson Brothers equipment and the Army equipment that was used in the construction of the highway were shipped home by loading it on boats, taking it down the west coast of the United States and then putting it on railroad cars.

George had become friendly with an Army Corps of Engineers major. One day George was called into the major's office.

"George," he inquired, "do you have a stencil?"

George didn't understand and he gave the major back a blank stare.

"Do you know what a stencil is, George?" the major asked.

"Yes, I know what a stencil is," George replied.

"Do you have one with your company's name on it?"

"Yes..." George said slowly, still not understanding what this conversation was all about. The stencil he had read "Johnson Bros. Litchfield, Minnesota."

"See that boat out there?" the major continued, pointing out the office window toward the dock.

George nodded his head.

"That boat is totally loaded with forty or fifty big units of iron (construction equipment). Do you suppose that you would know how to use your stencil on some of that equipment down there?"

"Well..."

"I'll tell you the truth," the major added, "We don't know where the hell to send it. I'm supposed to ship it back to the States but I don't know where."

George looked at all the equipment and shook his head. "Typical government operation," he thought. SNAFU...Situation normal, all "fouled" up.

"You use your stencil and put your name on that equipment," the major said, finally revealing his plan. "We'll ship it home to you."

George went out to the boat and looked at the millions of dollars of equipment and he started visualizing trainload cars of tractor after tractor coming into Litchfield and Grove City with the Johnson name on the sides. What would his brothers say? Then he started visualizing himself behind bars somewhere.

George walked slowly back into the major's office. "I've got the stencil all right," he said, "but I ain't gonna put our name on any of that equipment."

The major had the equipment taken off the boat and hauled out into the woods. It left there for the Canadians to worry about.

From that point on, whenever the brothers got into an argument about the integrity of a job, one of them would quietly stop the argument by asking, "Do you have a stencil?"

A Toast

Several times over the years, I've been asked to make a toast at an anniversary party, a retirement dinner, or just a family get-together. I make one every time my family gets together for the holidays. I decided to write a toast of my own and make it adaptable for any occasion. I did that and I offer it to you for your use.

A Toast

May your life be filled with love
and kindness everyday.
And may the ones you love
be just a touch away.

Chapter Twenty
The Rosemary Home

The doctor had bad news for the couple sitting across from him in his office. Dorothea's pregnancy had taken a turn for the worse. There was a problem.

"I'm sorry to tell you this, but if you bring this baby to term," the doctor said, looking at the young distraught woman, "it will most certainly kill you."

Edwin grabbed his wife's hand. "Isn't there something you can do, doctor?"

"Terminate the pregnancy, but I know your wife's feelings on the matter."

"I will not kill my baby," Dorothea exclaimed.

"Yes, I know," the doctor said quietly, shaking his head. "You understand then that you will probably die in childbirth?"

The woman bowed her head and nodded.

The doctor told Dorothea that the best chance for her baby's survival was for Dorothea to stay in bed. As the days turned into weeks, she had a lot to think about in that bed.

"I was told," she said, "I could not live to bring up my children."

She wouldn't be there to guide her new child and give her advice as she had started to do with her son, and that bothered Dorothea the most. She set out to do something about it. She had come to Litchfield to teach high school English, which she did only briefly because she met an up and coming businessman from a prominent family in town named Edwin.

Because of her interest in reading, Dorothea had started a collection of her favorite sayings. She added to this collection more inspirational sayings and little bits of advice for the baby and for her son, Edwin, Jr. She wanted something to "serve as a substitute in their lives." "The task," she went on, "was to bridge the gap in education not filled by church or schools." She wanted to leave "a chart or blueprint for guiding and teaching such a way of life." She wrote on items in her collection, adding her own thoughts about them that she wanted to tell her children.

In April of 1928, by a miracle or because of the bed rest or a combination of the two, both Dorothea and her baby survived the birthing. The Dorothea and Ed Kopplin named the little girl Rosemary.

The Kopplins seemed to have the Midas touch. Buildings were built and businesses started all over town. Dorothea's parents died and she was left with fourteen farms and some businesses in Minnesota and Wisconsin. Then tragedy struck. Rosemary had leukemia. She died on March 6, 1934 at the age of six.

Rosemary Kopplin

Dorothea and Ed were devastated. It seemed so unfair, yet they never lost their faith, especially Dorothea. She decided to publish a book of her collection of inspirational sayings along with her added thoughts to help others in times of tragedy. Maybe others could benefit from what she had collected and wrote about. That's how *Something To Live By* was born and Dorothea Simons Kopplin became a world famous author.

The book was published in 1945 and it became a best seller. The book wouldn't die. Years would go by and it would resurge in popularity. During WWII, the book was given to GI's by various groups and the royalties for their sale were turned over to the Minnesota Federation of Women's Clubs to be used for nursing scholarships.

Dorothea Simons Kopplin

Dorothea wrote another book called *Scripture To Live By*. It was published in 1955. Ed's business flourished and he began spending more and more time away from home. The couple took over the Kopplin family's beautiful mansion[46], which had been built in about 1885, about the time that Ed's grandfather, Fred, had come to Litchfield to buy a lumberyard. Ed's dad, Fred, Jr., had taken the lumberyard over and also sold coal. When fuel oil became popular, the Kopplins switched over to sell it. Ed also sold cars for a while and switched his company over to natural gas when it came through the area.

The word around town was that Ed started drifting from Dorothea and was a ladies' man in town. I don't know if that was true or not but he and Dorothea divorced in 1956. Dorothea's world started to crumble. On top of everything else, she discovered she had breast cancer. Except for two German Shepard dogs named King and Queenie and a very small circle of friends, which included Norma Berke, Dorothea was alone in the mansion at the corner of Sibley Avenue South and McQuat Street. Her son Ed Jr. was grown up and had moved away. Dorothea saw other mansions in town go to disrepair and get torn down to make room for office buildings and hospitals and she decided that wasn't going to happen to her beloved house.

---

[46] After it was built, there were about four different owners before jeweler David Elmquist bought it in 1891. Gustav Settergren bought it in 1904 when Elmquist moved to Willmar and Fred A. Kopplin, Sr. bought it in 1928.

Always community minded and giving much to many charities, especially medical ones, Dorothea Kopplin, who was named Minnesota Mother of the Year in 1949, decided to will her mansion to the city, with some stipulations. The main floor must be kept exactly as it was and the entire house kept in repair. She put money in a trust to make that possible. Then, the house must not be turned into a museum or any such thing where it wouldn't be used as a home. Female college-level students, such as nursing students studying at the hospital, nurses themselves, student teachers at the public schools and businesswomen could use it. They could live in the house rent-free. The reason was that Dorothea never forgot the care and loving concern nurses had shown her daughter during her illness.

The Rosemary Home today.

So the second floor of the mansion, following Dorothea's wishes, was converted into a dormitory with five bedrooms, housing two students each. Also community groups could use the main floor for meetings, especially charitable groups. The rent for that would be free also. Finally, the house would be named after her beloved daughter who had survived the miracle birth. The city graciously accepted the house under the stipulations and that's how the Rosemary Home was born.

Dorothea became very ill and went to the Meeker County Memorial Hospital. There she had her own dresser, bed, chair and curtains brought in so she could feel more at home. She died on September 14, 1970 at the age of 72. Her divorced husband Ed died a few months later on February 23, 1971. The Rosemary Home at 724 Sibley Avenue South has been in use since it opened to the public in late 1973.

An open house was held on November 25, 1973. Over one thousand people lined up outside the mansion, standing in the cold rain, to get a glimpse of how Litchfield's famous author lived in her lonely mansion on Sibley Avenue.

Chapter Twenty-One
Baseball and Litchfield – Part One

Abner Doubleday invented baseball in Cooperstown, New York. Correct? Wrong. It's universally believed now that the story of the beginnings of our national pastime was made up. How did we come to believe that story in the first place? Well, sporting goods manufacturer A. G. Spaulding wanted to prove that the sport was "all American" so in 1905 he made up a committee and gave them instructions to prove his premise. After two years of research, they couldn't do it.

One day a dejected Spaulding received a letter from Abner Graves, who claimed that he and his friend, Abner Doubleday, had invented the game. Spaulding didn't bother checking on the claim. He was glad that he finally had the "proof" he wanted. The unsupported claim went on as fact for decades until some researchers finally proved that, although the two Abners had played a form of stickball as kids, they didn't invent the game.

What does all of this have to do with Litchfield, other than the fact that Litchfield has produced some great baseball teams over the years? Well, the February of 1890 newspaper told us that the great American game was growing so rapidly in England, that A. G. Spaulding proposed sending a group of base ball[47] "experts" over there to teach the game to the Brits. (I don't suppose the effort had anything to do with expanding the baseball equipment buying territory?) Who did Spaulding pick to send to England? Included in his group were B. E. Harris, Hiram S. Angell[48] and R. Chinnock from non other than Litchfield, Minnesota.

Litchfield has always been in love with the game of baseball. You might be surprised to learn that the town was barely eight years old when Litchfield fielded its first town team. Yes, in June of 1877, the Litchfield Terribles took the field to play Forest City. W. D. Joubert reported in his *News Ledger* that "The game of base ball has broken out in the county at a great rate. Nearly every town in the

---

[47] In the early days, the game was referred to that way. The words weren't combined until much later.
[48] Hiram S. Angell, pioneer photographer Clark L. Angell, Sr.'s son, and Alex Roehl bought the Branham grocery in April of 1892. It was located where the Ed Olson Agency is today.

county has a club and matches are being played every few days." Litchfield's first team consisted of Joubert, Charley Myers, son of William H. Myers, owner of Litchfield's first New Bakery, A. McCarger, S. W. Frasier, owner of a restaurant where the Main Street Café is today, C. Pixley, son of millinery owner Mary L. and insurance agent B. F. Pixley, Charles Taylor, owner of a butcher shop where Larry's Barber Shop is today, George E. White, future State Senator and son of machinery business owner W. M. White, attorney C. Bowen, and H. Hines.

A late August of 1890 Litchfield newspaper reported "Charlie March[49], while in Glencoe last week, made arrangements for the Glencoe nine to meet the Litchfield boys at Hutchinson next Tuesday to play for $50 besides the gate. We are informed Glencoe has a very slick team so the game should be a good one." Imagine how popular the game of baseball must have been at that time for people from Glencoe and Litchfield to drive a buggy fifteen or more miles one way to watch a game. People won't even drive their car a few blocks in town now to support the town team.

Well, the Litchfield nine showed up in Hutch to play the Glencoe town team and found that Glencoe "appeared with four of her nine players (from Glencoe) and five from some other point." Apparently Glencoe wanted to beat Litch so badly, they had brought in ringers from all over the state.

Litchfield refused to play and Glencoe called them scabs and advised the team to disband if they were afraid to play them. Over two hundred people had shown up at the Hutchinson fairgrounds and paid 40¢ each to watch the contest. They were upset also. So Litch relented and said they'd play but the $50 bet was off. This time Glencoe refused to play. The players had been drinking and it looked like trouble was brewing. Finally Litchfield said they would go home, practice up and return to play Glencoe anywhere, anytime with the proper team. I don't know if the match was ever played.

---

[49] Col. Charles Hoyt March and his brother Nelson D. were lawyers in Litchfield. They both served as mayor in the early 1900s. In August of 1900, they moved their law offices to the rear room of the "new bank building", which is the Pizza Ranch today. Charles' house at 218 South Sibley Avenue became the first home of radio station KLFD.

Some of my earliest childhood memories are of going to watch the town team play on Sunday afternoons and some evenings. Howard "Howie" Pennertz [50] managed the team and one of the stars was our Lake Ripley lifeguard and friend first baseman Gene McHugh. Pat and I later got jobs selling pop and candy in the stands, which were full in those days, by the way, and Mom and her friend Kathryn VanNurden worked the concession stand under the bleachers. I took the stand over later and because of my experience there I was given the Lake Ripley stand that Dingo Rangeloff had operated for so many years. But I digress.

Litchfield currently has a great town team named the Litchfield Blues. But if you speak to anyone who knows the game and the town, you can't talk Litchfield baseball without first mentioning the fabulous and elite Litchfield Optimists of the early fifties. I will tell you about them and their great season of 1951, but first I must tell you of another great Litchfield baseball team: The Litchfield Blacks.

Most people have never heard of the Blacks, but during the 1895 and 1896 seasons, they racked up a 27 and 6 record. In 1887, the Blacks played in a league with Glencoe, Sumter, Arlington, Howard Lake, Dassel and Hutchinson. The players, recruited from the town's surrounding area, received a dollar a game and got fifty cents for showing up at practice. Sometimes a "ringer" from a Minneapolis league was brought in and there was even talk of an umpire being "bought" by some Hutchinson players for a very important and highly bet on game with Hutch's rival Dassel. Hutchinson won 9 to 6 and irate Dassel citizens chased the team and the Hutchinson judge holding the bet money all the way to the McLeod County line.

The Blacks were so popular in town that all of the stores would close when they played so that the proprietors could go to the game. The team "mascot" was little Van Artis Spence. Called "Tonk" or "Art, the little black boy was the son of Litchfield's resident sole black man and town lamplighter Van Spence.

The curve ball was just beginning to be used and the only pitcher in the area that used it was from Lower Prairie. His name was Johnny Miller. The manager and ace pitcher for the Blacks was Charlie Anderson. His catcher was Joe Hannan, who would later become a

---

[50] Howard was a postal clerk on the mail train that ran from Willmar to Huron for many years. In 1961, he became a mail carrier on Route 1 out of Grove City until he retired in late 1997.

priest in Montana. I wouldn't doubt that he was a relative of the Optimist's leading hitter Jim Hannan. More about Jim later.

In the early days, the "stands" usually consisted of some cracker boxes, kitchen chairs and milk stools. Whatever could be conveniently brought to the game on horseback, buggy or by walking. The fields were just that...mowed farmer's fields. The outfield fence was more likely than not a cornfield. The games would often stop while outfielders searched through the corn for the one good game ball. The games got pretty rowdy. Drinking was allowed in the stands and fights would break out and bottles would get thrown at umpires. So, in the summer of 1919, a bunch of church groups got together and forced the city to ban baseball from the town. Not the team, mind you. You just couldn't play ball in Litchfield. So the town team played all their games on the road in Darwin, Forest City, Watkins, Kimball and Eden Valley. Some of the players on the team that year were Butch Koerner[51], Vern Miller, Art Krout[52], Charles Hatch, Baldy Ackerman[53], and Francis Ackerman.

Bill Brandt was pitching a game against Litchfield for the Eden Valley team and he was getting upset with the ump's calls. After several disputed calls, another batter came to the plate and Bill threw one right down the middle of the plate, or at least he thought he did, and the ump called, "Ball!" Bill gave him a look, spit, wound up and threw another one down the middle. "Ball two," the ump called. The catcher threw the ball back to Bill and Bill stood there at the mound looking down at the ground and snorting. Suddenly, he whirled and threw the ball as hard as he could...right out into the cornfield. Time was called while the outfielders searched for the ball. They couldn't find it. It turned out that the game ball was the only one they had, so the game was called. The Litchfield boys went home without finishing the game.

Although it's hard to believe, (even harder after you have read this chapter), Litchfield's baseball teams weren't always winners. The 1925 town team lost all their games but one. I wonder whom

---

[51] Son of famous Litchfield butcher Mrs. Gottlieb Koerner.
[52] See Chapters Thirty-Six and Thirty-Seven about Art. He later built and owned the bowling alley by Lake Ripley.
[53] Baldy was a barber for Ray Wheeler, who had his shop under what today is the Pizza Ranch. Baldy moved to Watkins where he had his own shop for many years.

they beat? Anyway, the team didn't draw either and they ended up with a deficit of $600 at the end of the season. Now in 1925, $600 was a huge amount of money. In fact, it was a year's salary for a lot of men back then. So you can imagine the pickle the team was in. I never found out how they made up the deficit but I do know it didn't destroy Litchfield's love of America's game.

Chapter Twenty-Two
Baseball and Litchfield – Part Two

Jim Hannan is a quiet, unassuming nice old gentleman who stops in at the G.A.R. Hall occasionally to talk with me. He continually surprises and amazes me with things he did in his life. I wrote about him in the chapter called *The Highway Shooting*. I was talking to Jim one day about baseball, a favorite subject of his. He related the following story to me.

Joe or James Shelley was playing left field for Darwin in 1941. Darwin's baseball diamond was right behind Jerry O'Brien's service station in town. Right next to the field, just in foul territory, sat a doghouse. Tied to the doghouse was a vicious barking dog. At every movement of the outfielder, the dog would run at him, straining at the short rope that tethered him to his house, while baring his fangs and barking all the louder.

Someone from the opposing team hit a shot that hit the grass in fair territory to Shelley's right and then rolled...you guessed it...into the doghouse. While the runner rounded the bases, Shelley wisely just stood there looking at the mad dog. Retrieving the ball just wasn't worth it. The runner got an inside-the-park home run. I don't know if they ever retrieved the ball. I wouldn't have.

Jim and I continued our talk about baseball and I brought up the famous Litchfield Optimists. I started telling Jim some of the facts I knew about the amazing Championship team.

"Yeah," Jim said, "they were a great team. I played a little for them."

"You did?" I said, suddenly embarrassed that I was telling him something about a team he played for. "You played for Siebert?" I went on.

"Yeah. Played a little for him."

A little? It turns out Jim was one of the Optimist's star players. Legendary Gopher baseball coach Dick Siebert[54] coached the

---

[54] Born in 1912, Siebert died on December 9, 1978 in Minneapolis, Minnesota. He began his Major League baseball career in 1932 with the Brooklyn Dodgers. He played for eleven seasons on three different teams and ended his big league playing career in 1945. He later became baseball coach at the University of Minnesota for thirty-one years, winning the College World Series in 1956 and 1960-64. He was

Optimists. Siebert had played in the major leagues for many teams, the last being the Philadelphia Athletics. Before he died in December of 1978, Siebert said, "The time I spent as manager of the Optimists here (in Litchfield) were some of the best times in my baseball experience. I'll never forget those days."

Left:
Jim Hannan
in 1951.
Right:
Dick Siebert
in his
Philadelphia
Athletics
uniform.

The ballparks in the early days left something to be desired. Litchfield's park was the cream of the crop. Jim and the Optimists were playing an early evening game in Fulda, Minnesota. Fulda's field was a disgrace. Just as in the movie *Field of Dreams*, the outfield had no fence. It just ended with the start of a farmer's field. Jim was playing outfield and he took off after a fly ball hit his way. Running to catch up with the ball, he suddenly slipped and fell onto his back. The cool night had brought on wet, slippery dew to the warm grass making it treacherous.

Jim slid on his back and finally came to a halt. As he started to pick himself up, he felt something made of metal by his head. There, sticking six inches out of the grass was a jagged piece of metal. Jim surmised it was a broken and buried fence post. Had he fallen a few inches to his right, it would've stuck right into Jim's back. Or he could've tripped on it causing other injuries. The home team outfielders must have known about it, but no one mentioned it in the pre-game ritual of discussing foul lines and the differences of the field. What Jim couldn't figure out was how the guy who mowed the grass avoided it and didn't wreck his mower.

---

named Coach of the Year twice, and in 1978 he won the Lefty Gomez award for his contribution to college baseball.

Regardless of the playing conditions, the 1951 Optimists cleaned up in the Class AA West Central League they were in. Other teams in the West Central were Willmar, Benson, Morris, Alexandria, Olivia, DeGraf and Glenwood. They played a 35 game season that year. Litchfield's record was 27 and 8 and they won the pennant. Litchfield men on the team were Jim Hannan, Dr. John "Jack" Verby[55], and Larry Rosenow. Verby was good enough that he had been offered a contract with the New York Yankees, but he chose the medical profession instead of working his way up through the minor leagues. Bob Kinsel from Kingston was another player. He pitched (a record of 6 and 1) and played outfield. The "ace" pitcher was John Herr, who had played for the minor league Columbus Redbirds[56]. Herr's record that year was 12 and 2.

The playoffs were a two out of three series of games with all league teams participating (except for Glenwood which folded before the playoffs began). Litchfield had a first round bye and advanced to the semi-finals. There they beat Alexandria in two straight games to advance to the finals. In the first game, Morris shocked Litchfield with an 8 to 3 ten-inning victory. Litchfield won the next game 4 to 3 and then crushed Morris 10 to 0 behind ace Herr winning the pennant. The batting star of the playoffs was Jim Hannan with a .500 average.

For the state tournament, held in Faribault, the team was allowed to draft a few players from other teams. They took pitcher Gene Kelly from the Willmar Rails, catcher Red Fischer from Benson, and Howie Schultz, also from Willmar. Howie was a former major leaguer, having played for the Brooklyn Dodgers.

In the first game against the St. Paul Nickel Joints, pitcher Dick Donnelly threw a no-hit, no-run game. The Optimists won 23 to 0. Jim Hannan continued his hot streak, getting three hits, including a home run, driving in six runs. Kelly threw another shutout in the next game. His three-hitter was too much for Cannon Falls. Our boys won 7 to 0. Ace Herr was picked to pitch the third game against Marshall. He threw another shutout for six innings and Donnelly cleaned up for the last three. The Optimists won 11 to 0.

---

[55] Dr. Verby's office was upstairs over Boyd's. Dr. Gregory Olson, our family doctor, took over Verby's practice when he left for military service.

[56] A farm team for the St. Louis Cardinals, the Redbirds were in the same league as the old Minneapolis Millers.

The Championship games were against the powerful Austin Packers. It was a double elimination tourney and Litchfield hadn't lost yet, so all they had to do was win one game. Herr came back and threw a four hitter, striking out ten, with left fielder Jim Hannan continuing his hot bat going 4 for 4. But Austin won the game 4 to 2. In the next game, Kelly pitched a five hitter and our boys won 10 to 2 winning the title.

"I think we lost tonight to the best team we've met in a long time," said the manager of the Packers. Manager Dick Siebert accepted the trophy and then handed it over to Jerry Schaber, who had managed the team in the championship game. Siebert had a scheduling conflict that night and was unable to attend until the game was almost over. The Optimists had outscored their opponents in post-season play 93 to 24.

The 1951 State Champion Litchfield Optimist team.

Back home, the victorious State AA Champs played an exhibition game against Watertown, the State A Champs. It was for pride only, but both teams wanted to show who was the "real" State Champion and put forth their best effort and players. Kelly pitched, Siebert hit two homers and good old Jim "Hot Bat" Hannan continued by hitting 3 for 5. Litchfield won easily 12 to 5. In his last nine games that season, Jim Hannan hit .459 with 17 hits in 37 at bats. Yes, Jim Hannon certainly played "a little" for the Optimists.

In July of 1994, a few members of the team were invited to Litchfield's dedication of its new ballpark. Dr. Jack Verby, Jim Hannan, Larry Rosenow, and Jim Madden signed a baseball, which was given to the Meeker County Historical Society and that's where I found it along with a box of newspaper clippings and programs while researching this chapter.

Don't Complain

*You know the old **adage**; "I complained because I had no shoes, until I saw a man who didn't have any feet." **Growing up relatively poor and having very little, I used to hate it when** my own children complained about not having the latest fad clothes, shoes, or toys. That's what this lyric was about.*

Don't Complain

Don't complain when times get bad.
Times ain't bad unless you've had.
If you've had, then bless your stars.
Some have never been that far.

What I'm trying to say is this…
If you ain't had, you don't miss.
And if you've been there before,
at least you've had your chance to score.

The world is round. You must know that.
No matter where you hang your hat,
men will be in front of you.
But they will be behind you too.

Is your cupboard ever bare?
Do you have something to wear?
Do you know someone without?
That is what it's all about.

Chapter Twenty-Three
I Remember

I wrote this chapter for my class reunion as a recitation piece. If you're not from my hometown of Litchfield in the fifties and the sixties, it might not mean much to you. Then again, you might find it interesting as to what stands out in the memories of my generation.

I remember the old high school being called Washington High[57] and not only graduating from there, but going to the first grade there; I remember little Senator Steve Dille wearing cowboy outfits to grade school and I remember the Longfellow grade school with its tube fire escape and the "Duck and Cover" drills about what to do in case of nuclear attack in the fifties.

The tube at Long-fellow school

---

[57] A new high school was built in 1964, the first class to graduate from it was the class of 1965, and the old high school at 114 Holcombe Avenue North was turned into a junior high and then a middle school. A new middle school was built in 1994 and the last classes to be held in the old building were in January of 1995. The inside was gutted and remodeling began in November of 1995. An open house was held in July of 1996 to show off the building. The first occupants were the Meeker County Family Services offices. Today various community and government offices are in the building.

I remember teachers Hazle Walters and Esther Settergren, who seemingly taught school forever; I remember all my male teachers wearing suits and neckties and all my female teachers having dresses on with high heels; I remember my beloved Dragons and our fight song, "Here's a cheer for Litchfield High, colors every flying, with a spirit never dying"; I remember always thinking "Wait'll next year"; I remember the green plastic hot lunch tokens; the hated raisin and carrot salad in the lunchroom; a quick noon lunch away from school consisting of 15¢ hamburgers at Janousek's or day old Bismarks at the New Bakery and I remember when the Janousek hamburgers were only 10¢.

Left: Janousek's café   Right: CJ Music Store

I remember the New Bakery being by the First State Bank building instead of across from the park and I remember the big fire that caused Wayne Rayppy to move; I remember decorating a homecoming float in somebody's garage; I remember Jerry Wimmer stalling Clarence Weber's one year old Plymouth Valiant on the railroad tracks at the Holcombe crossing and a freight train plowing through it; I remember our school bus getting stoned by angry Willmar Cardinal fans after we beat them in the district semis in 1962 and I remember the 6 o'clock, 7 o'clock, 12 o'clock, 1 o'clock, 6 o'clock and 10 o'clock whistles[58].

---

[58] The siren or "whistle" was situated on top of the "old" power plant. In January of 1992, in anticipation of the plant being torn down, the siren was moved to a place three quarters of the way up a leg of the new water tower. Later in the year, it was "silenced", that is it was only used for emergencies.

I remember calling people "hoods", "skags", "fairies", "queers", "dorks", "squares", "whores", and "teacher's pets" and not knowing for sure what they meant and I remember being called all of the above myself except for two of them; I remember the round gold "virginity pins" that the girls wore on the upper left side of their sweaters; I remember smoking in Fransein's after school and smoking in the bandstand all the time; I remember monster, cowboy and Bowery Boys movies at the Unique Theater and sitting in the first seven rows for only 20¢; I remember Friday night band concerts in Central Park and nickel bags of popcorn from the popcorn stand and I remember going to the bathroom in the hotel's basement in the early sixties and seeing "White" and "Colored" signs over the doors.

I remember standing against a wall at the sock hops after the game wishing someone would have the courage to ask me to dance, but not having the courage myself to walk the long walk across the gym floor to the "girls' side"; I remember dancing the Twist, the Stroll, and the Calypso and I remember the *Pepsi Platter Parade* on KLFD on Saturday afternoons; I remember town characters like Freddie Williams, Roy Peipus and Len "Buck Buck" Inselman, who sold his wonderful melons on the street; I remember not wearing a cap for fear of messing my hair up and I remember walking to school with frozen hair in the winter; I remember my mother buying Duz detergent so she could get a free towel inside the box.

I remember climbing the water tower on a dare at fourteen; I remember Lake Ripley's water wheel; skating at the ice rink and the warming house; I remember Evan "Dingo" Rangeloff at the skating rink and at the candy stand at the lake; I remember driving around the lake in somebody's dad's car and bushwhacking at the Beehive on a Friday or Saturday night; I remember the test pattern on our B&W TV in the morning after the five minutes it took to warm up, and "You hoo, it's me, my name is Pinky Lee" in the afternoon right before "Hey kids! What time is it? It's Howdy Doody time..."; I remember seeing *Bonanza* or the *FBI* for the first time in "living color" on NBC; I remember Axel and his dog and his Birdie jokes (Birdie wit da yella bill...) and I remember seeing him in person at Sandgren's shoes and at our high school.

Axel at the Litchfield High School.

I remember playing pool in Bull Johnson's pool hall after school and on Saturday afternoons; I remember Norb's Cut-Rate service station in the round "Merry-Go-Round" building next to the Community Building; I remember dances in the back of the Western Café, which was the old bowling alley; and I remember the Halloween dance there in 1958 when Bugs Bokander got splattered against the Depot by a train; I remember science teacher Ruthie Burns winking and sticking her tongue out of the corner of her mouth and sometimes dropping her dentures out of her mouth onto her desk and I remember class plays directed by Floyd Warta and Floyd swearing in class (damn and hell).

Floyd Warta and Phyllis Koenig.

I remember Phyllis Koenig, who taught for fifty-three years, almost twice as many years as I did; I remember being self-conscious taking the mandatory shower after Phy Ed; I remember the day we got our class rings and giving it away immediately because I was going steady; I remember football coach Howie Felt crying during his speech at a pep fest; I remember getting caught chewing gum in Willard Erickson or Rolly Scharmer's classes; I remember Rolly throwing erasers at sleepers in his class and getting Wally Stubeda to talk away the hour about his World War II experiences; I remember stinking up the entire school in Bonkrude's chemistry lab; I remember little 2¢ bottles of milk in the lunchroom milk machine and getting out of class because I belonged to the projection club; I remember not wanting to be called out of class by Harry Lindblom and the hair standing up on the back of my neck when I was.

I remember penny candy at Axel Johnson's or at Batterberry's; I remember milk being delivered to my house in glass bottles with cardboard stoppers at the top; I remember dances under the west wing of Spotty's A&W drive-in during the summer; I remember the shoe x-ray machine at Sandgren's and Greep's, the Milk Bar and the smell of the Produce; I remember Mudballs at the Travelers' Inn and a "Suicide" phosphate soda at Johnson Drugstore's soda fountain; I remember new car unveilings at Lund-Hydeen Pontiac, Nelson Buick, Quinn Motors, Fenton's, and Swartzwald's and I remember always being proud of Litchfield's Christmas decorations, even if outsiders said they looked like glasses or upside-down bras.

I remember black high top Keds sneakers and PF Fliers; I remember when my phone number was Oxford 3-8278 and I even remember when it was 214-J; I remember my mother watching Dave

Moore, Bud Kraehling and Hal Scott on Channel 4 on TV at ten o'clock; I remember not having air-conditioning at home or in the car; I remember someone painting "Class of '58" on the water tower and I remember someone from my class painting graffiti on the side of the hotel that read "Booze is cheap, sex is free. We're the Class of '63"; I remember being closer to the beginning of my life than to the end of it and I mostly remember never being ashamed to call Litchfield my hometown.

Chapter Twenty-Four
The Baby Boomers

My generation has been named the "Baby Boomers" because we were a part of the post-World War II crop of babies born from 1946 to 1964. I feel blessed to have grown up a Baby Boomer in the fifties in a small town in mid-America. The years of my childhood were innocent, trustful and without fears. No fears, that is, except for the "Duck and Cover" drills in school teaching me what to do if there were a nuclear attack from the Russians. I was to *duck* under my desk and *cover* my head, I presume so that my charred lifeless body could be found under the desk instead of sitting in it. But movie monsters, snakes, spiders and the bogeyman were much more terrifying to me than the threat of any commies.

I respected my mom and my teachers. I went to church every Sunday, I did my best in school and I dressed up for both. I didn't expect an allowance for doing chores around the house, two gifts at Christmas were enough to satisfy me, and a perfect day was one that included a 10¢ bottle of soda pop. My heroes were movie stars, Davy Crockett, my teachers and my mother.

The fifties was an innocent time, but it was also an exciting time. We Baby Boomers were there for the birth of so many wonderful things. We were there for the birth of Rock and Roll, with the debuts of Elvis and the Beatles. We were there for the birth of the space program, with the launching of Sputnik, and, because of it, an increase in the Cold War. And we were there for the birth of the peace movement and civil rights. We were there for the beginnings of drive-in movies, canned soft drinks, television, the Barbie doll, microwave ovens, satellites, stereo records, portable transistor radios, 3-D, K-Mart, Wal-Mart, Disneyland and McDonald's.

For a period of time, I was able to listen to one episode of *The Lone Ranger* on the radio with William Conrad as Matt Dillon and then see a different episode on TV with fellow Minnesotan James Arness in the lead. We played marbles during recess at school and other games with unusual names such as *Red Rover, Red Rover* and *Captain (or Mother) May I*. At home we played *Cops and Robbers, Cowboys and Indians* and *Annie, Annie Over*. We Boomers started such fads as Hula Hoops and Davy Crockett coonskin caps and dances like the Twist, the Limbo, and the Stroll, the real first line dance. Our major decisions were made by saying "Eeny-meeny-miney-mo" or "My mother told me to choose you." Mistakes were corrected by simply yelling, "Do over!" We would do anything stupid on a dare and if we backed down, we were forced to do it anyway by something called a "double-dog dare."

Blue jeans were the "uniform of the day" for Baby Boomers. Dress pants were for Sunday church only. We hated new blue jeans. They were always over starched and stiff as a board. I would take mine, soak it in water and then kick it around the block a few times to "break it in". I had seen Spin and Marty, two teenage characters on *The Mickey Mouse Club* show on TV, do it so I knew it'd work. I'm sure that my mother loved washing those jeans before I had even worn them one time. We never wore shorts or "cut-offs" in the summer in the fifties. It was jeans year 'round.

In our small town, we never wore baseball caps in the fifties, except when actually playing baseball. I didn't even wear one then. We didn't want to look like a dork. We called each other names like "square", "dork" or "fairy", which were our terms for nerds. "Fairy" had nothing to do with being gay in those days, by the way. If you wore glasses or got good grades in school or helped your mother with the housework, you were a fairy. I had all three strikes against me. "Terry the Fairy" was what they called me.

We also didn't wear caps because we didn't want to mess our hair up. Cool hair was important in the fifties. I spent hours training my hair to go back on the sides with some sticky goo from a jar labeled "Butch Wax". It was used for crew cuts and I bought it from my barber. That hair was going to go back, even if I had to glue it to my head.

I froze my ears many mornings walking six blocks to the high school, sometimes with my head turned sideways so that the bitter Minnesota January wind wouldn't mess up my "do". I arrived at the school door with "frozen hair" and red ears, but looking cool. My ears burned during most of my first hour class while my hair slowly thawed out.

Being cool always went before safety and warmth. We never wore "rubbers", which is what we called boots or overshoes in the fifties, so we always had cold, wet feet and salt stained shoes in the wintertime. And we never wore gloves. If we saw someone with mittens on, we'd fall down laughing at them. "Did your mommy dress you today?" Or "Are those pinned to your coat?", we'd taunt some poor little kid. Some of the bullies would take the kid, pull off one of his mittens real hard and he'd hit himself in the head with his other mitten-covered hand. The two mittens, of course, were tied together with a long string around the kid's neck inside his coat.

Like most Boomers, I had a paper route when I was little. I earned about $3.00 a week. $1.00 went into a mandatory savings account with the paper, $1.00 went into the mandatory "Bank of Mom" for safekeeping and rainy days, and $1.00 was cautiously spent on candy or movies. There are a lot of reasons for my mother's generation being called "The Greatest Generation" by authors and politicians. The lessons they learned about saving money and care in spending while in their teens in the Depression and in their early twenties during WWII were passed on to my generation, their children, the Baby Boomers.

Chapter Twenty-Five
Baby Boomer Toys

Tim Bergstrom was interviewing me on KLFD in November of 2003. I was promoting my upcoming appearance at the GAR Hall on the following Sunday. I had been asked to lead a discussion about living in the fifties. Tim asked me a very good question.

"Now, what about toys? What kinds of toys did you have in the fifties?"

Without thinking, I pointed to my head and said, "Our brains. Our imaginations. (We) Ran around with sticks playin' war. They were rifles, you know. (We) Made our own rubber band guns, things like that. But we played a lot of board games. Monopoly and Clue. Games like that. We played a lot of card games. Of course there was the Hula Hoop. Things like that. That came out then. We weren't deprived, mind you. We had real toys, but we didn't get very many. At Christmas time, we were lucky to get two gifts from 'Santa'. One would be a toy and the other would be clothes. Now, my kids, when they were little...we would spend the whole Christmas morning opening up their presents. Of course, like the old story goes, most of the time they'd end up playing with the boxes."

Tim got me to thinking about the real toys we did have back then. What were the things that we just had to have, if we could get Mom to buy it for our one toy gift or if we spent our paper route money on something? What were the things my friends brought to school to show off or that I saw over at their houses and wished I could have?

At the very top of my wish list was a double gun and holster set so that I could be like my heroes, such as Gene Autry, Roy Rogers, Hopalong Cassidy and the Lone Ranger.

"They cost too much money," was the answer I usually got from Mom. But one Christmas, she and my absent father (they were divorced when I was three) must have gone together on our gifts because Pat and I both got double gun and holster sets. They were beautiful! I couldn't believe how beautiful they were.

Hopalong Cassidy and a gun set similar to mine.

The holsters were real brown leather, not plastic like my friends had. There were silver plastic bullets in each of the tiny bullet loops on the belt. The guns themselves were silver with white plastic "ivory" on the handles. Pat and I ran off and chased each other around the house making gun noises with our mouths. The guns were cap guns but caps cost money and rarely worked very well, so we didn't bother buying them very often.

I wonder what ever happened to the guns and holster? I think one of my stepbrothers took one of the holsters for a revolver he had. By that time I was too old to care for them anymore. The plastic "ivory" on the guns' handles got cracked and eventually fell off. I imagine we helped the handles' demise by using the guns like a hammer pounding caps on the concrete steps leading up to our front door. The caps were the ones on the long red rolls. They didn't fire inside the gun like they were supposed to, always jamming up. You could never rapid fire a cap gun.

I got caught up in the Davy Crockett fad at the age of nine in 1954, wanting to own a coonskin cap. But they cost $1.98. That was a lot of lawn mowing money. Mom couldn't afford to give me the money. Wisely, I thought it out. How often would I wear it and would my friends make fun of me? I did collect Davy Crockett bubble gum cards and I had the entire collection. Like a dummy, I glued them into a Davy Crockett scrapbook that I bought for 50¢ at the Ben Franklin store, thereby ruining the value of the cards.

Fess Parker as Davy Crockett.

We Baby Boomers never thought of those things when we collected bubble gum cards. We played with our cards, clothes pinned them to our bike spokes to sound like a motor scooter, and we traded them to each other and enjoyed them. When I remarried and moved to Willmar, I had an auction at my old house. I sold the Davy Crockett scrapbook. I don't think I got more than a couple of dollars for it. What a shame.

Some fifties toys go for quite a bit on eBay.com and in antique stores. An erector set in the original box ($450 to $800) or an Easy Bake Oven ($50) or a Chatty Cathy doll ($75 to $400), for example, will bring quite a bit.

I saved up for and bought model airplane kits and painstakingly assembled them. After I tired of them, I burned and smashed them and put them into crash and war scenes that I made out of cardboard boxes and real branches and twigs.

We put together puzzles while listening to our favorite programs on the radio or just sitting around a table. Mom gave us an old large square board that she used to roll bread dough out on and we did the puzzle on it so it could be moved off the table when Mom needed it.

One time I knew my Uncle Dean Shaw was coming to visit and I wanted him to see my accomplishment. So I carried the board upstairs and put it under my bed for safekeeping. When Dean stopped by, I told him I wanted to show him my puzzle. I ran upstairs, retrieved the puzzle from under the bed, and started to hurry back down the steps. Suddenly my feet, clad only with my socks, gave way under me on the slick gray enameled stair. The next thing I knew, I woke up on the living room couch with Dean and Mom standing over me. At the base of the stairs were 300 puzzle pieces scattered all over, the board and a neat little hole the size of my head in the wall facing the steps.

I never had an electric train set. Too costly. My oldest brother Dennie had one for a little while. He also had some little car that he put a CO_2 cartridge into, hooked the car to a long wire and then tapped the cartridge to set it off. The car would zip quite a distance in a few seconds. Dennie talked the men at the new power plant into letting him string his wire in the huge room the generators were in. He let me go along to watch the three-second show. Clink, zing, bang...it was over.

I got some white building blocks for Christmas once. They came in a round tall tube just as Lincoln Logs and Tinker Toys did. It took me half the night to figure out that the blocks wouldn't stay together unless I overlapped the next row over the one I had just made. Pat had a set of Lincoln Logs and we built things to dive bomb our model airplanes into.

Dennie also had a chemistry set, but Pat and I weren't allowed to buy one. We used to ask Mom prior to purchasing something like that. Dennie subscribed to the "It's easier to ask forgiveness than to ask permission" theory.

"They're too dangerous for you to have," Mom told Pat and I. "You'll blow yourselves up or set the house on fire."

You know, she was probably right. I was kind of a firebug back then, lighting matches in the basement, playing with gasoline out on the driveway. I did burn down the doghouse next to the garage. Only the quick action of Grandpa Bill Shaw, who was staying with us, saved the structure.

We also had to fight with Mom for a BB gun. We ended up buying our own. Pat and I were over by the new power plant shooting at some cans we had set up on a big square concrete block. We had no idea what the block was or contained. Some BBs ricocheted of the block and hit one of a couple of little girls who were playing by us. I think one of them was dogcatcher Smokey Schmidt's daughter Avis. Anyway, the girls ran off and told on us. Police Chief George Fenner[59] drove into our driveway later that day and confiscated the BB guns and took Pat and I upstairs at the firehall where the police station was. There he lectured us for about a half an hour and then turned us loose to "sin no more". We never got our BB guns back and, although we had bought them with our own hard earned money, we were afraid to go and ask for them.

There were ViewFinder viewers, Cootie games, Etch-O-Sketch, Spirograph, Barbie dolls and Slinkys. Girls played with paper dolls, which they bought in booklets by the coloring books' racks in the stores. Silly Putty came out in the fifties. You could press it on the Sunday paper comic strips and the image would appear on the putty. (Wow!) Then you could stretch the picture out. (Hilarious!) The advertising geniuses worked overtime selling that one to us. There were Magic Rocks. They were little colored rocks you put into a glass container, added a teaspoon of water and then colored crystal things grew all over the container, ruining the glass. Mom liked that one.

---

[59] George Fenner came to Litchfield in 1949 and started a furniture business with a man called C. I. Eddy on Depot Street near Greep's on Depot Street. He joined the police department on April 1, 1951 and became the Chief of Police on January 15, 1953. George died at the age of sixty-nine in September of 1978 while shaving one morning. He had just told the city council that he was going to retire after being the chief for twenty-five years.

I sent away for an official Roy Rogers miniature ranch set, which was sold on Roy's Saturday morning program. It had a tiny molded plastic Roy, Trigger, Dale Evans, her horse Buttermilk, their dog Bullet, sidekick Pat Brady and his jeep Nelly Belle and a cardboard ranch house.

We Baby Boomers sent away for lots of things such as the Winky Dink screen I'll write about in a later chapter or things like Sea Monkeys. We got back a small envelop containing some seed-like looking things, which we dropped into water and watched daily. In a week or so, we had some tiny organisms floating around in the water. They didn't look anything like the cute little monkeys we saw in the ads in our comic books. In reality, they were nothing but tiny brine shrimp.

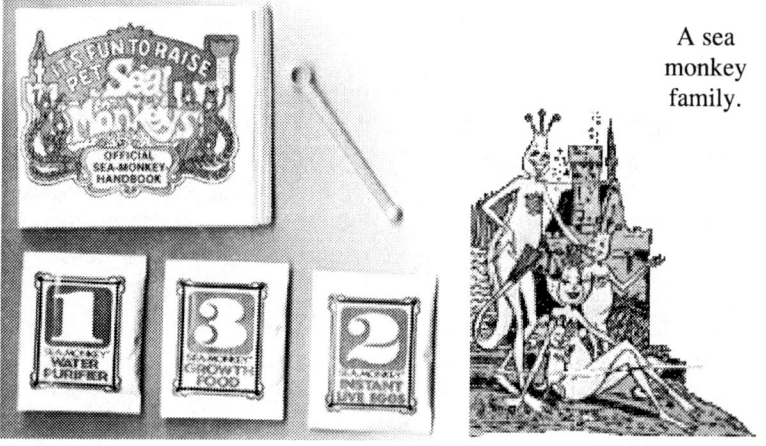

A sea monkey family.

A man named Harold von Braunhut came up with the Sea Monkeys idea. He found them in dried up lake bottoms, not the sea. He started selling them in 1960 for 49¢ a packet. They came back in the nineties and CBS-TV briefly had *The Amazing Live Sea Monkeys* show on Saturday mornings from 1991 to 1993. Four hundred million of the "monkeys" went into space with John Glenn in 1998. Harold was the P. T. Barnum of the Baby Boomer generation. There literally was a sucker born every minute. Harold once sold "invisible goldfish" by guaranteeing the buyers that they would never see them. Duh!

Harold wasn't all fun and games. Another invention of his was a pen-sized coil-spring weapon, which unfurled a deadly metal whip.

Burt Reynolds used one in the movie *Sharkey's Machine*. Harold advertised it as the "ideal weapon". "If you need a gun, but can't get a license..." he lured buyers. It sold for $60 and Harold kicked back $25 of it to his favorite "charity", the Aryan Nations defense fund. It turns out our "P. T. Barnum" was a racist of the first order. He belonged to the Ku Klux Klan also and once said, "Hitler wasn't a bad guy. He just received bad press."

Harold died from an "accidental fall" at the age of seventy-seven in November of 2003, but his Sea Monkeys are still being sold today. Amazing.

Pat and I bought a lot of things that were advertised in the back covers of comic books. X-ray glasses that never worked (another von Braunhut "invention"), magic tricks and disappearing in that did work. Comic books were treasured and traded. We found out that barber Roscoe Keller would let us trade comics with him so we were always running up to his shop under the New Bakery next to the First State Bank to sort through his collection.

The Shaw boys had an aunt named Mabel Shaw Connor who was a teacher in Long Prairie. She gave us old library books that the school had tossed or old textbooks. She also worked part-time at a drugstore. When the new comics came into a store, the storeowners would tear off the banner on the cover with the old comic's name and return it to the distributor for a refund. They were supposed to throw away the old comics without the banners but Mabel would save them up and give them out to her nieces and nephews. So we had lots of comics from her. They were a little harder to trade, especially to Roscoe. They were supposed to be in the same condition as the comics you were trading for and, of course, ours had the banners torn off the front covers. Bummer.

I Like To Sing

When my daughter Andrea had just turned four years old, she saw me writing and singing songs all the time in the living room and she wanted to join in. She loved to sing and she loved to perform. So one day I asked her, "Drea, how about you writing your own song? I'll help you."

Andrea Shaw Peterson singing.

We went to my "Fun Machine" synthesizer (like an organ) and I lifted her up on my lap. We started writing the song with me prodding her and prompting her into the right direction. I had her tell me things that she liked and like to do, I wrote them down and then I helped her arrange them into rhyming lyrics. Next came the melody. I started playing a chord and a rhythm on my Fun Machine and she just started to sing along. I followed her, changing chords when she changed her melody. I had to help her with the Bridge melody.

When it came time to record the song, I recorded the background track and then asked her to dub in her voice. All of a sudden she got stage fright with the headphones on standing in front of the mike. She wouldn't do it. So, I tricked her. I brought a cassette recorder into her bedroom and asked her to sing her song into it. That she'd do because we often played with the little cassette recorder out on the front steps. Luckily for me, she sang her song in the right key, but not in the same tempo. Stopping and starting the cassette recorder on playback, I was able to dub her voice onto my background track in the right tempo.

The resulting recording made a nice gift for her mother and her grandparents.

I Like To Sing

I like to swing.
I like to slide.
I like to jump.
I like bike rides.
But, most of all, I like to sing.

Candy
and popcorn too.
Dresses
with pretty shoes.
But, most of all, I like to sing.

Singing makes me happy.
Singing is real fun.
Singing is for me
and for everyone.

I like to play.
I like to dance.
I like TV.
I like snow banks.
But, most of all, I like to sing.

Chapter Twenty-Six
The Bernatson Boys – Part One

I had a couple of chapters in *Terry Tales* about characters in town, like old Bing Schultz and Len "Buck Buck" Inselman. Some people didn't like being called a "character" or having a relative called one. I understand that, but it doesn't change the fact that those particular people stood out for some reason and were considered "characters" by others in town; others who themselves might be considered characters. As I said in the first book, "Unfortunately, if you had a physical or mental handicap, you were likely to be called a character, although those weren't the sole requirements. You generally had to do something odd along with your appearance."

A person came up to me one day and said, "Say, how come you didn't have anything about the Bernatson brothers in your book?" Well there were two reasons. First of all, I forgot about the old characters and secondly, and probably the reason I forgot, they weren't actually Litchfield characters, although the only time I ever saw them was when they came to Litchfield.

Harry and Henning Bernatson, both born in Ellsworth Township, actually lived in Greenleaf Township near Lake Minnebelle, just off Highway 22 on the east side. You could see their small green one room shack from the road. The county had built the shack for them to live in. The boys lived off of the county, what they could "find" to eat and off of the little money they got for sharpening saws for people. The Bernatsons came to town about once a week for supplies, usually on Friday nights. While most of the town was attending the Friday night band concert in Central Park, the Bernatsons would be walking the alleys behind the stores digging through the trash, looking for discarded treasures. Gee, that's sounds familiar. My brother Pat and I used to do that too, only we did it in the mornings. They were probably finding better treasures at night.

Bill Krueger, who had a dairy farm to the south of the Bernatsons, was sure he knew where they were getting their milk. Many mornings he would bring his herd in for milking and there would be one dry cow. Where was the milk going? Bill was sure that the Bernatsons were "rustling" milk in the middle of the night from a cow. But how do you prove a thing like that?

The manner in which the Bernatson boys came to town caused people to stand up and notice. They came to town in one of their two old Model Ts. Five years older, tall and thin Harry drove a 1925 Model T and short and squat Henning drove a 1923 Model T Ford Roadster, complete with wire wheels. They would change off, one driving his car one time and the other driving the other time. Until July of 1960, that is.

On the 10th of July, Harry and Henning were making a "water run". They had no well on their little piece of property so they would go to a neighbor's well and help themselves, or go down to the 4-E resort on Lake Minnebelle and help themselves to the water hose. If someone was around to stop them at either of those two "outlets", the boys would go to the Lake Minnebelle itself with a trailer behind Harry's '25 T and load up a bunch of old milk cans with lake water. I assume they drank it and made their moonshine out of it. For sure they didn't bathe in it. More about that later.

Finished loading the trailer with lake water in the cans about sundown, the boys started for home. The trailer had no taillights. Seventeen-year-old Jean Ryan of Cedar Mills was driving her ten year old sister home from Litchfield in a '53 Buick around 10pm. It was dark now and Jean never saw the trailer as she came up behind an old Model T car chugging south on the highway at about 30mph. She jackknifed the trailer, demolishing it, and pushed Harry's car into the other lane. Her sister got a cut on her forehead, but no one else was hurt.

The Bernatsons and the Ryans got out of their vehicles and talked. Someone drove up behind the Ryan car and said, "You'd better try to get these cars off the road if you can before somebody else comes along and you cause another accident." The Bernatson's Model T's lights were out now and the car was sitting in the northbound lane. "I'll run ahead," the Samaritan added, "and flag down anybody coming from the other direction."

The man grabbed a flashlight from his glove compartment and ran up the road, but not in time to stop Orville Burress' 1958 Pontiac, which drove right past him and plowed into the Model T, totaling it out. When the police arrived, Harry was ticketed and fined for pulling a trailer with no taillights and, oh yeah, for driving without a license. The Bernatsons didn't bother with such trivial matters.

Harry's 1925 Model T at the accident site.

Everyone coveted the remaining Model T. Henning's 1923 Roadster, unlike his brother's car, was in top running condition and appearance. Henning took it to Nelson's Buick, two blocks from our house, for servicing. The workers there would love to see it roll in.

"Hey Henning," Virgil "Bud" Rangeloff, son of Dingo, would yell. "Wanna sell your car?"

"No, I don't tink so," Henning would always answer as he walked his funny walk up to the inquirer. Henning's right foot turned in almost ninety degrees, pointing to his left foot. Probably it had been broken in his youth and never properly set. Uneducated but wise, Henning knew his car was worth something. People in town took him and his brother for slow-witted people, however, and a group of men thought they'd finagle the car away from him. The sight of cash would surely get the boys attention, they thought. So the men took a shoebox, filled it full of one-dollar bills, and took it out to the boys' shack.

"Here boys," one of the men said. "We'll give you all of this money for your car."

"No, I don't tink so," was all they got from Henning.

When the car dealerships would have their "new car unveilings", the two men would get dressed up in their old suit coats and hit the showrooms. There they would help themselves to cups of coffee and the free donuts and cookies. They would always stuff their pockets with cookies for later too. The rest of the time, they would come to town dressed in bib overalls and farm boots. The men were always unkempt and filthy. You assumed that they never bathed or washed their clothes. But for some reason, they didn't smell, except for an odor of kerosene about them.

Rumor was that the Bernatson boys had owned quite a bit of land around their shack at one time. Some said that it was their parents Emil and Emma Bernatson's farm that they were slowly selling off in chunks. But they had gotten down to a small parcel of land and just a lean-to shed on it for shelter. Social Services stepped in and had that little green shack built for them. The boys didn't seem to have any source of income anymore, since the land had been sold off. So, they helped themselves to whatever they wanted.

When they walked into a store, you could be sure one of them was going to shoplift something. A lot of times, the storeowners just looked the other way rather than raise a fuss and contend with the boys. It was sort of a charitable contribution on their part.

Paul Brunkin lived across the highway from them and one of the boys started coming over every morning and helping himself to Paul's *Minneapolis Tribune* newspaper. Rather than fight with the boys, Paul just bought them a subscription to the paper.

The boys were spearing fish in Lake Minnebelle and the game warden knew it, but he couldn't prove it. He set out to catch them in the act. Observing them around their shack, the warden surmised correctly that the Bernatsons had to be doing the spearing at night. So, the warden set out one night to catch them. Sure enough, along they came one summer evening carrying a gunnysack and a pitchfork.

"Say fellas," said the game warden, "watcha up to?"

"Aw, we're gonna git some gravel from the shore dere for our driveway," Harry said.

"You're gonna have one helluva time scooping up gravel with that pitchfork, boys."

"Pitchfork?" said Henning. "What da hell. You grabbed the wrong ting," he said, turning to Harry. "Dat's not the shovel."

Harry and Henning had a pet horse. They didn't ride him or use him for any work that anyone could tell. They just kept him around for years. The horse got sick enough that the two men broke down and called a veterinarian to come out to their place. When he arrived, the vet couldn't believe his eyes. Using pulleys and a crane-like contraption in their lean-to shed, Harry and Henning had the horse propped up on its feet.

"He shits and eats just fine," Henning said, "but he just can't stand on his own anymore."

The Joe Tacheny farm was a couple of miles south of the Bernatsons. Joe had an additional eighty acres right over by the Bernatsons. One day the boys inquired of Joe if he had any hay to sell them for their horse.

"Sure, I got a couple of extra bales," Joe told them.
"How much you gotta have, then?"
"Oh, give me 75¢ a bale."
"Okay, then. We'll come over tonight and get some," Henning said.

That night the boys came over and got two bales. Then Harry reached into his big overalls and pulled out a handful of pennies, which he proceeded to slowly count out into Joe's hand. Joe thought they were paying him that way on purpose, thinking he'd get tired and say, "Oh, that's enough. Go ahead and take the bales." But he didn't.

After Harry had counted out one hundred and fifty pennies, Joe said, "Say, I've got a couple of bales that broke out on the eighty by your place. You can have them too if you want to clean them up." And clean them up they did. The Bernatsons must have used some fine rakes because there wasn't a trace of the hay on the field the next day.

Chapter Twenty-Seven
The Bernatson Boys – Part Two

It was said that the Bernatson boys were moonshiners. The sheriff's department had visited them several times but the law could never find the boys stash or still. Maybe it was just a rumor. Lots of stories floated around about the Bernatson boys.

The neighboring farm was owned by a man name Christenson. Mr. Christenson put up a brand new gate at the end of his long drive. The next morning, it was gone. A few days later he noticed a new gate at the end of the Bernatson boys' drive. Confronting the two, Christenson demanded his gate back.
"Your gate?" Harry asked. "That's our gate. We bought it and you can't prove otherwise."
Christenson couldn't. Somehow, though, he stayed "friendly" with the boys, friendly enough that they sold him the main part of their original farm. The boys had been selling off parcels of their land. This particular piece of land had probably been their parent's actual home site, as it had a barn and a shed and a big pile of hay nearby. In finalizing the deal, Harry said to the buyer, "You can have the buildings and all, but we want that pile of hay there."
"No problem," said the buyer. "Just come and take it anytime that you want."
Well, the boys didn't come and months passed. The buyer warned them that he'd like to get it moved.
"Sure," Henning assured him. "We'll be over and get it." But again they didn't come. So one day, the buyer had had enough of it, working his way around the pile all the time. So he decided to burn it down. He started the hay pile on fire and the damp old musty hay started to smoke. Suddenly, the man heard some yelling. He looked up and saw the Bernatson boys running across the field towards him.
"Put it out! Put it out!" they were screaming.
Running up to the man, they gasped one more time, "Put it out!"
"Well, you never..." the man started saying and then stopped as the boys grabbed what ever they could and beat the flames out, pulling clumps of smoldering hay out of the pile. Then the man saw why the boys wanted the pile but didn't know how to move it. Hidden inside was their stash of moonshine in every conceivable type, shape, color and size of bottle and container. What a fireworks display it would've been had the fire gotten to them.

One day at Nelson's Buick, the two had the grand old Roadster in for something. By this time, they had "upgraded" to an old Chevy, replacing Harry's demolished '25 T and they didn't drive the Henning's Model T as much. Mechanic Bud Rangeloff thought he'd give it another shot.

"Hey fellas, I sure like this here car. How about selling it to me?"

Bud was shocked when Henning replied, "Yeah, maybe I will."

"What? Really?" Bud was stunned. "How much would you have to have for it?"

"Well, let's see," Henning said, scratching the stubble on his chin. "How 'bout $200?"

"Sold," Rangeloff replied.

"When you want it then? We need to git home you know."

"How 'bout tonight?"

"Okay, you come tonight after supper then."

Bud, a lover of old cars was beside himself. He borrowed the wrecker from the dealership and took a friend along to help him with the car. There it sat in the yard by the old green shack when Bud pulled into the Bernatson place.

"Whatcha got dat ting for?" Henning asked Bud, looking at the big wrecker. "It runs, you know."

"Well, I thought..."

"You drive it home. It runs."

"Well, okay," Bud said, not wanting to "queer" the deal by insulting the boys. Reaching into his pocket, he pulled out his checkbook.

"I'll write you a check for the $200."

"No, I don't want dat," Henning said. Bud was in shock. "Sure," he thought, "I knew it was too good to be true."

"You give me $10 a month for twenty months, okay?"

"Sure," Bud said, relieved. "I can do that."

"S'long as you got dat wrecker here, you can take what's left of da old '25 for spare parts if you want."

"Sure thing," Bud said, happily. The Bernatson boys had hauled Harry's wrecked '25 T home somehow. You don't suppose they fixed up the old trailer, do you?

Bud still has the Roadster at his place on Lake Ripley and he drives it once a year.

155

The Rangeloffs take the 1923 Model T Roadster for a drive.

Henning had some health problems that necessitated he go to the clinic to see Dr. Harold Wilmot. Dr. Wilmot told him he would need to have a series of penicillin shots.

"I'll turn you over to my nurse and she'll give you the shot and then you come back tomorrow for the next one," Dr. Wilmot told him.

Wilmot left the room and a minute later Ethel Ackerson, Wilmot's nurse, came walking in with a tray on which sat a small bottle and a needle.

"Okay Henning," Ethel said, "I'll need you to stand by the table here, drop your pants and lean over."

"Drop my pants?"

"Yep. Shot's gotta go in your butt. That's the only way I can give it to you, Henning. It won't hurt."

"Don't care 'bout hurtin'. No way I'm gonna drop my pants in front of you."

"Then I can't give you the shot Henning. You want to get better don't you?"

"Yeah, but I ain't gonna be droppin' no pants."

"We can argue like this all day, Henning, but that's the way I'm gonna give you the shot. The doctor's busy and he can't do it."

"Don't like droppin' no pants…"

"Henning…."

"Don't like this droppin' pants," Henning continued as he slowly undid his big overalls, let them slide down to the floor, and leaned over the table.

"Shot tomorrow gotta be done this way too?" he asked after Ethel had finished.

"Yep. Same way, Henning."

"Okay, then," Henning said as he dressed and left.

The following day he showed up for his shot and was ushered into the doctor's office. Ethel came walking in with her tray.

"We gonna have problems with you today, Henning?" she asked, getting her needle ready.

"No, we ain't," Henning shot back. Then he dropped his bib overalls revealing a pair of long underwear covered by two pair of pants. All three had been cut through with a small circular hole exposing a tiny portion of Henning's buttock.

Harry brought Henning to the emergency room of the Meeker County Hospital one afternoon in the late sixties. Henning had a strangulated hernia and was in extreme pain. The nurse, a friend of mine who told me this story, thought that Henning was dressed in black leather.

"How appropriate for a farmer," she thought to herself. But on closer examination, she found that it was just regular clothing, so dirty and filthy that it had become black and shiny. The doctor told the nurses to prep Henning for surgery, and so, much to Henning's objections, the ladies fought to hold him down and remove his clothing. They were sure that, other than Henning's mother Emma, they were the first women to attempt this act.

My friend and her nursing partner began to wash old Henning down. His long dark hair was so unclean and matted with dirt that it looked like dreadlocks to the nurses. Strangely, Henning didn't smell, although it was obvious that he hadn't had a bath in months or years. There was a strange line under the skin of Henning's lower stomach where the hernia was. My friend started to feel around it and she had a suspicion.

"What's this Henning, under your skin?" she asked to the still fighting patient.

"Bailing wire," he growled. "Hold the hernia in."

Henning had "trussed" himself up with bailing wire and his stomach had overlapped it and skin had grown over the wire. It had to be cut out. When Henning had recuperated from the operation over a week later, the nurses took up a collection and bought Henning some new clothes from the Penney's store downtown. They had thrown away his "leathers".

Henning's health was failing and Harry couldn't care for him anymore. So the county stepped in and had Henning taken to the Cosmos Nursing Home. His failing body couldn't take the normal life and he got worse and worse. Finally, Bud Rangeloff's wife, who worked for Social Services, was asked to take Henning to the hospital in Litchfield. The nurses and aides at the nursing home couldn't find any clothes for Henning, who just worn the nursing home pajamas and gown all the time he was there. Apparently, his clothes had been thrown away when Henning was admitted to the home. The nurses scrambled to get something on poor Henning's body for the chilly ride to the hospital. They came up with a shirt, a lady's dress and a scarf to wrap around his head in lieu of a cap. That's how Henning was "dressed" when he came into the Meeker County Memorial Hospital.

Henning died in March of 1972 at the age of seventy-three. Bud Rangeloff dug into his own closet and found an old suit that he had worn to his high school graduation. He took it to the funeral home and that's what Henning was buried in.

At 4:45pm on December 27, 1972, seventy-nine year old Harry was attempting to cross Highway 22, returning to the shack. He waited in the late afternoon darkness while a car, heading north, sped past him. Then Harry started across the road, forgetting to check the southbound traffic. It was a fatal mistake. Eugene Fitterer's right fender of his car slammed into Harry even though Eugene stood on his brakes and skidded into the ditch. Harry died on the way to the hospital.

What happened to the Bernatson boys' green shack? Bud Rangeloff's sister Helen, who lives in Indiana, bought it for a summer cabin to stay in while in Litchfield visiting each year. But first it had to be cleaned out and disinfected. It's funny the sheriff couldn't find the boys' moonshining stuff. There it was, stored away in the little green shack. Copper tanks, tubing and boilers. It was all thrown away.

"I'd love to have it all today, just to show," Bud told me. Well, he's got the Roadster and a lot of fun memories of the Bernatson brothers.

Chapter Twenty-Eight
Prospecting For Babbit

Growing up in a small rural town in the fifties in a one-parent house made my younger brother Pat and I keenly aware of money or, in our case, the lack of it. I guess you could say we were poor, although we didn't know it. We made our own way with many different income sources. Of course, we had the mandatory paper routes working for Dean Schultz and we raked leaves and mowed lawns for our neighbors Alma Colman and Mary Jensen. For that we got a quarter or "two bits" each, which is what the older people in town called a quarter. Pat and I also found other ways to acquire money. Searching for pop bottles to redeem for the 3¢ deposit was one but we came up with a couple of unusual monetary pursuits.

Pat and Terry Shaw

We lived a block away from both the railroad track and the First District locker plant. Whenever we learned that the locker plant was slaughtering pig, we'd go behind the plant and dig through the garbage cans looking for meaty bones nestled beside pigs' eyes, noses and other unidentifiable parts. We put the bones into paper bags we brought from home. Then we went door-to-door selling the "bone bags" to people for their dogs. We asked for twenty-five cents a bag. It seems that every job we had and everything we did was for those two bits.

Someone told Pat about money he could get by selling babbit to the junkyard. Babbit, I later learned, was a soft white metal, an alloy of tin, lead, copper, and antimony, used by the railroad to line the bearings of the boxcar wheels to reduce friction. Isaac Babbit developed it in 1839 for use in steam engines and it bore his name. Because it had a low melting point, it would heat up inside the wheels, drop out onto the tracks and cool into shiny silver-looking clumps or nuggets. All he had to do was find it amongst the rocks on the bed of the railroad tracks. Pat told me the good news and that was all I needed to hear. We made up our minds we were going to go prospecting for babbit, even though, at the time, we had no clue as to what it was or what it looked like. Pat had been told that he'd recognize it when he found it and what to do with it when he did find it.

Early one morning, Pat and I each made a couple of peanut butter and jelly sandwiches, threw them into a paper bag, grabbed an empty coffee can to put the treasure into once we found it, and we set out west on the railroad tracks with the warm sun on our backs in pursuit of our fortune. At first, walking on the granite stones in the rising heat of the summer morning, I was leery of this venture; searching for something I had never seen or heard of before. Maybe somebody was playing a joke on us like snipe hunting.

We had hardly walked a block from the railroad crossing by our house though when Pat stopped, bent over and picked up a shiny little nugget of something. It looked like dime-sized clump of solder. I knew what solder was. My big brother Dennie was always soldering some electrical gizmo together.

"I'll bet this is it," Pat said, holding the clump out in front of my face before he dropped it into the empty can with a clink.

"Yeah..." I replied, letting the word hiss slowly out of my mouth. We were on our way to riches.

We walked all morning and into the afternoon, nearing Chicken Lake woods, finding more and more of the nuggets, but it seemed that the farther we got from town, the fewer nuggets we found. Along the way, we had stopped to sit on the tracks and eat our sandwiches and we had thrown rocks at the blackbirds sitting on the power lines or at the glass insulators on the tops of the poles. Neither one of us had good enough aim nor strong enough arms to every hit any of the things we were throwing at.

When we had the coffee can about three quarters full of clumps of babbit, I said to Pat, "I think we got enough for now. Let's turn around and go home."

"Yeah," Pat replied, "we can come back tomorrow for more."

We turned around, anxious to sell our treasure and divide our riches. We headed back home on the other set of tracks, finding more babbit as we walked. Occasionally we would have to run to the ditch beside the tracks to let freight trains roar by us. The windy breeze caused the fast moving train cooled our small warm faces peaking up from the ditch's tall weeds. When the train had gone by, we'd crawl back up to the tracks and feel its hot steel. Then we resume our trek.

It was mid-afternoon when Pat and I arrived at home. By now our coffee can was full, actually overflowing. We were hot and tired but all smiles as we put the heavy coffee can on the stove at the medium setting, as Pat had been instructed to do. We stood and stared at the can, waiting for the clumps to melt down. At first nothing happened.

"Turn it up," I suggested to Pat, reaching for the temperature knob.

"No, just wait," he said, stopping me.

Minutes went by, it seemed, and then suddenly, as if by magic, the clumps turned shinier and then all flowed together into a brilliant silver soup. We grabbed a pair of Mom's potholders, picked up the can and set it in the kitchen sink, which we had half filled with cold water. The half blackened can hissed while it quickly sunk and then it thumped as it hit the bottom of the sink. Cooled down, the large shiny and heavy block of metal slid easily out of the blackened coffee can onto the bath towel we had spread out on the kitchen table.

"Wow," I said to Pat, "that was easy. Let's get this place cleaned up and sell it today." We rushed around the kitchen, cleaning up any evidence that we had been there so Mom wouldn't have a conniption. Then we dropped our treasure into a paper bag, hid the blackened coffee can behind the garage and got on our bikes. We biked out to the Meis Brothers' junkyard two and a half miles away to make our fortune.

"Can we sell this to you, mister?" Pat asked, holding out our shiny treasure.

161

Mr. Meis reached across the counter of his small office shack at the junkyard and took the clump from Pat into his big oil blackened hands.

"Where'd you boys get this?" he asked out of the corner of his mouth, a cigarette dangling from the other corner.

"Found it on the tracks," we answered in unison, looking up at him in anticipation.

"Well, let's see here," he said taking it over to an old black iron scale on the corner of the counter. He weighed it, pulled open a drawer, looking at some piece of paper, and then he reached into his pocket and pulled out two quarters.

"Here you go, boys. That's what she sells for," he said, as Pat took the money. He handed me my quarter. Two bits. Yeah, that seemed like a fair wage for a full day's work of prospecting.

There was plenty more babbit to be found, but that was the last time Pat and I prospected for it. We found quicker ways to earn two bits.

It's Getting Late

My daughter Andréa was getting to be a pretty good little singer. So, when she was about seven, I decided that we should record a duet together in my little basement studio. But first I had to have the right song for us. I decided to write my own.

Every father knows that he never seems to have enough time for his kids when he's a young workingman. Then when he's older and doesn't have to work so much, freeing him up, his kids are grown and gone. Where did the time go? I wrote about that dilemma, making it a dialogue between Andrea and I.

It's Getting Late

DAUGHTER: Daddy, will you read me a book...
huh, please, will you?

DAD: Honey, I would, but can't you see, I've
things to do?

DAUGHTER: Daddy, you promised that you
would...it's getting late...

DAD: I know. But this is so important. Can't it wait?

DAUGHTER: Daddy, just read one book to me.
Just one, not two.

DAD: Honey, don't bother me right now, I'm working.
And I'm too busy to be reading books to you.

DAUGHTER: Daddy, you finish all your work and
I'll just wait.

DAD: Can't you hear me now? Go on to bed, it's
getting late. Tomorrow, I'll spend some
time with you, if you'll just wait...

DAUGHTER: Daddy, I hope you do,
before it gets too late...

Chapter Twenty-Nine
Mosquito Days

They say we have two seasons in Minnesota: winter and road construction. We actually do have four seasons and the only one I hate is the brutal winter. The snowmobilers, skiers and ice fishers here love it. "Think Snow" is what they put on stickers on their car bumpers. The summers in Minnesota can be brutal too, but they are beautiful. Brutal when the humidity is high and beautiful when it's not. But even the beautiful summers can get brutal in the warm evenings just before sundown. That's when the "Minnesota State Bird", the mosquito, comes out.

Minnesota State Bird

When I think back to my childhood, growing up in the fifties, I don't remember the mosquitoes bothering me all that much. There couldn't have been less of them. There might even have been more. Kids just aren't aware of pests as much. I guess because they're large pests themselves. But the adults were always complaining about the mosquitoes. In 1957, the adults in my hometown decided to do something about it.

Just after supper one hot summer evening, my younger brother Pat and I were sitting on the floor of our living room in front of the lone fan our mother had, trying to hear the little black and white Emerson TV above the fan's roar. We had put a bowl of ice cubes in front of the fan to try to get some "air conditioned" relief from the heat. That was about all you could do in the fifties. Pat and I would always sleep in the basement in the summer. Our bedroom on the second floor was just too stifling hot.

Suddenly, we heard a whooshing roar above both the TV and the fan. It sounded like a large engine combined with a windy sound; like an airplane flying down our street. We both jumped up and ran to the front-screened door. Peering through the screen mesh, we saw a truck coming down our block. There was a man sitting up on the back of a contraption on the truck. With a steering wheel, he was aiming, and moving back and forth, a giant bent rectangular tube that looked like a cannon. He was shooting a fog all over our neighbors' yards. When the truck was in front of our house, the man "shot" us. We quickly closed the inside door until he had passed, not knowing what to expect, but all three of the windows in the living room were wide open. A sweet smell permeated the room. The man was spraying for mosquitoes.

Spraying for mosquitoes in '57.

Our city had decided to hire an outfit from Morris, Minnesota for $972 to come to town and get rid of the pests...the mosquitoes, that is, not us kids. There had been something about the spraying in the newspaper, our mother told us later, but no mention of a spraying schedule; just the fact that there would be three sprayings over the summer and they would "entirely rid this area of mosquitoes." Yeah, right.

It took three days to cover the town. People would be out in their gardens or on their porches when the spray truck came by. The sprayers didn't care. They went right down the street spraying DDT on everyone and everything. They gave no warnings, nothing. You'd think the driver could at least have beeped his horn.

Sometimes a group of us kids would be playing ball in the yard or in a park, and the truck would come by and just spray us. It burned my eyes and smelled sweet. By the way, neither the guy driving the truck nor the guy spraying us wore any kind of protection like a facemask. Sometimes there'd be a cigarette dangling from their lips.

The spraying must have worked because the next year our little town bought its own spraying "cannon" and mounted it on a city truck. A neighbor of ours, Ernie Radunz, ran the sprayer. An army of kids, including myself, would follow him and the truck down the street oblivious to the dangers of the fog we were walking in. We had gotten used to the sweet smell and kind of liked it.

I was reminded of the spray trucks a couple of years ago when New York City environmentalists got up in arms over the spraying in their city for the West Nile virus mosquitoes. They were worried about what the spray would do to their pets and the homeless people on the streets. We lived in a different time in the fifties. "Shoot first, ask questions later" must have been the motto. I've never heard of a study about the increased cancer in us "Baby Boomers" of the fifties from the spray either. Would too many of us be suing our hometowns?

Chapter Thirty
Our First TV and Winky Dink

Television was still in its infancy and a novelty more than the norm, when I was growing up in the early fifties. I can't imagine not having a TV today, but there was a time, of course. The first mention of the modern marvel in Litchfield's local newspaper was in August of 1948. There was an article, not an ad, telling the public that one of the two local electric appliance stores had a new Motorola television in the store. The article stated that the television "projects a clear image of the radio program" and rightly predicted that someday it would be as common as radios in everybody's homes. A year later, the other electric store in town, John Colberg's, had a press release in the newspaper telling the public that the store owner had a new TV in his home at 224 North Gilman Avenue and people were invited, by appointment, to come and view "this new entertainment".

    We got our first television in 1953, when I was in the third grade. Before that, I would listen to *Arthur Godfrey*, *Gang Busters*, and *The Lone Ranger* on the radio during the week and a kid's radio program called *The Teddy Bears' Picnic* on Saturday mornings. My mother told us about the new TV the night before we got it. I couldn't wait to get home from school the next day.

    "We're getting a TV at our house!" I told all my friends. I hardly impressed them though, as almost all of them had televisions at home for a couple of years already. But it was a big deal for me.

    I got off the bus, ran into the house, and saw the brand new shiny television standing along the north wall of our living room. My heart was beating fast and it felt like Christmas morning. The TV had a deep reddish brown mahogany cabinet about a yard high and eighteen inches wide with two brass lions' heads holding rings in their mouths on fake doors in the bottom half. The entire bottom half of the cabinet served absolutely no purpose, as the tiny speaker was right on the top of the TV. The top half of the cabinet contained a small twelve-inch black and white screen, and gold letters spelling EMERSON on a pull down door that concealed controls right under the screen.

Sparky, Terry, Dennis and Pat Shaw in front of the Emerson.

Mom had bought the television for about $150 from a friend, Ernie Aveldson, who sold Emersons out of his house. On top of the television was taped a note, which read, "Don't touch until I'm home. (signed) Mom" Rats! Mom didn't get home until 5pm!

When she finally got home, my brothers and I started pestering her to turn it on.

"Come on, Mom. We're missing all the good shows!"

"We're not turning that TV on until we've eaten supper and all of the dishes are washed and put away," she said.

We rushed through the meal and were extra helpful that night clearing the kitchen table and washing the dishes. Mom had also started insisting that we pray the Rosary every night while we did dishes. There was a national campaign called the Rosary Crusade going on in the Catholic Church in the fifties to get people to pray together again. "The family that prays together, stays together." Our minds already wandered while repeating the *Hail, Mary* over and over, but this night the prayers didn't do us a bit of good as we mumbled our responses to Mom's lead as fast as we could.

Finally, just before 7pm, we all gathered in the living room, jockeying for the best place on the sofa, which Mom had pulled to the center of the room facing the TV. The single easy chair off to the side had been declared hers. She turned off all of the lights, except for a special "TV lamp" sitting on top of the television. The 40W light bulb of the TV lamp was in a red upside-down cone, which was perched on the middle of a little red settee; on which sat two miniature plaster Chinese people, a boy and a girl, dressed in red. Mom had been told to have a TV lamp so that her children's eyes wouldn't get ruined watching television.

The big moment had arrived. Mom reached down and turned the volume knob to the right with a click. The small screen started to flicker. A small white dot in the center of the screen slowly grew as the picture tube warmed up. This was taking an eternity. Suddenly the dot jumped to fill the screen. We sat and stared at a full screen of...nothing. Nothing but snow, accompanied by a roaring hiss from the tiny speaker. Mom turned the volume down and then, clunk, clunk, clunk, clunk...she turned the channel tuner dial, which had numbers on it from one to twelve, until she came to a stop at a channel that wasn't all snow. Somewhere in there was the faint image of...*The Goodyear TV Playhouse.* An hour-long live drama without any cowboys or police shooting at bad guys. We had waited for this?

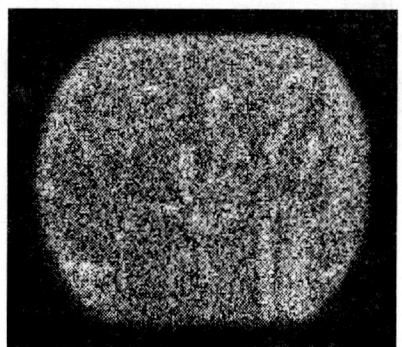

"Mom, isn't there anything else on?" I pleaded. I had heard about the cowboy shows, like *Gunsmoke*, the police dramas, like *Dragnet*, the comedy shows, like *I Love Lucy* and *The Jack Benny Show*.

Clunk, clunk, clunk, clunk...she turned the dial.

"I'm sorry, boys. That's all I can find. Just this one channel comes in."

"Why didn't you buy a better TV?" I cried.

169

"It's not the TV," my older teenage brother Dennie said. He knew about these things. "It's the antenna, dope," he said to me. "Mom," he said, turning to face her. "We need a better antenna."

"Well, we'll just have to do with this for now." We sat through the drama, bored to tears.

Over the next few days we did everything we could to improve reception, including moving the TV set closer to the window, but all we could get were four snowy channels from Minneapolis and St. Paul, which was sixty miles east of us. Mom called Ernie and he came over and went up on the roof.

He yelled down, "Is it clearer yet?" over and over until Mom finally said, "Well, that's the best we're gonna get it, I suppose."

It didn't get any better until a few years later when the stations started building bigger transmitters. Our little town was just too far away from the transmitting towers in the Twin Cities. Cable was decades away.

Television shows didn't come on until 6am. Before that, all you got was a test pattern. I never knew what in the world you were supposed to do with that test pattern. I suppose use it to adjust your contrast, brightness and vertical and horizontal hold knobs. Those were the four controls on the TVs, besides the volume/on/off knob.

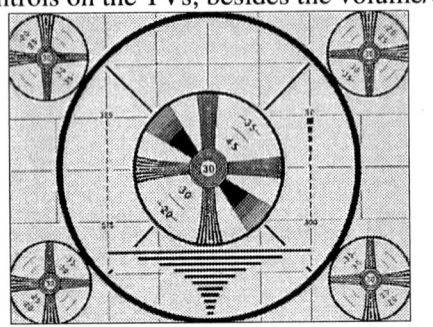

A typical test pattern.

We'd be watching a TV show and suddenly the picture would start twisting sideways. One of us would have to jump up, run to the set and delicately turn the appropriate knob until the picture straightened out.

"There...there...there...that's it...no, back the other way...no...here let me do it."

"Now the picture's rolling...put it back the way it was."

Then, at midnight, everything went off after the National Anthem was played with a movie of jets flying in front of the American flag.

I sat on the floor right up by the screen, because I couldn't see the television very well. I wouldn't be getting my glasses for two more years. Mom kept telling me to back up from the screen because I was going to ruin my eyes, but I would just inch forward back to where I had been. So I became the official knob turner. I became quite good at keeping a nice straight picture for my family. Plus I got to "surf" the channels after shows ended.
"There...leave that on."
"No, we ain't watchin' that junk."
"Mom...make him put it back to where it was."

There were lots of cartoon TV shows on the air in the fifties and they all had the same format. A host wore a costume, such as a cowboy suit, a spaceman suit, or railroad engineer outfit, like local celebrity Casey Jones, and he would perform skits and introduce cartoons. But, there was a clever television show on Saturday mornings from 1953 until 1957. It was called *Winky Dink and You* and Jack Barry hosted it.

What was different about the Winky Dink show, which featured the adventures of Winky Dink, a star-headed cartoon boy, and his dog Woofer, was that Jack Barry wore a plain suit, and the show was interactive. For 50¢, I was able to send away for a light green plastic Winky Dink screen and a "magic" black crayon. When I put the Winky Dink screen on our TV screen and wiped it with a cloth, it "magically" stuck.

Jack Barry and Winky Dink.

171

Winky Dink would get himself into jams in the cartoons and end up being chased by some villain. Suddenly he would find himself at the edge of a cliff in front of a canyon. The cartoon would freeze and Jack Barry's voice would come on giving us instructions.

"Quick kids," Barry voice would say, "connect the dots and draw a bridge for Winky Dink."

I'd grab my magic crayon, draw the bridge, Winky Dink would run across it, I'd erase the bridge, as instructed by Barry, and the villain would be foiled again. I saved Winky Dink's life many times.

At the end of each segment, we were instructed to trace parts of letters at the bottom of the screen so that we could eventually complete and read a secret message at the end of the show. I guess *Winky Dink and You* was the world's first interactive video game.

Pat and I bought our own TV on Crazy Days when I was about fifteen years old. I can't remember for sure where we bought it. It might have been at Don's TV, which was in a front room in Dahl's Goodyear tire shop at the corner of Third Street West and Ramsey Avenue, but Pat thinks it was out on Highway 12 East, just past the Traveler's Inn. Regardless, I remember what we paid for it. Two dollars.

It must have been a chore for us to carry it home, as it was in a cabinet similar to our old Emerson. Again Pat thinks we might have enlisted the aid of some of our older friends with cars, like Skeeter Anderson, but get it home, we did, and we deposited it in our clubhouse in our section of the garage. That was where we slept in the summer and spent most of our time when we were home and not chasing around town.

We had one problem. We had no antenna. I can't remember if we found some "Rabbit Ears" (a simple antenna which sat on the TV with telescoping antenna hollow wires sticking out opposite each other like a big V), or if we just hooked up a wire coat hanger, but somehow we "Gerry-rigged" the TV so that we could get one very snowy channel. We then discovered we had another problem. The picture tube was going out and we had a black smudgy 3" diameter circle in the middle of the small 19" screen. So we had to watch around the black smudge. After a while, if we could get enough of a picture to watch in the first place, you got to the point where you hardly noticed it. After all, how many other kids in town had a real TV in their clubhouses?

Eventually the black smudge kept widening and it got to the point where we didn't have enough screen left to watch, so we junked the TV, but not before Dennie got into it and removed the single speaker and the good tubes. I don't know what he planned to do with them and he probably didn't have a clue either, but he wanted them. Before too long, Mom had married Floyd Young and they had bought a console TV for the living room and put the old Emerson in the basement. Once again, we had our own TV to watch, although we were back to antenna problems in the basement and down to watching one snowy channel again. Upstairs the new TV was bringing in six, if I remember correctly. They were channels 2 (PBS), 4 (CBS/WCCO), 5 (NBC/KSTP), 7 (NBC/Alexandria), 9 (Independent/KMSP), and 11(ABC/WTCN). I think channel 9 was ABC at first until 11 took it over and then 11 and 5 swapped networks.

Litchfield finally got cable television service in October of 1972. Imagine, if you can, the viewers in town now had to choose between not six stations but an unbelievable twelve!

Chapter Thirty-One
Bikes

Because my mother didn't drive and I didn't have a father while I was growing up in Litchfield, my world didn't include any place that I couldn't get to by walking or riding my bike. My "Frankenstein" bike, thrown together from parts of other "dead" bicycles, was my most prized possession because it expanded my world. There was enough entertainment and adventure for me right in my own backyard and that poor, ugly bike had just made that backyard much bigger.

The frame, handed down from an older brother, had been painted so many times that it didn't have a distinct color of its own. I guess it was bluish and greenish, if I had to name a color. The wheels came from other discarded bikes. My Frankenstein bike had bald and cracked tires, no chain guard, no handlebar grips, very little for a seat, one side only of which had springs, and no fenders. If I rode it through a mud puddle, I got sprayed with a streak of muddy water up my back. The local police department gave out safety reflectors to the kids in town to put on their bike fenders. I had nowhere to put them. And my bike had no kickstand, meaning I had to lean it against something or lay it down on the ground when I wasn't riding it.

Because my Frankenstein bike had no chain guard, I was forever catching my blue jeans in the chain. I would coast over to someone's lawn, fall down to the grass, and then stand and crouch down to peddle the bike with my hand so I could walk my jeans out of the chain. There would be a black tattoo of the chain track on the bottom of my pant leg. Of course, if I had only rolled my pant leg up, it would never have happened. But I chose the possibility of catching the jeans in the chain rather than look like a "square" or a "dork".

My Frankenstein bike was very important to me. I vividly remember meeting my mother at the corner of our block, as she was walking home from her job at the turkey processing plant to eat her noon lunch, and having her watch me peddle wobbly down the street in front of her for the first time.

Terry Shaw with his Frankenstein bike.

None of the bicycles in my circle of friends were much to talk about. Some of my friends didn't even own one, so we would "buck" them around town. That meant they would either sit sideways on the frame behind the handlebars and in front of the person on the seat or they'd sit right up on the handlebars with their feet carefully resting on each nut of the front wheel's axle. This type of "bucking" was dangerous. First of all, the rider blocked the peddler's view. Secondly, the rider sometimes got his shoe into the spokes, which caused all kinds of calamities.

Those of us who had bikes were always fixing and tweaking them; pumping air in the tires, oiling the axles and the chain, trying to make the bike go faster. It seems that my bike was in the upside down position on our driveway as much as right side up. Generally the wheels were so bent from jumping curbs and hitting things that I was always adjusting an axle so the tire wouldn't rub on the frame.

One of my friends put a car steering wheel on his bike somehow. It was hard to steer though, so he took it right off. Not before parading it around town for laughs, though. Then there was always the kid who would put a smaller wheel from some cart on the front, just for kicks and laughs. Pat did that once to his bike.

It was hard for us to imagine existing in town without a bicycle. It seemed to be such a necessity. Of course, like everything around us, from radios to refrigerators, we were always amazed to hear from a grandparent or some other older person that those things weren't always around. Even the bicycle had only been around about a half a century. Grandpa never had one when he was young. In my research of the downtown buildings, I read an article in the April 5, 1890 edition of the Litchfield newspaper that a man named Vernon Brokaw had just bought a Columbia Safety bicycle. Arthur and Ernest Campbell and Jewell Fuller owned the only other two bicycles in Litchfield. They were all adults and Fuller owned a clothing store in town at that time.

One day my brother Pat and I were playing in our front yard, when he looked down the street and exclaimed, "Wow! Look at that bike!" I looked up to see old Bing Schultz, a local town character, riding down our street on a brand new shiny black '55 Schwinn Hornet. I knew what it was from an ad in my comic books.

"Hey Kids!" the ad screamed. "Bike back to school on the best!" Yeah, right.

"Mom, I need a new pair of jeans and shoes for school. And, oh yeah, could you get me this bike in this ad too?"

Whatever it cost, I knew we couldn't afford it. As I mentioned, Mom, who was raising four boys on her own, didn't even own a car.

Bing Schultz was also called "Ding" by some people and that name fit him better as a "ding dong" was what we called what we thought were crazy people. Bing was a little "off center". He sat outside the pool hall most afternoons catching flies to feed his pet toad Johnny, which he claimed, "understands me when I talks to him." The old man was a gravedigger, by trade. Just the thought of that alone gave us the "willies" and we stayed away from Bing, thinking only people like Egor in the Frankenstein movies dug graves. But his bike sure got our interest. We stared at it as Bing rode past us, talking to himself, as he always did.

Bing's beautiful bike had shiny black fenders with a single white stripe on each side. The front fender had a light attached to it and the back fender had a large red reflector. I think the tires even had white sidewalls. On Bing's handlebars was a bell, which he rang to say "Hi!" as he peddled slowly by. The bicycle also had that metal cover between the two support bars, which served no more purpose than the fins on a '57 Chevy, except to remind us that we didn't have one. The name "Schwinn" was embossed into it.

Extending over the back fender was what we called a "buck seat". It was a flat metal thing that we assumed a passenger could sit on. But Bing had a black saddlebag draped over the one on his beautiful bike. The saddlebag looked like it was made of leather with fringe hanging down from the flaps. The compartments on each side were loaded with something. Later, Bing added some kind of a rack back there, in which he carried his shovel and pick, tools of his trade. And Bing's beautiful bike had a chain guard; on which were painted the white words "Schwinn Hornet". It could have said "Cadillac Eldorado" as far as we were concerned.

We drooled over and talked about Bing's beautiful bike for weeks. He'd let us look at it, leaning on its kickstand in the alley by the pool hall, but he never let us touch it. I'd say, "Nice bike, Bing," to him and then walk away mumbling to myself that someday I'd have one just like it or better, as I climbed up on my Frankenstein bike. Of course, by the time I could afford such a beautiful bike, my thoughts had turned to cars. Cars with big fins that served no purpose.

One day, a couple of years ago, my wife bought me a brand new bike for my birthday because we were going to start bike trail riding with some friends for exercise. I'm sure it cost as much or more than Bing's beautiful bike. My brand new shiny red bike wasn't a

Schwinn though. It had no metal compartment between the support bars, no fenders (when did they stop putting them on bikes?), no bell, no light, and no "buck seat" over the back wheel. But, luckily for me, it had a chain guard. At least I wouldn't have to look like a dork riding it around town with my pant leg rolled up.

Schweiss Chicken Pluckers Jingle

I was asked to write a radio commercial jingle for a local inventor/manufacturer. I had a melody already. I had written it for another song, so my brother Dennie and I sat down together one evening when he was visiting me and, in about half an hour, we came up with these lyrics to go with the melody.

Schweiss Chicken Pluckers Jingle

Chickens come with feathers.
Isn't that a shame?
'Cause chickens cooked with feathers
just don't taste the same.

Now Schweiss makes chicken pluckers.
It plucks them really fine.
Your chicken will taste better
and you'll save lots of time.

So go see Schweiss, this guy is nice.
He's built one just for you.
Don't get uptight, the price is right.
Schweiss never would pluck you.

Chapter Thirty-Two
Letter Stories: Herbert

If you haven't read the Forward to this book, you should. It is about letters I received after *Terry Tales* came out. For the most part, I'm thankful to tell you, the letters were positive; thanking me for the wonderful job I did researching the history of Litchfield and writing the stories about the people in town. The book jogged many memories in people. Some of the people, who took the time to write me, call me, or talk to me in person, told me some additions to my stories. Sometimes the writers inspired me to write complete chapters in this book and other times they gave me little tidbits that I thought I should share with you.

For example, I got an email from Herbert Schuermann, who now lives in Prescott, Arizona. He was looking for a copy of *Terry Tales* and wondering where he could get one. Herbert was a graduate of the class of '58 from Litchfield High and his story was interesting.

Herbert came to Litchfield at the age of sixteen in November of 1956 from Herborn, Germany. He wasn't a foreign exchange student. His mother, two sisters named Ellen and Brigitte, and Herbert came to America to escape the post-war poverty in Germany. His father had left them and, as in my case, didn't pay any child support. There was no welfare in Germany at that time. The Schuermanns went to bed hungry many nights. Herbert's life paralleled mine in many respects.

Herbert, in the middle, with his sisters and brother in Germany.
They are wearing wooden shoes.

Times were hard in post-war Germany. The Schuermann children would scour the countryside for scrap iron, tin cans, copper, rags, and paper; anything that wasn't tied down. They would sell it to the local scrap dealer for cash. That's what they bought groceries with. At night they would go to farmers' orchards and steal fruit off the trees and in the daytime they would help the same farmers harvest their potatoes. For every ten sacks they filled with potatoes, they were given one to take home.

Herbert's dad had been a heavy crane operator in Germany. During WWII, the German Army had used his expertise in France repairing bombed out bridges. In 1944, he was taken prisoner by the Americans and shipped to a POW camp in Connecticut. The American government was looking for volunteers to work on farms in the Midwest, so Herbert's dad volunteered. He ended up on the Borg farm in Cokato, where he became friends with Torre Borg[60].

I'm going to stop my story here to tell another little personal story. My grandpa, Louis Rheaume, worked for Green Giant in LeSueur, Minnesota during the war. They were short handed and so prisoners from the POW camp in nearby Montgomery were brought in to work. Grandpa was made foreman of their crew. He had trouble with the prisoners. At first, they refused to go into the seed house to clean peas because it was too dusty in there. "Nix! Nix! Nix!" they'd tell Grandpa. So Grandpa had them husk the seed corn and separate the grades of corn. They started sabotaging the operation, mixing the grades and throwing corn at each other. So, the prisoners were shipped back to the camp. Where did Green Giant get the much-needed replacements? From the State Mental Hospital in St. Peter.

Back to Herbert's story. When the war had ended and Herbert's father was sent back to Germany in 1946, he continued his friendship and wrote to the Borgs. After Herbert's mother and father divorced in 1947, Torre Borg suggested that Herbert's older brother and sister come to the United States and live with them and help on the farm. This they did.

---

[60] Torre was a brother of George Borg who owned the Northland Canning Factory in Cokato.

Herbert's older sister married and moved to Litchfield with her new husband. Then they sponsored the rest of the family to move to Litchfield. Herbert and his mother and two sisters, Brigitte and Ellen, came over on the SS New York and lived with them for about two months. The older sister and Herbert's mother got into a big fight and the family had to move out and be on their own.

Brigitte got a job in Minneapolis, and Herbert and his mother and sister Ellen moved into the big old white building by the old library called the Lien Apartments[61]. They lived there for three months. The apartment building was home for a lot of Litchfield's characters, whom you met in *Terry Tales*. Herbert never had much of a chance to see them, however, as he came home around 1 or 2am from one of his jobs and then he left early in the morning for school. Herbert's mother worked at the Produce, as did my mother. Later Herbert's mother got a job as a seamstress at the dry cleaners in town. Herbert's younger sister Ellen went to school at St. Philip's elementary around the same time I did.

Herbert did many of the crazy things my buddies and I did to entertain ourselves in town and he had multiple odd jobs, like pin setting at the bowling alley, to earn spending money, as I did. Art Krout, the owner of the bowling alley gave all of the pinsetters a ride home after he closed up every night. He drove a big old '49 Hudson[62] and, according to Herbert, that car always started up on the first crank, no matter how cold it got at night.

One of Herbert's several jobs was as a bus boy and dishwasher at the Colonial Café at the hotel. Herbert would work until 12:30 in the morning and then rush home to catch some sleep before getting up for school the next day. Sometimes he would hang around in the lobby to look at the girlie magazines until old John Fischer, the night clerk, would politely remind him that it was late and he had school in the morning. A young man's hormones would always win the battle with any other part of his body, however.

One night Herbert was the last person working in the café. Somehow, he locked himself in the big walk-in cooler in the kitchen.

---

[61] Built in August of 1869, it had once been a grand hotel called the Litchfield House.
[62] Art had owned a Hudson dealership in town, which he bought from Harry Radunz. It was located where the REA building is today. In fact, it was the same building.

It was very cold in there, at least forty degrees. Herbert kept himself busy and warm all night by snacking on the five gallon containers of fruit pie filling. There were apple, blackberry, blueberry, and cherry and Herbert found a big spoon to eat them with. After he got tired of eating the fruit, he found some other things to snack on. He told me, "I was very busy inside that cooler and I didn't have much time to think about the cold." The next morning Dick Simmons and Claire Foss found a grinning Herbert, with strange colors all around his mouth, sitting in the cooler when they came to start the morning shift.

Another evening, while working the late shift with Dick Simmons, Dick urged Herbert to come with him to the Darwin Dance Hall on the following Saturday.

"Jerry Wheeler's band is playing and it'll be fun," Dick told him, while mopping the floor. "You'll meet lots of girls too."

"I don't know how to dance," Herbert said.

"It's easy. Here, I'll show you." Dick went over to the counter and turned on the radio. He found a southern station playing some rock 'n roll music and then he took the mop handle and started dancing with the mop.

"See? All ya gotta do is move your feet like this and hold the girl like this," Dick said, sliding around the room. "Here," he commanded, holding out the mop, "try it."

While the German boy was trying his best to dance to that crazy American music with the mop, Dick advised him.

"Try to hold it tight to your body and squeeze it a bit," Dick said, holding back a giggle or two. Herbert said to me, "Did I really squeeze that mop? I don't remember, but anything was possible in those days."

The *Independent Review* had a picture of Herbert on its front page in 1956 getting his first American haircut in Hubert Dedrickson's barbershop. In woodworking class in school, Herbert made a beautiful coffee table, which he showed at the Birch Coulee Industrial Arts Fair, getting First Prize. He took Third with it at the Minnesota State Fair. Back home, Edna Whitaker, his social studies teacher, offered him $65 for it. Herbert desperately needed the money but he couldn't bring himself to part with something so beautiful that he had made in this new country with his own hands.

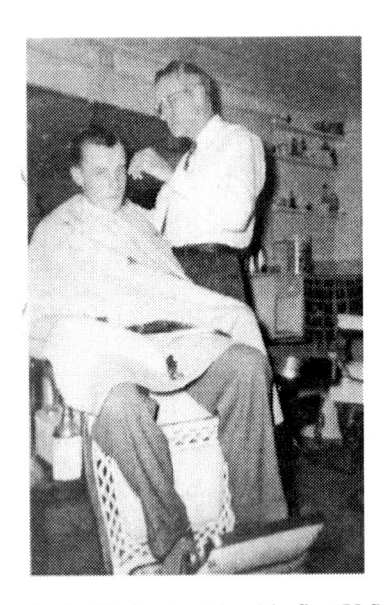

Left: Herbert getting his first U.S. haircut from Hubert Dedrickson.
Right: Herbert's senior class picture.

Herbert couldn't speak a word of English when he arrived in Litchfield, but he claimed that the teachers and students at the high school taught him to speak our difficult language in one month. Not fluently, but enough to get by. The high school principal, Howard Buska, had a different volunteer student[63] come to his office during four periods of each day to tutor Herbert. He learned to spell and write in English by taking a beginning typing class. Can you imagine being that teacher, trying to communicate with and help Herbert along with her thirty other students?

The fact that Herbert learned the language so quickly enabled him to find the three part-time jobs he had to help support his mother and sister. His mother struggled with the language for about a year. Because of that, she was unable to find work for a long time.

Herbert still had a lot to learn and he made some big mistakes, struggling with the language at times. When he heard the other students say, "Excuse me," Herbert thought they were saying, "Kiss me." So he thought that was the right phrase to use when being polite. A girl was standing in front of his locker one day and Herbert

---

[63] Mariann Braatz, Geraldine Chase, Patricia Farnquist, Diane Tiemens, David Van Nurden, and Judy Curtiss.

walked up to her and said, "Kiss me". Through a volley of giggles from the other girls nearby, Herbert found out very quickly that he was saying the phrase incorrectly.

Herbert adapted quickly to the American ways and, like any American teenager, he was determined to have his own car. So each week, he put away two or three dollars out of his pay to achieve his goal. A year later, he had the $100 he needed to buy an old '46 Nash. He was extremely proud of what he had accomplished and, better yet, now he wouldn't have to walk out to the bowling alley by Lake Ripley four times a week in our brutal winters. Soon, however, Herbert's Nash started giving him problems. Before long, it died. Herbert went to Quinn Motors and found a '51 Plymouth that he really liked. It was blue with a white top. He dickered on a price, traded in his dead Nash, and, short of cash, he asked if he could buy the Plymouth "on time". The salesman agreed but didn't want the teenager to drive the car until it was paid for. He would hold it on the lot for Herbert.

Herbert's car on frozen Lake Ripley in '58.

The German youth couldn't stay away from his beautiful Plymouth. Somehow he found a spare key to it and almost nightly he snuck it off the lot after he had finished work at the Colonial Café, in the wee hours after midnight. Sometimes Herbert would drive the car around until four in the morning and then he'd sneak it back onto the lot. He did that for three months until he finally had the car paid for, and broken in to his way of driving.

One evening, while cruising around town in his finally paid for car with some school buddies, Herbert turned onto the gravel road on

185

the south side of Lake Ripley. He got too close to the shoulder of the road and got his car stuck in the sand.

"You guys stay here," he told his buddies. "I'll walk back to the bowling alley and call a tow truck."

After he left, his friends got bored and started digging around in Herbert's car. Inside the trunk they found a saw and an ax. Herbert had been building a doghouse at home and had thrown all his tools into the trunk of his car. Now what could a couple of bored teenagers do with a saw and an ax late at night by Lake Ripley? They started cutting down trees along the lakeshore.

Herbert came back later with the tow truck and saw what they were doing.

"Stop!" he yelled. "Are you guys crazy?" By that time, they had cut down three trees. I wonder what the tow truck driver thought. Herbert must've thought the Gestapo was going to come and get him in the middle of the night. He was learning the ways of the bored American teenager who didn't always think things out.

Herbert returned to Litchfield in September of 2003 for his 45th class reunion. The class toured the old high school, which at that time was an office building. Dr. David Harder, who now lives in Willmar, took him for a horse and buggy ride down some farm roads around town. Herbert loves Litchfield and the great friendly people who gave of their time to teach him the difficult language and the sometimes-strange American ways.

Class of '58 reunion: Front row: Holly Tostenrud Duininck, Monica Klose, Mrs. Rodney Johnson, Elizabeth Widmark Rueter, Elaine Beckman Bock, Rosalie Krussow Schwenzfeier, Sandy Rayppy
Back row: Gary Klose, Herbert Schuermann, Rodney Johnson, Dick Simmons, David Harder, Jim Kuckler, Carol Schneider Marshall, George Marshall, Doug Engelson

Chapter Thirty-Three
Letter Stories: Dickey

One friend I wrote about quite a bit in *Terry Tales* was Dick "Dickey" Whelan, stepson of Harlan Quinn. I guess one way to describe Dick was "an imp". A little guy in stature, he was involved in everything that went on in Litchfield, it seems, especially with the Shaw boys.

As related in *Terry Tales*, Dick used to come over to our garage in the mornings in the summer to wake up whomever was staying over that night. He would flash twenties and take us uptown to Fransein's to treat us to breakfast. Whenever we asked where he was getting this money, he would tell us that he would sneak an occasional twenty-dollar bill out of his new stepfather Harlan Quinn's wallet. We had no reason to doubt that story.

Now Dick informs me that Harlan gave him a weekly allowance of twenty to eighty dollars and he was too embarrassed and afraid to tell us about it so he made up the sneaking story. He thought it would be "cooler" if we thought of him as this great sneak thief rather than "Ritchie Rich", the rich little kid in the comic books. He was probably correct. My friends and Pat and I were all so poor, our jealousy would definitely have affected our relationship with Dickey.

This was in the very early sixties when I was making $2.80 a week delivering papers, so you can understand how amazed I was that Dick was getting that kind of money in any way. I honestly believed what he told us and so I suffered for years from a very guilty conscious, knowing that I had "accepted stolen goods" from my friend and had not made restitution. I was sure St. Peter was going to bring it up to me some day when he checked the Giant Ledger. What a load off my "soul" when Dick made this revelation to me.

Dick, or Dickey as we called him, related a story to me about a rare time when he wasn't with the Shaw boys. Instead he was with another "friend" of ours, whom I wrote about in the first book also, but who will remain nameless this time around. This "friend" asked Dickey to go with him to visit some other friends one afternoon. Arriving at the house, the friend, let's call him JB, then told Dickey he was picking something up and the people weren't home. He asked Whelan to wait outside while he went inside to get whatever he came for. Dickey should have been leery of this whole affair, because his friend then proceeded to actually break into the house. Dickey knew he should go home, but he obediently waited outside.

Minutes and minutes passed and Dickey was starting to get worried and a little scared standing in broad daylight out in front of the house. Again, instead of just leaving, he decided to go inside the house himself and find out what was going on and what had happened to JB.

"I thought he couldn't find what he was supposed to pick up." Dick said. Working his way around in the strange house, whispering his accomplice's name, he heard a noise upstairs. Creeping up the stairway, he saw that the noise was coming from behind the bathroom door. Inside he found JB sitting on the toilet doing his thing reading a magazine as if he owned the place. In front of him, on the floor was a bad of "goodies".

"What in the hell are you doing?" Dickey hissed.

"Takin' a crap. What does it look like I'm doin'?"

"I'm outta here," Dickey said, turning. "You're nuts," he added. He finally did the right thing and left. And Dickey was right. Our friend JB, Dickey's friend, was nuts and his later activities did nothing to change our minds about that fact.

Dickey was in the same class at St. Philip's Parochial School as JB. My brother Pat was in that class too. The seventh and eighth grades took turns singing at funerals or at the 10am Sunday mass. On this particular Sunday, it was the seventh grade's turn, thank God. So Dickey and Pat and JB were singing. After mass, Pat took off for some reason and Dickey and JB snuck into the room off to the left of the altar and got into Father Foley's wine cabinet. They found a bottle of wine and poured it into some big cups they found and then ran downstairs to the basement where the popcorn machine was. It still had some popcorn left in it from Saturday night bingo and the boys scarfed it up for breakfast with the communal wine.

Although it was a weak wine, the boys were young and had empty stomachs, so before long they were feeling no pain. The giggles set in and a nun came down to investigate. Dickey had finished his wine but JB stood there with his cup half full of evidence. The nun grabbed a handful of ear with each hand and pulled the two up the stairs, out of the church and down the sidewalk to the rectory next door. Father Foley must have been having a good day because he didn't spank the boys. He just called their mothers and the two criminals started six weeks of penance, both at home and in school.

Dickey was told to stay home and watch his little sister Frannie while his mother went to visit her sister Alice and Alice's husband Jack Harris, the manager of the new Super America station. The only problem was the Meeker County fair was in full swing and the fairgrounds were only a few blocks from the Whelan house. Mrs. Whelan hadn't married Harlan Quinn yet. The sounds and smells started to wear Dickey down and he finally gave in to temptation and snuck out to the fair. There he met up with Andy "Monk" Schreifels and the Wimmer brothers, Jerry and Dougy.

Dougy had thick glasses and an intestinal problem, which enabled him to throw up at will. We used to treat him to the cheap hamburgers at Janousek's and then have him throw up on the police car parked on Sibley Avenue or Third Street. The group headed for the booth in the Dairy Barn where they had seen a sign that read, "ALL THE MILK YOU CAN DRINK FOR 5¢". Dougy, never one to pass up a deal, drank about thirty cold glasses and then he surprised everyone and held it all in.

The boys left the fair, dropped Monk off at his house two blocks away, and were walking home past Dickey's house.

"Okay," Dickey said, "see you guys tomorrow."

"Hey," Jerry asked, "got any food? We're hungry."

"Guys, you know Mom won't let me have friends in the house when she's not home."

"Come on, you big baby," Dougy chimed in. "How's she gonna know?"

"Listen, she'll know. Tell you what. You wait here on the steps and I'll get you something."

Dickey went into the house and raided the fridge and cookie jar and came back outside, only to be met with Dougy standing up and saying, "I don't feel so good. I think I'm gonna throw..." And he did. All thirty glasses of white milk all over the steps. Somebody got the bright idea to run and get the garden hose and just hose down the steps. Well, it worked, but no one had thought to close the screen door and water got inside the house. Just as Dickey was lamenting about how he was going to clean that up, he saw his mother's car coming down the street.

"Geez guys! It's my Mom!"

His "friends" took off running and Dickey got grounded for life...well, three weeks, but that meant the rest of his summer. To add insult to injury, he had to do Fran's chores for two months. But good times were right around the corner. His mother would soon meet and marry Harlan Quinn and Dickey would be rolling in the money. But for a long time, Dickey grew up in the same fatherless boat that we did.

Dickey had lived in Hopkins with his mother and sister Frannie after his mother had divorced his dad. I suppose they came to Litchfield because Dickey's Grandma and Grandpa lived here. "I remember it like it was yesterday," Dick said. "Mom, Fran and I had stayed in the apartment above the Horseshoe Cafe where Grandma and Grandpa Bauer[64] lived."

Frannie and Dickey Whelan.

"Grandpa was a beer man through and through," Dick went on. "Grandma let him think he was helping out at lunch standing behind the bar collecting the money for the lunch tabs, but all he was really doing was drinking with his buddies and having fun. By the time lunch was over, he'd be the happiest guy in the place. But a finer man never walked this earth."

The Bauer's son, Dickey's Uncle Jerry, was a track star for LHS. In 1951, he took first place in the West Central Conference in the

---

[64] George and Francis Bauer owned the Horseshoe Café at 26-30 Second Street East until November of 1960, when they sold the restaurant to George Schoultz.

100-yard dash. In 1952, he took first place in District 20 in the 100 yard dash and also first in the Broad Jump.

Dickey's mother gave him a little cowboy outfit, complete with a two-gun holster. His grandma didn't like it, but George would lift Dickey up onto the horseshoe shaped counter in front of his buddies and ask Dickey, "What kind of cowboy are you?" to which Dickey had been taught to respond, "A helluva cowboy!" Grandma Francis would come out of the kitchen and put George back to work.

Dickey's mother took him with to the post office one day. It was just across the street from the Horseshoe. Dickey was left to wander around the waiting room in his cowboy outfit while his mother stood in line in front of the post office "cage". She finally made it to the front of the line and was doing her business when she heard smirking and laughter behind her. She turned around to see little Dickey doing his business too. He was peeing into one of the spittoons, which used to be scattered around the waiting room. She grabbed Dickey and ran him out the door. Dickey, who wasn't finished, left a stream of urine in his wake. Grown up Dick said, "Well, it looked like mine (kiddy potty) at home that I used in Grandma's bathroom."

The only time I really spent any time with Dickey was when he was over in our garage or when we were smoking up in the bandstand. Because he was younger than me, he ran around more with my brother Pat and a kid named Dale Curtis. Dale was a lanky, skinny kid who had, what I thought was, an enormous Adam's apple. Not having a lot of tack, when I'd see him I'd say, "Hey, it's D-gale Cur-ca-urtis," making a guck guck sound in my throat, much like that tribe in Africa. I thought it was funny, but I don't remember anyone else laughing.

One summer, Dale, Pat and Dickey worked in Darwin for Harry Linderholm who hauled and laid sod. Harry lived in a filthy trailer about a quarter of a mile down Highway 12 from the world's largest ball of twine, which has since been moved into Darwin proper. The boys only worked weekends to begin with until school got out for the summer, but then it was six days a week after that. Dickey said he never worked so hard in his life.

The boys had to be at Harry's at 5am sharp, which was very early for three teenagers on summer vacation. It never occurred to the geniuses that Harry couldn't leave until they got there and other teenagers weren't breaking down any doors trying to replace them. They'd drive to open fields that Harry either owned or leased, where he would slice three foot long pieces of sod. The boys would roll them up and carry them to a flat bed truck. Harry had three trucks and each would hold five hundred rolls of sod. That was just the morning's work. After a break for lunch around noon they would drive to the site Harry had been hired to sod and unload the trucks and lay the sod.

Dickey and Pat were short and could barely reach their rolls up to the platform of the flatbeds, but another kid named Farley worked for Harry too and the guys thought he was Superman. Farley would grab a roll in each hand and place them up on the flatbed. At the site, he'd get up there and toss them down like beanbags, knocking the three young Litchfieldites all over the place.

Pat dated Farley's younger sister for a while and Pat said that Farley "was a nut case, loved to fight, drive about a hundred miles an hour, drive into a ditch and laugh his ass off. He would actually look forward to going to Cold Spring (Ballroom) on Friday or Saturday night to fight."

It rained hard the night before the third day the boys went to work. All the extra moisture in the sod rolls made them three times as heavy. Getting them up on the back of the trailer was almost impossible for my friend and they were yelled at all morning. So, the boys, riding to the job site on the flatbed, just happened to "lose" a few sod rolls (called sod balls) on a cloverleaf. For their hard labor, they ended up getting paid $10 a day. They had agreed on an hourly wage but this only broke down to about $1 an hour. What could they do about it?

Dickey told Jerry and Dougy Wimmer what had happened. Jerry and Dougy were big athletic types and they went to pay him a visit that weekend but when they got there his trailer and flatbeds were gone.

Chapter Thirty-Four
Letter Stories: Two Guys

Guy Shoultz wrote me a nice letter about my book. In the letter he told me how his dad, David, called "Mickey", was part of the Shoultz-Lenhardt family. I know that now, but I didn't know it when he and I crossed paths when I was in ninth grade. Actually his Grandpa William was a son-in-law to old Erhardt Lenhardt, Meeker County's first brewer. Lenhardt's brewery was out by Lake Ripley on the northeast side. He also owned the grand hotel, which had been called the Howard House[65]. William Shoultz, whose wife was the pastry cook at the hotel, ran the hotel for Erhardt starting in 1898. William and Erhardt's son Edmund bought the brewery in 1910 and William took sole-ownership in 1911. He also was part owner of the old icehouse over on Commercial Street and he owned the building where Nicola's is today.

Guy lived around the corner from me at 324 West Depot Street. He ran around with some of the same friends as my brother Mick. That meant Guy and I couldn't be friends because in our pre-teens, Mick and I didn't do anything together at all, let alone run in the same pack. One of the mutual friends of Mick and Guy was Jerry Koehn. Jerry and Guy, both twelve at the time, were hanging around the new power plant just west of our house looking for something to do. The two power plants that we lived between offered many possibilities of things to climb on or get into.

Jerry and Guy came across the official Litchfield rain gauge. The device had an eight-inch collection funnel at its top, which led down to the glass container. As luck would have it, a heavy rainfall started. The boys pulled off their T-shirts to make another "funnel" to collect more water in the gauge and then added a little more "liquid" of their own. After the rain quit, they ran away from the plant. The next day, Jerry ran to Guy's house with the Minneapolis Star newspaper. The headline read "Litchfield Receives 8 Inches of Rain". The boys were elated. They were famous! Of course, according to Guy, the headline should have read, "Litchfield Receives 8 Inches of Rain and Urine."

One day, Guy, still twelve, decided to hitch a ride on a freight train from Jerry's house on the east side of town to the Swift Avenue

---

[65] See Chapter Eleven, "Mrs. Howard's Monument".

crossing by Guy's house. The freights would load up at one of the elevators in town and slowly move west out of town, or, as I recounted in *Terry Tales*, they would just move back and forth switching cars and blocking crossings, exasperating motorists all over town. This particular freight train was very short and didn't need much time to get up to speed, however, something Guy didn't notice.

After he climbed into a boxcar, Guy knew right away that something was wrong. The train was picking up speed way too fast. He didn't want to jump off right downtown by the depot where everyone would see him, so he thought he'd just jump out, as originally planned, by his house.

Whizzing by the Swift Avenue crossing, he thought better of that plan. Guy gulped as he watched his house disappear behind him and then the entire city of Litchfield disappear as the train rounded a bend by a grove of trees. Guy was overcome with fear. Where would he end up? South Dakota?

Luckily for him, all the trains stopped at the roundhouse in Willmar, Minnesota in those days. Guy bailed out there, walked from downtown Willmar out to Highway 12, and hitchhiked the twenty-five miles back to Litchfield.

The driver who picked him up let him out downtown by the hotel. The "hobo" ran home and into his house just in time for supper. He sat down at the table grinning and looking at his family, wishing he could tell them of his great adventure. But he knew that what they didn't know wouldn't hurt them...nor his own hind end.

My stories about treks out of town on the railroad tracks to Chicken Lake brought back memories to Guy. He told me, "Trips to Chicken Lake were frequent for my gang. Half a pack (of cigarettes) on the trip out, half a pack on the return trip."

"Those trips were not always law abiding," Guy added, "and I wonder if we are still being sought for some of the things we did?" Speaking of smoking, he confessed that he "learned to French Inhale in the Shaw clubhouse, "probably at the age of eleven or twelve." The clubhouse was, of course, the Shaw garage, which was the subject of an entire chapter in *Terry Tales*.

Another twelve-year-old boy named Harvey Curtis joined Jerry and Guy in another adventure. They were all sitting next to one of the two metal Quonset huts at the Swift crossing one day, as my brother Pat and I had done so many summer days. The sheds offered privacy for a smoke and you could also look down the tracks and see downtown Litchfield or see the farmers stopping off at the tractor dealership and maintenance building on an angled piece of land one block to the east. Next to it, where Depot Street and Second Street met up and joined together, was a small triangle of vacant land. Occasionally a car would be parked there or a piece of machinery stood on the lot.

"Look there," one of the boys said, nudging the others. A Greyhound bus had just pulled onto the triangle of land. The driver opened the door, got off the bus, lit a cigarette and then started walking towards the hotel downtown. Obviously, he was going for lunch before picking up passengers at the hotel for a run to the cities or to Willmar. He left the empty bus just sitting there…with the side door open.

Talk about opportunities just waiting to be capitalized upon.
"Betcha I could drive that thing," Harvey said.
"Yeah, right," Jerry answered.
"Could too."
"I'll dare you to," said Guy.
"Nah, it's the middle of the day. I'd get seen."
"Chicken. I double-dare you."

That was enough. A double-dare could not be ignored. Harvey got up and took off running for the bus. Jerry and Guy stood up for a better view and to allow room for their jaws to drop. Harvey got into the bus, ground the transmission for a while and then turned the big wheels and slowly drove off the lot. Not only did Harvey drive the bus, but he drove it right through downtown. Jerry and Guy ran up the street to watch the bus' journey. Soon it turned onto Second Street and came back to the triangle of land, where it stopped in its original location, the door opened up and Harvey triumphantly stepped down.

"Somebody had to see you and recognize you, Harvey," someone said. "Let's get the hell out of here."

The trio spent the remainder of the day under a railroad overpass at Jewett's Creek waiting for the long arm of the law to root them out. But no one came and Harvey achieved legendary status amongst the gangs of pre-teens in Litchfield.

Guy also related to my stories about climbing the old water tower, which was next to the "old" power plant at the corner of Third

Street West and Miller Avenue North. Both the tower and the plant are gone today[66]. Guy had climbed the water tower too. Climbing the water tower was a right of passage for a lot of the gangs of kids that ran around Litchfield in the fifties. You **had** to climb it on a dare. Back then, there was no guardrail or padlocked "gate" to the tower to keep us off.

Guy told me something I didn't know. He said that scaling the side of the tank to climb over the roof to touch the light bulb on the very top of the tower was the real test. A burned finger, from the heat of the bulb, was required as proof of reaching the summit. I didn't know there was a ladder on the tank itself, thank God. Now that I think of it, there had to be a way to get to the top to service the light, which was there to warn airplanes. My stepfather, Floyd Young, used to be the guy who went up there doing those things, including hanging garland and lights around the top at Christmas time, yelling down to my bewildered mother who was hanging her laundry on the clothesline in our backyard a block from the tower. She must've thought God was talking to her.

I mentioned in *Terry Tales* that Bill and Ida Johnson started a restaurant at the East Side Shell gas station in May of 1959 at the very east edge of town on East Highway 12. Guy reminded me that the Johnson Cafe did open in 1959, but not exactly on schedule. Bill Johnson, Guy's step-grandfather, died of a heart attack five minutes before opening the café on the restaurant's opening morning, May 9, 1959. Ida Johnson opened the cafe several weeks later as the "Ida-Way Cafe". Guy helped paint the sign for the cafe, assisting his first cousin Jim Gunter in Jim's sign painting shop in southeast Litchfield across from the Deb Thomas Trucking Company. Gunter was in a building with Klitzkie's Body Shop. Jim promised to pay Guy but he didn't, so Guy stole a pack of his Chesterfields in lieu of payment. Cigs, as we called them, were an important commodity to a teenage boy in the fifties and sixties. Sometimes they were needed to calm us

---

[66] The "old" power plant east of our house at the corner of Austin Avenue North and Third Street West was torn down in February of 1992. It had been built in 1890, so it was 102 years old. After the new power plant was built in 1941, this plant was used sparingly, mostly as a backup. The generators had been on standby since 1961. In 1985, the generators were turned off for the last time. The building sat idle for almost seven years while the city tried to interest somebody in taking it over for something useful. But there were no takers. The water tower was torn down in May of 1996. It was eighty-two years old at the time, having been built in 1914.

down before and after we did something dangerous and stupid on a dare.

I mentioned that Guy and I crossed paths when I was in the ninth grade. Actually, I was in fear for my life for about two weeks because of Guy. One day, in Bernice "Ski Jumps" Slinden's English class, I had a feeling that someone was looking at me. I looked up to see cute dark haired Cheryl "Cherie" Fuhrman giving me the most wonderful coy smile that shot right through my eyes and landed in my heart. I smiled back and then I tried to concentrate the rest of the class time on my work. But every so often I would peek a glance her way and then she'd turn to me and smile again.

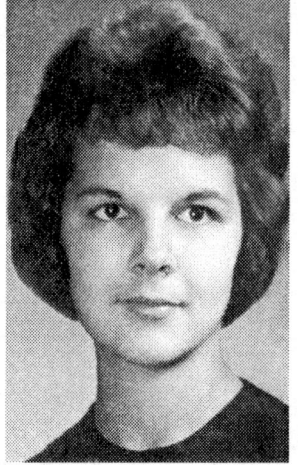

Cheryl "Cherie" Fuhrman Olson

Cherie was the daughter of the high school counselor, Bill Fuhrman, and she was the cutest girl I had seen since Jeanette Oliver in the eighth grade over at St. Philip's Parochial School. After class Karen Holtz came up to me and said, "I think Cherie Fuhrman likes you. Why don't you call her up tonight?" Now, Karen was almost a stranger to me at that time and I could smell a set-up here, but I didn't care. A girl was interested in me? I couldn't believe it.

That night I agonized over trying to get up enough courage to call her, and somehow I finally did. We talked about unimportant things and then I laid the big question on her. "Are you going steady or something?"

"Well," she said, "I have been seeing Guy Shoultz, but we're not going steady. We're just friends."

Friends? I didn't like this.

"I'd better leave you alone then. I don't want to interfere or anything."

"No, you're not interfering. I told him I wanted to see other boys."

"What'd he say?"

"Well..." she paused, "he doesn't like it."

My heart took over my brain and the next day in school, I persisted in staring at Cherie in class and finally I passed her a note: "Hi! Can I walk you home?"

"Yes," she wrote back.

As we strolled down the street, Cherie as cute as ever and me as nervous as ever, I saw a boy walking along in the next block parallel to us. He was matching our pace exactly.

"You know that kid over there?" I asked Cherie.

"Yeah, that's Guy."

"Oh, boy."

"Don't worry, he wouldn't do anything while I'm around."

Was that supposed to be reassuring? I got Cherie home and she invited me in for a while for a cookie or something. When I left, I walked home fast and kept my eyes peeled for the stalker. But, I never saw him. I was sure he was going to track me down like a dog and kill me, but I continued to call Cherie up nightly and even went over after supper one night to go in her basement and listen to records. Then, suddenly, just as suddenly as the romance had started, Cherie lost interest and moved on to an older boy with a car, I think. All I know is that both Guy and I lost out.

Throughout my high school career though, Cherie and I remained close friends and I felt something in my chest when we were dancing slow at the hops after the games or at parties. I always wondered what could have been with her had we both been more mature. She's still a very good friend with a great husband and lots of beautiful kids. She lives by and works in Litchfield.

Oh, Guy wrote to me and said he didn't remember the incident and "at 5'6" and 115 lbs., I don't think I was in any position to beat the crap out of anyone." Well, Guy, you had me scared 'cause in the ninth grade I was about 5' 4" and 95 lbs. I remember my weight because I won the championship in intramural wrestling in ninth grade gym class.

Another Guy wrote to me also. This time it was Guy Robeck. In *Terry Tales* I wrote about my mother's Christmas rules. Christmas was a special time for Mom and she had rules concerning the holiday. My brothers and I would each get one toy gift. The other gifts "from Santa" had to be clothes. The tree wouldn't go up until one week before Christmas and it wouldn't go up at all if her four boys didn't pitch in picking it out, carrying it home and decorating it. My favorite decorations were our bubble lights and we always topped the tree off with a lot of tinsel and Angel Hair. Only Mom could put the Angel Hair on the tree because it was made from spun glass and too dangerous for us to handle, she told us. A plastic Santa in his sleigh pulled by eight reindeer on top of a sheet of sparkling cotton usually went on top of the TV, with the manger scene on one of the lamp tables beside the sofa. Sometimes Mom would switch them around.

We would open gifts on the twenty-third of December because of another rule. We had to be in Le Sueur, Minnesota for Christmas Eve Midnight Mass with Mom's parents, Grandpa and Grandma Rheaume, every year. Getting to Le Sueur without a car was quite a task for Mom, but somehow she did it. I remember taking the bus a couple of times, where we had to go to Minneapolis and then to Le Sueur from there. Grandpa or Uncle Bud drove up to Litchfield to get us a couple of times.

Most often there was a family of three, Clinton Robeck, and his wife Caroline and son Guy, who had relatives also in Le Sueur and they would give us a ride with them. The back seat of their old sedan would be crammed with Guy and us noisy Shaw boys, having to go to the bathroom, fighting amongst ourselves and yelling everything we said. God bless the Robecks. We never missed a Christmas Eve in Le Sueur.

Guy Robeck wrote me and thanked me for "writing such a refreshing book". He wrote, "It was such a joy to bring back the memories of when times were simpler and the pure joy of just being with friends." Guy's dad Clint was still living but his mother Caroline had passed away in April of 2004. Guy talked about our Christmas trips together to Le Sueur.

"How did all us boys fit in the back seat of that car at one time and still be able to walk away with a smile on our faces?" he asked me.

Life played one of its tricks or oddities on Guy the day he retired from working at the Minnesota State Security Hospital in St. Peter, Minnesota. At 6am that morning, his mother died. "It was my wish," he said, " for her to see me retire and she held on just long enough."

Guy finished his letter by thanking me for the "walk around Litchfield".

"Too soon, he went on, "we forget what a wonderful place Litchfield was and still is. I stop at the City Park every now and then, just to watch people and to see if Litchfield still smells the same. I can almost smell the popcorn coming from the Popcorn Wagon. My mind can drift across the street and can see Helen Anderson standing behind the counter in Janousek's. Man! What a delicious burger."

Then Guy said something very nice to me that I agree with. "When we were young," he wrote, "we really were closer to heaven."

Right you are Guy and the fifties and sixties in Litchfield were a little slice of that heaven.

Chapter Thirty-Five
Letter Stories: The Askeroths

The history of Litchfield has certain names that stand out or keep cropping up over and over. Askeroth would be one of those names. An Askeroth descendant named Todd wrote to me that he and his dad, Jerry, were enjoying my book. The Askeroths are most known for their wallpaper and paint store that was just behind Sandgren's Shoes[67] on Second Street East, just west of the alley.

The Askeroth family had been involved with painting and decorating in Litchfield since 1885 when Andrew O. Askeroth started a business in town at an unknown location. In 1893, Andrew's son, Olaf O., came into the family business. Andrew finally retired in 1912. Olaf brought in his son Clarence M. "Skip" in 1917, after Skip got out of the Navy, and his son Vernon joined the business in 1921. Olaf and Skip moved the family business to a building on main street, which eventually had my favorite pool hall, Johnson's Rec, in it after the Askeroths moved tot the Second Street location. Today, it's a vacant lot next to True Valu hardware. Olaf retired from the business in 1941.

Jerry Askeroth said that Litchfield used to have a foot race downtown every Saturday morning in the early 1900s. It was open to anyone. The race would be run from one end of downtown to the other on main street in front of the stores. Skip told his son Jerry that the "Gray Eagle", legendary football coach Bernie Bierman, used to win all the time. Bernie Bierman was the son of Litchfield clothing merchant William F. Bierman, whose store preceded Viren-Johnson's. Bernie was the captain of Litchfield's high school football team and a 1913 graduate. He coached at Tulane University and took that team to the Rose Bowl in 1932.

Returning to Minnesota to coach the Gophers, Bernie brought on what has since been called the "Golden Era" of Minnesota football and the reason the team is now called the Golden Gophers. Before the dome was built, the Gophers played at Bierman Field on the university campus.

On the return train trip from a victorious Rose Bowl and National Championship in 1948, Bernie had the train stop in Litchfield. He then had his players get off and greet the town folk.

---

[67] Nicola's today.

Future Vikings' coach and Hall of Fame legend Bud Grant was one of those players.

Back in 1917, Skip Askeroth had been a bugler while in the Navy. He had played in the Great Lakes Band, which was conducted and led by none other than the famous "March King", John Philip Sousa. Skip had also been a great baseball pitcher, so his son, Jerry, went out for baseball in high school, following in his dad's footsteps. But, Jerry was a mediocre pitcher. His athletic talent, and his towering height, showed up more on the basketball court, where he was a star. Anyway, Litchfield was playing a game at Howard Lake and Jerry was pitching. Some guy got hold of one of Jerry's pitches and hit it out of the park. But the Howard Lake player only got a double. The ball had cleared the fence all right, but it hit a tree and had bounced back onto the field. The lone umpire behind home plate was watching to make sure the runner touched first base and he just saw the ball bounce back onto the outfield grass. He assumed it had hit the top of the fence. No amount of arguing from the Howard Lake coach or from the poor kid standing on second could change the ump's mind. Howard Lake "was robbed!"

At one time, the Askeroth sons also owned a bowling alley in town. It was at 27 Depot Street East, where America's Racquet & Fitness Center is today. Skip and Vern built a new building there in April of 1940 and put in the bowling alley. They leased the front of the building out to Frank L. Fransein for his Bowling Café. The Askeroth sons dissolved their partnership in April of 1945. Skip kept the bowling alley while Vernon took over the paint shop. Eventually the Western Café was in that building where my brothers' bands played in the back room, where the bowling alleys had been. I also went to many teenage record hops there.

I wrote about a character in *Terry Tales* who was a teacher and a coach. His name was Howard Felt and he did things one way and one way only...Howie's way. Besides being the football coach, Howie was also the track coach. Todd Askeroth reminded me of the spring when the weather was bad so that the track team couldn't practice outside. Howie had the shot putters practicing by throwing their shots in the gym. Thud, crack. I believe it. The custodians and principal Curtis McCamy must've put a quick stop to that.

Howie had an unusual way of teaching Phy Ed, which I wrote about in *Terry Tales*. Most of the time, it seemed, he would just have his favorite athletes pick teams to play basketball and those of us not chosen would play Ping-Pong on the sidelines. Then he would go off into a corner and read *Esquire* magazine. I was a straight "A" student, but could only muster a "B" from Howie, no matter how hard I tried. The "B" was only because of my drawing ability. I got a "C" in Phy Ed, but an "A" in Health class, which Howie taught in tandem with Phy Ed. We'd have gym a couple of days a week and Health class a couple of days. In Health class, Howie had us draw posters against smoking and such, hence my "A" in that class.

John Klug, the other Phy Ed instructor who eventually took over head football coaching duties when Howie left before getting fired, would share study hall duty with Howie in the huge room upstairs in the middle of the old high school. The teachers sat up behind us on a raised desk in the rear of the huge room. We were told not to talk and not to turn around. Come report card time, Howie would quiz Klug on students.

"This Johnson kid, first row, second chair. He in your class or mine?"

"He's in your class, Howie," Klug answered.

"He out for sports?"

"Yeah, he's on your football team"

"Okay," Howie said, as he marked an "A" next to Johnson's name in his book.

"Okay, then...this Anderson kid, third row, second to last chair. Whose class is he in?"

"Yours again, Howie."

"Out for sports?"

"Nope."

"Okay," Howie said as he wrote a "C" down in his book.

"Now, this kid over in the last row...."

A Simple "I Love You"

Try as hard as you can, when you write poems or song lyrics, you are always drawn back to the theme of love. It goes hand in hand with poetry and music. But how many ways can you come up with different words to tell someone you love them? I decided not to search for a different way just once and keep the words simple. K.I.S.S.: "Keep It Simple, Stupid." Sometimes simple is simply the best.

A Simple "I Love You"

It's so hard to say
it any other way.
To let you know how I feel.
A simple "I love you.
That will have to do.
Anyway, it's real.

I wish that I could say
it many other ways.
But too many words might conceal
feelings of true love,
feelings worthy of
what you mean to me.

Chapter Thirty-Six
Art Krout – Part One

A late snowstorm in March of 1916 stalled the train Art Krout was on in Pipestone, Minnesota. Jacob Krout has entrusted his livestock and personnel goods to his son Art, another son, and hired hand and friend Frank Manion for the move to Forest City, Minnesota where he had purchased a farm.[68] Jacob had gone ahead with his wife on a passenger train. Everything he owned had been loaded into three boxcars in Elkton, South Dakota. Now, just across the Minnesota border, the train had run into the snowstorm.

Stalled for three days, it was decided on the third day that the horses and mules had to be walked and fed. So Frank, Art and Art's brother unloaded them, put the cattle in the stockyard and started walking the horses and mules to the local livery stable for fodder. On the way, a dog suddenly came out of nowhere, yipping and snapping at the ankles of the animals. When it succeeded in biting one of the colts, Frank calmly drew his revolver from its holster and shot the dog dead.

While Art and Frank were tending to the animals at the livery stable, the door opened and the town marshal strolled in.

"Which one of you shot the dog?" he said, brushing snow off his coat.

"I did. He had it comin'," Frank said. "He bit one of our colts and was tryin' to bite the others."

"I've got to take your gun, fella," the marshal said, strolling up to Frank.

Frank turned to face the marshal, spread his feet apart, pushed back his jacket revealing his revolver in its holster, and calmly and slowly said, "Do you want to take it right now?"

The marshal looked down at the exposed side arm, looked up at Frank's eyes and saw that this cowboy meant business.

"No more shootin' in my town," he said, turning on his heels and heading back out into the storm.

A scene from a Hollywood western? No, that was the way things still were in the early 1900s in the Dakotas, according to Art. "Just about everyone back in South Dakota those days carried a gun," Art told Stan Roeser in an interview later in his life.

---

[68] Once operated by Otto Berg, the Marlin Booth family later owned the farm.

Art Krout was born in 1900 on a farm in Cherokee, Iowa, but he spent most of his younger years in Brookings County, South Dakota, moving there when he was nine. His dad moved the family around an awful lot, which was common in those days. Art grew up on horseback, taking care of a neighbor's 180 head of livestock. The neighbor was the local sheriff. After the harvest, the livestock were turned out into the pasture, which would grow over with various plants. It was called "winter pasturing" and it was pretty much open range in the Dakotas then. Very few fences were around, so someone had to ride the herd.

Art had a special rapport with horses and felt he could communicate with them. The work was hard and sometimes sad. Cholera wiped out the family herd of hogs. Over a hundred died. Every day after that, Art harnessed up the mules to a wagon and carted dead pigs out on the prairie where he buried them. Art got along with the mules too and he just told them what to do and they did it. He didn't have to use a whip or pull on the reins. Neighbors came by to see the kid who got mules to work by just talking to them.

When Art was sixteen, his dad told him they were moving to Minnesota, where he had bought a farm. A neighbor had a brother who worked for dairy farmer Charles Nelson here and he told them there was good cheap land here. The Charles Nelson farm was where the Meeker County Fairgrounds are today. In fact, the old barn is still there being used by the fair.

"You're good with the stock. I want you to take your brother and go with Frank and ride in the boxcar with them and take care of the animals 'til we get to our new place," his dad told him. It was still the winter of 1916 when they loaded everything, farm machinery, livestock, and furniture into the three boxcars and took off for their new home. One boxcar held nothing but thirty-two head of cattle and ten brood sows. The four horses and the farm machinery were in another and four mules and the furniture were in the third. They left at one in the afternoon. It was brutally cold in the boxcar and Art kept warm the way he had herding on the prairie. He and his brother would climb up on a horse or mule, pull a blanket over themselves and feel the warmth from the animal rise to their bodies. Frank was too big to do that. At least he couldn't sit up on the animal. So Art showed him another trick he'd learned on the prairie where he would get between two animals and make a tent over them with a blanket.

When the train got to Pipestone, Minnesota, the boxcars were parked on a sidetrack to transfer to another locomotive. Before dark it started snowing and it never let up. Before the engine could come and hook them up, the track got closed because of all the snow. So there they sat. Frank and the boys took the three kerosene lanterns they had and put them into a large washtub for safety. Then they sat around the washtub for warmth with the heat of the horses and mules' breath warming the back of their necks. When the storm kicked up and freezing eight below zero air and snow started coming through the cracks of the boxcar's siding, Art and his brother crawled through the hay chute in the cattle car and tacked tarpaper and whatever they could find on the windward side of the car.

They had eaten the sandwiches they brought along for the one day trip, so the only food they had left were some ginger snaps, Frank's beer and fresh milk right from the cows. There was no water and very little feed for the livestock, so it was decided to unload them. The cattle went to the stockyard and the horses and mules went to the livery stable.

Finally, after the run in with the marshal and three days of misery, the storm lifted and a snowplow train engine opened up the tracks just before daylight of the fourth day. Art's father found out what was going on and he came to Pipestone on the passenger train to help them load the livestock back up again. They were on their way again and when they arrived in Litchfield in one piece, cold, hungry and tired, they looked out to see snow up to the tops of the fence posts. They wondered what they were getting into here in Minnesota.

No sooner had the livestock been unloaded in Litchfield at the stockyards east of town near Highway 12, than a non-stopping mail train came screaming through town with its whistle blowing from one end of Litchfield to the other. The stock got spooked and stampeded west down the tracks, almost as if they were trying to chase the train out of town. One mule stayed because he couldn't jump the three-foot fence around the stockyard. Like a Wild West cowboy, Art saddled the mule up, jumped on, and took off after the spooked animals.

A half hour later, the men at the stockyard dropped their jaws in unison as they saw the lanky, skinny kid from Dakota bringing the entire herd back by himself. He rode past them and into the stockyard. The herd all followed him right in. Art had caught up with them and then just whistled them back into a herd, just as he had done back home on the Dakota prairie.

The Krouts and Manion drove the herd from Litchfield to Forest City trying to follow the sled track there. There was no regular road such as Highway 24 in those days. Occasionally a cow would get off the track and fall into deep snow in the ditch and all the men would have to lift the stray back onto the track.

"We lifted more tonnage of cattle back onto that track," Art said, "than I lifted in my whole life."

The tracks on the trails got pretty deep sometimes and the middle would be crowned up so that when automobiles came along a couple of years later, they would get hung up on the crown. The wheels would just spin.

Back in Dakota, Art had dropped out of school during his eighth grade year to help on the farm. Now in Minnesota, settled on the new farm, he was suddenly stricken with appendicitis and he had an operation. As he was recovering, his dad decided that because he wasn't any help on the farm, he should go back to school. So Art enrolled in Litchfield High (the old original one that burned down) and stayed with the Angier family in town. But he had to pay his way, so he got a job at the Mellquist Department store, which was in the building occupied by Penney's, Woolworth's and Hardware Hank over the following years.

Emil C. "E.C." Gross, one of the town jewelers, saw him working in the store and liked what he saw.

"Say kid. How much do you make here?" he asked Art.

"$5 a week, Mr. Gross."

"You come and work for me and I'll double that."

So Art ran to the jewelry store after school everyday and cleaned up the store. He worked the whole day on Saturdays and shined up the glass in the display cases and helped clean pendulum clockworks.

The jewelry store was at 227 Sibley Avenue North, where Gervais Jewelry is today. Out front on the sidewalk was a large clock on a metal pole, much like the clock at the corner in front of the new library. Krout used to watch dogs come down the street, see the clock pole, sniff it, and then lift their leg and mark it. He thought it was funny, but made sure not to laugh in front of E. C. It drove E. C. Gross nuts, especially during the winter when a large deposit of yellow ice started growing at the base of the pole. Gross' watchmaker, Art Gainer, came up with an idea. He went into the basement and wired the pole with electricity. When a dog came along and urinated, his stream completed the electrical circuit and he got a jolt in a very sensitive spot. After the dogs went whimpering down the street enough times, the problem ceased.

In the spring, things started melting and there was a large puddle on the street in front of the pole. Along came farmer Tom Farley with his team of black horses, which he parked in front of the Gross jewelry. Krout noticed the team out of the corner of his eye and then looked up when he heard the familiar sound of distressed horses. Somehow the horses standing in the puddle made a connection with the pole and, of course, they got the resulting jolt. Rearing up, they started going crazy in front of the store. Luckily Gainer saw what was happening and he was able to run down to the basement and disconnect the electricity before the horses could come through the store window.

In school, Art met up with Hugo Esbjornsson.

"I kept my eye on him whenever he was around 'cause you never knew what he'd be up to," Art said.

Hugo did things like writing notes to the pretty girls, not signing them and having some other boy deliver it, or putting a statue of *September Morn* (a naked girl washing herself in a pond) on the principal's desk.

Hugo was out hunting prairie chicken with Don Putzier in Hugo's car one Saturday morning. Some guy was ahead of them on the road in an old Model T putt putt putting along. It got even worse when they got to a hill.

"Why, for a 10¢," Hugo said, "I'd push that guy right up over the hill."

Don reached into his pocket, took out a dime, and threw it into Hugo's lap. So, Hugo stepped on it, bumped into the Model T and then sped up more, pushing the T up over the hill.

The driver pulled over to the side of the road and got out. Hugo pulled up behind him, got out of his car and walked up to the man.

"What the hell's wrong with you", the man asked the grinning Hugo. "What'd you do that for?"

"Well," answered the smug Hugo, "I told my friend that for a dime I'd push you up over the hill, and he threw a dime in my lap."

"For a dime," the driver snorted, "I'd hit you right in the nose."

Don reached into his pocket, took out another dime and threw it down at the man's feet.

BANG! Hugo took one right on his nose and down he went. He got up and came at the man and...BANG!...down he went again.

"Wait a minute!" Hugo said, dusting himself off. "That's enough of this. Pick up your dime!"

With that, Hugo turned and went back to his car.

Chapter Thirty-Seven
Art Krout – Part Two

After Art Krout finished high school, he played baseball for the town team and went to work for Northwestern Bell installing phones. Litchfield had two phone companies in those early days, the other one was Tri-State, and most business places had two phones. Northwestern acquired Tri-State and either replaced all the old Tri-State phones or just took them out.

"I suppose I was in just about every home in Litchfield that existed then, replacing phones," Art told Stan Roeser.

One day the telephone service went out in an apartment at the Litchfield Hotel, called the Lenhardt at that time. Art traced the line to a hallway that was locked. He went to old man Lenhardt and asked for the key.

"No, I don't like anyone using that hall," he was told.

"Well, I have to get in there. That's where the trouble is," Art said. "If I can't get in there, I can't fix it."

Lenhardt relented and let Art in. Art had heard about a secret passageway at the hotel used by "ladies of the evening" who came out to Litchfield on the weekends to ply their trade for the locals. A close friend of mine who worked the night shift at the hotel had also told me of this passageway and he confirmed the story about the ladies.

Two or three ladies came at a time on the train on Friday afternoons and left on Sunday mornings. They never caused any trouble and they had their meals sent to their rooms. They paid in cash and bought a lot of cigarettes from the night clerk. Most of the ladies were in their twenties or early thirties and not particularly good looking. The downtown stores were open on Friday nights because it was payday. Sometimes, as in December of 1958, the bank cashed the Produce checks with $2 bills. Some of the ladies changed stacks of $2 bills into larger bills at the front desk before leaving on Sunday morning. The "business" was still going into the sixties.

When Art had the bowling alley later in his life, he employed a great cook named Lil Anderson. The restaurant part of the alley was almost as popular as the alley. Lil was known for her lutefisk during the holidays. Anyway, for years the bowling alley had the only restaurant in town that was open on Sunday evenings. Old man Hanson, of Hanson Silo by Lake Lillian, would come to the courthouse every Monday morning with a bus and hang around the court. The judge would sentence misdemeanors, drunks, etc. to either go to the city workhouse or go with Hanson and work making cement stays or putting up silos. Many jumped at the opportunity to get out into the open air. A lot of them came into the bowling alley for a late Sunday supper. Art would overhear their conversations, which confirmed to him the rumor about the ladies at the hotel.

In 1919, Art enlisted in the Army. He was sent to communications school. In 1920, the troop train he was on, heading from Fort Dodge, Iowa to Camp Lewis in the state of Washington, happened to stop in Litchfield for water. Art and the other soldiers stepped off the train to stretch their legs and Irene Lenhardt and Blanche Settergren, two pretty Litchfield girls who happened to be at the train station, noticed him and ran up to him.

"Art!", they screamed, hugging him. Then they both planted a big kiss on his cheeks. Red-faced Art's stature among his fellow soldiers went up a few notches as the soldiers climbed back on the train and headed west. But he didn't hear the last of playful and jealous razzing all the way, either.

After Art's discharge from the Army, the country was in the Depression and he luckily got a job in Tacoma, Washington where he worked in a copper-smelting refinery. But, he didn't like that job so he got a job on a dock loading lumber on ships for the Weyhauser Timber Company. He went from there to the Todd Shipyard, working in the foundry building ships. Jobs were short-lived because when the work got done, companies laid people off until they got another contract.

The last year and a half of Art's army career had been spent being a mess sergeant feeding the troops. So, Art hired on as a cook on a construction camp working on the railroad. From there he ended up in Des Moines, Iowa where he was a cook in a restaurant. Then it was back to construction camp cook in Perry, Iowa.

Back in Des Moines, Art jumped on a freight train and road to Minneapolis where he got a job at a creamery. He stayed with the creamery for seventeen years and finally came back to Litchfield in 1942. Here he went to work at Land O'Lakes, driving truck. He also rented some land from Armour by Minneapolis and started a feed cattle operation on the side. All he had was a hoe and a wheelbarrow, but he got by borrowing and renting. He worked three days for Land O'Lakes driving truck, putting in sixty-two hours, and four days on the farm. The farm was so successful that Art took his profits and bought another farm in the Litchfield area.

In 1946, Art heard that Harry Radunz wanted to sell his farm machinery, REO truck and Hudson car dealership and new building[69] out on East Highway 12. Harry Radunz had built his new Harry's Tire Shop out there in 1936. So, Art bought everything and started Krout Motors. He mostly sold used vehicles and machinery because the war was on and everything was rationed. Oh, and he bought another farm north of town too. A few years later, Art decided he couldn't keep the business going with the shortage of new goods and so he sold everything at a public auction in December of 1949.

Art went to work for Clarence Weber, selling farm machinery. His farmland was still bringing in good money, although he was still working two jobs. It caught up with him when, in early 1954, Art suffered a heart attack. He decided to change his lifestyle and buy a more relaxing business. Clarence "Skip" Askeroth had built a bowling alley at 27 Depot Street East and he sold it to Walt Schranz and Walt sold it to Ray and Jacob "Ollie" Olson in May of 1949. Art got together with his friend, builder Warren Plath, in November of 1954 and they bought the bowling alley. It was where Beckman's Appliance store is today and it had four lanes. My brothers Dennie and Mick worked there as pinsetters for a while.

At the same time, Art started the residential development in the Morningside area of town. He also bought ninety-one acres of the old Peterson farm out by Lake Ripley. When he heard that a group, ironically from Art birthplace, Cherokee, Iowa, was going to build a new bowling alley in town on East Highway 12, he and Plath quickly put up the Ripley Lanes[70] on some of his Peterson land in September of 1956. Other pieces of the farmland were sold to Arvid Reinke for his Custom Products business and Oscar Schwartzwald for his dealership and Litchfield's first motel. The rest of the land became the Melodie Heights addition to Litchfield.

---

[69] The REA bought the building from Krout in December of 1949 and had their office at that location.
[70] Art and Warren sold the Ripley Lanes to Martin Pedley in September of 1961 and he sold it to Joe Nelson who had it for many years. An earlier bowling alley in Litchfield, other than the one Art owned where Beckman's is, was where the King's Wok is now.

Art was married to his wife Myrtle for fifty-two years before she died in 1980. Art said of Myrtle, "She brought me peace and contentment. It was just a joy living with her."

In his nineties, Art lived alone in an apartment at 802 Second Street East. My friend Cheryl Almgren lived in the apartment above him.

The first thing Art said to Cheryl, when they met in the building, was "I remember you. You tipped over my toilet."

When Art had lived in the Forest City area about forty years prior, some teens had done that on a Halloween night. Apparently Art had spied Cheryl as one of the pranksters.

Late one morning, Cheryl heard a loud "WHUMPH" and felt herself rise up a little as she was walking in her apartment. She opened her door to the hall and ran into Peggy Larson, who had the apartment across from hers.

"Did you hear that?" Peggy asked.

"I sure did."

"Must've been a big gust of wind."

"Wind? I went off the floor!" Cheryl answered.

Just then the ladies heard a smoke alarm going off on the floor beneath them.

"That's gotta be coming from Art's apartment," Cheryl said and the two took off down the stairs and ran to Art's place. Sure enough, that was where the alarm was the loudest. They rang Art's doorbell, but got no answer. After another attempt, they tried the door, which they found open. Inside, in a cloud of smoke, stood Art Krout.

"I can't get the damned thing to shut off," said Art, referring to the alarm. Then he quickly explained that he had been cooking, had a grease fire, and had mistakenly thrown water on the burning pan. There had been an explosion and there was grease everywhere. The ladies went to make sure that everything was okay and suddenly Art disappeared. They couldn't find him anywhere. The pain of Art's burns had set in and he had driven himself to the hospital where he was treated for bad burns on his hands and arms.

Art Krout at 95 years old.

Art Krout lived to be 103 years old, dying in July of 2003. When Stan Roeser asked him to what he attributed his longevity, Art replied, "I was pretty fussy about who my grandparents were."

Art's paternal grandfather was very strong. Twice, Art saw him do something on a bet to show his strength. Art's grandpa was working with a road graveling crew and some of his co-workers bet him a pony keg of beer that their team of horses could pull him out a barn door. They tied a rope around Art's grandfather's waist and to the team of horses one hundred feet away. Then old grandpa put his hands against the doorjamb and his feet against the sill and the horses couldn't pull him out.

Three of Art's grandparents lived into their nineties and the fourth died from a fall. He was on his way to the outhouse in the wintertime and he slipped and fell on ice on the pathway.

My older brother Dennis William "Dennie" Shaw wrote a couple of chapters for my first book Terry Tales. *I only published one in that book. It was called "The Gun" and a lot of people told me it was their favorite chapter. Here is the other one Dennie wrote. He was a little leery of my publishing it because of the "instructions" he gives in it. I told him not to worry because he wasn't specific enough, but I'll add this disclaimer: Kids, don't try this at home...or anyplace else.*

Chapter Thirty-Eight
Dennie's Chapter:
The Missing Ingredient - Part One

I believe everyone has a guardian angel. My guardian angel worked overtime, especially during the summer of 1954. Up to that time, my simple life consisted of going to school, working odd jobs for spending money, trying to learn how to play guitar, and fishing in Lake Ripley. In stark contrast with the normal days growing up in my hometown is this story of how I was led into a dangerous experiment that almost terminated my young life.

At 6:30am each summer morning, Jack Lawrence, manager of the Litchfield Seed Store, would drive around town picking up his corn detasseling crew, which consisted of twelve young people and a supervisor, who was a high school senior. Jack leased out the crew to corn farmers in Meeker and other surrounding counties. The crew's job was simple; walk up and down the shoulder high corn, while pulling the tassels out of the tops of the corn stalk.

This effectively "castrated" the corn plant so it could not self-pollinate the corn silk coming out of the ears to produce seed. Other crews from seed companies came behind us a few days later and "cross pollinated" by hand those selected plants to produce hybrid seed for the next new strain of hybrid seed corn.

Brother Dennie with the dark jacket and cap and the rest of the crew.

The pay was decent, but it was dirty and muddy and every insect God ever created would end up on you. They would get in your hair and up your nose or other body cavities while you were working. The day was long and hot. We looked forward to the end of each day and the long truck rides back to town.

Six of us found that we could climb up on the roof of the cargo box on the back of the truck. It was a special club open only by invitation. Laying flat on our stomachs on the roof literally holding on to the edges for dear life, we could cool down as air blew across our bodies and dried out our sweat soaked clothes. Sometimes we would get the driver to stop at Lake Ripley and we would literally jump in the lake, clothes and all, to wash the dirt and sweat off.

We never gave much thought about what could have happened if a tire blew or if our driver had to stop quickly. It was a macho thing. We would tell dirty jokes, sing stupid songs and talk about "guy things", away from the ears of the girls in the crew or the other guys who were too chicken to ride on top of the truck. The ride's dangers were paltry compared to the scheme that grew out of one of those mobile discussions.

The truck top riders were usually Art Bryntenson, Dennis Current, Jerry Kohlhoff, Dick Nordlie, Ludwig Andreen, Jr. and myself. Ludwig lived about a block away from our house. He constantly dominated the discussions and talked about things he did or was going to do. Many of these things were not the normal things you would expect.

Ludwig read science fiction comics, went to monster movies and spent lots of time in his parent's basement experimenting with electricity, mixing up strange concoctions and inventing smells. He was smart, loved chemistry and knew a lot of chemical formulas. Ludwig and I shared a mutual interest in electricity and radio. He had a peculiar interest in explosives. He showed me how to make a firecracker gun, a .22 "zip" gun and a "farmer match bomb". He constantly talked about guns, rockets, bombs and chemicals that exploded or made a big stink.

Ludwig Andreen, a junior in high school.

"Hey, Shaw," Ludwig would say, "You know if you mix aluminum powder and sugar, it will burn. And if you put it into a bottle," he'd go on, now that he had my attention, "cap it, and then heat it, it will explode!"

"If you mix sulfur, charcoal and potassium nitrate (salt peter) together," he'd say another on a different occasion, "you get gunpowder."

I would listen politely and intently and usually say something asinine like, "When are we gonna to do it? When are we gonna make it?"

"Ah...I can't find any powered aluminum," Ludwig would reply, or saltpeter or something else. There was always the missing ingredient that he couldn't obtain.

I tired of hearing his stories so many times, and had a tendency to pass them off as idle talk. It was always the same; the missing ingredient always prevented him from making "the big boom".

"You know what the most powerful explosive in the world is?" Ludwig asked Jerry and I one day on the truck.
"Atom bomb," I said.
"TNT," Jerry said.
"Nah," Ludwig instructed us. "You guys don't know nothin'. It's nitroglycerine."
We raised our eyebrows as Ludwig proceeded to tell us about "nitro".
"A thimble full," he told us, "could blow up a car."
I have to admit that at the time I didn't believe it, but years later it was explained to me that a tiny amount, such as a thimble full, could actually blow up a car and much more. It was powerful stuff, if it was used correctly.
"You know what?" Ludwig asked us, as he continued. "I know how to make it."
Jerry and I looked at each other with smirks on our faces.
"Oh, sure you do," Jerry said in disbelief.

The gauntlet had been thrown. A challenge. Ludwig always responded to a challenge, especially if his integrity or honesty was at stake.
"Okay," Ludwig said defiantly. "You guys come with me down to the library and I will show you."
I suddenly suspected that Ludwig really did know what he was talking about this time. I guess Jerry knew it too because he called me at home that evening. He sounded nervous. He warned me not to get involved.
"Dennie," Jerry said, "you had better not mess with that stuff. I heard that it's pretty unstable."

I was not totally sure what unstable meant. I was about to find out and reassure myself that Ludwig was unstable himself. I don't want to give the impression that Ludwig was stupid. To the contrary, he had a very high I.Q. and was proud of telling people about it. But he was very impulsive and would do almost anything on a dare.

The next morning, shortly after Mom woke me to get ready to go to work, it started raining. The phone rang. It was the crew chief calling to say that corn detasseling would be cancelled because it was lightning, raining and muddy in the fields. A day off! Forty-five minutes later, after Mom was on her way to work, I heard a pounding on the back door. It was Ludwig.

"Ready to learn something?" he asked.

I knew that Ludwig would call me a coward or worse if I did not go with him.

"Sure," I said, surprising myself. We took off for the library.

Our local library was well stocked and staffed. Ludwig, a regular patron, headed right to the stacks that contained books on chemistry and pulled out several large tomes. One chemistry manual was like a phone book. You could look up a compound or substance, a chemical formula or a trade name. It was some kind of chemical engineering reference book, referencing all ingredients and detailed descriptions of sources and uses. I recognized some symbols for basic elements but not much else. Turning to compounds of nitrogen, Ludwig excitedly showed me chemical descriptions on all kinds of explosives that I had never even heard of.

I saw the words nitrocellulose or "gun cotton", TNT, blasting gelatin, and then there it was... nitroglycerine. It was a very simple compound made by combining three ingredients, sulfuric acid, nitric acid, and glycerin. It had a chemical formula of $C_3H_5(ONO_2)_3$. It appeared that Ludwig really wanted to make dynamite, but did not know where to find diatomaceous earth. Dynamite is a mixture of diatomaceous earth, sawdust and nitroglycerine. The reason Mr. Nobel, (yes, the peace prize guy), invented it was because nitroglycerine by itself was so unstable. Just moving it quickly could cause it to detonate. Nobel found that mixing it with the inert ingredients mentioned would allow a person to move it, ram it and stuff it down holes for mining without a premature detonation.

I knew what glycerin was. My mother used it on her sore and bleeding hands. She had a bottle of "Rose water and glycerin" in the medicine cabinet. I did not say a word about it, thinking to myself, "Where are we going to find nitric or sulfuric acid? Ray Johnson, the pharmacist at Johnson's Drug Store, surely wouldn't sell us any of that."

Ludwig made some hurried notes and announced that we were going to make it, saying, "Let's go over to your garage."

Chapter Thirty-Nine
Dennie's Chapter:
The Missing Ingredient - Part Two

My section of our unattached garage had been an office where my Great-Aunt Millie, the former owner of our home, had a business office. It was like a small apartment. It was my "clubhouse" and my brothers were not allowed in it. It had a deadbolt lock and I had the only key hidden under a rock behind the garage.

Dennie Shaw in front of the locked garage door.

As we walked home, Ludwig told me he knew where we could get the nitric acid.

"Where?" I asked, mystified. "In the high school chemistry lab?"

"No, it's right downtown and all we have to do is go pick it up."

"What about the sulfuric acid?"

"That's easy," Ludwig replied. "We're going to walk right past some of it on our way to your garage." I could not think of any place where that could be, but imaginative Ludwig had it all figured out.

We walked down the alley behind the hotel and down the middle of the block by the seed store to the back of the old power plant. Ludwig stopped briefly and looked at the lock on the door of a small building near the water tower. He boldly tried the doorknob. It was locked. I thought to myself, "Well if it is in there, we can't get at it." I was wrong. Stacked along side the backside of the little building were three or four large ten-gallon glass carboys or large colored bottles, each individually boxed in a wooden container. The neck and stopper of each carboy stuck up out of the container. Stenciled in large red letters on the side of each were the words "Poison - Dangerous Chemical – Corrosive - Sulfuric Acid. 87 % pure" with lots of other warning labels and writing. The carboys were empty...almost!

At the garage, Ludwig told me his plan, as we smoked cigarettes. He had learned that the power plant had recently started using sulfuric acid in the cooling towers for the big Fairbanks Morris Diesel Generators. The acid was to control algae and scum from forming and plugging up the cooling systems of the big engines. The engineers had burned sulfur in small metal boxes on the outside of the cooling towers. The sulfur fumes purified the cooling water as it fell through the cooling tower. It always smelled of rotten eggs around there, a characteristic of sulfur. After being burned, the sulfur made a mild acid when mixed with water.

To the right:
The power plant's cooling tower.

Ludwig had discovered the bagged sulfur when he saw a worker open up the little building one day. He told me that he had "borrowed" some to use when he tried to make gunpowder. Evidently the power plant decided, for some reason, that they could mix small amounts of pure sulfuric acid directly into the cooling water and quit using the powdered sulfur.

After dark, Ludwig and I tipped each of the big "empty" carboys upside down into a plastic pail and requisitioned about eight ounces of sulfuric acid. We then filled an old Coca-Cola bottle with it. We had spilled some on the outside of the bottle in the process and had to leave the bottle and return with a pair of pliers to pick the bottle up without burning our hands and get it back to the garage. Ludwig got a drop or two on his shoe and it promptly ate a hole in it. He stuck his foot into a neighbor dog's watering dish to stop the burning on his toes.

Ludwig had done his homework and had read up on nitric acid. His research revealed all of the many uses for nitric acid. He found that it was used in the newspaper business to etch pictures into the zinc plates used to transfer black and white photos onto newsprint. Several nights later, we acquired the nitric acid. "Fuming Nitric Acid, 98% pure", the label on the pint bottle read. The *Independent Review* had several brown glass bottles of it in the dark room in the basement of the building. They now had one less. Ludwig had seen it while using the bathroom down there.

Ludwig slipped through a basement window that night to "borrow" the bottle. As I stood outside in the dark alley, as the lookout, asking myself, "What are you doing getting yourself into this situation for?" We had only one ingredient to go. It was the simple one, the easiest one to find. Glycerin. Enter my guardian angel, ready, willing and able to watch over me.

The next day was Sunday, again no corn detasseling. Ludwig and I had agreed that I would call him as soon as the coast was clear. My mother was going to have to be at St. Phillip's to help with serving a supper for some church activity. She would not be getting home until seven or eight that evening. She had made up a big pot of her wonderful goulash and given me specific instructions to feed my brothers at five o'clock. As soon as she walked out the kitchen door on her way to church, I called Ludwig.

Curiosity and excitement had taken over and I just went along with whatever the mad scientist wanted to do at this point. Ludwig ran over, but in his own excitement, he had left the notes from the library that indicated the proper ratio of nitric to sulfuric to glycerin. "No big deal," he assured me. "I remember it."

I later learned that there was a very specific sequence to be followed. It was important which ingredient you added first and many other cautions. We totally disregarded them. I brought Mom's bottle of Rose Water and Glycerin out to the garage and started mixing the ingredients by the "shot in the dark" method. Ludwig put what I think was about three ounces of glycerin into a water glass he had brought from home and then he added what he thought was the proper amounts of acids.

We waited and we watched the light yellowish and oily looking mixture but nothing happened. Then, ever so gradually, a reaction started. The glass started to get warm. Ludwig was holding it in his hands. He set it down on the floor of the garage because it quickly got real hot. He almost dropped the glass, which would have been the end of this story and of us. We noticed a strange smell and the mixture soon looked like the color of weak coffee. We were standing directly over the glass when suddenly...whoosh...our mixture evaporated in an instant with a loud sound, like water hitting a hot frying pan. A thick cloud of smoke that choked us and made our eyes burn filled the garage. The whole place smelled like very strong Clorox bleach. You could taste the acid in your mouth. Then there was a crack! The glass broke into pieces.

We ran outside and then cautiously went back in and used the pliers to pick up the broken glass. We scraped the gooey mess off the floor with a tin can cover. Not happy with the results, our hearts pounding, we were scared but just inquisitive and foolish enough to want to see what would happened if we changed the amounts a little. The first results were fairly sensational but we were driven on to perform the experiment again.

I ran into the house and grabbed a heavy one-ounce shot glass from the cupboard. I theorized that it could take the heat. It was a darn good thing that I did. The smaller capacity of the container and the shape of the glass were consequential. The tapered sides, larger at the top than the bottom, did not confine the ingredients, a very important point, I learned later. Ludwig ran home to get his instruction notes.

Had we confined the nitroglycerine to a closed container or restricted the reaction in any way, it would have become even more unstable and almost certainly would have resulted in an explosion. Ludwig and I would be memories and they would still be scraping pieces of us off the walls. I learned later that when the professionals made this explosive under controlled conditions, they kept the temperature constant at about fifty-five degrees and used wooden containers and utensils to mix the ingredients to avoid sparks or static electricity discharges.

Here Ludwig and I were in the middle of July in Minnesota, using whatever containers were available and not paying any particular attention to anything. In fact, at one point I think Ludwig had a lit cigarette in his mouth. We moved the ingredients out of the garage to the concrete driveway with the direct afternoon sun hitting them full force. Again we mixed up the concoction using an eyedropper I took out of one of my brothers' eardrop medications. Counting drops to get the proper ratios, Ludwig did the dripping and I did the counting, again both of us standing directly over the shot glass. I counted about fifteen drops from the eyedropper into the shot glass.

The reaction was much more brisk this time. The mixture turned darker and darker and then, with a loud whoosh, it was over. This time the whoosh was accompanied by a bright orange flash and blast of heat. The heat wave was pretty dramatic. We were terrified! We knew we were messing around with something pretty scary and, thank God, we ended the experiments right on the spot. We had made a very unstable and obviously very unsafe version of nitroglycerine, in a very incorrect way in a very hot July sun.

During my tour in the military several years later, I had the opportunity to casually talk with a munitions expert. I told him about my adolescent experiments. He told me we were remarkably lucky that day. We had done everything wrong that could be done wrong. What we had done was comparable to playing Russian roulette with a six-gun with only one bullet missing instead of only one in the chamber.

"You must lead a blessed life," he said. "The only thing that saved your ass was that you did not use pure enough ingredients!"

"Oh, you mean the 87% sulfuric?" I asked.

"No."

"You mean the 98% pure nitric acid?"

"No!"

"I don't understand," I said.

"I know you don't, blockhead. It was the glycerin. The formula called for 100% glycerin, not Rose Water and Glycerin. The alcohol, water and fragrance included in that mixture diluted the chemical just enough to cause the compound not to work."

Once again, indirectly, my mother had saved my life. The missing ingredient was the glycerin. The wrong ingredient was the lotion that my mom used nightly to soothe her sore hands after working all day to provide for me. Thank you Mom and thank you God for sparing me from my own stupidity. As Archie Bunker once said about his wife Edith on the TV show *All In The Family*, "God watches over drunks and dingbats."

Note: Ludwig Andreen, Jr. died at the age of thirty-two in a car accident near Alexandria, Minnesota in October of 1974. His younger brother Larry had preceded him in death. He was involved in the terrible accident in August of 1962, which I wrote about in Terry Tales. *Six people had died in that accident and my friends and I were a couple of miles behind the cars involved.*

Terry Shaw

He Is The Key

I decided to try to write a religious song. It's hard to come up with something that hasn't been said before or a new way to say it in that type of song also. After all, it is a love song.

He Is The Key

When you're feeling low,
it's good to know
that there is always someone
Who is loving you and loving me.

Jesus is the one
Who'll get it done
no matter what your trouble.
He will set you free.
He is the key.

Just open up your heart and say,
"I'm with you Lord, all the way."
And set your soul at ease.

He is loving you
no matter who
you are or what your color.
You must love all too
to be with Him.

Chapter Forty
The Rockin' Shaws – Part One

One of the few good memories I have of my father, before he left our family, is of him playing guitar in the living room and my mother singing along with him to *You Are My Sunshine*. He was a self-taught musician and one of those people who could pick up any instrument and play it. He played the accordion and piano also and he had a big old white metal stand-up bass, but his first love was the guitar. Dad played in a weekend band out of Eden Valley. They were called The Valley Ramblers.

I remember my father setting his guitar amp out on the front steps and playing in the evenings. Neighbors would gather around outside of our house to listen to his impromptu concerts. Dad wasn't the only one to do this type of entertaining. My neighborhood was full of old-time fiddlers and pianists, like Pete Lindberg, Axel Roman, Eldor Ericson and Pedar J. "Pete" Marstad, whom we called "Pete Mustard". With music all around us, it's no wonder the Shaw boys joined in. Of course, our type of music, early Rock and Roll, probably wasn't exactly "music" to our neighbors' ears.

It took a long time for Rock and Roll to get to Litchfield. Once it did, the Shaw boys grabbed hold of it and never let it go. We started seeing movies with Rock and Roll music in them as early as late 1956, yet the half-dozen dance halls around us never had a Rock dance for teens. Finally in September of 1957, the Silver Horseshoe[71] ballroom in Darwin, Minnesota ran a newspaper ad for a "Teen-agers Only" dance featuring Jerry Wheeler and His All Modern Band. This wasn't Rock and Roll, believe me, but it wasn't "oom pah pah" Old-Time music either. The tidal wave was finally on the way.

On Tuesday, May 13, 1958 most of the youth in Litchfield were conned into thinking that a national touring band from Texas was real Rock and Roll. A dance, at the four-year-old Armory Building, sponsored by the Chamber of Commerce and WDGY radio, was attended by about four hundred of the town's young people, including the Shaw boys. We heard WDGY's "Brother" Bill Bennet introduce

---

[71] The Silver Horseshoe went the way of most ballrooms when times got hard. It burned down one night in November of 1960.

The Big Beats, who did instrumental renditions of *In The Mood*, *Sentimental Journey* and *Raunchy*. It was close enough to Rock and Roll for us, but still light years away from the Jerry Lee Lewis and Chuck Berry songs we were listening to on late night radio out of Little Rock, Arkansas or Shreveport, Louisiana.

The Big Beats

At the Big Beats' dance at the armory. Back row: Smiling at the camera is Dennis Shaw, with the glasses is Connie Olmstead and in the center rear is Jerry Wheeler. Front row: In the middle is Sandy Vick and to the right is Sharon Shelley.

The turnout was so great for the Armory dance that the band was brought back on June 12 along with The Crescendos. The big turnout also inspired someone to bring in a real rocker. On Saturday, July 19, 1958, one of the fathers of "Bop", Gene Vincent and his Blue Caps, came to Litchfield. Gene Vincent was most noted for his songs *Be-Bop-A-Lula* and *Lotta Lovin'*. He performed with and was idolized by the Beatles in Liverpool. Now we were getting somewhere.

The Big Beats returned to the area several times. They were at the Armory again on Saturday, August 23, 1958. The newspaper ad, giving the admission price as 90¢, stated "No Slacks, Blue Jeans, or Leather Jackets. Dress Right, Feel Right, Act Right." Ah, the old dress code. It carried well into the sixties. The Big Beats were in Willmar with Sonny James of *Young Love* fame on August 30, 1958. Over a thousand teenagers showed up at the National Guard Armory for the artists, who also signed autographs earlier that day at Margie's Record Shop in downtown Willmar. Five hundred people showed up there and Willmar Chief of Police R. H. McLane had to come to control the crowd. The area teens were starved for Rock and Roll.

My brother Dennie started playing the guitar in his early teens. There used to be a little white building on Second Street East between the Post Office and Mutt's. It was a radio and television repair shop owned by Dick Baldwin. Dennie liked to hang around Dick and learn how to hook up speakers and other things electric. Dennie was walking by Baldwin's one day when he saw two guitars hanging up on the inside wall of that little building. Dick had them for sale. Dennie bought the cheaper of the two, a Hohner, and he started turning finger blisters into calluses.

Our absent father came by once on one of his extremely rare visits and showed Dennie some chords, but most of what Dennie learned was on his own with the help of a Mel Bay guitar instruction book. Dad did show Dennie how to tune the guitar and, being a wiz with electronics, he also built Dennie an electric pickup and helped him install it into the sound hole of the old Hohner. I don't remember Dad spending that much time around us, so Dennie must have been in heaven. Then Dad showed Dennie how to hook the guitar up to his old Ward's Airline Radio for amplification. Dennie immediately turned our big console in the living room into an amp, much to Mom's objections. Dennie was on his way to Rock and Roll, which had been given birth about the same time as Dennie's guitar playing.

In the fall of 1957, Dennie met Connie Olmstead in Litchfield's Milk Bar[72], a teen hangout downtown on Sibley Avenue North at the time. Connie was also into electronic[73] things. He and Dennie made a trade. Dennie agreed to teach Connie guitar chords in exchange for which Connie would teach Dennie how to drive a car with a stick shift. As a bonus, Connie threw in teaching Dennie how to drink orange and lime flavored vodkas.

Connie Olmstead and Dennie.

One day, Connie showed up at our garage with a brand new Fender guitar and a used Fender amp. Fender was the Cadillac of guitars. Dennie was jealous and with his limited finances he decided to buy a real electric guitar too. He searched through the catalogs at home and found a blonde semi-hollow Kay K-161 ThinTwin. After proving to Mom that he could pay for it, Dennie ordered the guitar from the Spiegel catalog in February of 1958, and he and Connie formed a band, which they called The Rockets, complete with the slogan "Rock with The Rockets." I don't know if you could call what they played "Rock and Roll", but it sure wasn't "Old-Time" like our Uncle Robert Rheaume played with Fezz Fritsche's band out of New Ulm.

---

[72] 225 Sibley Avenue North, where Pizza Plus is today.
[73] Connie later went to work for Don Test, whose "Don's TV" repair shop shared the brick building at 224 Ramsey Avenue North/35 Third Street West with Dahl Tire. Connie was a repair technician.

Back row: Terry and Pat
Front row: Mick, Helen and Dennie, smokin' with his Kay guitar.

Early Rockets: Sherm Robb, Bob Peifer, Connie Olmstead, Dave Thompson and Dennie.

The members of Dennie's band were always changing and sometimes the band included some very odd instruments for Rock and Roll, such as Dick Blonigan's trombone. I remember Sherman Robb's drums. The bass drum was so big it almost hid him. There

233

were no toms and his cymbal was no bigger than a dinner plate. Sometimes Dave Thompson played sax and Bob Peifer, Jr., whose dad was an assistant manager at the Produce, where Mom worked, and who married Darlene Oliver, sister to Jeanette, my first love, plunked away on the piano, when one was available. I don't remember them having a bass player.

Above: Sherm Robb, Dick Blonigan, Dave Thompson and Dennie at the Community Building. Below: Dennie with his Kay guitar.

234

For The Rocket's first "booking", the band performed two songs at a March of Dimes Benefit Dance and Talent Show held at the Litchfield Armory in September of 1958. Dick Newman was brought in to play lead guitar and the group decided to change the band name to something more like the names of the current hit groups, such as Danny and The Juniors or Little Anthony and The Imperials. So the band members gathered in our garage one night and started throwing out possible names. Still influenced by The Big Beats, the names thrown out were The Night Beats, The Beat Kings, and The Dance Beats. Finally somebody tossed out The Beat Offs. After much laughter and giggling, the band got back to work. Dennie came up with Chance and The Chancellors, but because no one wanted to be Chance, that part was dropped from the name. The Chancellors it would be.

Dick Blonigan and Dennie.

The group went to Plate's Toggery and ordered black and white plaid cardigans and black jeans. Now they looked professional. Dennie painted "The Chancellors" on the door of his section of our garage. It stayed there long after he went into the Marine Corps in June of 1960.

Dennie borrowed Gary Rayppy's Wollensack reel-to-reel tape recorder and recorded some of his own compositions, such as a tune called *Dear Barbara*. The band liked that song enough that they had Larry Graf from Hutchinson record the group doing it on an acetate record on his home record cutting machine. Dennie played the record on Litchfield's KLFD radio station where he was working for free as a guest teenage disc jockey.

235

The big Litchfield Armory dances of the Big Beats inspired Dennie and Connie to put on their own dance at the armory. A local DJ was hired to emcee and it went over well enough that they started to get a few jobs in some local ballrooms in the winter of 1958 and summer of 1959. Also in the winter of 1958, Mike McKenzie was hired to replace Peifer on the piano. Mike ended up on the drums when Sherm Robbs couldn't get out of his athletic commitments.

BENEFIT HOP	RAINBOW	RAINBOW
"Bishop's Burse Fund"	BALLROOM	BALLROOM
MAY 10	2 miles North of Eden Valley	2 miles North of Eden Valley
8 to 11 P.M. — Admission 50¢	Saturday, July 25	Friday, Aug. 14
"The Chancellors"	Arnie Wolf's	The Chancelors
(Formerly The Rockets)	Deutchmeisters	Rock & Roll Hop
Sponsored by the Youth of the Litchfield Deanery		
SILVER HORSESHOE BALLROOM	Thursday, July 23	Saturday, Aug. 15
Darwin, Minn.	"The Chancellors"	JERRY'S BAND
	Teen-Age Hop	
	For Booth Reservation Call GL 3-2178 Eden Valley	For Booth Reservation Call GL 3-2178 Eden Valley

Ads for Dennie's band.

The Chancellors playing for the Bird Island prom. Left to right: Dick Newman, Mike McKenzie, Dennie and Connie Olmsted.

Chapter Forty-One
The Rockin' Shaws – Part Two

The earliest days of Rock and Roll dances were as I described in the last chapter. The ballroom owners just didn't get it. They didn't understand the power the teens had to generate big money for them. They just kept having Old-Time dances. So anyone who wanted to bring in "Rock" groups, promoted the dances themselves in armories and town halls. The first time I saw a local ballroom bring in a legitimate Rock and Roll performer was in October of 1958. The Playland Ballroom in Kimball brought in Dale Hawkins who had a hit called *Suzy-Q*, which is now a Rock standard. But those dances were few and far between. The next legitimate Rock star that came around was Buddy Knox (*Party Doll*) in May of 1959 in Glencoe and Eddie Cochran (*Summertime Blues*) in Kimball in September of 1959.

Small time "garage bands" like Mick's and my band, The Defiants, played most of their dance jobs in self-promoted venues. I think we played in every armory in southern Minnesota. And there is no place less suited for music than an armory that echoes so bad you can't understand what song is being played.

The Chancellors practiced in Dennie's section of our garage. Many times, when neighbors called to complain, Mom went out to the garage to plead with Dennie to "Please turn it down. I can't hear myself think!" After much yelling, Dennie would break into a Sonny James' song called *You're The Reason (I'm In Love)*. It seemed to magically shut Mom up and sometimes bring a tear to her eye, as did another song; *I Can't Help It (If I'm Still In Love With You)*. She would turn on her heels and head back to the house, beaten again.

Mom seemed to lose control over us when we grew to her height. Dennie had long ago surpassed her in that area. His greasy pompadour hair-do, which was piled high on his head, culminating into a "duck-tail" both on the top of his head and in the back, added a few more inches to his six foot one inch height.

Mick began to nose into Dennie's musical sessions. Mick didn't get shooed away as Pat and I did. Dennie's band broke up in April of 1960. Dennie was graduating from high school and he had enlisted in the Marine Corps, for some crazy reason. I think he thought the dress uniform was cool looking. After he left, Mick found Dennie's old

Hohner guitar in their bedroom closet and he started learning to play. Mick also learned drumming before he settled on the bass.

Mick's first band was called The Nightbeats. (Doesn't that name sound familiar?) In the late summer of 1960, Mick met up with the remnants of Dennie's old band and enlisted them to play with him. There was Dick Newman on lead guitar and Jerry Wheeler on drums. Danny Bates, a guitarist from Atwater, Minnesota, was added to round out the band. After a while, Jerry left to join the Air Force so Mick switched over to the drums and another old member of Dennie's band, Connie Olmstead, came aboard to play the bass.

Beginning on August 22, 1960, Sylvester "Spotty" Lohr began running occasional Teen Hops on Friday nights to drum up business at his A & W Drive-In, which was out on Highway 12 East. Spotty had the dances under the west canopy of his double-winged establishment. The dances went over so well that Spotty hired The Nightbeats to play one Friday night. About half-way through the dance, Mick asked Alvie Watkins, Terry Kohlhoff and myself to get up on the hay wagon with his band and sing background on a couple of songs. We did some "doo-wops" and even threw in some back and forth dance steps together that we had kidded around with to some records at Terry's house, just like we had seen the acts do on *American Bandstand* on TV. That's probably where Mick had seen us do it before. Alvie and I also harmonized on *Rip It Up*. That was the first of thousands of times that Mick and I would be on a stage together doing Rock and Roll music.

Alvin "Alvie" Watkins.

Connie left the band and Mick went back to the bass. Jerry Wheeler was once again brought in to play the drums. The Nightbeats also practiced in our garage or in our basement in the wintertime, just as The Chancellors had. I was allowed to hang around them this time. I would sit high up on the basement steps, watching my drumming idol Jerry Wheeler's every move. I had fallen in love with the drums and I used to play along with records in my room on my makeshift drum set, which consisted of boxes. The round Quaker Oats boxes were great sounding, by the way. My sticks were two butter knives. They had unbelievable bounce.

Jerry Wheeler on the drums.

When the bands would leave the basement to go uptown for coffee breaks, I would sneak downstairs and bang away on the real drums, teaching myself to play them the correct way. Mick came home unexpectedly once and caught me. He yelled at me, an argument ensued, and he hit me, but I had planted the seed in his head. He now knew that I could actually play the drums. My drumming is what eventually brought us back together. Music also brought Dennie and I together in later years as we started co-writing songs. Before that there was this natural division in our family where Mick and Dennie did things together and Pat and I did things together.

In 1961, Danny Bates got married and left The Nightbeats, so the band broke up. Mick was hanging around Jerry Olson's music store in Willmar one day, (he would eventually work there), when he met Doug "Tamba" Spartz. Doug was in a band called The Embers, with another old Chancellor, Mike McKenzie, playing the drums. Also in

239

the band was a crippled guitarist named Doug Herman, who had to be helped up on the stage every night. Mick joined the band.

There was a band playing the mid-west ballroom circuit called Roscoe and the Green Men. They drew huge crowds. One of their gimmicks was that they sprayed green dye in their hair and wore green jackets. So, The Embers decided to emulate them. They bought some red jackets and started to dye their head red.

The Embers: Mick Shaw, Mike McKenzie, Doug Herman and Doug "Tamba" Spartz. I painted their drumhead.

Mick would come home in the wee hours of Sunday morning with his red hair dripping red dye down his neck from the previous Saturday night's sweat. Mom would insist that we always made it to Sunday morning mass, no matter what, so sometimes she'd be sitting next to red-haired Mick and later, during the Beatle era, she'd have to sit next to long-haired me. But we were in church.

Mick had our old friend Alvie get up and sing a couple of songs with The Embers one night. Alvie sang and did *The Twist* and then he did some Jerry Lee Lewis songs. The audience loved him. Soon the band's posters were advertising the group as "The Embers featuring Little Al Vee" and then as "Little Al Vee and The Embers".

▼▼▼▼▼▼▼▼▼
PLAYLAND
BALLROOM
KIMBALL, MINN.

Put Joy in Your Life
—Go Dancing!

FRIDAY, JULY 13
Carnival Days
THE AMBERS
Featuring Little Al Vee
Rock 'n Roll
Ultra Modern

A poster with "Embers" misspelled.

    Mick graduated from high school in 1962 and he decided to go to Brown's Institute in Minneapolis to learn to be a radio announcer. He left The Embers. While at Brown's, Mick roomed with members of another band called The Trashmen. The Trashmen would eventually have a number one national hit called *Surfin' Bird*. Mick came close to joining the band. The bass player had quit, Mick was asked to join and before he played his first job, the original bass player came back.

    Mick started skipping classes and also began running out of money, so he came back home to Litchfield. Steve Henslin, from Clara City, heard that Mick was home again and was available so he called Mick and asked if he'd like to join his band, The Defiants. Mick jumped at the opportunity to get back on stage, his first love.

    But before long, Henslin left for college and the drummer also quit. Mick took over the band and replaced the departing members with old Nightbeats' drummer Jerry Wheeler, just back from the Air Force, and Dick Newman on the guitar. Mick also found a great guitarist in Willmar, a young kid named Loren "Wally" Walstad. The band was back in business and Mick's Defiants were born.

The Defiants in 1963: Mike Shaw, Jerry Wheeler, Loren Walstad and Dick Newman.

Dick Newman decided Rock music wasn't for him, so he left. Mick replaced him with a Bird Island guitarist named John Collins. John could play "Surf" music, which was just coming into vogue. Wheeler was in the Air National Guard and he got orders for Temporary Duty in South America or someplace. Out of desperation, Mick asked me to fill in. As I wrote earlier, Jerry was my idol. He was all over those drums. I could just keep a steady beat without any flair, but I had the added dimension that I could sing Rock and Roll. Jerry didn't sing.

The first job we had was a "Battle of Bands" against Mike Glieden and The Rhythm Kings at the armory in Willmar, Minnesota. I was scared to death but once we got into the songs, things went well. Mick looked up to Mike Glieden because he had been in the business longer and had a very professional band. He had even recorded some records.

Glieden didn't know who I was and he came up to Mick after the job and said, "Hey, keep that drummer you got tonight and get rid of that redhead." I think it had more to do with my youth and looking like a Rock band drummer than with my drumming abilities, because Jerry could drum circles around me. But Jerry was older and his style was more suited to big band and jazz. That was all Mick needed to hear. Upon Jerry's return, Mick told him I was going to take over. I felt bad about it and told Jerry so.

"That's all right, Terry. I've been looking for a way out myself," Jerry said. "Rock isn't really my thing."

On top of everything else, Jerry drove me down to the cities and helped me buy my first set of drums. Then he taught me a few drumming tricks. This final incarnation of The Defiants was together for almost four years. When we eventually broke up, the band name ceased to exist.

The Defiants at the Willmar Armory: Terry Shaw, Loren "Wally" Walstad, John Collins and Mike Shaw.

Because of The Trashmen's success, every band in the state was rushing down to the Twin Cities to record a 45 record. Our band was no different. We bought a package deal at Kay Bank Studios where The Trashmen had recorded and also Bobby Vee. For $300, we would get two hours of recording time and five hundred records. All we had to do was pick the songs. Mick loved Chuck Berry and saw Jerry Lee Lewis do a song of Chuck's called *Bye Bye Johnny*. He decided he wanted to do that song. I saw that everyone was doing Bob Dylan songs and having hits, so I picked an obscure song of his called *Maggie's Farm*.

When we received our records, I started promoting it, sending out copies to all the local radio stations. I was even interviewed on our favorite Rock station, KDWB. But the record flopped and we ended up giving most of them away at our dances. In 2003, a friend of mine sent me an email and told me to go to eBay.com on my computer and type in "Maggie's Farm". I did and I discovered that someone was selling a copy of it. I monitored the auction and saw that the record went for an astounding $45! I couldn't believe it. A German record company had bought it to put it on a "Garage Bands of the Sixties" CD. The company contacted me to see if I had more copies of the record. Unfortunately, all I had left was one copy and I'm hanging on to it.

Chapter Forty-Two
The Rockin' Shaws – Part Three

On a summer morning during Crazy Days in Litchfield in the early sixties, I walked by the Greep-Trueblood department store, looking at the men's clothing hanging from racks on the sidewalk. A red-haired guy was sitting on a stool in the doorway playing his guitar through a small amp and singing into a microphone. I stopped to watch him. He was a good-looking guy and a great singer, but he was just singing folk songs, which, at the time, I hated. If it wasn't Rock and Roll, I wanted nothing to do with it.

The guy's name was Jim Allen and he was dating my perennial classmate Cathy Osdoba. I watched him for a while and then walked off thinking the guy had a lot of courage doing a single act in front of a store, performing for people who didn't care a thing about him or his music. I didn't think I'd ever see him again.

Another drummer in Litchfield at that time was Marvin "Bill" Stewart's son, Marv Jr. He played drums with my stepbrother Gary in a band they called The LeSabres. They also practiced in our basement. Poor Mom. One band left and another one replaced it. Marv also had sat in with Mick in The Nightbeats.

Mick and I had seen Jerry Lee Lewis perform at the Lakeside Ballroom in Glenwood in the early-sixties. Jerry Lee, who I saw three times and never once saw sober, had two drummers playing for him. It made an impression on Mick. He suggested that we try it in our band, The Defiants. Mick ran the band, so I went along with the suggestion, although I didn't like it. I was nervous about it because Marv had taken drumming lessons and played in the high school band and I was self-taught and hadn't started playing until I was out of high school.

At that time, Dick Blonigan, who had briefly played trombone in a very early version of Dennie's band, The Chancellors, was doing some booking for The Defiants. Dick also drove a big old Buick that had a trailer hitch. We were still borrowing and using Jerry Wheeler's band trailer to haul our equipment around in. Dick was also my college roommate in Minneapolis although he didn't go to school. He worked selling TVs in an electronics store. Dick had co-owned a TV repair and sales store in Olivia, Minnesota and his partner had left him with debts and so Dick had shut down and moved to Minneapolis. We recruited Dick to set up the two-drummer job in his old haunt, Olivia, at the armory and also to drive our equipment and us there.

We played the old armory on a Saturday night. We were to get "the door", or the admission money, after paying the expenses of $15 rent, $5 for a policeman, Dick's gas and 10% to him for the booking fee. He also took the money at the door and one of our girlfriends pitched in. We'd usually get a hundred or a hundred and fifty kids paying $1 each to get in at our dances. We thought it was great if we made $20 apiece. We had a good turnout that night so we expected a big payday.

Marv and I set up our drums on opposite ends of the stage. The stage was made up of large gray eight-inch high four by eight foot platform sections that were pushed together. We piled up extra sections on the stage's corners so that Marv and I were up higher than the band so that we could see each other. We had to be able to see each other. You couldn't depend on what you heard in an armory. It was like playing inside of an echo chamber or farm silo, which was used as the first echo chamber in recordings, by the way.

I don't think the experiment went that well because we never tried it again. Maybe the guys didn't like dividing up the money five ways instead of four. *Wipe Out* is the only song I remember doing that night. It was like a "battle of the drummers" between Marv and I on that song, especially with all the echo in that armory. I finished the song after Marv so I'll have to say that he won the battle.

When the dance was over, we looked for Dick, but he was gone. The girlfriend watching the door and our money said that another cop had come and arrested Dick.

"Arrested him?" I yelled. "What the hell for?"

"I don't know."

"Well," Mick said, "we've got to go and get him. He's got the key to the trailer and we can't leave our stuff here."

Marv had driven himself to the job, so he volunteered to drive Mick to the jail while the rest of us packed up the equipment. At the jail, Mick asked to see Dick, who was sitting alone in a room.

"Dick," Mick said. "What the hell's goin' on?"

"Hey man. They're saying I owe rent money on the TV shop building. That sonofabitch (his former partner) didn't pay it and the owner had me arrested." Dick nervously tapped the ash off his cigarette, took a big drag and continued. "I can get the money from my mother, but you gotta bail me out tonight, man, so I can get home."

"We gotta get home too, Dick," Mick said. "Give us the key to the trailer so we can at least pack up our equipment and get it out of the armory."

"No way, man. You gotta bail me out first."

"Bail you out with what?"

"With the dance job money. There's gotta be $150 there, at least."

"You gotta give us something so we know you'll pay us back," Mick bargained.

"I'll give you my trombone to hold, man. It's worth more than $150."

"Oh all right. We'll go get the money and come back. The rest of the guys ain't gonna like this."

"You think I like this, man?"

Dick got out of jail, we got home in the wee hours of the morning, Mick got the trombone to hold and we eventually got our money.

Another Minneapolis band that had a national hit was The Underbeats (*Foot Stompin'*). They heard Wally play one day at a jam session and when their lead guitarist got drafted, they asked Wally to join them. He felt bad deserting us, but he couldn't turn it down and we told him not to. We picked up another guitarist from Bird Island named Alvin "Bud" Setzaphant. John Collins also got drafted, so he joined the Marines instead and The Defiants broke up in 1967.

I didn't play for a while, except for some pick up jobs with an Old-Time music accordion player. Mick had joined a Country band called The Sterling Strings, so I joined a Country band from Litchfield called The Country Ramblers. Country music was getting more and more popular in the mid-sixties. One of the members of The Country Ramblers was Jim Price, who had "stolen" my high school sweetheart, Vi Haggart, from me. Small world. My tenure with the Ramblers was short-lived, however. I got drafted in December of 1967. After I left, a red haired guitarist/singer from Litchfield named Jim Allen joined the band.

Myself, Jim Price, Russ Vilhauer and Keith Miller.

When I returned home from my Army service in mid-October of 1969, I went walking the streets of Litchfield once again on a Monday afternoon, soaking in the warmth of my hometown. Jim came running out of his CJ Music Store, by Janousek's café at that time, and he grabbed me.

"Hey, Terry!" Jim started. "Welcome home! Hey, how're ya doin'?" Meanwhile, I'm trying to remember who the heck this redheaded guy is and where I had seen him before.

"Say," Jim went on, "we're starting a band and you're gonna play drums for us."

"Who's 'we' and who's gonna be in this band?" I cautiously asked, thinking that this guy's got a lot of nerve telling me I'm playing drums in his band.

"Well, your brother Mick and I. Didn't he talk to you?"

I shook my head.

"No?…Well, we're gonna rehearse on Thursday at Mick's house 'cause we play on Friday night here at the Legion Club."

"I haven't heard a thing about it…but if Mick's gonna be in it, I guess it's ok with me."

"Great. See ya Thursday night then." Off he went and I went home to call Mick to find out what the heck this was all about.

As much as Mick and I didn't get along early in life, music had made us closer and I respected his taste, judgment and business sense in the music business. In the winter of 2000, the Minnesota Music Hall of Fame showed that they respected him too by electing him into the Hall. The following year, the annual "Rock and Roll Reunion", held in St. Joseph, Minnesota, presented Mick with a Lifetime Achievement Award.

Mick, Jim, and I played that first job at the Legion club without a name for our group, so the newspaper ad stated that the music would be by "Jim Allen & his band." That was the start of a seven-year non-stop run with the band that we first called the Shaw-Allen Trio, then Shaw, Allen & Shaw and finally Shaw-Allen-Shaw. We played every single night for those seven years while I started my teaching career in Glencoe, Minnesota. I remember one December having Christmas Eve and one other day off. That was it. It ran me ragged, burning the candle at both ends, but being a teacher, I had my summers off. I devoted them entirely to my children with our camping trips, which included telling my kids the stories of my childhood while we sat around the campfire. Those stories led to the book *Terry Tales*.

★★★★★★★★

FREE
MEMBERSHIP
Dance

**American Legion
Clubrooms
Litchfield**

SATURDAY NIGHT
Saturday, Oct. 25th

Music by
Jim Allen and his Band
(3 piece)

★★★★★★★★

Above: The first ad. Shaw

Jim Allen, Mick and Terry Shaw in the Shaw-Allen Trio.

    The band became quite famous, recording two albums (*This Side – That Side* and *South Fork Crow River*), appearing on television, receiving a national award every year from the Entertainment Operators of America (ballroom owners) convention held in Kansas and setting and breaking ballroom attendance records all over southern Minnesota.

Shaw, Allen & Shaw albums released in 11/71 and 12/72.

    When Mick and I were teens, we used to hitchhike down to the Kato Ballroom in Mankato, Minnesota to see the biggest recording stars. You name the group, The Beach Boys, Jerry Lee Lewis, Roy Orbison; they all played there, even Buddy Holly on his fateful last tour. Mick and I were there in the summer of 1962, when our idols, the Everly Brothers, just out of the Marines, set a Kato Ballroom attendance record. From that day on, my dream was to play the Kato. In 1975, Shaw, Allen & Shaw played the Kato for the first time. We broke the attendance record and our record stands today.

The Everly Brothers, the way I saw them perform at the Kato Ballroom.

On our second album, Jim and I wrote all the songs except for two. Our recently hired keyboardist, Dewey Larson, wrote one and brother Dennie wrote the other, a song called *Love Is Gone*. The band continued to play every single night. Multi-talented musician Danny Grossnickle, who could play drums, keyboards, steel guitar and lead guitar, replaced Dewey, after Dewey had quit the band. Danny brought the group up to a higher level. The constant playing and teaching was wearing me down, however, and I started praying for an end to it or an "out". I didn't want to leave the others hanging but I wanted it to be over.

Danny Grossnickle, Mick, Jim Allen and myself.

One night in 1976, we were driving in my van to Willmar to play at the Buccaneer Lounge, when Jim leaned over to me and said, "Say, Terry. I've been thinking about leaving the band. I've had enough, I think." I could have kissed him.

"Really? Great," I said, surprising everyone. "Then I'm gonna leave too." So the band broke up. We did get back together a month later to play a wedding dance for some friends, but then it was over. I felt like a huge weight had been lifted off my shoulders.

Chapter Forty-Three
The Rockin' Shaws – Part Four

The doorbell rang at my house in Glencoe a few months after Shaw-Allen-Shaw had broke up and I went to see who was selling something or which neighbor was coming over to see my wife. There on my doorstep stood Mick and Jim.

"We've thought it over and decided to start the band up again," Jim said.

"Yeah," Mick added. "Why turn down all that good money and start all over again with some other musicians?"

"Sorry guys," I said. "I've really had enough. I want to spend some time with my family." I think I took them by surprise. I was always the one who couldn't turn down the money.

Jim and Mick hired a drummer from Willmar named Terry Jessup and they called the band The Shaw-Allen Band. I went into a year of staying at home, but I needed music in my life. So I taught myself how to chord on the piano and play guitar and I started writing songs. I also taught myself how to "score" the songs, that is writing the notes out on a lead sheet. I got good enough at it that I started a side business scoring music for other songwriters.

In May of 1977, Van Johnson, from Sleepy Eye, called me up. He had a band called MacArthur Park and he asked if I could help him out for a weekend job in Essig, Minnesota. I thought it'd be fun so I said, "Okay". After the weekend, Van started on me to play full time with him. I begged off, but he was convincing. I finally gave in with a promise that we'd only play weekends and I'd get some vacations, especially in the summer. I played with Van and bass player Bobby Krause for twenty more years.

Van Johnson, Terry Shaw and Bob Krause.

Jim Allen left Mick again in 1979, and Mick continued the band calling it simply The Shaw Band. Mick kept that band going until Saturday, May 22, 2004, when The Shaw Band played its last job at Buster's in Mankato, Minnesota. Some of the members wanted to wind it up, so rather than audition replacements and rebuild a repertoire, Mick, at the age of sixty, thought he would simply join a band for a change, instead of leading it and booking it. Who did he join up with? Mike Glieden's Rhythm Kings. Mike, you might recall was the one who talked brother Mick into hiring me full-time as his drummer in The Defiants, when I was just starting out.

When Mick's three sons were in high school, they also started a band and it's still going today. They call themselves The Shaw Brothers band.

Van had a bad car accident in the winter of 1997. He couldn't play anymore. Bob Krause and I hired a keyboardist named Bob York and called ourselves SKY (Shaw, Krause and York). It didn't last however, as York wanted to play more jobs than we did. So I was back to being a "civilian" once again.

I thought I'd had enough of long drives and late hours every weekend, but in May of 1998, I thought I'd try it again with a local Willmar, Minnesota band named TASZ. They didn't drive very far for their jobs, staying in the immediate area. I played with TASZ until the summer of 2003, when I quit playing for the last time. Well, I quit playing in bars and ballrooms. I now play drums in church every Sunday (Dennie plays guitar in church in Montana) and I have just begun a different musical career. I've put together a one-man act with my guitar and I play in area nursing homes for free.

I told John Dean, the guitarist in our church group, that I was putting together a little "act" to do nursing homes. I knew he'd done it himself with a couple of other guys in a group called The Golden Oldies a few years ago. I wanted to know if he had any advice for me.

"Be prepared for anything," he told me. "I was doing a nursing home job," he went on, "and we asked if there were any requests. A little old lady in a wheelchair in the back of the room slowly raised her hand. 'Can we watch the TV?' she said."

I called my little show *Terry Tunes* and I nervously set up my amp, microphone and guitar at the Bethesda Nursing home in Willmar in the early spring of 2004. I was about to do my first job. I finished my first song and a drooling gentleman to my left, who was sitting by the activity room piano, looked at me and said, "This here your piano?"

"No, sir," I answered, and then thinking quickly I added, "You can have it."

No laughter. Oh well, maybe they didn't hear my "joke". I did a couple more up tempo numbers and then, looking out at the dozen or so women in wheelchairs and the single drooling gentleman, I said, "I'm going to slow it down for a song, so this next dance will be a lady's choice." No laughter. "Okay, skip the jokes," I thought to myself, "and stick to the songs."

Terry Shaw performing as Terry Tunes in a nursing home.

I finished my last song to applause and then I thanked the wheel-chaired audience for coming to my "show". I don't know why, but I expected them to leave the room. Instead, they sat looking at me. "Thanks again," I said, "I hope to come back soon and sing for you again." Again, no movement. The silence was unnerving. "Do they expect another song?", I thought to myself. "If I start packing up in front of them," I thought some more, "that'll be rude." I looked at a couple of women who I had picked out during the show as the most interested. "Where are you ladies from?" I asked. Some lady said something that I couldn't understand so I got up, set my guitar down and walked over to her. Just then, a couple of aides came in to wheel my audience out, one by one. They couldn't leave without help, I finally realized. As I talked to the ladies, I also realized that I had hit upon the perfect way to end my show. Get up and talk to the audience, mingling amongst them. Touch them, shaking their hands. They loved it.

If you ever walk into a nursing home in the evening and walk down the halls, you'll discover that most of the TVs in the individual rooms have the Minnesota Twins' baseball games on during the season. The old people love to watch the Twins. At the beginning of the 2004 season, the Twins weren't on TV for a long time. The Twins were trying to market their games themselves on their own cable channel and the cable companies were buying it, literally. Finally, the dispute was settled and the Twins were to come back on TV for a 3pm Saturday afternoon game. I was scheduled to play for the Emmanuel Nursing Home in Litchfield at 3pm on Saturday. "Great!" I thought to myself.

Even greater, I walked into the nursing home and discovered I was to set up right in front of the big screen TV. The show went on. After a couple of songs, I apologized to the audience for the poor timing and said, "If I knew the Twins' score, I'd pass it on to you."

"It's one to one," a gentleman in the back said out loud. I looked over at him and he was sitting in a wheelchair with an earphone in his ear. He was listening to the game while I sang.

I was asked to do twenty minutes for the Meeker County Historical Society membership banquet and meeting. I was told that previous entertainers had conducted a sing-a-long with the members after they had performed. So I made up some sing-a-long sheets of songs I liked to do. The evening's performance went over well. I thought to myself, "If these people love a sing-a-long, how about my nursing home audiences?" I had noticed many of the old ladies in the nursing homes singing along with me as I performed.

So, at my next job, I announced, "This next song will be my last one, but if anyone's interested, I'll stick around and sit among you and we'll have an old-fashioned sing-a-long for a half hour before your dinner." I saw some faces smiling and heads nodding, so I did my last song, thanked my audience, and got up and moved among the people. Unfortunately, most of them wheeled themselves out of the room or walked out and left. A sleeping woman, a nice looking old gentleman sitting apart from everyone else and a smiling little grandma remained. "What the heck," I thought. "What do I care if it's two people or twenty people?"

"Okay, what would you like to sing?" I asked sitting down next to the little old lady, handing her one of my booklets.
"How about *When Irish Eyes Are Smiling?*" she asked me.
"Sure," I answered, proceeding to play and sing it along with her. The old gentleman smiled and played an imaginary keyboard on his tabletop. I finished the song and said, "What next?"
"How about *Sentimental Journey?*" she said.
"You bet."
Finishing the song, which the old man loved, by the way, playing along furiously on the "keyboard", I said, "That was good. What would you like to do now?"
"How about *When Irish Eyes Are Smiling?*" she asked me.
"We just did that song, ma'am."
"We did?"
"Yep. Anything else?"
"How about *Sentimental Journey?*"
I decided not to fight her and we sang the song again. When we finished, I looked at the old man. "Sir?" He smiled back at me. "Anything you'd like to hear?"
"You're doing fine," he said.
"Well, I see they're coming in to set the tables," I said, noticing two young girls walking into the room with silverware and napkins. "Maybe we should finish up. What should we do for our last song?" I said, turning to my singing partner.
"How about *When Irish Eyes Are Smiling?*" she asked me.

Most of the time, a good many of them stay and sing with me. I usually have a full room. Some have told me it's the best part of my show. I've been doing about an hour of sing-a-long in addition to my hour-long "show". The old-timers are fun to play for and they really appreciate the music.

One gentleman was playing drums on his knees along with me at Bethesda Nursing Home in Willmar.
"Are you a drummer, sir?" I asked him.
"Used to be," he replied.

"I used to play drums myself," I told him. A lady next to him identified herself as his wife.

"Tell him who you used to play for," she encouraged her husband.

"Who'd you used to play for, sir?" I asked him.

"Tommy Dorsey," he answered me, matter of factly.

One lady came up to me after one of my shows and she tried to hand me a dollar.

"Here," she said, "I want to give you something for singing for us."

"No, ma'am," I said. "I do this for charity."

"But you need to be paid," she insisted.

"Okay," I told her. "Give me a hug." So she gave me a hug.

As I was loading up my equipment that afternoon, a little old lady with a black t-shirt on shuffled slowly past me. The t-shirt read, "I'm up. I'm dressed. What more do you want?"

The ladies may be old and some have a touch of Alzheimer's, but the fire's not out yet, if you know what I mean. They love to flirt with me, especially when I do my sing-a-long. I was flirting with the lady sitting to my left during the sing-a-long after a 10am show in Litchfield's Bethany Nursing Home. Afterwards, the lady who was sitting to my right came up to me in the hall and said, "Do you do evening performances too?"

"Why, sure," I answered her. "I'll come anytime of the day."

"How 'bout midnight in my room?" she said, winking at me.

Dennie and I never had the opportunity of performing together on "stage". Not until June of 2004, that is. Dennie came back, with his wife Shirley, to Minnesota to visit his brothers. They arrived at our house on a Wednesday night. On Thursday afternoon, I had Dennie come with me to the local nursing home I was booked in and we did about two and a half hours together on our guitars. That night I dragged him off to a coffee house in Spicer, Minnesota where we got up on stage and did about an hour there.

I found out that our church group didn't have a bass player for our upcoming Sunday service, so I borrowed a bass from an old TASZ member and recruited Dennie to play it instead of guitar for our church service.

Finally, that Sunday afternoon, we had a Shaw family reunion at a local park and Dennie and I played guitar for the family sing-a-long for over three hours. Pat and Mick joined us on a few songs, marking only the second time the four Shaw brothers had sung together in our lives. The first time was for our mother and stepfather's Twenty-Fifth wedding anniversary party.

Mick, Pat, Terry and Dennie at the reunion.

Dennie left for home on Sunday night with blistered fingers and many new musical memories. The following Wednesday morning, Pat joined our "zipper club" and had quadruple by-pass surgery. That makes three of us four boys to have the surgery and Dennie has had a mild heart attack and a shunt installed.

Mick occasionally talks of a Shaw-Allen-Shaw reunion tour, but I'm not keen on it. He will continue playing somewhere, somehow, just as Dennie and I will until they can't lift our wheelchairs onto a stage or church altar somewhere, I am sure. You can't take the music out of a Shaw. As I wrote in one of my song lyrics, "the song goes on".

259

The Song Goes On

One song lyric that I did publish in my first book was my biographical song, The Song Goes On. *The lyrics are about how music has played an important part in the Shaw family through the decades. It is a common thread that runs through the family, possibly for generations to come. Grandpa Bill Shaw used to entertain socially on the piano, but I think my father Florian Shaw was the first in the family to be in a formal band, The Valley Ramblers. Next came my older brothers' bands, my bands and now my nephews' band.*

The lyric was in Terry Tales *in "installments", so to speak. That is, a verse was in the book whenever it tied into a story I was writing about. Here are the verses put back together and updated. When I first wrote the song, my mother and stepfather were still alive. The verses tell of incidents that I recall. Then the verses lead into other songs that were important in our lives and then back to my verses again.*

The Song Goes On

The first thing I remember
was my Daddy's old guitar,
plugged into an old amp
that he used when playin' bars.

Florian Shaw, second from the left, on guitar with The Valley Ramblers.

He'd set the amp out on the steps
so everyone could hear.
The neighbors would soon gather 'round
and sit and share a beer.
Dad played accordion and bass
and tried piano too.
In my small eyes there wasn't
anything he couldn't do.

A young Florian Shaw with his accordion.

He and Mom would sing duets,
that's something that I miss.
Mom would harmonize my dad
and it would sound like this…
[Go into *You Are My Sunshine* in harmony.]

The next thing I remember
was my brother Dennie's band.
They practiced in the old shed
and I was their biggest fan.
His guitar was from a catalog,
and it was called a Kay.
After coming home from school,
he'd go up to his room to play.

Dennie Shaw and his Kay guitar.

He wrote some songs, we were impressed
because they sounded fine.
The band just had a few jobs,
but they practiced all the time.

The Chancellors: Connie Olmstead, Sherm Robbs, Dick Blonigan on trombone, Dennie and Bob Peifer on piano.

Mom would yell, "Please turn it down.
I can't hear myself think!"

Dennie would start singing this
and Mom's heart just would sink...
[Go into *You're The Reason (I'm In Love)* by Sonny James.]

Brother Mick took up the drums
and joined the music race.
Then he tried to play guitar,
But settled on the bass.
How many bands, I can't recall.
I listened to them all
But, I remember one night
at the A&W in the fall.
Mick let me get up on the stage
and sing some background stuff.
The bands still practiced at our place;
on Mom, it sure was rough.
I'd sneak downstairs when they were gone
and beat the drums; "crash...bang!"
When Mick asked me to join his band,
together we both sang...
[Go into *Rip It Up* by the Everly Brothers.]

The Defiants: Mike Shaw, John Collins, Terry Shaw
and Loren Walstad

Brother Pat, he never sang
nor played in any band.
But he was always at the shows;
he was our biggest fan.
Brother Dennie went out state
to be a businessman,
while Mick played on and I "G.I.ed"
across in German land.
I came home and Mick said, "Hey...
we've got another band,"
and we took off on a never-ending
string of one-night stands.

Me, Jim Allen and Mick Shaw in the Shaw-Allen-Shaw band.

We made some records and it seemed
that we could do no wrong,
and on one album we recorded
one of Dennie's songs...
[Go into *Love Is Gone* by Shaw-Allen-Shaw.)

Now time has passed and Mick and I
have gone our separate ways.
We now play in different bands,
unlike the early days.
Pat and Dennie work in business,
gainfully employed.

Dad's been gone for many years
and so are Mom and Floyd.
Dennie and I get together
and we write some songs.
Mick's three sons now have a band...
the music marches on.
Though our family's spread apart,
the memories sure aren't gone.
Our love for music's stayed with us
and so the song goes on...
Oh yes, the song goes on.

Chapter Forty-Four
Lenora's Disappearance

There's a tombstone in the Ness Church Cemetery for the Clausens, Herman and his wife Lenora. In the center of the tombstone is a heart and inside the heart is the date the couple was wed. Or it was supposed to be the date they were wed. The tombstone carver put the wrong date in the heart. According to the date, Lenora would have been nine years old.

Old Herman, born in Germany in 1879, was livid.

"I'll sue the sonofabitches," the quick-tempered German yelled. He contacted the carver who said he'd make it right for $25 more. That made Herman even angrier and more determined to sue. Finally, an acquaintance pointed out to Herman that it would cost more than $25 to sue.

"I won't talk to the sonofabitch, I won't," Herman said.

"Why don't you give me the $25," the acquaintance said, "and I'll take care of it for you. Then you won't have to talk to him and it'll be cheaper for you."

So, that's what old Herman did. Ironically, his wife wasn't even buried in the grave under the tombstone. When Herman died at the age of 85 in a Naperville, Illinois hospital in July of 1965, his body was brought back to rest along side his wife's empty grave. Where was her body? No one has ever found it.

There's nothing like a mysterious disappearance to get people talking and rumors to start flying. I was asked why I didn't tell the Clausen story in *Terry Tales*. Well, I couldn't tell every story in that book. I never would have finished it.

It was a nice Indian summer morning on Thursday, October 6, 1960 at the Clausen farm two miles south of town near Highway 22. The Clausens were in their eighties and didn't work anymore so they had gotten up late and had breakfast before starting to do their daily chores.

Herman's first "chore" on Thursday mornings was to read the *Independent Review* newspaper, which came in the mail. So it was up to eighty-one year old Lenora to get her first chore done right away, besides the chore of making breakfast, that is. Her first chore was to go down the drive to get the mail, which included the paper, for

Herman. A little after nine, she shuffled down the gravel road, dressed only in a light sweater thrown over here navy blue polka dotted dress. It was so nice and warm outside; she didn't feel the need for her jacket.

When Lenora got back to the Clausen's white two-story house, she gave Herman the paper and took the garbage burner container that was attached to the stove. It was full of ashes and Lenora took the container outside to empty it. Herman, glancing up from his newspaper as she went out the door, looked at the clock. It was a little after 9:30am. He never saw his wife again.

Lenora Clausen

"I was reading my paper," Herman told the newspaper reporter interviewing him, "when I noticed the house was unusually quiet. I looked around the house and the yard, but I couldn't find her." It was just before 11am. Herman searched for about forty-five minutes before he decided to drive to town to report Lenora missing. Why drive? The Clausens had no phone.

Herman went to the police station in the Community Building in Litchfield. He told the dispatcher on duty that his wife was missing.
"I'm worried," he said. "She's had lapses of memory and maybe she's wandered off into the swamp next to our place."
"Do you think she might've gone over to visit a neighbor and just didn't tell you?" the dispatcher asked.
"No, she wouldn't do that, I'm sure."

267

"Okay, well, being it's out of town, I'll call Sheriff Hardy and you go home and meet him. Okay?"

Herman left and started thinking about the neighbor idea. Rather than go back into the police department and use their phone, he drove over to the telephone office building on Ramsey Avenue North. There he had an operator call his neighbors, Mr. and Mrs. Melvin Beckstrand and Kenneth Archibald, and ask them if Lenora had walked over to one of their places. She hadn't. The neighbors got together about 1pm and started searching around the Clausen farm.

Sheriff Hardy went out to the farm and talked to Herman. Satisfied he had a missing person case, the sheriff called his office and asked for help in conducting a search. The Meeker County Civil Defense rescue unit arrived around 3pm and also the Sheriff's Posse. It was a twelve man mounted patrol of volunteers. The search was on.

By nighttime, the two groups, plus many more volunteers, had searched the cornfields and swamps in a two-mile radius of the farmhouse. The Clausen place was near a large slough area and many speculated, as Herman had first told the police, that Lenora had wandered into it for some reason and drowned. But surely her body would turn up?

Sheriff Eldon Hardy called off the search for the evening and it was resumed the next morning at eight. During the night the temperature got down to 40 above and there was concern that Lenora couldn't have survived in the wet swamp ground. The number of volunteers was increased to close to one hundred and Civil Defense chief Ervin Radunz was kept busy coordinating all of the search teams.

The Clausen's son, Rudolph, drove out from Minneapolis and he joined the searchers. They re-searched every acre of ground, concentrating on the swamp ground. Airplanes owned by the local fliers were added. Again, nothing turned up.

Saturday, the search continued. This time a National Guard helicopter out of St. Paul was added. Once again nothing turned up, so the entire group, including the helicopter, went out again on Sunday.

The search helicopter.

Finally, on Sunday night, Sheriff Hardy called the search off.

"We're fresh out of theories as to what happened to Mrs. Clausen," Hardy said. Herman offered a $500 reward to anyone who could provide him with information, which would lead to finding Lenora. He never had to pay it.

The rumors started. Someone said they had seen Lenora sleeping on a golf course green one morning prior to her disappearance. She said she had gotten lost. Did she have Alzheimer's? Herman was known to have a quick-temper. Did he have a fight with Lenora and do away with her. The Natural Gas Company had been laying a pipeline near the Clausen farm. One theory was that Herman had put Lenora in the ditch and covered her just prior to the gas company's heavy equipment coming to bury the line. Melvin Beckstrand firmly believed that she was buried under the cement when the addition on the old Reinke building by the bowling alley was built. A previous county attorney told a friend of mine that Herman had been brought in twice and given a lie detector test. He had failed both times, my friend told me.

In 1985, on the twenty-fifth anniversary of Lenora's disappearance, Sheriff Hardy's lone deputy in 1960, Marvin Johnson, was interviewed. He simply said, "We never did consider the case closed...but we also never found a clue of what could have happened to Mrs. Clausen." Maybe the answer died with old Herman and is buried with him under a corrected tombstone next to an empty grave.

Chapter Forty-Five
Jerry and Edgerton

Litchfield has been blessed with some great families of athletes. The current Carlson family comes to mind, two brothers of which led Litchfield to its first ever State Basketball Championship in 2002. When I was in school, I had two close friends who came from athletic families: Alvie Watkins and Jerry Wimmer.

Alvin Cecil "Alvie" Watkins was short in stature but tall in talent. He was a gifted athlete, but he never went out for sports in high school even though he was as good or better than any of our school's stars. It had something to do with his grades. Alvie thought the pursuit of music and girls much more important than grades or even showing up for school.

Alvie Watkins today.

His other brothers played school sports though, such as his brother Maynard who ran on the track team. Still living in Litchfield today, Maynard's an expert on Litchfield sports. Anyway, the Watkins boys were something else. In 1957, the Presbyterian championship softball team consisted of fourteen year old Alvie and his brothers Maynard, Harold, Arnold "Ray", Marvin (whom we called "Muck") and a couple of actual churchgoers.

In the early sixties, Alvie, Maynard, Donald, Ray and Muck had a very good bowling team competing in the local league for Becker Shoe Service. Their substitute bowlers were, of course, their brother Harold and their dad, Emery. Then in March of 1967, the Miller

Motors bowling team consisted of Emery and the six Watkins boys. They scored the second highest single game total in twenty-five years.

Then there were the Wimmer boys. Kevin was the star of every team he played on in high school, Brendan or "Jopey", as we called him, was a great wrestler and football player, young Dougy, although hindered by bad eyesight, kept up with his older brothers, but my classmate and close friend Jerry has been called by some Litchfield sports experts as the best all-around athlete to ever put on the green and white colors of Litchfield High. My friend Maynard Watkins, the Litchfield sports expert, disagrees with that. He told me that Kevin was better than Jerry and then he added that he thinks Litchfield's greatest all-around athlete was Jim Harder.

Regardless, Jerry Wimmer was on a different level. Whatever sport he participated in, he dominated the play. He was even great in sports he didn't go out for, such as wrestling. In ninth grade gym class, teacher Howie Felt had us wrestle. At the end of the school quarter, he put on an intramural wrestling tournament of all the grades. He had us wrestle the championship round during the noon hour lunch period free time.

Jerry Wimmer not only won the championship, but I never once saw him down on the mat in any kind of a hold. He'd walk out to the center, shake hands, Howie would blow his whistle and in a flash, as quick as a panther, Jerry would have his opponent on his back and pinned. Two seconds here, four seconds there…that's all the matches lasted. I won the 95 lb. championship by the way. Claustrophobic fear can put added strength into your body.

Jerry Wimmer, senior year.

Jerry and Dougy came over to our house all the time. They almost lived there, sleeping with us in our garage in the summer. We

271

shot basketballs on our driveway until the weather forced us indoors to our basement. Mom had a four foot high cardboard barrel down there for a giant wastebasket. The barrel's foot and a half diameter opening at the top was rimmed by a metal edge. Anderson Chemical would discard the barrels and people took them home for trash bins. Ours sat on the floor up against the stairs next to our oil-burning furnace right underneath a bare light bulb. We would stand back from the barrel about ten feet away where there was a crack in the cement floor, and shoot buckets with our basketball. Usually we just played Horse, but sometimes we'd try to play a little Two On Two. Often the ball would bounce up off the "rim" and just miss the light bulb above it. A couple of times it didn't miss.

In the fifties and sixties, the Minnesota State High School Basketball Tournament consisted of one "class" only. The big and little schools were thrown together, with the bigger schools of the metro area usually winning the tournament. Occasionally a large school from out state, like Bemidji, would come down to St. Paul with a bunch of thick-thighed lumberjack descendents and knock off the Twin Cities' powerhouse. You couldn't help but root for the little giant killing schools like Wabasso or Annandale that would occasionally sneak their way into the semi-finals and then lose. But to win the State Championship? It had never happened and probably never would.

When I was a freshman in high school in 1960, a little Dutch town near Pipestone called Edgerton, population 1,017, sent eleven of their young citizens, an undefeated team called the Flying Dutchmen, to the tournament. These boys were different from a lot of the other tournament participants in another respect. Most had never seen a movie or played a pick up game of buckets on a Sunday like every single other kid in the United States. The reason? Their parents belonged to one of Edgerton's four Dutch Reform Churches where those things were frowned upon[74].

Most of the one thousand Edgerton citizens or so left in town followed the team up to the "cities". Edgerton turned into a ghost town for three days that March. Four-year-old Cindy Achterhoff

---

[74] A couple of years ago, a Minneapolis newspaper ran a "Where are they now?" article on the team. In the article, many of the boys admitted to sneaking over to Slayton, Minnesota for an occasional film or into the high school gym on a Sunday to shoot some buckets away from their parents' eyes.

probably stayed home. Fourteen years later, while attending Southwest State College in Marshall, Minnesota, she met and fell in love with black student athlete Lionel Bolden. Edgerton eyebrows rose when Cindy brought him home to marry. They had a daughter named Shannon, the Big Ten All-Academic defensive stand out for the University of Minnesota who helped her team make a run at the National Championship in 2004.

There were rumors floating around in March of 1960 that the Flying Dutchmen, these "little town hicks", were all cousins and stuff, but the boys were just neighborhood kids who had grown up together, playing pick up games each night on one of their folks' driveways. They immediately became everyone's "Sweetheart", "Cinderella" or "Jack the Giant Killer" Team. We all knew they didn't have a chance but they at least made it to "the big dance", something Litchfield could never accomplish because we played in the same District as perennial powerhouse and bigger school, the despised Willmar High Cardinals.

The Cinderella team of 1960 – The Flying Dutchmen of Edgerton.

Prior to the State Tourney, we had never even heard of Edgerton the town, let alone Edgerton the team, even though they had cleaned up in their conference by averaging 75 points to their opponents' 46. They teased their fans by coming close to 100 points several times during the season in the days when even the Minneapolis Lakers weren't scoring 100 points. The kids had odd sounding names like Kreun, Graphenteen, Wiarda, Veenhof and Verdoes.

The Shaw boys were poor but the Wimmers were even poorer. They didn't have a TV set, so they begged us to let them come over to our house to watch the basketball tourney. I tried to beg off because I knew that Mom would be gone those nights and every time the guys were over when she was gone, they'd be digging in our cupboards for something to eat. The Wimmer boys had voracious appetites and I knew Mom couldn't afford to feed them. But they came over, never the less, and we watched the games...well, most of us watched most of the games. In between games or at half times, we'd run downstairs and shoot some buckets ourselves. Jerry was terribly superstitious and usually a nervous wreck at sporting events. He was betting playing in the sport because his only way of relieving his tensions was to do something competitive.

"If I make ten shots in a row, Edgerton will win tonight," he'd say, and then he'd proceed to sink every shot from the ten-foot line. If he'd miss one, and it did happen once in a while, he'd make it tougher on himself.

"Okay, if I sink fifteen in a row, then they'll win."

As if the Dutchmen didn't have enough going against them, their coach was a first year teacher and a first time coach. His name was Rich Olson. The entire team, including their baby faced coach, would surely buckle under the pressure of playing on TV in front of packed houses in the loud and famous home of the Minnesota Gophers, Williams Arena, lovingly called "The Barn", in the awe inspiring Twin Cities with its sole skyscraper, the Foshay Tower. The big city boys must've been thinking, "Don't even bother to unpack, farm boy. You ain't gonna be here for long."

Besides being the smallest town[75] in the tournament, the Edgerton team was the only undefeated team left in the state that year. Everyone would be gunning for them. In the first game against Chisholm, a town from the other end of the state, six foot four Dutchmen center Dean Veenhof scored the first eight points for his team and then quickly got himself in foul trouble. Just after the start of the second quarter, he picked up his fourth foul and Coach Olson was forced to set him down.

---

[75] Edgerton wasn't the smallest town ever to play in the tournament. That "accomplishment" goes to little Lind, Minnesota. But Edgerton was the smallest town to ever win the whole thing.

"That's it," Jerry Wimmer said. "He's the heart of the team." Jerry left the room and went downstairs to shoot some buckets.

But unbelievably, the Edgerton team seemed to get strength from Veenhof's absence instead of getting down. They slowly started to pull away. Veenhof came back in the game in the second half, stayed out of foul trouble and proved his worth by leading his team in scoring with 24 points. When the final buzzer sounded, the scoreboard read Edgerton 65 – Chisholm 54.

Everyone's joy was short-lived however when the Dutchmen found out that they would have to face Richfield in the semi-finals. Richfield, the biggest school in the tourney, was the pre-tournament favorite to win it all. It seemed that the entire state, lovers of the underdog, jumped on the Dutchmen's bandwagon.

The Friday game against Richfield seesawed back and forth with Richfield jumping out to an immediate 10 to 3 lead and they still led at the end of the first quarter. The largest crowd ever at a semi-final tourney game saw Veenhof and teammate Dean Verdoes kick it up a notch and by the halftime buzzer Edgerton led by two. But, once again, Veenhof had gotten himself into foul trouble.

In the third quarter, the unbelievable happened. With 5:09 left on the clock, the star center fouled out. My buddy Jerry resigned himself to the fact that the bubble had finally burst for little Edgerton. He rolled his eyes and left the room when Dean Verdoes also left the game with five fouls.

"No, no, no…" Jerry said, heading for the bathroom.

The Dutchmen had a six-point cushion, but that evaporated and, with about 1:36 left in the game, Richfield tied it up at 56. Gaining the ball, Richfield went into a stall in an all or nothing strategy. They were going to run the clock out and take the last shot. With just six seconds left, the whistle blew and the ref called the Richfield center for too much time in the lane. There wasn't time for an Edgerton shot and the game went into overtime. Everyone was on the edges of their seats.

How could Edgerton keep going with their two stars on the bench? Richfield suddenly got aggressive, thinking they could rattle the little Edgerton guards who had the fate of their team dumped on their shoulders. The plan backfired on Richfield and their aggressiveness kept sending the Edgerton guards to the free throw line and LeRoy Graphenteen and Darrel Kreun were almost perfect from the charity stripe. Edgerton was out shot from the field but shot an unbelievable 81% from the free throw line. In the end the Cinderella team came out ahead, winning 63 to 60.

Jerry Wimmer was a nervous wreck, but he loved the way the underdog Edgerton team wouldn't die and kept fighting back. That was Jerry's style of play also: Never say die.
On Saturday night, March 26, 1960, he and Dougy showed up early for the biggest game we had ever witnessed in high school basketball. Edgerton would face another big school, but this time an out state school...Austin.

We went downstairs and threw some balls into the barrel. I kept running upstairs to check on the TV. Finally I yelled down, "Okay, the introductions are about to start." Everyone ran upstairs and we gathered around our little black and white Emerson TV. Jerry couldn't sit. He kept pacing the floor.
"Sit down Jerry," my brother Pat yelled at him. "You're blocking the TV!"
"Jerry!" Dougy yelled.
"Come on Jerry, sit down," I pleaded.

Could little Edgerton complete an undefeated season and win one more time? The game had just got going when Jerry exclaimed, "I'm too nervous. I gotta shoot some buckets." He turned and ran downstairs. We kept yelling the score down to him. Edgerton led from the very start. It seemed they had saved their best game for last. Jerry came upstairs to witness the phenomenon, but the minute he sat down, Austin started coming back. So, he jumped up and ran downstairs again. Edgerton would start to pull away, the 19,019 fans, the largest crowd to ever see a basketball game of any kind in Minnesota, would start going crazy, and Jerry would run back upstairs. The minute he did, Austin would come charging back. Pretty soon we were screaming at Jerry to stay down in the basement. He was so superstitious anyway that he actually thought he was helping Edgerton win by staying down there.

"What's happening?" Jerry yelled up the stairs. "Who's ahead? How many fouls does Veenhof have?"
We kept yelling back and forth. Austin was refusing to go down, just as Edgerton had in the first two games. The banging of the ball into the barrel was increasing down in the basement, almost drowning

out the screaming of the Williams Arena crowd through our little Emerson TV speaker. We were going hoarse yelling a play-by-play down to Jerry.

"What happened? What happened?" he yelled each time he heard the crowd roar. Slowly Edgerton pulled away and they started to slow their game down, controlling the ball. The game was in their hands now, but we refused to let Jerry come back upstairs. Finally the buzzer sounded and the game ended. The score was 72 to 61 and the Flying Dutchmen picked up the youngest coach to ever win a State Championship in Minnesota history and carried him around on their shoulders.

Jerry Wimmer, on the left, today.

Jerry came upstairs and we let him watch the awards ceremony where the All Tournament Team was announced. For the first time ever, the All Tournament Team had four players from the same school. They were Darrel Kreun[76], LeRoy Graphenteen, Dean Veenhof and Dean Verdoes. Our school's greatest athlete sat on the arm of our sofa staring at the tiny TV screen knowing that he had just missed seeing the greatest basketball game in Minnesota State Tournament history[77]. But maybe, just maybe, in his nervous demented way, Jerry Wimmer also thought to himself that he had just helped Edgerton do the impossible.

---

[76] Darrel Kreun recently retired as a very successful boys basketball coach at Sibley East High School. (Arlington and Gaylord)
[77] Not to be outdone, another Edgerton school went on to perform an amazing feat. Edgerton's Southwest Christian High School won the state title four years in a row from 1999 to 2002. It was and probably will forever be the only school to ever repeat four years in a row in Minnesota or any other state for that matter.

Chapter Forty-Six
The Hoochy Coochy Show

When I was about thirteen, I came home early one Saturday morning. I had gone out for the day to hook up with my buddies but found none. "No big deal," I thought. I was very content doing things alone. I had a vivid imagination and could entertain myself for hours in my room with my things or just some blank paper and a pencil.

Because it was a chilly morning, I opted to sit down by the furnace duct in the wall by the kitchen door instead of going up to my cold room. That corner was a favorite spot of the Shaw boys on cold winter mornings. We used to fight for it. I would get up in the morning, grab my clothes and run downstairs so I could dress in that corner.

Our bathroom was just off the kitchen and its door was a mere three feet from me at the most. I could see that the door was closed and someone was in there. Probably Mom. I was busying myself with some book or newspaper on the floor feeling great snuggling close to the warm slightly oily smelling air coming from our oil furnace in the basement when I heard the bathroom door open. I glanced up and there stood Mom in her entire nakedness. Embarrassed she reached back and grabbed a bath towel to cover herself with.

"I didn't think anyone was home," she said, rushing past me towards her bedroom just down the hall.

"I...I..." I stammered, not knowing what to say. I had never in my life seen a woman's body. Not the whole thing, anyway. Just an occasional glimpse of a bosom in a men's magazine down in Roy Peipus' garage. A little breast was all you saw in those magazines. Much was left to the imagination. Today's kids see more in Victoria's *Secret* catalogs or "fashion shows" on TV than we ever saw in most men's magazines like *Stag*.

Mom was a wonderful woman, by no means ugly, but her body was not anywhere near what I had imagined behind the skimpy clothing in those girly magazines. The vision of my mother had the totally opposite effect of the simplest photograph in any of the magazines I had seen.

A couple of years later, one of my favorite times of the year rolled around. It was August and the Meeker County Fair was going on. The boys in our gang didn't give a rip about the fair itself, except for the freebies we got in the commercial building. What we liked was the carnival that set up next to the fair. The Tilt-A-Whirl, the Bullet, the Scrambler, those were the main attractions to a teenage boy. The Digger in the "arcade" strip of games of chance was another. For a dime you operated a model steam shovel in a glass box trying to grasp an illegal switchblade knife or a fake Zippo cigarette lighter.

Then there were the sideshows. Freaks of nature, odd looking people and more fakes and cons. We didn't really believe that the Monkey Girl, born in the dark jungles of the Amazon, would be naked except for the fur and the tail like the poster taunted us, but we had to pay our dime or quarter and see it for ourselves.

When I was sixteen, a new "show" tent had been added to the fair's carnival. How it got past the seventeen churches in town and the faithful within who protested the slightest "filthy" movie shown at the Hollywood Theater downtown, I never knew. The "Legion of Decency"[78] in the Catholic Church gave the bad movies a "C" rating.

---

[78] The Legion of Decency was formed in 1934 to combat immoral movies. We took a pledge, in church, against "Condemned" movies, pledging not only to never go to any "morally objectionable" movie, but also never even to go to any movie theater that had ever shown a morally objectionable film! That made it hard for us in Litchfield as both the Hollywood and the Unique theaters occasionally showed them. For the curious, here's the pledge: "In the name of the Father and of the Son and of the Holy Ghost. Amen. I condemn all indecent and immoral motion pictures, and those, which glorify crime or criminals. I promise to do all that I can to strengthen public opinion

279

That meant "Condemned" and we were told it was a Mortal Sin to go to those movies. A green sheet with movie listings hung in the vestibule of the church and we never went to a movie without first checking the list. "Darn it. It's rated 'C'!" we'd say after checking out a movie on the list that all of our Lutheran friends had told us we just had to see.

But, anyway, there it was...a real live "Hoochy Coochy" show tent at our fair carnival. Inside the wall of brown canvas was the forbidden fruit of our imaginations. The carnival barker promised us that we'd see "everything", with nothing left to the imagination. The cost? A mere eight bits...one dollar. One problem: our age. Brother Pat and Dougy Wimmer, fifteen years old each, and Dougy's sixteen year old brother Jerry and I would never be able to pass for the required age of eighteen. Buying cigarettes was one thing, but getting past this wise old Carny guy would be another.

"No one under eighteen or over eighty will be allowed to see this show. If you're under eighteen, you just wouldn't understand it and if you're over eighty...well, you just couldn't stand it! Look at her, gentlemen. She shakes like a bowl of Jell-O on a cold frosty morning on Grandma's kitchen table."

There next to the barker stood a fairly attractive young blond with a shiny, glittery red robe around her hidden naked body. At least we assumed she was totally naked underneath the robe. And those X-ray glasses we had sent for using an ad in the back of our comics never worked, either. There was only one way to find out the truth.

"Come on let's go," Jerry urged me.

"Naw," I said, "we'll get caught for sure." Besides, I didn't want every man in town see me go into that tent. Someone would surely tell my mother or Father McGowan would find out about it and bring it up in the confessional. Fear of the confessional was real.

"Come on, all he can do is turn us away," Jerry urged.

"What about Pat?" I inquired. My diminutive blond brother looked like he was still in grade school instead of high school.

---

against the production of indecent and immoral films, and to unite with all who protest against them. I acknowledge my obligation to form a right conscience about pictures that are dangerous to my moral life. I pledge myself to remain away from them. I promise, further, to stay away altogether from places of amusement which show them as a matter of policy."

"Well Jopey got in last night and so did Pokey." "Jopey" was the Wimmer's seventeen-year-old brother Brendan and "Pokey" was Donald Schreifels, seventeen-year-old brother to our pal Andy or "Monk".

"You gonna?" I asked Pat.

"Sure...I will if you will," he said with a frightened look.

Okay, it was decided. We were going to make that big leap into the adult world of sex. We took out our dollars. I took out a cigarette and lit it, letting it dangle from my lips to add to my "disguise". Then I pulled up the collar of my shirt, fluffed my hair up and tried to stand a little taller as we slipped into the small line of about a half dozen men entering the tent. As we passed the old man sitting on a stool, we held out the dollar, he took it from each of us, never even looking up, and we were in. We were in!

Inside the dark tent, illuminated by one bare bulb hanging from the center pole of the tent and a smaller bare bulb hanging over a wooden platform stage, were two dozen metal folding chairs facing the small stage that had a lone curtain to its rear. It might have been just an old blanket hanging over a rope. In front of the stage was a rope fence making a small arc from stage corner to stage corner. The single rope passed through eyelets on top of three-foot high metal stakes.

We sat down on the chairs in the second row trying to make ourselves smaller to hide from view in the middle of the small crowd of men. We giggled, nudging each other with our elbows. The anticipation and excitement coupled with the fear of getting caught was a high I can't imagine any drug could give. I could hear the shuffling of feet on the dirt floor behind me but I was afraid to turn around lest I see a businessman or a farmer I knew in the row behind me.

Suddenly, the light bulb dangling above our heads went out, leaving only the dim light bulb glowing over the small stage. Some tinny music came on over an unseen speaker and the "curtain" was pushed aside by the arm of the robed girl from out front. Okay. Now we're talking.

"Yeah..." I heard Jerry hiss, under his breath. I glanced over in his direction, but quickly turned my gaze back at the girl who had started "dancing" (shuffling) around the tiny stage. She didn't seem to have any rhythm whatsoever. She acted like she couldn't hear the music as she stepped barefoot around the small stage, moving her feet in every direction. She wasn't even trying to appear sexy. Instead of slowly baring a shoulder or leg or doing something to tease us, she suddenly just opened her robe and took it off. Underneath was nothing. No tassels, no G-string, no high heels, nothing. Not even a bra and panties or even plain shoes. Although I could suddenly see everything I had wanted to see, I felt cheated. There wasn't anything exciting about this at all.

Then the girl laid down on the stage and started gyrating her hips. "What the hell is she doing?" I thought. It made no sense to me. The music suddenly stopped, the girl got up, bent over picking up her robe and put it on. "That was it?" my mind screamed. "I spent a dollar for that?"

"You gentlemen like what you just saw?" a voice from the rear of the tent said. We turned around and saw the old guy from outside strolling around the seated crowd to the stage area. He turned to face us.

"She'll give you a close up view for a mere dollar more fellas. Who wants more? Come on up to the rope." A few men left saying "Bullshit!" or some other expletive, but most of the ten or so of us remaining marched up to the rope. I followed like a lamb to slaughter. I reached into my pocket and took out another dollar bill, my last one. There go the carnival rides I had been looking forward to. I was so nervous and scared standing there, I fumbled for another cigarette and lit it up as the man went down the rope and collected the bills from us, while the girl behind him looked at us with a blank stare on her face.

The man turned and left, the music came back on and the robe came back off. No dancing this time. The girl just stood there in front of us naked. That close to her, I couldn't look at her breasts or anything for fear she'd see me staring at her body. So I just looked at her blank face. Then she walked up to each man and did something like brush his hair back or unbutton a shirt button.

"What would she do to me?" I thought. I was worried how I'd react. "I've got to make sure the others don't see how nervous I am and that I've done this before," I thought to myself. "Seen a naked woman before, that is…even though it was my mom." My mind was racing and my skin felt clammy.

Suddenly, there she was, standing in front of me. She reached down and tugged on my pant zipper. I took a drag off my cigarette, acting as cool as I could under the circumstances, and blew smoke in her face.

"Got a problem, babe?" I hissed, hearing giggling all around me.

I was cool, all right, and thanking God that she had moved on past me. I was in a nervous stupor, sweating and shaking. I have no idea what she did to Pat, I was still recovering, but next to Pat was a drunk. This guy was unbelievable. He just reached up and put one hand on a breast and buried the other between her legs. She never protested or said a word. Then the guy walked her from one end of the rope to the other, while we scrambled out of his way. The whole time he was holding his hand between her legs. I couldn't believe it. After over forty years, that sight has never left my mind. It, like the entire show, was not sexy and did nothing to excite me. I found it disgusting.

The "show" ended and we filed out into the darkness outside the rear of the tent. I felt dirty and angry that I had given up all my "Carny money" for what I had just seen. Gypsy Rose Lee was truly an artist, demanding top money and billing and never showing a single thing while she turned on legions of men. I had just seen everything and yet I had just seen nothing.

It wouldn't be the last time I would lose all the money I had in the world in a "strip joint". To celebrate my turning twenty-one, my college roommate, Dick Blonigan, took me to a strip bar on Hennepin Avenue in Minneapolis. It was a Monday evening. Dick bought me a beer and we toasted my manhood, drinking it quickly, watching the stripper. Our waitress came back to our table.

"Another round, boys?"

"Sure," I said, even though I didn't really want another one. Alcohol and I never have gotten along. But, I felt obligated to buy Dick a drink in return. I grudgingly reached into my wallet and pulled out everything I had in the entire world; a twenty-dollar bill that I had earned playing a dance on the previous weekend. I needed that money to last me the entire week, with enough left to put gas in my car so I could get home the following Friday night.

The waitress brought us the beers and took my twenty from my hand. She laid a small black rectangular tray down in front of me and put some coins and several bills on it. My change. I decided that I would just leave it there, just in case Dick wanted another beer later. Rather than grabbing the money and stuffing it in my pocket, I was being cool, acting as if I had done this before. Besides, my attention was elsewhere on a small raised stage in the corner where a woman was making her tassels twirl in opposite directions without using her hands.

A few minutes later our waitress came walking by our table.

"Thank you," she said, doing a little dip with her body and picking up the black tray. She was gone before I could say a word.

"Dick!" I yelled, "she took my money!"

"You left it on the tray?"

"Yeah."

"That means it's a tip."

A very expensive lesson for a very naïve lad. "Hoochy Coochy" shows and I don't get along. Did I learn that lesson? No.

Donna Sure Is Actin' Strange

I got so tired of writing the standard love songs that I decided to really stray about as far away as I could from them and write a "sick" love song. I imagined having a girlfriend who was into kinky stuff and took my reaction a step further than normal.

Donna Sure Is Actin' Strange

Donna sure is actin' strange.
She scares me right down to my veins.
I love that girl but the fact remains...
Donna sure is actin' strange.

First it was some whips and chains.
Then came those two Great Danes.
I worried for that mind of hers,
especially when she bought those spurs.

Now, of course, the whips and chains
must've been for those Great Danes.
I asked her why the boots and spurs and
she made a sound like a wild cat's purrs.

I played along for a change and
didn't mind the whips and chains, but
the chamber was the final straw.
I'm sure it is against the law.

After goin' through great pains,
I cleaned up all the stains and
then I hid her remains 'cause
Donna sure was actin' strange.

Chapter Forty-Seven
Moving The Bank

Wayne Rayppy had a fire at his New Bakery in Litchfield on December 30, 1961. The bakery was next door south of the First State Bank. Wayne and his helpers were installing a new oven in the bakery, when sparks from welding ignited insulation in the walls. The place went up so fast that people in the offices above the bakery didn't have time to grab their coats as they left. Roscoe Keller's Barber Shop, which was below the bakery, was flooded with the firemen's water.

Fighting the fire at the New Bakery when it was next to the bank in 1961.

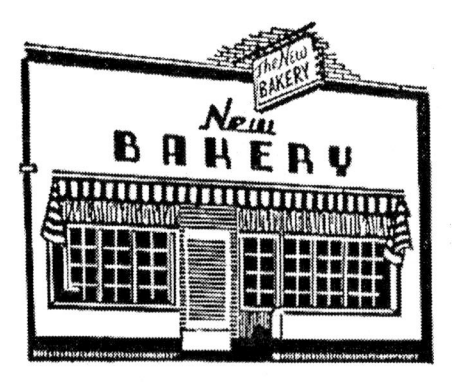

Bank president Garry Hollaar got a call at home and he and his son Lee went down to see what could be done at the bank. People kept asking Garry if their valuables in the vault would be all right. Garry told them that the vault was fireproof and airtight, and behind his back he crossed his fingers. He had no clue. "It's got a time lock," he told the worried citizens. "I couldn't even open it if I wanted to." Now, that was the truth.

The Hollaars gathered up all the paperwork on desks and storage files in the bank and moved them to safer places. The fire triggered numerous moving of businesses in town, starting with the bakery and the barbershop, and some changes to others, such as the bank.

This was not the first fire affecting the bank while I was growing up in Litchfield. Some years before, the bank janitor had left a mop soaked with wax or something on the floor by the back door, next to the stair going downstairs. It started to smolder and burn the tile floor. Somebody walking by outside noticed the smoke and put in the fire alarm.

The fire department didn't have far to go. The firehouse was just north across from the bank on Second Street. I don't know if they even had to sound the siren on the truck. And they didn't have to break down the door, since Bob Breitenbach, a bank employee, was one of the firemen and he had a door key.

The firemen tried to put out the smoldering mop with the stuff on the truck, but they weren't very successful. So Bob picked up the mop, walked across the street to the firehouse, and put it in a sink, which he had filled with water. Later, back at work at the bank, Bob was kidded, "If it doesn't work for the fire department to come to the fire, then you bring the fire to the fire department."

The bank owned the bakery building. After the bakery burned down, Hollaar decided that it would be a good time to build a new bank building. The old bank stretched from Sibley Avenue, Litchfield's main street, a half a block west along Second Street to the alley behind it. Since the bank had to keep operating, a plan was thought up. They decided to tear off the front of the building, just before the vault, reconfigure the back of the building and the upstairs to be the temporary quarters of the bank, and then build a new bank building next to Sibley Avenue.

The First State Bank in the thirties.

The bank in the late fifties. Notice the front steps have been removed. In the foreground are Andy Schreifels and Stanley Lunderby.

By the way, if you look closely at the two pictures above, you might notice a slight change to the entrance of the bank. Mr. Hollaar had the outside steps removed because of the danger of somebody slipping on the ice and snow that would build up on the steps. The steps were moved inside the front door. Also, just inside, there was a new entrance to the shops in the basement. An after-hours depository was added to the left of the door (not shown in the picture). The clock above the door was likely added about that time also. It was a pain to set when daylight savings time started and ended. There was a knob at the bottom of the clock, which you could only turn by climbing up on a ladder.

The new bank building would be twice as wide, using the bakery lot, but only half as deep. After the new building was finished, they would move the bank into it, tear down the old bank in the back, and have a parking lot where it was. There already was a parking lot behind the bakery, since that building wasn't as deep as the bank. A trailer would go there to house the bank's insurance agency during the construction period.

The move was done pretty much in one weekend although the construction took about a year and a half. The time came when the vault door had to be taken off the old vault and moved to the new building. The door weighed seven tons, so it wasn't an easy job. It took a day or so for Thulin Bros. Construction to jackhammer around the door to get it loose. Then another day was needed to move the door though a hole left in the basement of the new building and into place. Finally, another day or so was needed to cement the door into place. During all that time, there was a concern about a robbery even though many of the valuables were temporarily placed in other vaults. So the police and others stood guard.

There had been a light above the vault in the old bank, which was left on at night. The police could see it from where they parked in front of the bank across the street. Since it was thought that it would take hours to break into the vault, the light provided pretty good protection.

The move was finally finished and it came time to tear down the back part of the old bank. Thulin Bros. tore the building down, leaving the big concrete cube of the vault standing in the open. They hooked a heavy ball to their dragline crane and swung it at the vault. Nothing happened. Nothing happened on the next dozen or so swings, except that some plaster on the outside of the vault got chipped off. The vault was eighteen inches thick with steel reinforcing bars every four or six inches. Finally, they had to jackhammer all around the vault and cut the top part off below the level of the new parking lot.

Knocking down the bank walls.

By the way, on the second floor of the old bank building, there were a bunch of offices. Bob Farrish had his dentistry up there, a beauty shop was there and Ed Jacobsen had his law office up there. Ed's desk was right over the bank's indestructible vault. Ed used to joke that he was going to put "Assets over $1 million" on his business card because his "ass sets" over the money in the vault.

The new bank opened on May 27, 1963 and the bank had an open house on June 29th. The bank moved again into a new building at 301 Ramsey Avenue North in May of 1978. This time the Diebold firm of Minneapolis was brought in to move the vault door. The bank opened up to the public on June 5, 1978.

The new First State Bank after it became the library in '79.

The Carnegie public library closed in late October of 1978 and moved into the old bank building on Sibley Avenue in December of 1978, but only opened for short periods during the day. So for a while, Litchfield was without a library until they officially opened up in January of 1979.

Today the bank building is occupied by Sparboe Farms and somewhere in the parking lot in back is buried the rest of the bank vault.

Chapter Forty-Eight
Keep Litchfield From Dying – Part One

My hometown radio station's call letters are KLFD. When the station started broadcasting for the first time in late December of 1958, it didn't take long for us kids to come up with things that the letters stood for. The most popular was "Keep Litchfield From Dying". I don't know if the station has had anything to do with it, but Litchfield "ain't dead yet".

I started researching the story of KLFD the same way I did the history of the downtown store buildings. I relied heavily on the old newspapers in the Meeker County Historical Society. After all, our very own radio station in the late fifties must have caused huge write-ups and banner headlines, such as "We're On The Air!" But, I found very little mention of the station in the *Independent Review*. There was a mention of the possibility of a station coming to town, the costs, the application for a license, the installation of an antenna and then, a month later, an ad for Kohlhoff's Super Valu advertising their "Dial For Dough" call-in radio contest on KLFD. What gives? I was finally struck with the realization that the radio station was thought to be a threat to the advertising revenue and news reporting of the newspaper itself. Editor/Publisher John Harmon probably purposely low-keyed the whole deal, just reporting the occasional facts, nothing more.

In September of 1958, "interested parties" approached the Litchfield Industries committee with the idea of a local radio station. The committee then proposed the idea to the city council. The proposal was approved and by December it was almost a reality. An antenna was put up on the Albin Johnson farm one mile southwest of town. A crew came all the way up from Oklahoma to do it. The antenna and the station's 500-watt power were to give KLFD a range of forty-seven miles.

When the radio station did come to town, a mock studio was set up in a room by the sidewalk window in Reed's Printing on main street where the American Legion club is today. They had a big single RCA microphone with the letters KLFD on it in the window, as well as a UPI Teletype machine. But, they didn't broadcast from there. The owners were just trying to build interest in the station by letting people see the UPI machine and the news stories from it.

The downtown windowed site was chosen because the owners wanted something downtown to generate interest and excitement while the site they had really chosen was being remodeled. That site was the old Charles Hoyt March house[79] on the south side of the railroad tracks at 218 South Sibley Avenue, a few houses south of Batterberry's store. A permit to remodel the house was taken out during the second week of December 1958.

The Charles Hoyt March house on Sibley Avenue South.

Some of the first announcers, such as Hal Boettcher, lived across the street from the March house, renting rooms in the old Hugh Fenton house. The announcers tape-recorded some stuff at the Reed's Printing site to get practice while the actual station was being set up. Banker Garritt "Garry" Hollaar's son Lee, although only in grade school, "helped" put the station together. He hung around the house and was befriended by chief engineer Larry Lawson, who was building the studio. Lawson, who was in a wheelchair and walked with crutches, let Lee hold things and pull wires through the soundproof wall.

The front parlor of the house, with a beautiful rounded southeast corner, was divided in two with that soundproof wall. The wall had a big window separating what became the studio in the front of the

---

[79] The O. G. Nordlie family had recently occupied the house, having bought it in October of 1901 from Peter E. Hanson, who had built the house.

house and the control room in the middle. The kitchen became the newsroom. The studio was used for interviews and live performances. KLFD's first actual broadcast was from that house and that room.

Polly Nordlie did a community interview and entertainment show from the parlor/studio room. The show was on Saturday mornings at ten and was called *Polly's Personality Parade*. Local singers and musicians would perform on Polly's show. I was in the house/radio station twice to watch heroes of mine broadcast live from that room on Polly's show. One hero was my brother Dennie, who performed with his band, The Chancellors or Rockets (they kept changing their name). The other time was to watch my hero Jerry Wheeler's Dixieland band play. Jerry was a great drummer and therefore I idolized him. Norma Berke used to stand in front of a mike in that room giving the town news. English teacher Phyllis Koenig, who taught for fifty-three years, would give the school news there.

Frank Endersbee and Lee Favreau initially owned KLFD, which was a small 500-watt AM radio station at that time. The station hadn't been on the air three weeks when Frank's seventeen year old son Greg rolled and totaled out the KLFD's green and white station wagon on Friday, January 23rd. He was driving the mobile billboard on Highway 12 two miles east of Darwin.

Frank used to air organ music at the end of the broadcast day. Announcer Jim Harrison referred to that show to his friends as "Music For People Who Died Today". Frank didn't like Rock and Roll music and in the beginning he wouldn't play any. Finally he let his son Danny, whose on-the-air name was Danny Parker, host a one-hour teen show on Saturday afternoons. It was called *Date with Danny*.

Jim "Jimbo" Harrison had come to Litchfield after he had found out that Frank Endersbee owned the radio station here. Frank had been a childhood hero of Jim's from the half-hour live kids' show Frank had done on radio station KWOA in Jim's hometown of Worthington, Minnesota. Frank was the closest thing to "show biz" that Jim knew as a kid. Jimbo was creative with his broadcasting and he had a cast of made up characters that he would talk to as he introduced records. Some of them were Hiram Hightower, Sam Turnbolt, and Mither McTavish. Harrison had a big old record with prerecorded voices saying short things like "You're darn tootin', cowboy," "You no good bum," and "Mind your own business, kid." Jimbo would say something like "Say, our maintenance man, Sam Turnbolt, is walking through the studio. What's the good word, Sam?"

"You no good bum!"

"Little testy there, Sam," Jim would come back with.

"You're darn tootin', cowboy." Things like that. My brother Dennie thought Jimbo was a genius and hilarious.

"This is the 500 watt clear channel KLFD coming to you from the heart of the state right here in Meeker County," Jim would expound as he would sign off for his shift, "where the blue of the sky meets the gold of the day. Say, I see by the old clock on the wall, there's a dead fly and that means we are out of time. We have to make room for big Frank Endersbee, so this is James Murray Harrison saying, 'Blow the whistle, Bartholomew', (river steamboat whistle from sound effects record and the show's theme music), ...See you tomorrow folks!"

Irv Kjelland was the news director at that time. His son James, a mathematical genius that we called "K J" was in my class in high school. At some time C.W. Doebler, who had worked at radio station WBBM in Chicago, bought the station. He and his family lived upstairs over the station. There may have been other owners between Endersbee and Doebler too.

KLFD was a daytime-only radio station. Signals in the AM band travel greater distances at night, which was why we could listen to WLS in Chicago or a Little Rock, Arkansas station at night for our only initial taste of Rock and Roll. Daytime-only stations had to go off the air at sundown so that they wouldn't interfere with the other stations on the same frequency. Some stations had to only lower their power at night. There were and still are "clear-channel" stations like WCCO and WLS that could keep their full power (50,000 watts) 'round the clock, because they didn't share their frequency with any other station.

That meant that the sign-on and sign-off times for KLFD changed every month, based on the sunrise and sunset times for the month. So KLFD had to have more programming during the summer. During the winter, the station might go off the air before dinnertime. Because of this, KLFD couldn't do live broadcasts of football or basketball games. They made up for it by doing some taped replays. There also was a Saturday show broadcast called *Coffee with the Coaches*. They did it by a live remote on telephone lines from the Colonial Café in the old Litchfield Hotel.

Of course one coach who could be counted on to liven up the show was crazy football coach Howard "Howie" Felt. Jim Harrison taped an interview with Howie and later, at the studio, he started the playback on the air like this: "Today I asked football coach **Howie Felt, how he felt** about the game last night." (Say it out loud and you'll see how silly it sounded.)

KLFD did a lot of live remotes, including Sunday church services, which the station rotated through Litchfield's thirteen churches. Police Chief George Fenner's son, Jim, was fascinated with the radio station and he used to usher at the Lutheran Church one block behind the radio station. He would sneak out of church and come over to the control room during the sermon. It was broadcast live so Jim knew when it was time to go back to church. Jim Fenner later introduced Jim Harrison to his future wife, Sharon Shoultz, a classmate of Fenner's. Sharon was the sister of Guy Shoultz whom you met in an earlier chapter. Jim Fenner later became an announcer at KTOE Radio in Mankato, Minnesota at the same time that Harrison was an announcer at the only other station in town there, KYSM.

One of the first live remote broadcasts done on KLFD was from the Meeker County Fair for First District Association or Land O'Lakes. That was one of the earlier fairs at the "new fairgrounds". Jim Harrison, who had just come to Litchfield, said, "It was hard to interview people I didn't know and to compete with the noises and smells of the animal barns". Stores having grand openings or big sales had live remotes also. Bernie Aaker, who came to the station in early 1964, broadcast all day long from Jim and Cathy Allen's CJ Music Store's first anniversary celebration in May of 1970. Ironically a few years later, after the music store closed down, KLFD was headquartered there.

During weekends, the station was run by a lone person who handled the control board, did the announcing, answered the phone, took the FCC-required transmitter measurements every half hour (or every few hours, making up the missing entries), and getting the news off the UPI teletype. Sometimes that meant running back to the newsroom, (the old kitchen at the house), to grab an hour's worth of printout by tearing off the news summary that UPI packaged for radio stations, and then running back to read it live on the air without having had time to review or rehearse it. This practice was called "rip and read" by the station personnel.

Sometimes the Teletype would go haywire and start printing gibberish in the middle of a story. If the announcer hadn't spotted it before beginning to read it live, he had to think quickly on his feet and come up with an ending to the news story. All the while, he was also keeping an eye on the clock, so that his newscast would end at the right time. UPI was pretty good about providing phonetic pronunciations for strange names in the stories, but hilarious mistakes were made. Unfortunately the station didn't record all the broadcasts back then, so the "bloopers" are lost forever. You can get an idea of what it was like on blooper records of big station's recorded broadcasts though.

In the early days, we weren't sure if anybody was actually listening to KLFD, including the announcer on the air. There was an "audition" circuit built into the control board, which allowed the playing of something on the control room speakers besides what was going out over the air. So the announcer could listen to his favorite records or the Twins' game rather than what he had to play on the air. This caused a problem sometimes, such as when the record being played on the air was skipping and the announcer didn't notice it because he was listening to something else. Worse, if he threw the switches the wrong way, he sometimes put what he was listening to out over the air.

Chapter Forty-Nine
Keep Litchfield From Dying – Part Two

My oldest brother Dennie was fascinated with the radio station and he hung around there all the time. He even got on the air a couple of times and did an okay job. In a couple of years, in the early sixties, a decision was made to move the station to rooms above Reed's Printing[80] downtown, where the Legion Club is today. Again Lee Hollaar helped Larry Lawson and the rest move the equipment. They signed off one Saturday at dusk and went back on the air on Sunday morning above Reed's with one microphone and one turntable. After Lawson left, the engineer was Jerry Urdahl, State Representative Dean Urdahl's older brother.

Lee Hollaar used to work at the station on Sunday mornings, playing the transcribed programs like the *Ave Maria Hour*. The show came to the station on two large twelve inch vinyl records that played at 33 rpm, so someone, like Lee, had to watch when one record ended so he could start the other one. Other programs came on larger eighteen-inch vinyl or acetate records, some as thin as a hospital X-ray negative, and then there were the 7 ½" reel-to-reel tape recordings.

Dennie kept working his way in to the station and finally got his own Saturday afternoon show replacing the regular announcer, who had replaced Danny "Parker" Endersbee. Dennie wasn't paid, unless you'd count all the free 45-rpm promo records he brought home. There was never a hit among them but we played them never the less. By now Frank Endersbee had decided to keep the good rock records. Dennie always claimed that Mom, my brother Pat and I, and Aunt Doris Johnson were his only listeners. Dennie's job only lasted about two months. He also used to sweep up, vacuum the studio and tear newssheets off the UPI Teletype machine in the back room.

In the early sixties, KLFD starting having a Saturday afternoon one-hour teen show called the *Pepsi Platter Parade*. Jon Kent, the *Platter Parade's* deejay, gave away gift certificates for six packs of Pepsi during the Saturday show to the caller with the correct answer

---

[80] Reed's was at 220-222 Sibley Avenue North.

to a music trivia question. I would call in every Saturday and win a six-pack. I knew a lot of Rock and Roll trivia.

In my junior year in high school, the station asked the school to send over three teen volunteers to do the Saturday show with Kent. Marty Foss, Jeanette Oliver and I volunteered. We were put into a small windowed room next to Jon Kent's larger studio. We sat at a table introducing records by reading from a yellow script Jon had typed up. We looked at Jon through the window for signals. When the song was over, Jon would ask us to adlib our thoughts about the record. It was kind of a Rate-A-Record, ripped off from TV's *American Bandstand.*

"It's got a good beat and it'd be easy to dance to," Jeanette or Marty would say, and then snicker when their mikes were turned off.

I told the truth though. "I didn't like it too much." I'd say. "It sounds like somebody trying to imitate Elvis and the lyrics are stupid."

Off the air, Jon asked us for trivia questions for the Pepsi giveaways. I was the only one who could ever come up with them, so it became my job. Marty and Jeanette got bored with the whole deal and quit coming. I asked my friend Alvie Watkins to fill in. Alvie was in my brother Mick's class and was friends to both of us. He had a great sense of humor, was a great dancer and later sang in Mick's rock band The Embers. His ease in front of the mike made him a natural for the *Platter Parade* but he also got bored and quit after a month or so. So it was just Jon Kent and I every week. The following year, we continued with that format, just the two of us. Just like Dennie, I got a lot of free demo records, and mine were worse than his were. I gave them to my younger brother Pat.

Robert Miller was the station manager in the mid sixties. On his staff were Maynard Troland, in sales and sports announcer, Jack H. Christensen, news director and announcer, Larry Crawford, announcer, Hal Boettcher, program director and announcer, and Bernie Aaker as the sales manager. Bernie came to the station in 1964. Kenneth Eidenshink was general manager next until Bernie Aaker took over in February of 1967. Then Don Sabatke took over until Tom Costigan, once a school librarian, became general manager in March of 1970. Christensen was still an announcer around that time. Ron Kragenbring came to the station in 1970 to answer phones and learn the trade. He started announcing part-time in 1971 and then left to work at some other Minnesota stations.

In the early-seventies, the announcers felt they had to have a unique identity or name. So we had announcers like J. B. Scotch, Smilin' Bob Greenhow, who came in 1969 and went on to own the station, and Darryl "Mad Hatter" Hensley. Hensley came in 1972 and left KLFD in the very late seventies and went to KZEV-FM in Clear Lake, Iowa. There he started the famous Winter Dance Party concert days at the Surf Ballroom in 1979. It celebrates the fact that Clear Lake was the last place that Buddy Holly, Ritchie Valens and The Big Bopper performed before their fatal plane crash. It has grown to become an international event bringing in people from all over the world.

Darryl Hensley, the "Mad Hatter".

"I wanted to get out of the building; get outside," said J. B. Scotch on Saturday, February 20, 1971. "But then, when I thought about it, I didn't know exactly where I would go." On duty announcer Smilin' Bob Greenhow said, "There really was nothing to do. I knew I couldn't run home and grab a gun and join the fight."

Program director Rick Stuart went on the air and he shakily read a prepared statement that a national emergency was in effect and KLFD was going off the air. What in the world was going on? The start of World War III? Well, the staff at KLFD wasn't sure. It could very well be something like that. A Teletype alert had just come through directing the station to go off the air. There was only one circumstance when that could or would happen: a national emergency that would threaten the well being of the citizens of the United States. Only then would small stations, such as KLFD, be asked to clear the airwaves so that the bigger stations would be able to get information out to the citizens without interference.

The staff's fear turned to anger when another Teletype came through five minutes later apologizing for the mistake. Then the anger turned to frustration when something went wrong with the station's transmitter and KLFD couldn't get back on the air for a long time to explain the mistake to its rattled listeners. After what seemed like an eternity, the station went back on the air and the red-faced announcers tried to explain what had just happened and they hoped that they hadn't lost their listeners trust.

Smilin' Bob Greenhow soon became "family" with me as he married Nan Osdoba, who was the younger sister of my perennial classmate Cathy Osdoba, who had married Jim Allen. Jim was considered a brother to my brother Mick and I as we practically lived together during the seven Shaw-Allen-Shaw band years. Many, many days we spent as much as twelve hours together, driving to dance jobs, setting up, playing, tearing down, and driving home, only to get up and do it all over again the next day. We played every single night in those days.

Bob played bass also and got involved with a local band called Beats Working, for a short time. He had gone to Brown Institute, as most local announcers have. He went into the Navy for a short time during the Vietnam War and then returned to Brown, where he saw a listing for an opening at KLFD in 1969. Little did Bob know that he would meet his future wife here, eventually own the radio station and probably spend the rest of his life in our little town.

Steve Neighbors came to KLFD a year later in 1970. He was the station's news director in the early eighties. Tom Costigan resigned as station manager in May of 1971 and Bernie Aaker, station sales manager, took over again in June. Around this time, the news reporters were Dik Ryan and Noel Sederstrom and the station's motto was "Full Time Radio". Wayne Tursso was the news director.

Bernie Aaker left to work for the *Independent Review* in October of 1972 and, in November of 1972, KLFD moved to a street level store on the west side of Sibley Avenue at 237 Sibley Avenue North. There was an open house for the public to view the new studio in December. Jim Ohnstad became an announcer at the station and then general manager in the late seventies. Jim Nabors was an announcer and news director. Not THAT Jim Nabors...ga-oll-oll-ly! Also Mike Miller was an announcer. At this time Herb Gross owned the station.

Ron Kragenbring came back to the station in January of 1980 to work as an announcer and operations manager. Bernie Aakers's son Tony was a part-time announcer at the station in '83, working the weekends. Another announcer/sales manager in the mid-eighties was Chris Lenz.

On a Friday afternoon in January of 1986, the station suddenly went off the air. The owner, Herb Gross, simply pulled the plug. Litchfield was without a radio station until November of 1988, when Dick Johanneck and Norman "Red" Jones formed Crow River Broadcasting, Inc. and started an FM station with the call letters of KYRS. Steve Neighbors was their general manager and Bob Greenhow eventually worked for them also. Their studio wasn't downtown, but in the former Neperud law office building on North Sibley.

Bob Greenhow and Steve Neighbors

Somehow Steve and Bob started doing a morning show together at KYRS and during commercial breaks they would chit chat about this and that and the subject came up one day about buying and reviving the old KLFD station. Chit chats turned into serious discussions and, in July of 1991, the two formed a company called Mid-Minnesota Broadcasting and purchased the rights to KLFD from Herb Gross, along with the tower and tower site. Bob already had the old Gambles store at 232-234 Sibley Avenue North for his wife's Prints Charming business and he said he would lease part of it back to the company for the station.

Old friend Ralph Anderson from Atwater, who had been the engineer at the old KLFD for thirty years, put together a shopping list of the equipment the men would need to get back on the air. Steve went out and bought it, much of it coming from Indiana. They hired two employees, news director Dean Tongen and sales manager Jay Weinman. Steve and Bob thought they would be back on the air by September but their old station KYRS fought their pursuit of a license. They nearly went broke fighting for their license. Both of them had to find part time jobs. Steve even worked for KWLM over in rival Willmar.

KLFD finally went on the air again on December 7, 1991 with the staff of Tongen, Weinman, and Randy Quitney helping Bob with sports. Bob and Steve continued their morning show, which had been so successful with KYRS. They are still doing it today. Later, Dan McGee and Randy Domstrand came to KLFD and Randy became the Sports Director.

Tim Bergstrom came along and started his "news breakers" morning show, which brings my story back to me. Tim interviewed me twice on his show concerning my book. KLFD has a new slogan: "A Meeker County Original". I still like "Keep Litchfield From Dying".

The Sleep Song

There was a time in my life when I was burning the candle at both ends; playing in a band every night until one in the morning, driving at least an hour home and then getting up at 7am to rush to school to teach. I slept 'til noon on Saturday mornings, loving every minute of it. You write about things you know and love.

The Sleep Song

I hate to get up in the mornings.
I'd rather lie here in my warm bed.
It feels so good, just sawin' wood,
and makin' "Zs". Don't wake me please.

Can't understand early risers.
Can't think of what's in their head.
Just close that door and let me snore.
Don't wake me 'til I've had my fill of
sleep, beautiful sleep, restful sleep, yes, yes, sleep.

I don't want a little "shut eye".
Give me a long deep sleep instead.
Turn off that light. Bid me "Good night".
Pull up my sheet and give me that sweet, sweet
sleep, beautiful sleep, restful sleep, yes, yes, sleep.

I always thought that the day would finally come when I'd be retired and I could sleep 'til noon every day. Well, the day has come and I find myself waking up around 5:30am, laying in bed thinking about what I'm going to do that particular day and then rolling out of bed around 6:30am to get the paper, make coffee and wonder what in the hell went wrong with my plans.

Chapter Fifty
The Highway Shooting

Sometimes stories are right under my nose and I don't see them. Over the last couple of years, a frequent visitor at the G.A.R. Hall has been Jim Hannan. He would go for a walk from his place at Lincoln Apartments and stop in to say "Hi" to his son Bill, who would come over during his break from work at the city electric plant to do a little genealogical research, or just to speak with the ladies in the Historical Society.

Bill introduced Jim and I one day and I started telling Jim some of the stories going into *Terry Tales*. He loved them and couldn't seem to get enough. Occasionally he would throw me a bone, that is, add a little to my stories. He wasn't one to talk too much about himself. I would be talking about the Colonial Café, for example, and Jim would add, off the cuff, "Oh yes, I ran that for a while in '69, I think it was." Or I'd be talking about the great State Champion town baseball team, the Litchfield Optimists. "Oh yes, that was a great team," Jim would say, "I played a little ball on that team." What? Was this guy pulling my leg? You read about Jim and the Optimists in an earlier chapter and saw that Jim played more than a "little" for the team.

My newspaper research is how I found out about Jim's brush with death. He didn't tell me or offer that story to me either. I had to read about it in an April of 1969 *Independent Review* newspaper.

Jim and his wife Charleen had been out Saturday night, March 29th, at the Velvet Coach in Hutchinson for dinner and dancing with friends. Later in the evening the other couples decided to get a snack before going home. Jim and Charleen decided to go home. Jim had to work early the next morning. They left on Highway 7 West around half past midnight heading for their home in Litchfield. As Jim passed the truck stop on the outskirts of Hutch and started to pick up speed, he noticed the headlights of another car in his rear view mirror. He also noticed that his car was pulling a little to one side.

"It feels like we got a low tire or something," he remarked to his wife. "I'd better pull over and check it out," he added, pulling over to the shoulder a couple of miles west of Hutch. Strangely, the car behind him pulled over too and crept up behind Jim's car.

305

"Maybe somebody is stopping to help me," Jim thought to himself. Whoever the driver was, he jumped out of his car and quickly walked up to Jim's car. In his hand was a .45 caliber pistol.

"I'm a highway patrolman," the young man told Jim. Jim looked at him and noticed the man was dressed in street clothes and his speaking was a little hard to understand. "I don't like the way you're driving," the "patrolman" added.

Not one to argue with a gun, Jim replied, "I'm sorry, sir. But, I don't know what I've done."

Suddenly, the man went into a tirade.

"You didn't pull off the road far enough," he screamed.

Jim apologized, realizing this wasn't an officer, but still not someone to be messed with, and he started to explain.

"I thought I had a flat and I didn't know where to pull off and..."

"Listen, you'd better shape up. That's all I gotta say."

With that, the man turned and left the open-mouthed Hannans sitting in their car. The man got into his own car, pulled back onto the highway and continued heading west on 7.

"What the hell was that about?" Jim asked Charleen, as he also pulled onto the highway, heading west.

"I think he's drunk," Charleen said.

"I think he's crazy," Jim added.

Jim continued to follow behind the young man for several miles but the man was driving very slowly. Jim had finally had enough.

"I need to get around this kook and put some miles between us," he said, pulling into the left lane and stepping on the gas pedal of his old station wagon to pass the car. The old car barely made it around the guy. Ahead of him, Jim stomped down more on the gas hoping to get away from the fool, veering off onto Highway 22 towards Litchfield. But, as Jim looked into his rear view mirror, he noticed the headlights still behind him.

"Oh, no," he thought, "he's chasing me."

Suddenly there was a shattering sound and Jim looked into his rear view mirror and saw that his rear window had exploded into a million pieces.

"There wasn't any loose gravel back there, was there?" he asked his wife.

"Jim, that guy's shooting at us!" his terrified wife told him.

306

Another shot rang out into the dark night and Jim saw a hole appear in his dashboard between his cigarette lighter and the clock. Jim knew that the .45 slug must've whizzed by his right ear to hit that particular spot on the dashboard. He reached across the seat and grabbed his wife's arm and pulled her down to the floor. Just then another shot rang out, this time a hole appeared in the glove compartment. The bullet had passed through the space his wife had occupied just seconds before.

The car behind him veered left to pass Jim and pulled up along side of him. Pop! The windshield glass in front of Jim shattered with cracks in all directions as a tiny hole appeared in front of Jim's eyes. Another bullet shattered Jim's side window, half of the glass disappearing. The car pulled in front of Jim's car and suddenly stopped. Jim quickly pulled over onto the shoulder, avoiding going into the ditch, and he stopped his car. He was near Coney Island, a lone bar on the highway near Greenleaf and Lake Minnebelle.

The lunatic jumped out of his car, and walked back to Jim's almost windowless station wagon. This time he was carrying a .22 revolver. Jim rolled down what was left of his left window, thinking he had to do something quick to protect his wife. Before he could speak, the gun was thrust through the opening and pointed at his head.

"I'll shoot you, damn it, but I won't shoot your wife," he said.

Charleen lost it, thinking the worst. She broke down crying uncontrollably. The man took the gun away from Jim's head, held it in the air and fired off three or four rounds. The spent casings flew onto Jim's rear seat, where they were found the next day.

"I want you to show me the way to Highway 7," the gunman said, pointing the gun at Jim again. "I want to go west."

"Okay," Jim said, "follow me. I'll show you."

Jim slowly drove up to the Coney Island parking lot and was getting ready to turn around when another car pulled onto the lot. It was Dick Baril and his wife Diane. Dick got out of his car and started walking back to Jim's car.

"Dick," Jim yelled out his window, recognizing him, "Get going! This guy behind me's got a gun."

Baril jumped back into his car and took off, spitting gravel in his wake. Jim was amazed the mad man didn't take off in pursuit, but he didn't, so Jim turned around and drove back to the intersection of 22 and 7, with the gunman's car following close behind. There Jim pulled his car off the road again. This time he stuck his arm out the window and waved his hand in a "Come on" gesture and then he pointed west. Apparently, the gunman didn't understand, because once again the man jumped out of his car and came up to Jim's.

"Is this 7 going west?" he asked, pointing in the direction of Corvuso and Cosmos.

"Yes."

"Okay," the man said and he turned, got back into his car and drove away.

During Jim's drive back to the Highway 7 turnoff, Dick Baril had rushed to Litchfield to report the incident to the police.

Jim and Charleen turned their car around and drove as fast as they could to Litchfield. They pulled into town, shivering from the cold air coming through the shot out windows and from the fright of the encounter and they went home.

"You've got to call the police," Charleen told Jim.

"Yes, I know."

The officer who answered the phone was Herman Klitzke. He interrupted Jim in mid-sentence.

"Jim, we've already got the guy. We need you to come down to the station and identify him."

"Oh…okay," a stunned Jim Hannan said.

Cosmos police officer Reuben Martin had already arrested twenty-one year old David Bartos of Delano. Bartos' car had run off the road three miles east of Cosmos on Highway 7. Martin had come to investigate an "accident". Bartos had called in to have a tow truck help him get his car out of the ditch. He had two pistols on his person.

At the police station, Jim was ushered into a tiny room that had a one-way glass on one wall. There in another room sat Bartos.

"Yeah," Jim said, relieved this night was coming to an end, "that's the guy." It was 2:30am and Jim had to open up the Colonial Café at 6:30am.

Jim drove to work that morning. Neither he nor Charleen slept any. Jim parked his car on the south side of the hotel on Depot Street. All day long he noticed cars driving by and people walking over to his car to look at it. Word had spread like wildfire around our quiet little community.

Charleen suffered from nightmares for many years after that night.

"We were scared all right," Jim said, "but everything went so fast, we didn't have too much time to think. I really can't put my finger on what my thoughts were when that gun was held to my head, but I wouldn't want to go through it again."

Nor talk about it thirty years later to someone writing a book about strange things that happened in and around Litchfield, Minnesota.

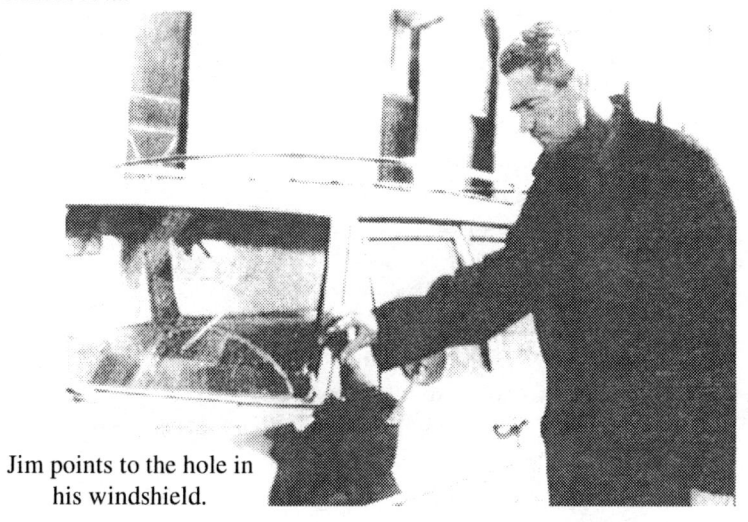

Jim points to the hole in his windshield.

Oh...Jim's son Larry got the car and drove it out to Rapid City, South Dakota where he had landed a teaching job. He drove it for a couple of years and then traded the "evidence" in on another car.

Excuses

Why didn't you do this? Why didn't you do that? Okay, who did this? I remember asking my kids those questions. Then would come a barrage of explanations from them. A parent sure hears his share of excuses. Add to that my occupation of being a teacher. More excuses. You start to think that no one wants to stand up for his or her own actions any more. I decided, out of frustration, to write about excuses, pledging that I wouldn't do it. Yeah, right. Should I tell you excuses why I didn't keep my pledge?

Excuses

I won't give and you don't want...excuses.
I won't hide behind a front like excuses.
You won't hear no "ifs or buts".
Everything will be clear-cut.
I won't jive or scuttlebutt with excuses.

It's the talk you don't want to hear...excuses.
People think it'll stop a tear...excuses.
It'll drive you up a wall.
People use it just to stall.
Then they have the gall to call with excuses.

Hey, please tell me anything but excuses.
Don't leave me hangin' on a string with excuses.
Why not say what you mean?
Don't put words in between...excuses.

Make up things to cover up...excuses.
Thinkin' it will help you out...excuses.
Talk is cheap. We all know that.
Don't try to be a diplomat.
Get in there. Step up to bat...aw...excuses.

Chapter Fifty-One
The Night An Angel Was Born

I got drafted in the early winter of 1967 during the Vietnam War. I was in my fifth year of college, studying to be a teacher, and my college deferment had run out. Lawyer Patrick Joseph "P. J." Casey III was assigned as my counsel for my automatic appeal, but it was to no avail. Uncle Sam wanted me. Mom, tired of sending loved ones off to war, such as my dad, her brothers, and my brothers and stepbrothers, suggested I go to Canada for a while. She knew I wouldn't and, being young, I felt invincible anyway. I even decided to enlist, thinking it would increase my chances of getting a decent job in the Army.

I was sent to Fort Campbell, Kentucky in January of 1968 for my basic training. "Great!" I thought, "I'm at least going to the warm south for the winter." Wrong! It was south all right but the temperature never got above freezing. We bivouacked or camped out for a week in our pup tents with the temperature always below 15°. I shaved with the dishwashing water at the mess hall tent because it was the only warm water I could find.

My mother's prayers were answered however and, after basic and AIT training, I got orders to report to an Army base in Pirmasens, Germany instead of Saigon. I had a month to get ready on base and train my replacement, after which I would be given two weeks leave to go home. So when I first got my orders, I called my fiancée from Lake Lillian, Minnesota and told her the news. Then I added, "Let's get married on my leave. Then you can be over in Germany with me."

She agreed and got the wedding plans going on her own, even sewing her own wedding dress. I came home and basically just walked into the wedding ceremony. I borrowed Pat's car and we drove up the North Shore Drive by Duluth for our honeymoon. My new bride came over to Germany a few months later after I had found an apartment off the base and had saved up enough money to pay for it and send for her. She had gotten pregnant on the honeymoon and had never been away from her parents or out of the United States before so it was a scary situation for her.

We were as poor as we could be over there. I was just a PFC with no housing allowance so most of my check went to the apartment rent. There was very little left for food. We ate popcorn for supper one night when the money ran out before the next payday. Somehow I was able to buy a used Volkswagen "Bug" for $200. It had been rear-ended and also hit something head on, so it looked more like a crinkled box than a car. A couple of G.I. mechanic friends of mine kept me on the road. And we got free prenatal care for my pregnant wife from the Army.

Discussing possible names, we had agreed that if the baby would be a boy, he would be named Christopher Adrian. We disagreed on the girl's name, however. My wife wanted Amy Beth but I thought it was old-fashioned sounding and too "cutesy". We finally agreed to stay with the Chris theme and decided on Christine Andrea.

When the baby's time arrived, late one dark moonless spring night, I loaded my wife into our little beat-up car and rushed her to the local Army clinic five kilometers away to confirm it. The medics said it was time, put my wife into an ambulance and told me to follow them to the Army Hospital up on a mountain in Landstuhl. I had never been there before. Off we went on a wild car chase up the unfamiliar curved mountain road.

I desperately tried to keep my VW close behind the speeding ambulance, praying I wouldn't get into an accident. I could barely do fifty M.P.H. up that mountain road with the gas pedal of my tiny car floored. I had some narrow misses as I blindly screamed around curves that dark night, which had become a dark morning by now. Finally arriving at the hospital, I was separated from my wife and escorted into a waiting room to pace and smoke cigarettes.

A little after two in the morning, a nurse came in the room and told me that I was a father for the first time. I wasn't allowed to see Christine, the name we had picked out if the baby was a girl, except through a nursery room glass. Officially born on April 30, 1969, Christine was tiny at five pounds, fourteen and a half ounces, but she looked fine. I was able to go into my wife's room. Exhausted, she mumbled "Did you see her?" and then she fell back asleep. I sat down in a chair, not knowing what to do. I was exhausted too, but I couldn't fall asleep. I just sat there looking at my wife, and occasionally walked down the hall to the nursery where Christine was also sleeping. Finally, daylight peaked through the hospital room's window.

A eerily strange thing happened that night at the hospital that would've made the hair stand up on the back of my head, had I known about it at the time. Thousands of miles from America, at a tiny Army Hospital on the side of a mountain in Germany, a woman from Lake Lillian, Minnesota, who had married a man who went to school in Litchfield, Minnesota, gave birth to a child on April 30th. In another room of the very same hospital, a soldier from Lake Lillian, Minnesota, who went to the same high school I did in Litchfield, died...on April 30th. His name was Dick Vick and he had been in a car accident on a curved mountain road that previous dark moonless night.

I waited until the daylight was full in the room and then I walked the halls in the big hospital again, glancing in at my sleeping wife and again stopping to look through the nursery glass at the sleeping or crying babies. Finally a shop opened up where I could send telegrams, so I sent one to each of the new grandparents back in the States. Trying to save money, I kept the message short and concise. "Christine born. She and mother fine."

I went back to the Army base after shaving at our apartment. I tried to get the day off to catch some sleep but Sarge said he needed me on the job. I called the hospital and told them to tell my wife I had to work but would be there in the late afternoon. After work, and still not having slept, I rushed back to the hospital expecting to see Christine in the arms of her mother. Instead, I walked into the room and saw my wife, in a robe, sitting on the edge of her bed. She obviously had been crying.
"What's wrong?" I asked. "Where's Christine?"
"I think you'd better sit down," she answered. "The doctor's going to come and talk to us. He says there's something wrong with the baby."
"What?" I was stunned. "What's wrong?"
"He says she's got Down syndrome."
A cold chill swept down my body from the top of my head to my feet.

Down syndrome is a type of retardation caused by an extra chromosome from one of the parents. The children used to be called Mongoloids because of their Oriental looking eyes. They have an enlarged tongue, which causes speech problems, poor muscle tone, which means they are slow to crawl and walk and a little less than half of them have heart problems. I hadn't sat down, but I did now. The words were shocking but not unknown to either of us. My wife's aunt had Down syndrome and my mother had babysat a Down boy named David Huberty when I was little. My younger brother and I had played with him on the lawn to help Mom out while she cooked our meals.

The doctor finally came to the room, my wife got onto a wheelchair as he instructed, and I pushed her down the hall, following the doctor to the glass windowed nursery room. The doctor told us to wait next to the window and he went inside. He walked over to a glass basinet, picked up our baby and then held Christine up behind the glass like a puppy at "Show and Tell" in school. He pointed out the various visual symptoms, like her eyes. When he bent her little double-jointed fingers all the way back, it was like a blow to my stomach. I grabbed my wife's shoulder as she shuddered and her head fell forward. We both cried. When the doctor came out of the room, he shocked us by telling us to consider putting Christine away in a home. The thought had never entered either of our minds.

I pushed my wife in her wheelchair back to her room. She climbed up and sat on the edge of the bed. Alone, in the room and in Europe, we sat and looked at each other for a while in a terribly awkward silent moment, not knowing what to do or say. Finally I said, "Let's write letters to our parents and tell them." So that's what we did. It was therapeutic and washed a lot of the pain right out of our bodies.

My mother, always one to see the silver lining, wrote back to us that God had picked us to be Christine's parents because He knew that we'd do a wonderful job raising a special child. That was the first time I had heard that term. Special child. In less than a week, we were allowed to bring Christine home to our apartment.

In the days that followed, I found myself distant from Christine, afraid to get too close to her. I thought I would have to give her up some day and I didn't want any more pain. But one night, some other

Army wives came over and "kidnapped" my wife, telling her she needed to get out. I was left to baby-sit Christine alone for the first time. She started crying, so I picked up and held her. She was so tiny I could literally hold her in the palm of my hand. I started talking to her, introducing myself. We bonded that night.

As Christine grew up, we discovered that she was indeed a special child, trying our patience at times, but bringing so much joy into our lives. We treated her like a normal child. She was our first of three children after all, so we had nothing to compare her with. So we didn't coddle her. I woke up one morning to discover her missing from the house. Frantic I ran outside and found her squatting on the sidewalk. She had taken a loaf of bread and a package of bologna from the refrigerator and was lining slices of each down the sidewalk. Down syndrome children are very orderly and neat.

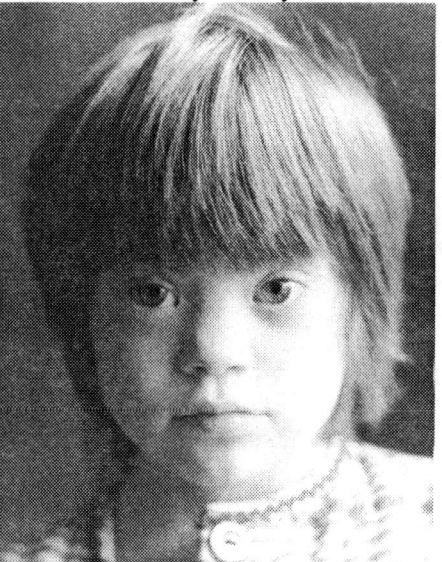

Christine at seven years old.

I yelled at Christine many times to catch up with her brother and sister as we were going for our nightly summer evening strolls. She was always lagging behind, stopping to look at every thing on the road. Down syndrome children are extremely curious.

I would stop and yell, "Keep up with us Christine or we'll leave you behind and go home and you won't get a treat." Then I'd think to myself, "People in their houses must think I'm an abusive father or awfully mean to the poor little retarded girl." As I said, we treated Christine like a normal child.

Christine has the prettiest blue eyes with little "stars" or white specks in them. I used to call her my "little angel with the stars in her eyes". Down syndrome kids are the closest you'll get to angels on God's green earth. Auntie Christine, as she prefers to be called now that her first nephew and niece have been born, has grown into a loving, gentle woman, who is "normal" in so many ways, still having her trying moments along with her good moments. If I introduced her to you, she would walk up to you and give you a hug and ask something about you.

Christine calls us occasionally from her home in Hutchinson and never talks to Lois, her stepmother, without ending the conversation by telling Lois that she is "pretty, perfect and beautiful". Then she tells me that she loves me. If we're visiting, she gives me a kiss on my forehead. She got in the habit of doing that when I had a full beard. Christine never liked my beard.

Christine goes to work every day in Dassel, Minnesota making time clocks and earning a living. I was told at a recent annual review that she does a job there that no one else can do. Only she has the patience and dexterity with her required small fingers needed to thread thirty wires through a series of holes in each of a particular time clock. She is not and has never been a burden on us or on society. Christine Shaw makes me proud to call her my daughter.

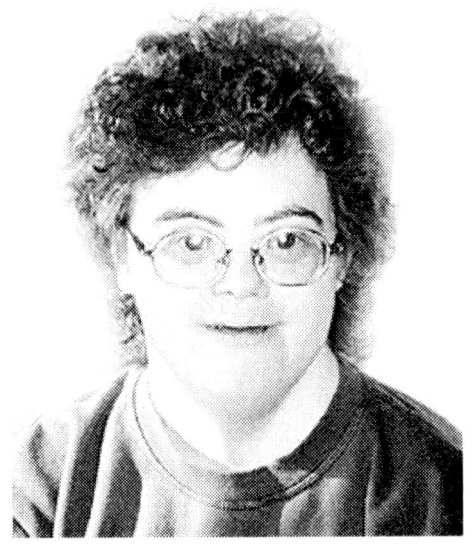

Christine Andrea Shaw today.

Chapter Fifty-Two
Bernie – Part One

When I got out of the Army and came home from Germany with my wife and baby daughter Christine, I rented an apartment[81] above the old Coast To Coast store, where Heartland Community Action is today. We lived there while I finished college and then got my first teaching job at the Middle School in Glencoe, Minnesota. I commuted to Glencoe until the fall of 1970 when we rented the downstairs of a house there.

While I was still living in Litchfield, I spent a lot of time down at Jim and Cathy Allen's CJ Music Store, just down the street from my apartment. Jim and I were playing every weekend at that time in the Shaw-Allen Trio, just before the music explosion when we started playing every night.

In May of 1970, Jim and Cathy celebrated their store's first anniversary by having a big week-long sale and having KLFD radio come in on the Saturday of the week to do an all day live remote broadcast. The announcer was going to be Bernie Aaker, who had come to Litchfield a year after I left home for college.

I had heard of Bernie. I knew that he had a low velvet-like voice, much like Charleton Heston, he was a good-looking man with a thin Clark Gable mustache, and he loved wearing hats. But I had never met the man. I was anxious to spend the day in the store and observe him at work. Radio announcers had always fascinated me.

When Saturday morning rolled around, I rolled out of bed quite late (we had played a dance the night before), and I shuffled down the street to Jim's store. When I walked in, Jim and Bernie were in the middle of a remote broadcast. I marveled at how at ease Jim was with the mike in his face. But, of course, his stage presence was one of the things that made our band so popular. Bernie masterfully led Jim through the long commercial and enticed listeners to "come on down and visit Jim and Cathy, have a cup of coffee and a doughnut and see the great deals."

With that, Bernie turned the broadcast back over to the studio for music and he lowered his microphone to his side and started chatting with Jim, who had noticed me sitting off to the side.

---

[81] My address was 221 Sibley Avenue North. The upstairs used to be called "Watson Hall".

"Bernie," Jim said, "come on over here. I want you to meet the drummer in our band."

He and Bernie walked over to me and Jim introduced us. Bernie and I shook hands. I complemented him on his great voice.

"You really handled that remote beautifully," I said. "You make it seem so easy."

Bernie thanked me and I could tell immediately that we would be friends.

Throughout the afternoon that Saturday, I stayed in the store, sitting in the storefront window watching Bernie work. He came over to me often and we chatted. The subject came around to children and I told him about my daughter Christine.

"That's a beautiful name," Bernie said. "How did you come to choose it?"

I told Bernie a short story about our selection and then I added, "My wife wanted to name her Amy, but I hate that name. I think it sounds so old-fashioned and cutesy."

Bernie looked me in the eyes and slowly said, in his low velvety radio voice, "My…daughter's…name…is…Amy."

Stunned at my stupidity and trying desperately to speak while extracting my foot from my mouth, I mumbled something apologetic. Bernie, nice man that he was, grinned and let me off the hook by saying something that I've since forgotten. Jim walked up to us and the two men started talking about the next live remote.

Amy Ann was the daughter's full name and she was Bernie's first of four children. He named all his children with "A A" names to go along with their last name, Aaker. Bernie, ever the salesman, thought he would some day get the AAA Insurance Company to do a story or a commercial on the family and maybe give him free insurance. So after Amy came Anthony Allen, then Andrea Allison, and finally Annette Alise. Bernie and I found we had something in common in that Annette had cerebral palsy as a baby and was mildly retarded, but not as much as my daughter Christine.

Bernie Aaker was born on August 24, 1937 on the family farm in Kenyon, Minnesota to Lutheran Norwegian parents. Aaker, pronounced "ah – ker", means "field" in Norwegian. Do you notice the similarity to the word "acre"? Neal Aaker, Bernie's dad, wasn't a "field man", however. He didn't like farming so he moved his family to Red Wing, Minnesota, where he became a leather tanner for the shoe factory. Bernie's mother worked there also, gluing souls onto the shoes.

In school, Bernie found himself drawn to the stage right from the first moment he stepped onto the platform at a grade school Christmas program, up to the full play productions of high school. He couldn't get enough of it. If he wasn't performing, he was working backstage or in makeup, absorbing every little detail about the workings of drama. He decided that this was what he wanted to do with his life.

While in high school, the lanky multi-talented kid also participated in speech competitions and vocal music. He found he had a knack for singing and harmonies, so he and three friends formed a singing group. They were good enough that they started getting a lot of bookings for parties and other functions. They went all out and bought themselves matching white dinner jackets. When you purchase uniforms, you mean business.

Bernie, on the far right, and his singing quartet.

There was a radio station in Red Wing and the group was asked to come and sing on some broadcasts. After the performances, Bernie would hang around the station, watching the announcer do his thing. After all, radio broadcasting was much like the theater. The station's owner was taken in by the skinny teenager with the nice deep voice and he offered him a weekend job of helping around the station and even signing on in the mornings. Sunday morning sign-ons were always given to the low man on the totem pole, but Bernie loved it and he leapt at the chance to make some extra money. He wanted to go to the University of Minnesota to study drama and his family couldn't/wouldn't help him with tuition.

Patricia "Patty" Christel from St. Louis Park, Minnesota was interested in drama also, but being more practical she decided on a career in teaching. She enrolled in the University of Minnesota, where she was assigned to a drama class as part of her pursuit of a degree in English and Speech. Patty walked into the University theater one afternoon while rehearsal was going on for a show. The sight of one of the actors on stage struck her. Tall, skinny and good-looking, the man was dressed in pink tights, of all things.

"What kind of idiot," Patty thought to herself, "would dance around in pink tights? What a weirdo!" She had everything she could do to keep herself from laughing out loud at the odd sight.

The man was Bernie, of course, and no sparks flew between the two fellow drama students. Patty even disliked Bernie, thinking he was quite egotistical. But they ran around in the same theater group, going for beers after shows and having weekend parties down at the Mississippi river flats near the campus.

Bernie was too busy for girls at this time. He ran back to Red Wing every weekend in his old beat up Ford to work at the radio station. The Ford had a hole clear through the passenger seat to the chassis. Bernie also did some broadcasting at KEOM, the University's radio station.

Patty was dating a boy named Tom, who also ran with the group. The theater kids were all down to the flats one weekend night partying. There was drinking going on and Tom had gotten himself good and drunk. All of a sudden, laughing and fooling around, Tom picked up Patty and threw her into the river. The river's strong current pulled Patty under and she started to drown, screaming for help. Tom thought she was kidding and he stood on the bank and laughed at her. From out of nowhere came Bernie Aaker to the rescue. Looking like Errol Flynn, both in appearance and in action, Bernie leapt into the cold water, swam to Patty and saved the drowning damsel in distress.

"He was my hero," said Patty Aaker, years later. "He saved my life. I was really drowning."

Bernie refused to let Tom take Patty home that night. From that point on, they were a couple. Their first official date was a movie, of course. Patty had to sit real close to Bernie in the Ford because of the hole in the seat. Maybe Bernie didn't fix it on purpose?

Graduating from college in the early sixties, the couple had to split up. Well, sort of. Patty had accepted a teaching job in San Diego, California and Bernie had enrolled in the famous Pasadena Playhouse acting school near L.A. They had to struggle to get together on weekends with Patty usually driving all the way up to Pasadena to meet Bernie, as he was usually involved in performing for the Playhouse.

Walking together down Colorado Boulevard one night, Bernie turned to Patty and said, "This is crazy, all this driving. You know, we might as well get married."

"What?" asked Patty.

"Sure, you could get a job teaching here and then we'd be together." And that was how smooth and suave Bernie Aaker proposed to Patty.

Catholic Patty knew she had to get married in her parent's church back in Minnesota, so off they went, back home. They married, but Bernie stayed Lutheran, promising to let Patty raise the kids Catholic.

Bernie and Patty Aaker with Simba.

Chapter Fifty-Three
Bernie – Part Two

After a summer in Minnesota, the Aakers went back to Pasadena, California where Patty did find a job teaching and Bernie continued his studies, which included directing and acting in plays. He received the Evelyn C. Hale Award at the Playhouse for "leadership and loyalty".

After Bernie graduated, Patty looked around and thought about raising a family in California. The idea didn't appeal to her. She yearned for the stableness and slower paced life of Minnesota and so she talked Bernie into looking for a job back home.

Bernie receiving the Evelyn C. Hale Award at the Pasadena Playhouse.

Back in the Twin Cities in 1964, nothing came up in the drama field for Bernie, but one day he saw a want ad in the paper for a radio announcer in a little town called Litchfield, Minnesota. Kenny Eidenshink, general manager of KLFD, interviewed Bernie, was rightfully impressed, and he hired Bernie on the spot. Patty, pregnant with Amy, had been raised in the metropolitan area. She didn't want to go off to the "sticks" or the "boonies", but Bernie won out this time and off they went to "farm country".

The Aakers rented a little house at 527 North Ramsey and Amy was born in December of 1964. That March, Minnesota was hit with a devastating blizzard and Bernie had to shovel one day for three hours to get out of the house and get to the station. Patty still wasn't keen on living in the boonies and this was the icing on the cake, so to speak.

There was another Bernie in Litchfield. His name was Bernie Felling and he owned the Fairway store downtown. He also had dark hair and a Clark Gable mustache. When Bernie Aaker would walk down the street, he must've thought, "My, this is a friendly town," because everyone was saying "Hi!" to him and some were even calling him by his name. "Good morning, Bernie!" What Aaker couldn't understand was the occasional "How's the grocery business going, Bernie?" He finally figured it out and had to go to the store to see and meet his double. It wasn't long though, I'm sure, as Bernie Aaker got known in the community, before the tables were turned and Bernie Felling was having people ask him about plays and radio stuff.

Bernie Aaker did everything at KLFD radio. He signed on in the mornings, a stickler for preciseness, he was always on time, then he went out to meet customers to sell ads, came back to the studio to do the noon news, sometimes grabbing a bite to eat at home, went out selling again and then came back to the station in time to do the sundown sign off. That meant he was very late coming home in the summer and early in the winter, if he didn't stay at the station several more hours doing production work, such as recording commercials.

When Eidenshink left the station in February of 1967, Bernie took over as station manager. That meant he would be there even more and home with Patty even less. It got to be too much and he finally told station owner Herb Gross he wanted to step down. Herb then hired Tom Costigan to be the manager.
Around this time, Bernie started butting heads with Gross. He didn't like one of the announcers Gross hired, namely the Mad Hatter. But when Costigan resigned in May of 1971, Bernie, for some reason, took over the managerial duties once again.

"I'm either gonna quit that station," he told Patty one evening after a long hard day at work, "or I'm gonna get fired."

323

"Why don't you quit, then." Patty told him. "Your health is more important than anything else and you'll find work somewhere."

So Bernie did quit and he did find work, managing the Legion Club. One day he was talking to his friend Vern Madson, who owned the *Independent Review* newspaper, the station's advertising revenue rival. Madson knew what a good salesman Bernie had been for the radio station, building it up from its meager beginnings.

"Why don't you come and work for me?" Vern asked Bernie, off the cuff.

"Are you serious?" Bernie inquired.

"Sure."

"I'll do it."

And so Bernie went to work for the enemy in October of 1972, selling ads. I've often wondered how he switched his "spiel" or "selling speech" over to the "other side". Bernie once gave his radio selling speech to me to show me how he did it, from the radio viewpoint.

"How do you walk into a business, Bernie," I had asked him one day when he came into Jim's music store to visit with us, "and convince the owner that he should buy a radio ad instead of a newspaper ad?"

Bernie grabbed Jim's newspaper and set it down on the counter in front of me. Then he slowly turned the pages, closed the paper and handed it back to Jim. He then asked me to tell him about the ads I had seen. I couldn't remember them. None had really grabbed my attention.

Bernie leaned close to my ear and said something like, "Buy a new Ford from Miller Ford. Check out the Back To School Sale at Penney's."

"Now," he said, "Tell me about the 'radio ads' you just heard." He got his point across. "You only see newspaper ads if you are actually looking FOR them. Radio, on the other hand, sneaks into your head." But somehow Bernie must have come up with a reverse spiel. He worked for the newspaper for thirty years so he had to have been good at it. In spite of his association with the paper, however, I still think of Bernie as a radio announcer first and foremost.

After Floyd Warta retired from teaching and from being the high school drama coach, Bernie was asked to take over the directing duties, which he did. One of his first productions was *The Music*

Man. Bernie was asked to share his duties with Keith Johnson, Litchfield's famous band instructor, who had turned the marching band program around into an envied and award winning one. Both men, understandably, had enormous egos. Once again, Bernie was a stickler for preciseness and he insisted on starting rehearsals on time.

During one of the final rehearsals, Bernie was up in the balcony, as was his custom, and Keith was down on the main floor in the "pit" with his orchestra.

"Okay," Bernie yelled to cast and crew. "This is going to be a timed rehearsal. I need to know exactly how long this thing runs. That means we don't stop for anything. It'll be just like a real performance. If you drop a line, if you flub something, if you make any kind of mistake, **you**...**do**...**not**... **stop**... **performing**! Do you all understand? Okay, let's start."

Keith tapped his baton on his music stand, raised the baton in the air and started the Overture. Almost immediately, someone in the orchestra made a mistake. Keith stopped the music.

"Okay," he said, tapping his baton on his music stand a second time, "let's try that again."

Suddenly a booming voice echoed through the auditorium.

"I told you not to stop!" yelled director Aaker.

Turning around and looking up, Keith Johnson yelled back, "And who the hell do you think you are?"

"I...am...God," came back the answer. "Any more questions?"

There were none.

Phil Ross was on the phone talking to Bernie in the summer of 1973. Phil, a professional singer in Minneapolis and a friend of Bernie's from the U of M days, was the husband of Marcia Fleur, KSTP-TV's news co-anchor.

"I've got a non-speaking part in a film Disney is making here for their TV show," Phil was telling Bernie.

"Anyway," he went on, "I heard they were casting a small speaking part too. They're looking for someone who's had more experience in the theater and they're gonna be filming out your way and so I thought of you."

Bernie drove up to the cities and auditioned for and got the part for the television movie *The Footloose Goose*. The movie was filmed for the *Wonderful World of Disney* TV show near Litchfield on the Bird Wing Farm near Star Lake and it aired on March 9, 1975.

Bernie and Phil's part in the movie was filmed at a Minnesota/Canada checkpoint on Highway 89 near Roseau, Minnesota where both men played American Immigration Officers.

In the film, a goose, named "Duke", had hurt its wing and it couldn't fly so it was walking from Canada to its home in Meeker County, Minnesota. In his scene, Bernie watched the goose walk up to the border and he leaned over and asked it, "Where do you think you're going?" It was silly, as was the movie, but it was a speaking part, even if it was only one line. That little scene took three days to film and Bernie got a nice check for it.

Then Bernie landed an acting role in a police documentary training film. He played a drunken driver and the film followed him through the pulling over of his vehicle and the entire arrest. Even though it was make-believe, Bernie felt strange being arrested, booked, photographed, printed and locked up. It all felt so real.

Bernie's mug shot.

Bernie was a perfectionist, as I already wrote, but he was fastidious about his dress also. Bernie always wore a suit and tie or at least a dress shirt and dress slacks.

"He was the only man I ever saw mow a lawn all dressed up," Patty Aaker told me. "He'd be out there mowing in his nice shirt and dress slacks."

Come to think of it, I only saw Bernie once in blue jeans. It was during the seventies' country-western dress fad days, spurred on by movies like *Urban Cowboy*. I can't remember where it was I saw him dressed like that, probably in Central Park, when he was doing some volunteer work, serving pies or something. But he looked so odd in those jeans that the image stuck in my mind. I'm sure he looked in the mirror also and thought, "This is not the Bernie Aaker I want people to know and see."

When Shaw-Allen-Shaw released our second album *South Fork Crow River* in the fall of 1975, we were asked if we'd be interested in doing an "album release" concert for the Litchfield Community Ed department as part of their concert series. We agreed to do it on two conditions. We wanted our good friend Wally Pikal to be our opening act and we wanted the great Bernie Aaker to be our Master of Ceremonies and introduce us. And introduce us, he did. I'll never forget the great booming voice we heard out front as we waited for the curtain to open.

"And now, ladies and gentlemen, here's the band you've been waiting to see. Setting attendance records all over the state, debuting their second album for you tonight, a *legend* in their own time, our hometown boys, I give you Shaw-Allen-Shaw."

"*Legend*?" I'm sure my face was blushing as the curtain opened at the old high school auditorium where I had attended so many pep fests and lyceums. Ironically, Bernie was in the process of creating his own "legend" and this same auditorium we were in that night would one day bear his name: The Bernie Aaker Auditorium. Why? Because of something Bernie and another person had been discussing just a couple of months before.

Chapter Fifty-Four
Bernie – Part Three

Charlie Blesener and Bernie Aaker were sitting over coffee one morning in early 1975. Charlie was Litchfield's Community Ed Director and he was also interested in the theater. The two men started to hatch a plan.

"Let's do a production," Charlie told Bernie. "You direct it. You'll be in charge of everything, you've got the know-how, but I'll do all the business dealings, the grunt work."

"Well..."

"We can do it Bernie," Charlie insisted. Bernie knew that it could be done but he also knew that he would end up doing most of the work.

"Wouldn't it be nice if Litchfield had a community theater?" Bernie asked Patty that evening over supper.

"What are you cooking up now?" Patty asked back.

"Well, Charlie and I were talking this morning and..."

And that's how it started and how Litchfield got its fine community theater. It took a long time to get the theater going from that morning coffee discussion though. Almost two years later, *The Unsinkable Molly Brown* debuted on July 7, 1976. One of the actors was Litchfield's famous high school director and Santa Claus, Floyd Warta. Twenty-five years later, Bernie directed his last play for the community theater. It was *The Music Man*. This time "God" didn't have to deal with Keith Johnson.

One of the musicals performed at the community theater was *Oklahoma*. Rehearsals are always fun in every play because anything can and does usually happen. This musical had its share of odd happenings. Dr. Bill Nolen's daughter Mary and Bernie's daughter Amy had a "fight" scene in the play. The girls really got into their parts and started to get more and more physical during rehearsals, tossing each other around. During a hot summer's night's rehearsal in costume, Amy grabbed Mary and flipped her. When she did, Mary's long 1800s dress went up over her head. Mary ended up on the floor on her back with the dress still over her head and nothing...yes, I wrote nothing... covering the rest of her body. "It was simply too hot," Mary must have thought, "to wear all that other stuff underneath." There was a long moment of silence from the stunned cast and then "God's" unmistakable voice boomed out, "Let's do that again."

John Benson, from Dassel, was a great singer and Bernie loved him. (He sang at Bernie's funeral.) Bernie gave John the lead part of Curly in *Oklahoma*. During dress rehearsal in front of a preview audience, John came out as Curly in the opening scene and sang *Oh, What A Beautiful Morning* as Auntie Eller (Bernie's wife Patty) sat and churned butter. When John got to the line "Everything's comin' my way," his gun and holster slid off his hip and crashed to the floor. The audience roared. Patty, who's back was to Curly, couldn't see what had happened and thought something had happened to her, such as her costume dropping off her front. She frantically checked herself out, trying to stay in character. Nope, it wasn't her. Meanwhile Bernie, the perfectionist, was backstage pacing, unable to yell at anybody...at the moment. Without breaking his character, John merely bent over and picked up his holster, gave the belt an extra cinch and continued on with the scene. But after the show was over John caught holy hell from Bernie for not tightening the belt when he had put it on the first time.

Larry Dahl is quite a character. You need only to look at him to see that he's an imp with his twinkling eyes. He's been in a lot of Litchfield community theater productions. I remember seeing him for the first time there in *On Golden Pond*. Another often seen local actor is Bill Peltier. Both of those actors could be called imps, I suppose. They both loved having fun with their roles and cracking up other cast members. Maybe Bernie should have thought twice about casting the two together, but he did it anyway in a play called *The Foreigner*.

One performance night, Larry came up to Patty back stage and said, "I'm gonna get Bill tonight."

"No, you'd better not do anything," Patty told Larry, fully aware of his past tricks. "Bernie's not in a good mood tonight."

Of course, Larry didn't listen. During the "breakfast scene", Larry's character was supposed to pour orange juice into glasses for himself and Bill's character as they sat facing each other at a table. It was important that the glasses had only a little juice in them as neither character was supposed to go on from that scene until they had downed their drinks, finishing their breakfast together.

Larry poured a little juice into his own glass and then he proceeded to fill Bill's glass to the very brim. Bill looked down and gulped. How in the world could he drink all that juice without holding up the show? Rather than panic, he stayed cool and in character, waiting for his opportunity to get Larry back.

In a minute, the opportunity presented itself. In the scene, Larry's character had to turn away from the table for a few seconds. Bill seized the opportunity and quickly and deftly switched the two glasses. When Larry turned back, he looked down to see the full glass in front of him. He had cooked his own goose. Momentarily panicking, but thinking very quickly, Larry simply reached down, picked up the glass, took a small sip, and then calmly turned again in his seat and tossed the rest of the juice into the potted plant next to the table.

Perfectionist director Bernie Aaker was not amused. Unable to contain his anger and frustration, he just left the auditorium and calmed himself down with a smoke outside.

Bernie in front of a wall containing cast pictures of
all the community theater productions he directed.

Towards the end of 1999, Bernie started complaining to Patty about back pains. Patty sent him off to see "Doc" Cecil Leach. Cecil thought it was a kidney infection and treated it as such. Bernie improved a little but then, in January of 2000, he came out of the bathroom one morning and told Patty he had blood in his urine. It was back to Doc Leach, who sent Bernie to Abbott Hospital to see a specialist named Dr. Utz.

The diagnosis was prostrate cancer.

"We've caught it early," the doctor told Bernie and Patty. He put Bernie on hormone therapy and Bernie was well enough to direct his final play, *The Music Man*, in the summer of 2001. But he kept bleeding, so he went back to Abbott. This time Bernie was told "We'll operate, remove the cancer, and that should be that."

So Bernie went under the knife and he almost died. Something happened during the operation and Bernie started bleeding. The doctors couldn't stop it. Bernie nearly bled to death before the surgeons were able to stop the flow. On top of everything else, the doctors found that the cancer had spread to Bernie's leg bones. Now the pain was going to come. Towards the end, the slightest movement or touching caused Bernie to have excruciating pain. Patty started putting pain patches all over his body.

Coming home from the hospital during Easter time of 2002, Bernie began thirty-nine agonizing radiation treatments and then he lost the use of his legs. He got up one morning and fell to the floor, unable to use his legs. Patty had a hospital bed brought into their living room and that was Bernie's last place on earth.

Bernie, wearing his hat, in his home hospital bed.

On November 20th, Bernie's Lutheran pastor, Reverend Al Bjorkland, came to visit Bernie as he had for so many days. During their talk, he told Bernie, "I believe you are on your final journey, Bernie."

Exhausted, Bernie fell in and out of sleep that morning. Bernie's children had been summoned and each time Bernie woke up he weakly asked, "Is Tony here yet?" He knew that his son Tony was coming that day.

When Tony finally arrived, the two talked for quite a while and then Bernie fell back to sleep. His breathing was labored and loud. I had heard that same sound just before my mother died.

After supper the whole family gathered in the living room to be with Bernie.

"Aren't you all going to bed?" Bernie asked the family.

"No, we want to stay up with you, Dad," someone answered.

"No, I think you should all go to bed."

The family finally relented and went off to various rooms in the small house on 4th Street East. Patty went to her bedroom just down the hall to put on her nightgown. She was going to return and sit with Bernie for a while longer before turning in. Then she heard Suzanne, Tony's wife, whom Bernie called 'Zanne, calling up the stairs to her husband, "Tony, Dad seems awful quiet."

Patty hadn't noticed the quiet, but she came running out of her room to Bernie's side. It was obvious that the final curtain had been brought down on the life of actor/director/broadcaster/loving husband and father Bernie Aaker.

Bernie's funeral was set for 1:30pm a couple of days later. At precisely that time, Pastor Bjorkland announced to the largest crowd to ever attend a funeral in his church, "We'd better get this funeral going and started on time or Bernie will rise up and give us 'what for'!"

"I think Bernie might be spinning in his grave right now," Patty Aaker told me.

"Yeah? Why's that?" I asked her.

"Well, Bernie stayed Lutheran all his life, never changing to Catholic for me. But all our kids were raised Catholic."

"And…" I inquired.

"And," Patty answered. "I buried him in the Catholic Cemetery."

I laughed.

"Well," Patty went on, "I want to be at his side when it's my time."

That sounds logical and loving to me. Logical, precise Bernie approves too, I'm sure.

The Child's Name Is Peace

Where do lyrics or poems come from? Sometimes a writer struggles and searches for words and other times they just pour out of him. The writer has no idea where they came from. That was the way with these lyrics. My older brother Dennie sent me a melody and he asked me to write lyrics for it. I was just trying to put words to his music, which, I guess, spoke to me. I don't normally write religious-type lyrics and this wasn't meant to be a Christmas song, but the child in the lyric was obviously the baby Jesus and the words were about our frugal attempts at peace on earth since His birth.

The Child's Name Is Peace

Lost in the wild stood a beautiful Child
who could make the night turn into day.
The Child has found the way home many times
but doesn't care to stay.

Once when the King graced the earth
and the spring chased the icicles down from the wind,
the Child set out for the Land of the Star
but soon returned again.

Who will give this Child a home?
The Child can't do anything alone.
Down through endless troubled years,
the Child has lived with our fears.

Out in the night then the sky brightens up
when the cannons explode. They won't cease.
The Child will die and the world will soon cry.
The Child's name is Peace.

Chapter Fifty-Five
The Perfect Christmas Gift

What is the perfect Christmas gift? At one time, when I was little, I thought it was a cowboy gun and holster set. But I've learned over the years that it's not always what I've wanted but what I truly needed at a particular moment in time. If I had gone looking for it on my own, I might never have found it.

My mother had several rules concerning Christmas, her favorite holiday, when I was little, growing up in the fifties. I wrote about several of them in an earlier chapter. One of her rules was that my three brothers and I had to buy gifts for each other with our own money. Mom wouldn't finance the gifts for us and she informed us that the gifts we gave to each other had to cost at least a quarter. Two bits. Now this was a goodly sum to little boys growing up without a father in the early fifties. We could spend more if we wanted to, but nobody ever did.

Helen Shaw with her four boys; Mike, Pat, Terry and Dennie.

I strived to find the perfect gift for my three brothers. My two older teenage brothers were easy. I forged a note from Mom and bought them each a pack of cigarettes. It was the perfect inexpensive

335

gift for a teenage boy in the fifties. But, the perfect gift for my younger brother Pat was a different story. I would search for a "neat" but inexpensive toy, a Herculean task.

I eagerly opened my gift from Pat one Christmas, expecting a cheap but "neat" toy back from him. When I had torn off the wrapping paper, I saw in my hands a piece of four inch by two inch white corrugated cardboard with about a dozen or so multi-colored pushpins sticking out of it.
"What the heck is this?" I asked him.
"It's a game," he instructed me with a smug smile on his little face.
"The heck it is. These are just some darned tacks!" I made sure Mom heard the anguish in my voice, trying hard not to say hell and damn in front of her.
"I thought it was a game," Pat said, looking to our mother for support.
"That's OK, honey," she said. "I'll take them back to the store and get your money back. Then you can buy Terry something else. Thank Pat for the gift, Terry," she added, turning to me.
"The heck I will. Darned tacks?"
"I thought it was a game!"
"Tacks?"
"I thought it was a game."

So much for his perfect gift. Pat and I would usually pool our meager savings together and buy Mom a cheap beaded necklace from Whalberg's variety store. Mom loved necklaces with large colored glass jewels on the strands, so we knew it was the perfect gift for her. At least she always got really excited and overly thankful when she opened our "perfect" gift of a gaudy necklace every year. She proudly wore our gift to church each Christmas Eve night. I don't know how many years we gave her necklaces but, once we saw her reaction, she got a lot of cheap jewelry from her four little boys.

My father left my mother and my three brothers and I in 1948, when I was three years old. He left us and gave Mom no support for our care. So our mother, too proud to go on welfare, got a job and went to work. Besides the enormous job of being a mother to four little boys, Mom worked all week and Saturday mornings at the local turkey processing plant, standing on a wet floor cutting oil sacks off the hind ends of the big birds which came by her hanging from a conveyor line.

A woman, who looks very much like my mother, is standing on the line at the turkey processing plant.

On Saturday afternoons, Mom walked across town to clean a local doctor's house and on Sundays, after helping us boys deliver our heavy newspapers, she cleaned Abe's pool hall downtown, cleaning out spittoons and then down on her knees in the filthy bathrooms scrubbing the floors, toilets and urinals. Sunday afternoons and evenings, Mom worked the concession stand at the town baseball games. Somewhere in between all of that, she found time to clean our house, do our laundry, shop for groceries, scrub our dirty faces and cook us simple but wonderful meals.

At Christmastime, things were usually bleak for Mom financially. We always got great gifts, but another Christmas rule of Mom's was that my brothers and I would each get only one-toy gift. The other gifts "from Santa" had to be clothes, except for a small brown bag of candy, nuts and fruit, which Mom always put under the tree for each of us. That tree wouldn't go up until exactly one week before Christmas and it wouldn't go up at all if her four boys didn't pitch in picking it out, pulling it home atop our little red wagon, and then decorating it with large shiny glass bulbs, tinsel, bubble lights (my favorite), strings of popcorn and Angel Hair, which only Mom was allowed to touch and put on the tree because it was made from spun glass.

We would open the gifts from Santa and to each other on the twenty-third of December because of another Christmas rule of Mom's. Mom went "home" every Christmas Eve. That meant we had to be in her hometown seventy miles away, with her mother and father for Christmas Eve Midnight Mass every year. We didn't have a car and Mom didn't drive so getting us there was quite a task for her. Somehow she did it. We never missed a Christmas Eve with Grandma and Grandpa. We had to get scrubbed and dressed up in time to go to the church early, march down the center aisle to the front pew with Mom and sit and listen quietly while the choir sang her favorite Christmas carol, *O Holy Night*.

Mom spent thirteen tough and lonely years after her divorce from my father because she was a devout Catholic and in her heart she believed she was still married to him. But after my absent father died in 1961, Mom met and married a good man named Floyd Young. Floyd was a wonderful stepfather to us and a loving and thoughtful husband to our mother. One of the first things he did, though, was buy Mom a car and teach her how to drive it.

When my brothers and I grew into adults and had families of our own, we always made it back to Mom and Floyd's house every Christmas Eve, just as Mom had taught us to do by her example. She would still have small brown bags of candy, nuts and fruit under the tree, but now they were for her grandchildren, not for us. We'd go to Midnight Mass with Mom and Floyd; early enough so that we could march down the center aisle to the front pew, just as we had done with Mom as little boys, and sit and listen quietly while the choir sang *O Holy Night*.

Mom died from pancreatic cancer in August of 1991. What I consider to be a small miracle happened just nine days before her death. Mom was extremely weak and wasting away from the ravages of the cancer. It was decided to put her into the Emmanuel nursing home in Litchfield in early June. Almost immediately, the doctor told us she was dying and wouldn't make the night. Floyd and I called the priest to come and we also gathered the family to say a final goodbye. Mom was given last rites.

Trooper, that she was, however, Mom rebounded that night and was pretty good for a couple of days. Then she got worse again and slipped into a coma. Florence Casey, P.J.'s wife, was a resident at the home and she would stop by the room every day in her wheelchair and say, "How's your mom today?" Sometimes she'd come into the room and reach under Mom's covers at the foot of the bed and feel her feet. We asked her why she did that and she explained that she had been a nurse. It was her way of checking a patient's terminal condition. She said to us, "It's down to a matter of days."

Dennie had been with us for a couple of weeks but he had to get back to his wife and job in Montana. He sat up with Mom the night before he left in June, hoping he'd be able to talk to her again. But she remained in her coma. About three in the morning, Dennie heard a soft moan from Mom, so he leaned over and started to sing *You're The Reason I'm In Love* softly in her ear, over and over. It was a song he had sung to her as a teenager when she'd yell at him to turn his guitar down. She loved that song and would always "melt down" and turn away. This time it was Dennie who left.

Being a teacher and having my summer's free, I drove to Litchfield from Glencoe every morning and sat with Mom every day, hoping that she would come out of the coma and I could have one more conversation with her. Floyd would come in and sit by the other side of Mom's bed and talk to me, all the while holding Mom's hand, caressing the top of it. She woke up briefly one day and asked Floyd to quit rubbing her hand because it hurt. It hurt Floyd to hear that. Then she slipped back into her coma. We went through June and July and into August like that. Mom stayed in her coma.

On August 16th, I walked into Mom's room only to be greeted by my mother sitting up in her bed. I was stunned. A nurse was in the room and was just finishing what she was doing for Mom. The nurse turned and said to me, "Your mother woke up early this morning and she's even eaten something." Floyd and my stepsister Julie Meis were in the room also.

"Hi Mom," I said to her. "How are you feeling?"
"Feel weak, but okay," she said, conserving her energy.
"Mom, do you know what day it is today?" I asked, wondering what response I'd get.
"Yes," she said. "It's Dennie's birthday."

339

"That's right Mom. You amaze me," I said, truly amazed. "Mom?" I went on. "Dennie was here, but he had to go back to Montana."

"I know." How did she know? She was in the coma the whole time that Dennie was around. I assumed she had misheard me.

"Would you like to talk to Dennie on the phone and wish him a Happy Birthday, Mom?"

"Yes, I sure would."

I reached for the phone and got a shocked and stunned Dennie on the phone, as I held the receiver to Mom's ear.

"Happy Birthday, Dennie," Mom said to her first-born son.

Dennie and Mom talked for five minutes or so. I could hear both sides of the conversation. Dennie told her he had been with her.

"I know, Dennie."

"How do you know Mom? You were in a coma."

"I know. You sang that song to me."

Then Mom said she was tired, we hung up the phone, and she took a nap.

I went home that night feeling better than I'd felt in a couple of months. Was it a miracle or just a coincidence that my mother had come out of her coma on the anniversary of the day she had given birth to the first of her four boys? My joy was short-lived. The next day Mom was back in her coma and there she stayed until August 25th when Floyd and I and my stepbrother Val Young were sitting with her on a Sunday afternoon. We were playing cribbage at the foot of Mom's bed. Her breathing was labored and then suddenly she just stopped. My mother Helen Rheaume Shaw Young had died. Floyd held her head, kissed her and said, "I'll see you in heaven, Helen."

My brothers and I were heartbroken and devastated. After the funeral ceremony, a strange but nice thing happened. A woman walked up to my brothers and I in the church basement and said, "I'm so and so (I can't remember her name). I worked with your mother at the Produce. We were good friends."

We acknowledged what she had told us and thanked her for coming to the funeral and being Mom's friend.

"Your mother was a saint," the lady added. "Now you don't have to pray **FOR** her...you can pray **TO** her." She walked away. What a nice thing to say to us.

Helen
Elizabeth
Rheaume
Shaw
Young

When Mom's favorite time of the year, Christmas, rolled around that year, we were uncertain if Floyd would want to carry on with Christmas as usual, but he told us he did. We all offered to help with the cooking and decorating but Floyd said, "Just come like always. I'll take care of everything."

I pulled my car into his driveway a little apprehensively that Christmas Eve afternoon. Not knowing what to expect inside the house, I loaded my three teenage kids up with gifts and we knocked on the door. Floyd greeted us with a smile and hugs. Then he took off with the kids to help them put the presents under the tree.

"Hi," I said to my brother Dennie and his wife, who had arrived the day before from Montana, and were sitting in the kitchen.

Of course, it didn't feel right in the kitchen that Christmas Eve afternoon. Mom wasn't there for the first time ever, dressed in her apron, standing by the stove.

I walked over to Dennie and quietly said, "How's Floyd doing?"

"Fine," he answered me. "I think he's gonna be all right."

We were still talking when my daughter Andrea came running back into the kitchen and grabbed my hand.

"Come here, Dad. You've got to see Grandpa's tree!" she said excitedly, pulling me by my hand towards the living room doorway.

"I'll see it honey," I said, stopping her. "I'm talking to your Uncle Dennie right now."

"No, Dad, you've got to come and see it, now!"

"Honey, I...oh...okay..." I sighed, looking at her pleading eyes. "I'll be right back," I said to my brother.

Andrea pulled me into the living room and I looked across the room to the tree. Floyd was standing in front of it with his arms around my other two children and I couldn't see what had made Andrea so excited.

"Isn't it neat?" she said, pulling me across the room. Something *was* different about the tree but I couldn't put my finger on it. Some different decorations, maybe? Yes...that was it.

"Isn't it neat?" Andrea repeated quietly, almost reverently, as we finally stood next to the tree. I stared at the tree's new and different decorations.

"It's all your mother's jewelry," Floyd said as he turned to me, referring to all the necklaces of different colored beads and glass jewels all over the tree, many that four little boys had bought for their mother many years ago. It was beautiful. It was perfect. The necklaces looked like they were right at home on that Christmas tree.

Floyd gave my mother thirty years of well-deserved happiness and he couldn't have given her four boys a more perfect gift on our very first Christmas without our mother. In one simple gesture, he showed us his love for our mother and for us and he gave us the perfect Christmas gift, exactly what we needed on our first Christmas Eve without our mother. The gift was given from his heart and it was wrapped in love. His gift showed us that Mom was still with us and would always be with us in our hearts and in our memories each and every Christmas. The rest of that magical Christmas Eve, I found my eyes, blurred by tears, drifting up to that beautiful Christmas tree over and over again.

Floyd died two years later, but we four boys still get together every year around Christmas. Pat has continued Mom's tradition of giving all the grandchildren a bag of candy, nuts and fruit. We raise our glasses and toast Mom and shed a few tears every time we hear or sing *O Holy Night*. And every year at least one of us goes "home" to Litchfield, the little town we grew up in. We go out to the cemetery and put a little Christmas tree on Mom's grave. Then we stand over Floyd's and say another "thank you" for the perfect Christmas gift.

Drawings I've made of Mom and Floyd.

Her Hands

When my mother's mother, Grandma Rose Anne "Annie" Connor Rheaume, died in 1982 at the age of ninety-one, someone found a little piece called "Her Hands" and I was asked to read it at Grandma's funeral. It was about a mother's hands; how they guided a child's first steps, cooked for the family, washed clothes and all the things that mothers do. It touched my own mother deeply that day, so much so that I remembered her comments about it and it stuck with me. When Mom died in 1991, I wrote a different version for her funeral. I share it with you in hopes that you can see your own mother in it and also will learn a little more about mine.

Her Hands

Her hands gave us life.
Her hands changed our diapers and guided our first steps.
Her hands showed us how to pray to God.
Her hands held ours as we walked to the front pew in
    church every Sunday morning.
Her hands pulled our little red wagon all over Litchfield to
    buy groceries for us.
Her hands clothed and fed us.
Her hands wiped away our tears when we fell.
Her hands washed our dirty clothes and scrubbed our dirty
    faces.

Her hands spanked us, when needed, but never touched us in anger.
Her hands were cracked, dry and bleeding with open sores from working at the turkey plant to support us.
Her hands helped us deliver our newspapers on cold, dark mornings.
Her hands covered her ears when an endless stream of Rock and Roll bands practiced in our basement.
Her hands raised four boys all alone until her hands were joined with Floyd Young's hand in Holy Matrimony.
Her hands cooked our favorite foods for us when we returned home for visits.
Her hands wrote volumes of letters and stacks of birthday cards to her children and grandchildren.
Her hands sold cases of candy and pop to hungry swimmers at the Lake Ripley Memorial Park beach.
Her hands fed thousands of school children in Litchfield.
Her hands carried both her cross and ours.
Her hands were held by all who visited her in her last summer at the Emmanuel Nursing Home in Litchfield.
Her hands held her rosary right up to the moment she took her final breath.
Her hands are now holding her parents' hands in heaven

It Wouldn't Be Christmas (Without You)

Mom taught us that Christmas means family and she couldn't and wouldn't celebrate Christmas unless she was together with her family. She believed, as I do, that without the family together you can't have a Christmas. You cannot celebrate Christmas alone. Impossible. At the center of any family is the mother and this lyric was a tribute to my wife, the center of our family and mother and stepmother to our children.

It Wouldn't Be Christmas (Without You)

Christmas brings love
with the gifts by the tree.
But it wouldn't be Christmas
if you weren't with me.

Christmas brings warmth
to a bitter cold heart.
But it wouldn't be Christmas
if we were apart.

Carolers singing Noel harmony
only mean Christmas
if you're here with me.

Christmas brings man peace
from angels above.
But it wouldn't be Christmas
without your sweet love.

A Christmas Tradition Explained

After my story of the perfect Christmas gift to the Shaw boys from our stepfather and my sharing of the Christmas songs that I wrote, I thought there was a need to insert something a little more light-hearted at this point.

Several years ago, I was told a Christmas joke. I thought it was a little crude, but too cute not to be retold. I decided to expand on the joke and rewrite it into a poem for inclusion in my annual Christmas card. Maybe you've heard the joke before, but not in this way. I hope you enjoy it and aren't offended by it.

A Christmas Tradition Explained

'Twas the night before Christmas and at the North Pole,
Santa was stressed! Things had taken their toll.
The worst of it was that the elves were on strike.
They'd said, "Mr. Clause, we want a pay hike!"

The reindeer were playing their "games" once again.
The smell in the air was of eggnog and gin.
Rudolph had slurred, "Let's go for a ride!"
Then they'd raced with the sleigh and smashed up the side.

Mrs. Clause had been crabby and words had been said.
She'd burnt Santa's cookies and he had seen red.
What really burned Santa and made him upset
was that this sad Christmas, he had no tree yet.

Oh, he'd sent Little Angel outside with the chore,
but since then a blizzard had started to roar.
She'd been gone for hours; Santa was pacing.
And drunken reindeer were still outside racing.

Then all of a sudden, there was a loud noise.
The door flew wide open, knocking down toys.
There stood Little Angel. She was quite a sight.
Snow blew in on Santa, turning him white.

She yelled out, "Yo, Fat Man, I'm cold as can be!
Now where do you want me to stick this here tree?"
So look at your tree. See the Angel on pine?
Yep! Santa had replied, "Where the sun never shines!"

Chapter Fifty-Six
The Proposal

    Second marriages are always tough when there's children involved. My first marriage to Linnet Johnson ended in a divorce and I met a woman named Lois Johnson at one of my dance jobs. The "L J" similarity didn't end there. Both ladies had graduated from Willmar High School and, although not friends, they had actually double dated once to the Meeker County Fair in Litchfield, my hometown, before I married either one.

Lois, my current wife, is at the front and Linnet, my ex-wife, is behind her.

    Lois had lost her husband in a car accident and, after a period of time, her friends had taken her out to the Legion Club to hear my band and just get her out of the house. A mutual friend introduced us. Lois and I talked that night and the next time my band was in Willmar, she and her friends were back. I noticed her again on a break and I said, "Hi", not even remembering her name. But, we talked again and over time we grew on each other.

At first we were just friends, until one day, close to Christmas, when I finally got up the nerve up to ask her out. I hadn't asked anyone out for over twenty-five years, so I was rusty and nervous. IN fact I did it "by proxy". I sent her a Christmas card in which I had written that I was interested in asking her out and if she was interested too, she SHOULD CALL ME! Thank God she wasn't as frightened as I was because she called, we dated for a year and, during that time, we fell in love. I decided I wanted to ask Lois to marry me.

My three children were grown and out of the house, but Lois' two children were still in school. They had lost their father in the car accident two years previously and they didn't want to share their mother with anybody new. I knew I had my work cut out for me. I decided that it would be wrong to ask her to marry me and then let her deal with telling her kids. So I took each one of them aside at different times and I talked to them about my intentions and how their lives might change, if at all. I told them that it was entirely up to them. I told them I wouldn't ask Lois to marry me if they both didn't approve and support us.

Amazingly, I was able to get a hesitant "okay" from each one to go ahead with the proposal. I knew I had my own three children's support, but I wanted to show that to Lois also. I came up with an idea that would kill two birds with one stone, asking Lois to marry me and showing her that all of the children supported us at the same time.

On Lois' birthday, we had a "family" dinner at her house. After the meal, I asked Lois to sit in a chair in the corner of the living room. I handed each of the children a big card I had prepared and had told them about. I kept one for myself. The six of us lined up in front of Lois. She thought we were going to do a birthday skit for her. On my signal, each person turned his or her card around, one at a time. Their five cards said, "LOIS" "WILL" "YOU" "MARRY" "ME" and I turned around the "?" card. Stunned, Lois put her hand to her lips, as tears welled up in her eyes.

All of us said, "Well?"
Thankfully, Lois said, "Yes."

My daughter Andrea was dating a boy at that time who I didn't really care for. Something about him bothered me. Just before the proposal, however, I took him aside and asked him to video tape us doing it.

"Sure," he said.

"You know how to run this?" I asked him, handing over the camera.

He gave me a "you've got to be kidding" look and I went off to organize the kids.

After the proposal and all the kids had gone off to do their thing, Lois and I sat down to watch the tape and relive the moment. The boyfriend had forgot to turn the camera on.

There's Always Someone Else

This lyric was written long before my divorce from my first wife and the meeting of my second wife, so I guess you could say I was predicting my own future. The point of the lyric was telling an imaginary friend not to do anything stupid over the loss of a love because in the long run everything in life seems to happen for the final good. I didn't know I was talking to myself. Thanks Terry for the good advice. It came in handy.

There's Always Someone Else

I must have cried a river of tears,
in days gone by.
Over loves I thought I must have
or else I'd die.

Time has proven me to be wrong.
I'll tell you so.
Pain's forgot and love blooms again.
Life goes on, you know.

There's always someone else to mend your heart.
Endings come before new starts.

I know you'll say that your love will last.
I hope it's true.
But if somehow love comes to an end,
don't be a fool.

There's always someone else to mend your heart.
Endings come before new starts

Chapter Fifty-Seven
Three Wedding Songs – Part One

Ever the romantic, I wrote my wife Lois a love song during our courtship. I called it *Lois, My Love*. It starts with those words: "Lois, my love…the hurt has passed." After we decided to get married, we started planning the wedding. We wanted it to be perfect, of course. I hadn't had any input into my first wedding ceremony and I went through it in a daze anyway. I decided I would be totally involved in this one and savor each and every moment.

Lois and I decided to write our own vows and we spent many evenings sitting together trying to come up with the right words. We finally came up with:

> Lois, (Terry), I love, respect and trust you.
> Today, before God, our children,
> our families and friends,
> I, Terry, (Lois), promise to do everything I can
> to never let that change,
> except to continue growing, as it has,
> since the day I met you.
> I will be your partner in life,
> until the day I die.

Three of our combined five children decided to sing a song together and my daughter Andrea asked to sing a solo. Friends pitched in with other prelude songs and instrumentals and then Lois shocked me one day by saying, "You're going to sing my song to me at the wedding."

"Oh no, I'm not," I said. I had never sung by myself in front of an audience before. I had always been in a band on stage, behind the comfort of my drums. I could play guitar but I wasn't that great at it.

"Please sing it for me?" she pleaded. What could I do? I said I would.

My daughter Andrea, who was a theater major in college at that time, told me once that during plays some cast member would do something in each performance that only the cast was aware of, just to be different. If it was thought out and done well, the audience never knew. As our planning continued, I stuck my neck out one night and

I said to Lois, "I'm gonna do something at our wedding that only you will know about. It'll be just our little secret."

"What are you going to do?" she asked nervously. "Are you going to paint HE – LP on the bottom of your shoes?"

"No. Everyone in church would know about it then."

"What then?" she pleaded. "You won't do anything embarrassing, will you?"

"No, I won't, and only you will know that I'm doing it."

"Come on. Tell me."

"Nope, I can't."

I really couldn't. I had no idea what I was going to do. What did I get myself into now?

As the weeks went by, I racked my brain for a good idea, but couldn't come up with one. What in the world did I say that for? One Saturday afternoon I was sitting on my couch at my home in Glencoe alone, watching a college football game while I rehearsed *Lois, My Love* for the umpteenth time. I was still scared to death of singing it. I wanted to make sure I knew it by heart. I knew I would be a nervous wreck at the wedding. Suddenly, an idea came to me. I knew what I could do. Only Lois would know I was doing it and it wouldn't wreck the marriage ceremony.

Rehearsal night arrived. At the appropriate time in the ceremony, I took my guitar and sat down on one of the altar steps. Lois, pretending to hold a microphone as she would in the ceremony, sat across from me on the same step, holding her hand out for me to sing into. "Lois, my love…the hurt has passed…" I began the song. Everything went well.

Wedding day arrived, hot and sunny. A typical Minnesota July Saturday afternoon. I was sweating from nervousness more than from the heat. Lois looked beautiful in her wedding gown. The ceremony was ready to start. Van Johnson and Bobby Krause, the guys in the band I was currently in, came out and sang *Let It Be Me* for the church full of people. When they finished, I came out of a door beside the altar and walked to my place in front of the right row of pews. The procession followed, our children were the groomsmen and bridesmaids, the minister said words, our children sang, and then my big moment came.

Van handed my guitar to me, I said a silent prayer, and Lois and I walked to the appropriate step and sat down facing each other. She smiled at me and held the mike out by my mouth. I strummed a chord on my guitar. Then Lois gasped and her jaw dropped as she heard me sing what sounded like a different song. I got her. Actually it wasn't a different song. I had written an introduction to Lois' song that she didn't know about and had never heard before. Instead of "Lois, my love...", she heard:

> This day has finally come.
> And soon we will be one.
> In front of God, I pledge my love
> and offer you this song....

It was perfect. Only Lois knew what I was doing. Everyone else in the church thought my introduction was always part of the song. The rest of the song goes like this:

Lois, My Love

> Lois, my love, the hurt has passed.
> You weren't my first love, but you're my last.
> You came my way, when I was down.
> Lois, my love, please stay around.

> Lois, my love, young love was sweet.
> But, though we are older, this love's complete.
> You were a lady, right from the start.
> Lois, my love, you've won my heart.
>
> Lois, my love, lady of mine.
> Stay in my heart, all of the time.
>
> Lois, my love, give me your hand.
> You be my woman. I'll be your man.
> Together we'll stay, with help from above.
> And you'll always be Lois, my love.
> Yes, you'll always be Lois, my love.

My mind played a trick on me during the singing of the song, refusing to let me get the upper hand over Lois. Instead of "though we are older...", I sang, "though YOU are older..." to Lois, almost cracking myself up and ruining the moment. But I made it through and Lois and I look at each other and smile every time we hear a playback of our wedding ceremony and my singing of "the wedding song".

The second "wedding song" story concerns my daughter Andrea Bree Shaw Peterson. Many years ago, I was watching a Dean Martin and Jerry Lewis movie on TV. Dean was on stage in a nightclub and he was singing a song with the lyric, "Who's your turtledove? Who's your little whozit? Who do you love?" Jerry Lewis was in the audience and started heckling Dean. I understand that this was how Martin and Lewis actually started in a nightclub out east. Anyway, Jerry was screaming echoes to Dean's lines with his funny high-pitched voice. I started laughing as it developed into a hilarious routine and I got to the point where I had tears in my eyes.

Later that same day when I was bending over to pick up and hold my daughter Andrea, who was about two or three at the time, I went into my version of a Jerry Lewis voice and sang to her, "Who's my turtledove? Who's my little whozit? Who do I love?" I kept singing the song everyday and it became our song, although I slowly changed the lyrics to "Who's my little turtledove? Who's my little whose ya love? Who's my little baby Bree...who's a-peein' on her knee?" It was dumb but she'd giggle.

I kept it up as Andrea got older and then I started telling her, "Some day I'm going to walk you down the aisle and I'm going to sing that song to you on the way to the altar."

"No you're not, Daddy," she'd plead. "Please don't. You'll embarrass me."

"I'm going to. A promise is a promise."

"Please don't."

And so it went over the years. I kept it up for a long time. Finally, in Drea's college years, I let it go and stopped it and then I forgot about it.

Andrea was working at a local bank in Willmar and acting in the play *The Rainmaker* in our local community theater while staying with Lois and I one summer. She, of course, had the role of the daughter who's taken in by and smitten with "the rainmaker" who comes to the family farm. A tall dark handsome boy named Ryan Peterson from New London, Minnesota was playing the part of Drea's older brother. Sparks must have flown between the two because they started dating and then one day Ryan came to me and asked for my little girl's hand in marriage. I told him I would be honored.

Ryan Bruce Peterson

On July 31, 1999, Andrea and I were standing in the back of the Catholic Church by New London, both nervously anticipating the moment we had both dreamed about for so many years. The rest of the wedding party, which included her brother Adrian and sister Christine, was standing in front of us in a line. Occasionally my two other children would turn around and look at Dad and Sis and give us a big smile. Adrian gave Drea a "thumbs up" and a huge grin.

Drea, in her beautiful white wedding gown, had her arm in mine and she turned to me, looked me in the eyes and said, "Do it now, Dad."

"Do what now, Andrea?" I asked, truly not understanding her request.

"You know. Do that song now."

"What song?" I said, and then slowly remembering and surprised by her, I added, "Oh yeah, that song."

My daughter had remembered my special promise to her as a little girl.

"No honey," I said. "I promised you that I was going to sing it to you as we walked down the aisle."

"No, Daddy, do it now."

"Nope."

"Daddy!"

The wedding processional music from Amy Grant's *Jesu, Joy of Man's Desiring* started, Andrea turned her gaze from me to her brother and sister ahead of us as they started to each walk down the aisle.

Adrian and Christine Shaw

Just before our turn came, I reached over and squeezed Andrea's hand, gave her a little kiss on her forehead, and then we started our slow walk, making sure that we both started out on the left foot.

Smiling faces of friends and relatives went by me in a haze as I slowly and nervously walked my daughter towards her future husband Ryan and the altar.

Terry and Andrea Shaw (soon to be Peterson).

About half way down the aisle, I turned to Andrea, leaned my head a little her way and then quietly sang, "Who's my little turtledove? Who's my little whose ya love?"

Drea started crying and I handed my bawling daughter over to Ryan, wiping a few tears away myself as I turned to sit next to my wife in the pew.

Andrea had a daughter on March 18, 2004. She and Ryan named my granddaughter Karra Bree. The first time I saw Karra, I bent down to her tiny little ear and I sang, "Who's my little turtledove? Who's my little whose ya love? Who's my little Karra Bree…who's a-peein' on her knee?" Then I wiped a tear from my eye. Here I go again…

The author and Karra Bree Peterson, who doesn't seem to appreciate his singing of the strange song.

Chapter Fifty-Eight
Three Wedding Songs – Part Two

The third wedding song story concerns some famous people. One of the early Shaw-Allen Trio's regular "gigs" in 1970 was in the Fireplace Room in the old Fireside Inn Restaurant in Willmar, Minnesota. It was a small cozy venue with a tiny stage in a corner. One night we were performing there when someone came up to us on our break, while we were sitting smoking cigarettes, and said, "Do you know who's in the audience tonight?"

"No. Who?" I queried.

"Peter Yarrow from Peter, Paul and Mary."

"Yeah, right," my brother Mick said. Jim Allen's head snapped around quickly as he peered around the room. Peter, Paul and Mary were one of the singing groups Jim idolized. We opened every show with their version of *Pack Up Your Sorrows*.

A more recent picture of Mary Travers,
Paul Stookey and Peter Yarrow.

"He's right," Jim hissed through his teeth. "I see him sitting over by the door."

The unmistakable mustached, and starting to bald, head of the glasses wearing musical legend was indeed at a small table with a beautiful dark-haired woman.

Peter Yarrow

"Do you know who the lady is?" our informant went on.

"No, who?" I asked, expecting to be told she was some famous actress or something also.

"That's Mary Beth McCarthy, the daughter of Doc (A. M.) McCarthy from Willmar. Her uncle is Senator Gene McCarthy."

Now my head snapped back towards the couple. Born in Watkins, Minnesota, "Clean Gene" McCarthy was one of my heroes. Minnesota's peace loving, kind, gentle and honest Senator had run for President of the United States in 1968. I voted for him, although he didn't have a prayer running against the polished political machineries of fellow Minnesota Democrat Hubert Humphrey or that of Richard Nixon. Now he was campaigning to get back into the Senate.

"Why would Peter Yarrow come and listen to us?" I wondered out loud.

"Well, he and Mary are gonna get married after the first of the year," our visitor informed us. "Maybe he's checkin' out bands for the wedding reception."

I don't know if that was why Peter was there that night with Mary but all three of us were too scared to even go over to meet him and ask for an autograph. We also figured that Peter would prefer to remain in the background and not be bothered by us lowly beginning artists.

Nevertheless, when we got back up on stage, we were all as nervous as hell and we kept watching for Peter's reactions to our music. He and Mary finally got up and left sometime during our third set.

I had just finished a half hour "set" at the Lake Avenue Cafe in Spicer, Minnesota in late August of 2004. The restaurant had an "open mike" night every Thursday and I had been asked to come over and sing. I had played my guitar and sung some 50s and 60s songs by myself.

Dr. Bill Hagen, a musician himself who was the "Master of Ceremonies" that night, came up to me when I got off the little platform stage.

"Say, if you got a moment, there's a lady here that would like to meet you," he said.

"What? What's this about?" I asked. I wasn't into "meeting" ladies, especially with my wife Lois sitting at a nearby table with friends.

"No," Bill said, understanding my misunderstanding. "She really liked the music you did and asked me if I could introduce you to her."

We strolled over to the table by the rear wall of the restaurant and Bill introduced us.

"Terry Shaw, I'd like you to meet Mary Yarrow."

"Yarrow," I said, reaching out my hand to the woman, "as in Peter Yarrow?"

"Yes, the same," the gray-haired woman said, shaking my hand. "I really enjoyed your singing tonight," she went on.

"Thank you. I appreciate that," I said putting my hands on the edge of her table and leaning forward. "I sang for you once before," I added and then I told her about the night in the fall of 1970 at the Fireside. She remembered the evening and the Shaw-Allen name and we chit chatted for five minutes. Mary told me she was still friendly with Peter, even though they were divorced, and that she was still living in New York and just home visiting friends and relatives. Actually Mary was home because her father was ill. After I ran out of things to say, I excused myself to get back to my wife and get up and do another "set".

Two nights later I was playing drums with our little church band at a private party for Willmar's elite. We had auctioned off our band's services for charity and the party's hosts had won the bid. It had been a lawn party under a giant tent by a lake and the band had just finished playing and we had packed up. Some of us, including our wives, had strolled back into the party to have some wine and eats when who should I run into but Mary McCarthy Yarrow again.

"Why Mary," I said. "I didn't know you were here."

"Oh yes. I enjoyed your music again. This time, you're on the drums. You are talented."

"Thank you."

I introduced my wife to Mary and we chit chatted again.

"Say Mary, as long as I have you cornered, so to speak," I said to the wine sipping lady, "can you answer a question for me that I've wondered about for years?"

"Sure, what is it?"

"Well, I heard a story that *The Wedding Song (There Is Love)* was written for your wedding to Peter. Is that true?"

"Yes, it is," Mary informed me.

The nuptial classic, written by Noel Paul Stookey, the Paul of Peter, Paul and Mary, may be the most popular wedding song ever written, other than the *Wedding March*[82] ("Here comes the bride..."). The first verse of Stookey's song is:

He is now to be among you at the calling of your hearts.
Rest assured this troubadour is acting on His part.
The union of your spirits, here, has caused Him to remain.
For whenever two or more of you are gathered in His name,
there is Love. There is Love.[83]

"Paul wrote the song as a gift for Peter and I," Mary went on, "and the first time it ever was performed was at St. Mary's Catholic Church in Willmar, Minnesota."

"Wow," I said, truly impressed. "I'd heard that also."

"Yes, and he played it on a very strange instrument. It was kind of like a mandolin, only it had an odd shape, like the old troubadours used in the Middle Ages," Mary continued on, sensing my interest. "Immediately, Paul started getting requests for the song to be used at other weddings and for him to record it, but he refused, saying, 'That song was my wedding gift to Peter and Mary Beth and it belongs to them now, not to me'."

---

[82] Written by Felix Mendelssohn.
[83] ©1971 Public Domain Foundation

"Peter told him it was too beautiful a song and it had to be put out for the public to hear and use," Mary finished her story, "so Paul said 'Okay, but we'll turn over all the rights to a charity'. And so that's what we did."

With the royalties, Paul set up a foundation called the Public Domain Foundation, Inc.[84]

"Over the years," Mary told me, "that song has earned millions of dollars for the foundation helping many, many people."

Now, that's a gift a little above a toaster, wouldn't you say?

---

[84] The foundation is set up to help new artists learn their craft, to help them write and sing songs with a social and political significance, to support other charities and to give counsel to budding artists.

Thank My Lucky Stars

I feel fortunate and grateful for each and every girl or woman on God's green earth who's ever told me and shown me that she loved me. Believe me, it's a short but treasured list. I'm appreciative of those sweet females because of my shyness and my low self-esteem, which has taken a lifetime to get over. I wrote about my appreciation in a song lyric. The "poetic gods" were with me when I did the writing because I think I came up with some clever rhymes.

Thank My Lucky Stars

She wakes me up with just her kisses.
She leaves the room. I hear the dishes.
And I guess I'm superstitious
'cause I knock on wood
and thank my lucky stars
that she loves me.

She answered all my dreams and wishes
when she became this mister's misses.
And I guess I'm superstitious
'cause I knock on wood
and thank my lucky stars
that she loves me.

Guess you'd say I'm mighty lucky and I know
that I won't disagree.
'Cause she's mine and she's so pretty.
And I know I'm fortunate to have that girl.

A lover's song, that's all that this is.
My love for her is so ambitious.
And I guess I'm superstitious
'cause I knock on wood
and thank my lucky stars
that she loves me.

Chapter Fifty-Nine
Some Unattached Thoughts

A Litchfield nurse friend of mine and I were talking about births at the Meeker County Memorial Hospital and she told me a few unbelievable stories. One of her fellow nurses was called out of the hospital to assist a large woman who had given birth on the way there. The nurse had to return to the hospital to get a scissors. It seems the baby had gone down the pant leg of the woman and the pants couldn't be taken off with the baby inside.

Of course there were stories of woman who couldn't or wouldn't believe that they were in labor.
"I can't be pregnant!" a slow-witted woman exclaimed. "All I've ever done was kiss a man."
Or the woman who insisted that she was just having an appendicitis attack. Informed she was in labor, she said, "That's funny. The same thing happened to me five years ago."
The saddest story was about the woman who came in holding a filthy baby. She told the nurses that she had to give birth in the barn because her husband wouldn't let her dirty up the house with the chore.

About births... My first grandchild's arrival, my grandson Ethan, had prompted me to write *Terry Tales*. I wanted to leave my stories for him and any descendants that followed. My second grandchild, Karra Bree Peterson, came in the spring of 2004 and her birth brought memories back to me of the birth of my own children, two girls and a boy. I thought I had some wisdom on the birth of a daughter that I could pass on to my son-in-law, Ryan Peterson. I decided to share with you what I shared with him. Here's my letter:
Ryan,
An old French saying is that "Daughters are the flowers of the home." Your life has now officially changed like you never thought it could. Your love for your son Ethan will never change, but this is going to be different. The Irish saying, "My son's my son 'til he finds him a wife, but my daughter's my daughter for the rest of her life" is not really true about the son, but it tells a little about the father/daughter relationship.

You will now know why Andrea means so much to me and why you had a funny feeling in the pit of your stomach when you came and asked me for her hand in marriage. (Thank you again for doing that. I hope someone asks you that same question someday.)
   When Karra walks out that door with her first date, a little piece of your heart will rip out of your body and go with her. You'll be quicker to run to her when she falls than you were with Ethan. All it means is that she is your daughter...and it's different.

Terry

   Karra Peterson was not only my second grandchild, but she is also my sixth cousin, twice removed. It turns out my parents, Helen Rheaume and Florian Shaw, were third cousins, legal but a little odd for 1941 when they married. It was quite common in the 1800s, I found. Mom and Dad shared the same great-great grandfather, Dennis Connor, who was born in 1785 and lived in Latrobe, Pennsylvania. My wife and I went out there a couple of years ago and found the house that he built. It looked identical to an old black and white photo I found in a Connor genealogical book except there was an antenna on the roof.
   Anyway, with my parents being third cousins, that made my brothers my fourth cousins, I was my own fourth cousin and my parents were my fourth cousins, once removed. Confused? It also made my children my fifth cousins, once removed, and my grandchildren my sixth cousins, twice removed. Yes, I know there's a song called *I'm My Own Grandpa*. I used to sing it to my students all the time, after giving them a genealogical lesson. I now sing it to the nursing home residents.

   Speaking of grandparents, they usually hold a special place in our heart. We get grandparents when they have mellowed out in life, they're not struggling so hard to make it anymore, they've accumulated both time and money and they spend both on us, their grandchildren. How can we not love them dearly? And, of course, Grandmas...Grams...Nannas...,whatever you called yours, are extra special. They always had a warm hug and a kiss and a great homemade cookie behind their backs or in the cookie jar. After my grandparents died, I was fortunate to get my Grandma Rose Ann's cookie jar.

If you think back about the image of your Grandma, working in the kitchen, or tidying up in the living room, or outside in the garden, she probably has an apron on. My grandma always did. An anonymous person wrote the following paragraphs about grandmother's aprons and I'd like to share it with you.

"The principle use of Grandma's apron was to protect the dress underneath, but along with that, it served as a holder for removing hot pans from the oven; it was wonderful for drying children's tears, and on occasion was even used for cleaning out dirty ears. From the chicken-coop, the apron was used for carrying eggs, fussy chicks, and sometimes half-hatched eggs to be finished in the warming oven. When company came those old aprons were ideal hiding places for shy kids; and when the weather was cold, grandma wrapped it around her arms. Those big old aprons wiped many a perspiring brow, bent over the hot wood stove. Chips and kindling-wood were brought into the kitchen in that apron.

From the garden, the apron carried all sorts of vegetables. After the peas had been shelled it carried out the hulls. In the fall it was used to bring in apples that had fallen from the trees. When unexpected company drove up the road, it was surprising how much furniture that old apron could dust in a matter of seconds. When dinner was ready, Grandma walked out on the porch and waved her apron, and the men knew it was time to come in from the fields for dinner. It will be a long time before anyone invents something that will replace that old-time apron that served so many purposes."

I was driving with my wife in Willmar and I saw a local beauty salon's sign. The name of the place was Hair We Are. I was mildly amused at the "punny" name and I thought about all the clever names I had seen on beauty parlors over the years. Why is it that just the hair salons have clever names? Doesn't it seem that way? Anyway, I thought I would list a few of the names I've uncovered for you, just in case you share my "pleasure" in their cleverness. The first one on my list is Shear Pleasure in Montevideo. Then there's Hair It Is, A Cut Above, Bangs For The Memories, The Mane Event, Hair Apparent, The Hair Port, Hair and Beyond, Just Cut Loose, Prime Cuts, Shear Delight, Upper Cuts, Curl Up & Dye, Deb On Hair, Dye Hard, Hair Raisers, Hair To Please You, Heads Up, Just Teasin', The Best Little Hair House, To Dye For, Scissors Palace, Hair To Stay, Blood Sweat & Shears, Combing Attractions, Hairway to Heaven, The Hair After,

Hair Ye, Hair Ye, Hair We Go Again, Get Your Locks Off, Hair 'Em, Cuts Both Ways, Hairobics, and finally...Hairborn. Mine would have to be Hair Today, Gone Tomorrow.

My wife and I were doing some closet cleaning, digging out clothes we hadn't worn for a year or so and piling them up to take to the Willmar Goodwill store. Our collective eyes fell to the floor of our closets onto all the shoes we had accumulated. Lois said, "I've never even worn some of those." The same was true for me because a friend had given me a bag full of fairly new athletic shoes. He was a school custodian and came across dozens of pairs each summer when he cleaned out school lockers. Then I had half a dozen sandals. For some reason, we had trouble parting with the shoes, unless they were obscenely out of style (in Lois' case only).

In my book research, I came across an article in the February of 1943 *Independent Review*. It was about rationing during World War II. Each family was limited to three pair of shoes per member per year. It makes you think a little about our parents' sacrifices for our freedoms. They were always visible to us Boomers.

An observation I've made over the years is that for a long time four items have always been the same price, until recently, that is. Each of the items cost 30¢ when I was a kid. A loaf of bread, a gallon of gas, a half-gallon of milk and a pack of cigarettes. In the seventies it went up to 60¢ and then to $1.00 in the eighties. In the nineties, cigarettes took off. Good. After starting smoking in the seventh grade, I quit in 1976 and today I hate the smell of it. But now gas and milk have soared ahead at over $2.00 and a loaf of bread has caught up to the cigarettes at $2.50.

Speaking of gas and cigarettes, it doesn't take a rocket scientist to figure out that the two don't mix. Recently, I was filling my tank up at a station in Fargo. As I went to get the windshield wash squeegee, I smelled a cigarette. I looked over at the guy filling his tank from the other side of my pump. He had the gas nozzle held into his tank with one hand and a burning cigarette in the other.

"Hey!" I yelled at him. "Get that damned cigarette out. You want to kill us both?"

He looked at me and then at his cigarette and then at me again.

"Oh, sorry," he said, moving to the rear of his car. "I'll stand here."

"Like hell you will," I informed him. "You'll put that out."

"When I'm done."

"Now!" I said approaching him with my dripping squeegee, "Or I'll put it out for you."

"Go to hell."

I turned on my heels, opened my car door and said to my wife, "Call 911. An idiot is smoking next to the gas pump."

"It's out," he yelled at me.

"Don't you know that's against the law and you could be fined $10,000?" I said to the fool. "I don't care if you kill yourself, but there's other people here."

"You're right, I'm sorry," he apologized. The sad thing is that this wasn't the first time that I had to remind somebody about cigarettes at the gas pump.

My brother Dennie worked for the Avon Company as a Division Manager for many years. He traveled a lot and flew into Minneapolis often, which afforded him a chance to rent a car and drive out to Glencoe to see me. One day we were sitting at the dinner table talking about teachers' salaries and vacations and benefits. He was totally in the dark about the whole thing, as I think most people are, thinking teachers get paid a year's salary and only work nine months. Anyway, Dennie, quite seriously, asked me, "What do you get as your Christmas bonus each year?"

"Christmas what?" I spat out.

"Bonus. Don't you get a Christmas bonus?"

"No. Are you kidding?" I scoffed. "Why, what do you get?"

"Well, I..." he stammered. I could see he was embarrassed for putting his foot in his mouth. He wasn't one to play one-upmanship with me concerning jobs. He realized that teaching was a noble but underpaid profession.

"I...I...," he continued, "this year I got $1500 and we had a big dinner party at a hotel."

"Well, here's what I get Dennie," I said, leaning forward and getting into my educating mode. "The school board's wives bake some cookies and invite us to the school library one afternoon before Christmas break for a cup of coffee and a cookie. Merry Christmas."

"Oh," he mumbled.

The two of us were sitting at Mom and Floyd's house sometime later, finishing up one of Mom's great meals. We were telling stories and jokes and I broke into the conversation with, "Wanna hear something funny? Dennie was asking me about my Christmas bonus and…" I went on telling my story, expecting a good laugh from Floyd for my effort.

"Ha," he said, when I finished my story, but the "Ha" was not said in a laughing manner. "You know what we city street maintenance workers get every year?"

"No," I replied, expecting to hear Floyd come back with some small figure.

"Well, the mayor gives all the department heads a box of candy and Louie[85], (Floyd's boss), comes around to each of us in the shop and holds out the box and says, 'Here, have a piece of candy.' That's what I get every year, IF I'm around the shop when he's passing around the box."

"Oh," I mumbled.

I enjoy messing with people's minds. One of my pet peeves is over friendly store clerks, whom I know are just doing their jobs, but they still drive me crazy. I just want to browse without having to be shuffled around and shown this and that.

One day Lois and I were shopping in the men's clothing section of a department store.

"Hello," a small twenty-ish store employee said to me, approaching me through the round racks of shirts and sweaters. "Do you have any questions, sir?"

"Yes," I answered her, "what's the capital of North Dakota?"

She looked at me for a few seconds, and then turned on her high heels and left.

"Good," I said to my chagrined wife, "maybe I can shop in peace now."

"That wasn't very nice," Lois reminded me.

"Yeah, but…" I had nothing to say for myself.

Later we were standing in the checkout line with our purchases, when I felt a tap, tap on my shoulder. I turned around to face the little female whom I had chased away a half hour earlier.

"Is it Bismarck?" she asked me, with a proud smile on her face.

Touché, my dear.

---

[85] Louis E. Nelson, head of the Litchfield Public Utilities Department.

Chapter Sixty
Pete Hughes

I was sitting in the G.A.R. Hall in Litchfield in my usual spot at a small round table surrounded by the shelves full of old newspapers. It was the summer of 2002 and I was researching my book *Terry Tales*. I heard someone enter the building and I saw Cheryl Almgren leave what she was doing and walk towards the front door to greet the arriving guest. That's how everyone who enters the Hall is treated, as a guest.

I went back to my work, but I could hear Cheryl talking to someone as they both came walking through the Hall and into the museum part of the building, the part where I was working. Behind Cheryl was a balding, plump, red-faced jovial looking guy with a white goatee beard. An Irish Santa Claus? I didn't recognize the man but he recognized me immediately and walked over to my table.

Peter Allen Hughes

"Hi Terry," he greeted me. "Whatcha doin' here?"
"I'm researching a book," I replied to the man giving him a "Do I know you?" look.
"A book? Great. What's it about?"
"Litchfield. It's stories about growing up here in the fifties and I'm adding a history of every downtown building."

"Fantastic," he exclaimed, pulling out the chair across from me and sitting down. Then it dawned on the man that I didn't know to whom I was talking.

"You don't remember me. I'm Pete Hughes," he said throwing a chubby hand out across the table. "Grew up not too far from you."

"Oh yeah," I said, vaguely remembering the name, shaking his hand. "I thought you looked familiar," I added, lying through my teeth.

I knew a Pete Hughes growing up. He was three years younger than me so we didn't pal around with each other, although his cousins lived near me. Could this be the same guy? The Pete Hughes I knew was thin with a thick head of red curly hair.

"What are you doing here, Pete?" I asked, mildly interested.

"Oh, I'm picking up a couple of books they sell here about Meeker County history. I'm looking for some pictures of the old schools here and stuff."

"Oh yeah? I've got some that I could share with you."

Pete and I settled into a nice long conversation about Litchfield, our mutual friends in town like the Wimmers, whom he was also related to, and more about my book project. He told me what he'd been doing for the last forty years or so. I was genuinely interested by this time. He knew all about me and what I'd been doing.

"My wife is a big fan of your band, Shaw-Allen-Shaw," he told me.

"Oh, she must be old," I said, laughing at my standard joke to people who remember that band.

Pete hung around for a couple of hours and even though I wasn't getting any work done, I really enjoyed our visit. He finally stood up and said, "Well, I've got to get going. I was only gonna stop here for a couple of minutes."

He did his business with the ladies, buying a book and then he came back to the table to say goodbye.

"Where do you live?" I asked him.

"Albert Lea, but I'm on the road a lot."

"Wow, that's some drive you've got ahead of you," I said, getting up to follow him to the door. We stood and talked some more at the door and finally said our goodbyes.

That was the start of our friendship. It was odd, because we grew up in the same town just blocks from each other, both went to the same school and we never were friends before. That's what the difference of three years in age means when you're a kid.

Pete came back to the Hall often, always wanting to talk about my book and give me information. We emailed each other almost daily from that point on and Pete sent me really long letters giving me great stories for the book. He had worked at both the old hotel and Greep's department store. He knew a lot of people and a lot of stuff. I told him, "I'm putting some of your stuff in my book almost verbatim, if you don't mind. It's great."

"Mind? Heck, I'd be honored," Pete told me. "Say, I know so and so and you should call him and get some more information. As a matter of fact," he'd always say, reaching into his pocket, "here's some phone cards so it won't cost you anything."

Pete sold phone cards in his business and he gave me a hand full of cards every time I saw him. He was always giving me things, emailing me pictures or stories or calling me.

I found out in our conversations that Pete had been in Vietnam and had health problems, which were never in evidence that I could see. He said that he had a whole planeload of Agent Orange dropped on him and that's what caused his problems. One of his problems was depression, which, again, I never saw. He was always so upbeat and laughing about things.

Pete was working on a book himself with the histories of Litchfield schools in it. It was also a school lunch cookbook. The book was for his upcoming class reunion. Pete came across handwritten recipes that my mother had written out and used as head cook at the Ripley Elementary School.

"I'll give them to you when I'm done with them," he told me.

In his quest for pictures, Pete discovered original glass plate negatives of really old pictures of buildings in Litchfield. The city hall had them and Pete got hold of them and had three sets of prints made at his own expense. He gave one set to the G.A.R. Hall, one to me and kept one for himself.

He turned his set and some other pictures of Litchfield over to an artist in Albert Lea whom he commissioned to make drawings of our downtown buildings. When the drawings were finished, Pete and the artist arranged them into a collage and had them printed on large poster paper suitable for framing.

"We're doing a limited edition of the prints," Pete told me. "They'll all be numbered and signed."

"Great," I said, anxious to see it, thinking it would've made a great back cover for my book.

Pete's poster.

"I want to give you a print," Pete said to me. "I promised print number one to someone else, but you can have any other number you want."

"Gee, you don't have to do that, Pete," I told him. "I'd be glad to buy a print."

"No, I want you to have one."

"Well, gee...thanks a lot. I'll take number sixty-three, the year I graduated."

"Okay, it's yours."

When I was having trouble with my printer in New York, getting books shipped to me on time, Pete called them up and spoke with them, trying to help me. He knew a lot about printing and he rattled the New Yorkers who thought they were talking to a mid-western farmer. That's the kind of guy Peter Allen Hughes was.

Pete could and would talk to anyone to find out about him or her. He loved to talk and learn. His wife Dar told me, "He was a unique individual and certainly could talk to anyone about anything, anytime! He would talk to people in line at the airport as we wound our way through security lines. And, of course, at every turn through the winding line, there was a new face, so he was in his glory. No matter where someone else was from, Pete knew someone or something about that place."

On Monday, December 29, 2003, suffering from the depression brought on by his medical problems, Pete Hughes shot himself. In doing that, Pete left a huge void in our world. All of us, who knew him and loved him for the great friend he was, now have an empty space in our hearts that Pete Hughes had occupied. Litchfield lost one of its biggest supporters and the city lost the countless things Pete would have done in the future for his beloved hometown. Pete's wife Darlene "Dar" lost a wonderful life partner and his kids Tony and Bridget lost a super dad. I understand his funeral at St. Theodore Catholic Church in Albert Lea was the second largest ever attended in that church.

Dar told me some things about Pete's "consideration" for his family, if I can call it that, before he took his life. He got important papers together with instructions and laid them out for Dar to find. Then he went out and sat in their old van instead of their two newer

377

vehicles. Pete left a letter for his family with the following poem, which I assume he wrote. It sounds like Pete. Dar wanted me to share it with you.

> "Remember me with laughter and cheers
> because that is how I will remember you all.
> If you remember me with sadness and tears,
> then don't remember me at all."

I miss you Pete. Thank you again for everything you did for me. Friends like you are very rare and I wish I had become yours much sooner in my life. I feel that I missed a lot by not being your friend until a later time in both of our lives. But I treasure the two years I had with you. I think you would've enjoyed helping me with and reading the stories in this book.

As instructed, I will remember you with laughter and cheers, but forgive me if I also throw in a few tears.

Myself

I've always been shy. I put on a great front (I call it acting) when I speak in front of a group or meet new people. But inside, I'm going crazy. I've heard that most actors are really shy. They pursue an acting career to hide behind a "mask" of another personality. I wrote these lyrics to tell of my problem.

Myself

You would think that by this time
I'd have it all together.
I should have learned enough to face
all kinds of stormy weather.
But when the voices criticize,
I hide behind a false disguise
and lie, like before,
and die a little more.
And make my life a little less
than dreams I've had, I must confess.
It' silly but it's so.
You would think that I could show…myself.

You would think I'd be at ease
when making conversation.
Others, who can hold their own,
I hold in admiration.
But unlike Jekyll's "Mr. Hyde",
my truer self is held inside.
I become just what you want
by putting on a front.
And, acting out a script of lies,
I disappear before your eyes.
It's silly but it's so.
You would think that I could show…myself.

Why am I afraid
to show you what I've made?
I'm only what I've made…
made out of
myself.

Chapter Sixty-One
The End

Digging through the old newspapers at the Meeker County Historical Society, I came across an interesting article in a local newspaper from January of 1918. It was about a man named G. H. Lockwood who was an art teacher in Kalamazoo, Michigan. He had grown up in Litchfield, played in the band, and moved away in 1888. Coming back thirty years later to visit his sisters, Mrs. Charles H. Dart and Mrs. Cora Quinn, Lockwood wrote a poem about the experience. He took the reader of the poem on a walk around town and talked about the different stores and buildings. I started to feel a little strange reading this. You see, I was an art teacher who played in a band, left Litchfield around 1970 and returned about thirty years later in 2001 to research my book *Terry Tales,* turning pages of books and old newspapers in the G.A.R. Hall. In my book, I took the reader on a walk around town to tell him or her about the different stores and buildings. Reading the article and Lockwood's poem made the hair stand up on the back of my neck.

Readers of my book *Terry Tales* and Litchfield historians will recognize the stores Lockwood wrote about in his poem: Revell's drug store, Mrs. Cary's millinery, the Harris drug, the Howard House, the Ledger office, the Court House, the Peterson brothers' candy shop, Olson's music store, and Mrs. Koerner's butcher shop.

Other stanzas in the poem are eerily as if Lockwood or I had written them about Litchfield just the other day. I feel they are an appropriate finish to my second "love letter" about my hometown, Litchfield, Minnesota.

I glance up and down main street now.
Just here and there I find
some building that is standing yet,
and old memories bring to mind.

The bandstand in the park is new.
The park, it looks like ever.
'Twas there in the band I used to play
and thought myself quite clever.

The G.A.R. Hall, still intact,
sad memories 'round it linger.
Right here I turn the pages back
with silent trembling finger.

Old Litchfield town, I'm glad
I've had a chance to greet you.
And you, my old friends, I am glad
at last, once more to meet you.

But even tho' I'm far away,
for my boyhood home I'll ever
have kindly thoughts, and I am sure
that I'll forget you…never.

                                        G.H.L. 1/2/1918

Thank you Mr. Lockwood. I feel exactly the same.

Terry Tales 2 Appendix

The History of Downtown Litchfield: The Next 30 Years

1970-2000

Author's note: To continue on with the history of Litchfield and its downtown stores, I will use my same "walk uptown" from my Swift Avenue North home that I used in my first book. With each site, I will give the first occupant of the site and the occupant most known by people of and around my generation before I pick up with the 1970's resident. I will also indent with a new paragraph whenever the new occupant was in a following decade.

I've included the present building address number to give you a general idea where the old stores were. You must know, however, that Litchfield had a couple of different numbering systems for their streets in the very early days and before the time of World War I. Before the turn of the century, for example, stores in what we know as the 200 block of Sibley Avenue had double-digit numbers in the 40s. DeCoster's store (Smith's Appliance), for example, was 42 Sibley Avenue North and Judge Harris' confectionery (vacant today) was 46 Sibley Avenue North.

Around World War I, the 100 block of downtown was numbered in the 800s, the 200 block was in the 700s and the 300 block, across from the park was in the 600s. The numbers also ran in the opposite direction. For example, the Sibley Antiques corner was 831-833 Sibley Avenue North, instead of 100 Sibley, and Nicola's corner was 801 instead of 134 Sibley Avenue North.

114 Third Street West. Heading east from our house on Swift Avenue North up Third Street West, I passed the old power plant on the south side of the street (gone today). Across the street, on the north side, was Andy Anderson's blacksmith shop. Andy's father, Hans Christian Anderson, started blacksmithing in Litchfield in 1904 at the corner of Miller Avenue and Second Street. Hans built a new shop here opposite the old power plant. His son, Andrew L. "Andy" Anderson, reopened the shop at this location in May of 1939 after

Hans had died. At some time, the shop here was torn down and a residential house was erected on the site.

In 1984, Litchfield Cablevision moved its office into the house.

Today the location is the house to the west of the drive-thru for the Center National Bank, which is at the northeast corner of the block.

301 Ramsey Avenue North. The Okesons' house was at the northwest corner of Ramsey Avenue and Third Street where the Center National Bank is today.

First Bank Center, the old First State Bank, moved here in May of 1978. The name was changed to First Bank Central at some time.

In July of 1987, CNB Financial Corporation, headed by Vern Smith and Bob Sparboe, bought the bank and the name was changed again to Center National Bank.

526 Ramsey Avenue North. In March of 1946, the bottling plant of the Litchfield Bottling Works was moved to its new building here.

Today Doug's Auto Repair is at this location.

227 Ramsey Avenue North/111 Third Street West. C. M. Tileston's roller rink was once at the southwest corner of Ramsey Avenue and Third Street starting in January of 1885, on the lot where the paper shack ended up (near the old power plant).

Today the Litchfield Fire Department is at this location.

221 Ramsey Avenue North. To the south of the lot, where the present VFW Post 2818 is located, was almost always a seed business. Oren Wilbert "Bert" Topping bought the old office of the Flynn & Bros. farm machinery business and moved it here in September of 1884 after he had bought lots 23 through 26 of this Block 60.

Walter Wogenson owned the seed/feed business here in the late fifties and early sixties until he went out of business.

Then the Admiral Benson VFW club bought the site in May of 1965 and started building their new club here in November. The building was completed in March of 1967. The VFW had been on Depot Street in the fifties, but met in the GAR Hall until 1943, then in the Community Building.

217 Ramsey Avenue North. A gas station went up in February of 1931 to the south of the present VFW. Joe Baden owned it and he sold "Lightning" brand gasoline for 16¢ a gallon.

The location is a part of the VFW building today.

213 Ramsey Avenue North. There was an alley to the south of the service station and after it was a small building which housed the Quinn (Tom) & Reitz (Fred) cigar factory in April of 1891.

Pat Woods' Black & White Café was here in the fifties and early sixties.

The site is a vacant lot today.

216 Ramsey Avenue North. Across the street from the present site of the VFW, in the middle of the 200 block of Ramsey Avenue, was A. Fred Grono's City Marble Works in the late summer of 1890.

Then the building here housed the Sigfrid W. Nelson and Sons' Nelson Implement business in the forties through the sixties.

Today this site is a city parking lot.

224 Ramsey Avenue North/35 Third Street West. Back at the southeast corner of Ramsey Avenue and Third Street was Dahl's Goodyear Tire Company for many years. Before that A. W. Dodge owned the first blacksmith shop in town at this corner.

M. Raleigh Dahl eventually bought the brick building here in May of 1957. Minar Ford had built it. Dahl moved into the building in July of 1957 and for years it was Dahl's Tire. David Binsfeld bought the business in June of 1995.

Today, the Binsfeld Tire Inc. business is here.

Joseph "Joe" Barth's blacksmith shop was just to the east of the corner building starting in April of 1882 and was torn down in August of 1938. It became part of the larger building erected at the corner. Next door to the east of the blacksmith shop was Josiah Payne's shoe store in the pioneer days.

It became a vacant lot and still is.

24-28 Third Street West. Joseph "Joe" A. Happ had an old wooden building here for his woodworking shop. He started his business in 1881 and moved to this site in May of 1883.

When Nelson's Buick dealership here finally folded, the building housed a toilet seat factory called Sperzel. It then had the Farm Bureau Insurance.

In March of 1987, West Central Community Services moved into the building. National Security Insurance, run by Robert and Linda Weida, was here also in the late eighties. Farm Bureau Insurance was here in the late eighties and early nineties in part of the building.

Divine Designs, a beauty salon owned by Kim Kalkbrenner, came to 30 Third Street West in June of 1990. John and Tina Young bought the business in November of 1992. It is now at 401 Sibley Avenue North. Edward D. Jones, Inc. came to the back of the building facing the west at 306 Ramsey Avenue North in April of 1994. West Central Community Service Center was here in 1990. I assume it changed to Meeker Center, a mental health services office connected with Woodland Center and run by Keri Kuhn, which came to 26 Third Street West in March of 1995. Images by Paige, a hair styling salon, came to the building in November of 1995. Steve and Paige Olson owned it.

Today the entire half block is called Courthouse Square and contains the Meeker Title Services, Inc. At 30 Third Street West is Images Hair Salon run by Bridget, Edward D. Jones, Inc. is still here and First Priority Mortgages at 304 Ramsey Avenue North. On the east side of the building, at 24 Third Street West, is the Crow River Obedience Club.

I reach the northwest corner of Sibley Avenue and Third Street where a large brick building still stands across the street from Central Park.

301 Sibley Avenue North. (50-52 Sibley in the early days.) (12-14 Third Street West in the rear.) This corner lot originally had a building on it eventually owned by Hiram S. Branham, son of Village Council President Jesse V. Branham, Jr. and co-owner of the Stevens and Company Bank. (While mayor of Litchfield and involved in a scandal at the bank, Hiram committed suicide by shooting himself in the chest. An embarrassed Litchfield took him off its list of mayors, never to be put back on it.) Jesse V. Branham, Jr. partnered with Edward A. Campbell to have a dry goods, clothing, and grocery store here in the fall of 1869.

Most people will remember the Ed Olson Agency being here for a long time. The Budget Beauty Shop, run by Mrs. George Anderson, was around the corner at 10 Third Street West, as was the Meeker County Farm Bureau at 12 Third Street West and Dr. W. B. Haugo with his veterinary office at 14 Third Street West in the early seventies.

The Budget Beauty Shop closed in July of 1980 and the Food Co-op moved in the building at 12 Third Street West in the summer of 1984. Natural Food Coop replaced the Farm Bureau in its part of the building sometime in the late eighties.

In the early nineties, the Edward D. Jones, Inc. office was in the front of this building along with something called Stor-A-Lot. New Horizon Marketing Company, owned by Dennis and Wendy Witthus was in 14 Third Street West in May of 1996.

The building stood empty for a long time until April of 2003 when Lillith's Natural Health & Beauty and Heavenly Hands Massage moved in from Library Square for a short time before it moved to Depot Street East. Then Mortgages on Main came. ABCO Etched Glass is in the rear at 12 Third Street West and Paul's Audio Video Service is at 14 Third Street West.

303 Sibley Avenue North. The also were businesses in the basement of the previous location. William "Billy" Hanley's two-lane bowling alley was downstairs in the early 1900s.

Hub Schiro moved his Schiro's Shoes to the basement here in the February of 1972 and downsized it to just shoe repair in the mid-seventies.

305 Sibley Avenue North. (54 Sibley in the early days and then 626 Sibley Avenue in the early 1900s.) Judge John Waldron was the owner of this next lot and one south of here in 1871. A house owned by Justice of the Peace James Benjamin "Ben" Atkinson, Jr., the druggist, was at this location.

Reed's Printing was here in the forties and fifties.

The First State Federal Savings bank was here in January of 1973. Then the U. S. Fish and Wildlife Service came here in December of 1978.

The building became TZ Heating and Air Conditioning in February of 1992. Joanne Holmgren and Bob Potter ran it. Then the Meeker County Economic Development and the Meeker County Extension Office was here in the mid-nineties. Kings Wok, a Chinese restaurant owned by Zheng Ting Zhi, Zheng Qiu Ping and Wayne Poirer, moved into the building in August of 1997.

The Chinese restaurant is still at this location today.

307-309 Sibley Avenue North. (56 Sibley in the early days and then 624 Sibley Avenue in the early 1900s.) Again, heading north, we had a location with quite a history. Judge John M. Waldron was the owner of this lot and the one south of here in 1871. At some point, the simple wood building was called the Kelley building. It burned down completely in a fire in April of 1882.

The well-known occupants of the lot were Johnson's Furniture and Rayppy's New Bakery.

Frank Forsberg's Bakery was here after Frank bought the business from Clarence Nelson in October of 1975. Nelson had owned it since April of 1964.

Forsberg shut down the ovens and closed the door on the bakery in October of 1985. He was a victim of super market bakeries, fewer downtown shoppers and increased government regulations. Litchfield's last bakery was gone. In May of 1986, The Best Sale Store In Litchfield, owned by Suzie Dalquist, moved in here. It was a novelty and gift store. Later that year, the name was changed to Susie's Best Sale. Then it was shortened to just Susie's.

Remax – Today's Realty came to the building in September of 1998. Janet Valen and Bob Sandstede owned it.

Today this building still houses Remax Realty and there are apartments upstairs.

311-311½ Sibley Avenue North. (58-60 Sibley in the early days and then 622 Sibley Avenue in the early 1900s.) This location and the next one shared a city lot, I believe. So the stores do get a little complicated. First, Judge Waldron and attorney C. Bowen built a new office building here in September of 1875.

The most known occupant of this site was the famous Janousek Brothers' Eat 10¢ Café, owned by Paul and his brother Henry in the fifties and sixties. It was changed in the late fifties to Eat 15¢.

I don't know when it happened, but many of the restaurants here shared the building with a business on the north side, such as Jim and Cathy Allen's CJ Music Store in May of 1969, H & A Television and Radio in the early seventies and A & C TV later in the seventies.

One of the rooms was used for DFL headquarters in September of 1972 and it became Margaret Breitenbach's Clay Pot Floral and

Gift Shop in December of 1973. Bob Gauer sold insurance from the north part of the building starting in 1978. He told Paul Janousek that if he were ever interested in selling the hamburger business half, he'd be interested in buying it.

So, in November of 1983, Paul sold it to Bob Gauer. Paul Janousek had been there for thirty-six years. Bob changed the name to the Parkview Lunch and expanded the restaurant to include the north half of the building.

Today the whole building is Parkview Lunch. Mark and Ann Lien owned it from July of 1991 until they sold it to Kevin and Donna Hartmann in April of 2003.

Janousek's and CJ Music Store in 1969.

313 Sibley Avenue North. (62 Sibley in the early days and then 618-620 Sibley Avenue in the early 1900s.) As far as I know, there was a vacant lot here for years. Silas Wright Leavett erected a building here in 1882. William Grono leased the building in January of 1885 for his marble works, which he moved all around town.

The famous Ole A. "Music Ole" or "Professor" Olson's Music House was here in 1901 with a wooden storefront stating "Pianos and Organs".

The Litchfield Coin-Operated Dry Cleaners was here in the summer of 1963, after a fire had destroyed the previous location on Depot Street East. Frank Anderson bought the business in February of 1964.

Before the building was torn down in the seventies, Anderson changed the name to Frank's Econ-o-clean.

The "300" block of Sibley Avenue.

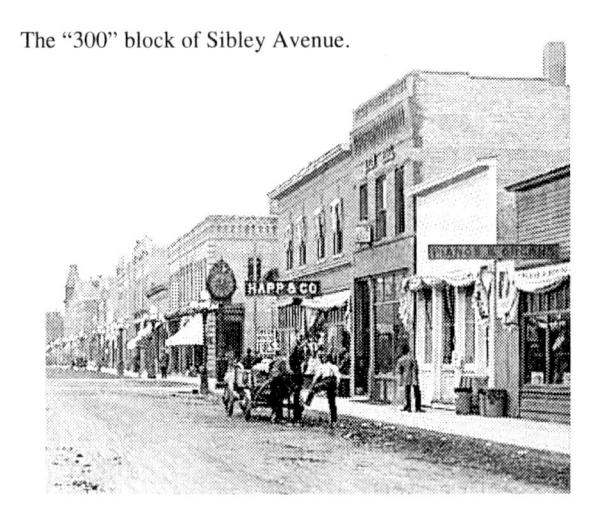

315-317 Sibley Avenue North. (616 Sibley Avenue in the early 1900s.) An alley was next followed by this location. In the 1880s, the News-Ledger, owned by Frank Belfoy and W. D. Joubert, was printed in a building here. Turner and Son had a blacksmith shop in the rear of the News-Ledger office, probably facing the alley. But there was a gas station here for years. The gas station was finally torn down in the early sixties.

Uptown Skelly in 1961.

In October of 1971, Harper Dollerschell started a used car lot here called Harper's Auto Sales.

People who bought cars from Harper didn't have to go very far to register them at the courthouse. The Meeker County Court House was just north of here finishing the block. The courthouse I knew, built in 1890, was closed in October of 1973 so that parts of it could be torn down to make room for the new courthouse.

The new courthouse, still here today, was moved into in February of 1975 and the rest of the old courthouse was torn down, starting in March. The jail to the rear of the courthouse was torn down in October of 1976, shortly after Sheriff John Rogers and his deputies moved into the new Meeker County Jail.

Going back south on Sibley Avenue, I'll cross Third Street to the southwest corner of the intersection and walk past the stores on the west side of the 200 block of Sibley.

Sibley Avenue west in the 1920s.

239-241 Sibley Avenue North. (48 Sibley Avenue in the early days and then 700 Sibley Avenue in the early 1900s.) Most Litchfield citizens knew this corner building simply as "Jacks", but the very first store on this corner was Samuel A. Heard's general merchandise store. Heard was partnered with C. D. Ward and their Heard and Ward general store was the very first store in Litchfield in 1869. It was the third building to be erected in town.

Falknor's Appliance and Electronics was here in August of 1970 after Bill Falknor bought the business. It was moved to the Second Street corner in the old bank building in September of 1972.

In June of 1980, The Barbers, a franchise beauty salon run by Rennae Kahl was here. Alissa (changed to Aleesa) Shaw, my first cousin, worked for The Barbers. Marv Alheim bought the business in February of 1983. North Central Mortgage and Pro-Vid-All Farms, Inc. was at 11 Third Street West and IDS – American Express was next to it at 15 Third Street West in the late eighties and early nineties.

391

Heartland Head Start came here to the front Sibley building in September of 1991 and it moved down the street in March of 1993. The Ed Olson Agency, Inc. took over the building in the late nineties.

The site is still the home of the Ed Olson Agency, Inc. The Classical Homeopathic Healing business, run by Julie Holmgren, is in the building behind the Ed Olson Agency, Inc. today at 11 Third Street West and Feistner Land Surveying, run by Sam W. Feistner is next to it at 15 Third Street West.

1880: Another view of City Grocery and City Drug Store on the west side of Sibley Avenue.

237 Sibley Avenue North. (46 Sibley in the early days and then 704 Sibley Avenue in the early 1900s.) George Merriam owned the next lot heading south in 1871 and also the next three lots after it. He must have had a bank here because the lot was referred to later as the lot that had the old bank building. Samuel A. Heard owned the lot and the building on it in 1874. I don't know if he used it for storage or to lease, as he had his store next door.

The most well known occupants were Judge Harris' Confectionery and Johnson's Drug.

Jim and Cathy Allen's CJ Music was here for a little over a year starting in November of 1969. Lowell Ruotsinoja's service shop, called Lowell's Radio & TV, came at the same time and was in the back.

When Jim left, Lowell took over the whole store. He closed, however, in December of 1971 and the Erlin Schultz' Budget Furniture Store came here in February of 1972. KLFD moved here in November of 1972. It was one of four locations I knew the radio station to be at in Litchfield. The first one was the Charles Hoyt March house at 218 South Sibley Avenue, a few houses south of Batterberry's store.

Second Time Around, a used clothing store, came here in October of 1989 along with Today's Concept, an exercise business. Mary Susa owned both.

Uppercut, a barbershop owned by Randy Leaf, came here in May of 1991. A tattoo shop followed and then a telemarketer was in here.

Today Rennie's China Closet is in the building.

233 Sibley Avenue North. The basement of the next location has always housed a barbershop or beauty shop. Originally owned by pioneer barber Ray Wheeler, who moved under the Northwestern Bank, it became Jack C. Hanson's Barber Shop in 1900.

Mac E. Steen's, who ironically had started out under the Northwestern Bank, in Ray Wheeler's location, had a barbershop down here for years.

Steen sold the shop to Larry Swenson in February of 1966 and it became Swenson's or Larry's Barber Shop.

Larry moved out in August of 1970 to another location and Jim Allen moved his CJ Music down here in February of 1971.

231 Sibley Avenue North. (44 Sibley in the early days and then 708 Sibley Avenue in the early 1900s.) George Merriam owned this lot in 1871. In 1874, Frank Belfoy had a law office here.

The Red Owl store and Thomas Furniture were here in the fifties.

John Kinsella moved a Sears catalog store in here in July of 1962.

In January of 1971, John Wiley took over the Sears and then Glenn A. Anderson bought it in November. Pat Meidal brought The Clothes Peddler store here in October of 1979.

The building now has Cliff Schaefer's Studio and Cameras, which began in 1973 elsewhere. Schaefer had moved to 725 Sibley Avenue North in January of 1981 and then here in July of 1982.

229 Sibley Avenue North. (42 Sibley in the early days and then 710-712 Sibley Avenue in the early 1900s.) William Henry Greenleaf had a general store here in early 1870. Greenleaf sold it to B. L. Perry and Company in the fall of 1870.

The site is most known for being the home of the McGowan sisters' millinery for years. Elizabeth or "Lizzie" had been a teacher for fifteen years and the County Superintendent of Schools and Sadie had taught in Salt Lake City, Utah. Lizzie was born in 1870. They were here from the early 1900s until late 1962.

In March of 1964, Ray Johnson moved his drug store here from just down the street.

Ray sold the store to Brad and Linda Teske in January of 1980. The store's name became Teske-Johnson Drugs and then to just Teske Drugs.

The business was moved out to the new shopping center on Highway 12 East in June of 1990[86] and Heartland Head Start moved into the building in March of 1993. It had been north of here at the corner. By the way, at this time my classmate John Ferguson, Ed Olson and Ray Doering, owned the building.

In August of 2000, Gary Smith and Amy and Joseph Berube brought Smith Appliance and Radio Shack to the building from their Second Street location.

This building still has Smith Appliance and Radio Shack today.

227 Sibley Avenue North. (40 Sibley in the early days and then 714 Sibley Avenue in the early 1900s.) The next site had a building called the James Building because it was built by Joseph James to be used as an office for his lumberyard, which was south of the railroad tracks. The building here was the third store building to go up in Litchfield in 1869. It also had Mrs. Mary L. Pixley's millinery in 1870. Another building shared this lot.

Setterberg's Jewelry and the Minnesota Valley Natural Gas Company were here in the fifties and sixties.

Minnegasco was still here in the seventies and eighties also. In May of 1987, Renee Regenscheid had a craft store here called Wood 'N Needle but it moved out in August of 1991.

---

[86] In August of 1994, the business became Teske Card and Gift shop, run by Linda Teske. Linda added Hallmark cards in October of 1998 and today it is called Teske's Hallmark and Gift Shop.

Stewart Jewelry, owned by Lyman and Sue Dale, moved here in July of 1991. Paul Gervais bought the store in November of 1996 and changed the name to Gervais Jewelry.

The building still has Gervais Jewelry in it today.

225 Sibley Avenue North. (38 Sibley in the early days and then 716 Sibley Avenue in the early 1900s.) Continuing down Sibley, the next lot was owned by shoemaker Louis Ekbom in 1871.

People will remember Nordlie's grocery, the Milk Bar and Thomas Furniture being here before Montgomery Ward came in 1964.

Herb and Lorna Roehn bought the catalog and appliance store in January of 1970.

In the late eighties and early nineties, Vern's Buying & Selling Service was here.

Then a Moose Bros. Carry-out Pan Pizza shop was here starting in July of 1992. Reid Van Brunt ran it. It closed down in October of 1996 and Jimmy's Pizza, owned by David and Vera De Rosier came in March of 1997. Jeff and Kelly Hecksel bought Jimmy's in December of 1999.

In November of 2000, Papa Sluigee's Pizzeria, managed by Debra Mankovich, moved into the building. Then in 2004, new ownership changed the name to Pizza Plus.

Pizza Plus is still at this location today.

223 Sibley Avenue North. (36 Sibley in the early days and then 720 Sibley Avenue in the early 1900s.) Louis Ekbom's shoe business was here in the next location in 1870.

For years the Coast-To-Coast store was here. Heartland Community Action Agency bought the building in November of 1993 and moved in. The Meeker County Clothing Center and Outreach Office moved into the building with its parent Heartland in October of 1994.

Stepping Stones, new clothing (donated by stores, etc.) for needy people to wear to a job interview, etc., was added to the Heartland Agency in July of 2000.

The Community Action Agency is still here today.

221 Sibley Avenue North. The upstairs at the last location was known for years as Watson Hall and was used for meetings and dances. But Watson was downstairs eighteen years after the building

was erected in 1886. The Odd Fellows met up there in October of 1889.

At sometime the upstairs here became apartments. I lived up there for a few months in 1970.

219-219 ½ Sibley Avenue North. I don't have much history on the next building. In June of 1876, Phineas "Pat" Cary rented the building that was here for his store but he moved out in a couple of months.

Marvin "Bill" Stewart's jewelry business was here for years until it was sold to Lyman and Sue Dale in November of 1985. The Dales kept the Stewart Jewelry name.

In July of 1991, the city bought the building for the Chamber of Commerce office. The jewelry stored moved a few doors north of here.

Today the Chamber of Commerce/Community Development office is here.

217 Sibley Avenue North. (34 Sibley in the early days and 722 Sibley Avenue in the early 1900s.) Next I arrive at the *Independent Review* newspaper building location. Originally, Andrew P. and B. P. Nelson started a general store here in a new building in May of 1871. It was called A. Nelson and Brother's "Skandanavian Store". (That's the spelling they used.)

John M. Harmon owned the newspaper for many years and Litchfield mayor Vernon "Vern" Madson bought an interest in the paper and became Harmon's partner in January of 1971. Stan Roeser bought into the paper in 1976 and he and Vern Madson bought out Harmon and became the owners on January 1, 1979 ending Harmon's family connection to the paper which went all the way back to its beginnings. Madson and Roeser retired in 1999, selling the newspaper to the Hutchinson Leader, Inc. in May of 1999.

The newspaper owners added Copy & Design Center to the business in May of 2000.

Today the *Independent Review* is still being published at this location along with the *Meeker County Advertiser*.

215-215½ Sibley Avenue North. (32 Sibley in the early days.) The first building here had Joseph Mills' jewelry store in it in 1870.

Doffing's Smart Wear, owned by Esther Doffing, opened here in March of 1960. Esther sold it to Mr. and Mrs. E. C. Chubb in the late sixties.

The Chubbs sold out to Ann and John Mattsfield in October of 1972. Doffing's was still here in the mid-nineties, but it closed and the building stood vacant until Maureen Jackman opened Treasured Keepsakes here.

Doffing's in 1969.

213 Sibley Avenue North. (30 Sibley in the early days.) The next store location was on a lot owned by Judge Virgil Homer Harris. Justice James Benjamin Atkinson, Jr. built and owned a building here. In August of 1872, John Patten and Jacob "Jake" Koerner had a meat market here for a while.

Sederstrom's Realty Company was here in the fifties and sixties. Larry Swenson moved his Larry's Barber Shop here in 1969.

Then Larry Ackerman bought the building from Swenson and moved his barbershop, also called Larry's, in March of 1972. Alva "Al" Larson Insurance (State Farm) was in a part of the building also in the mid-sixties and on.

The West Central Youth For Christ, operated by Bruce Kaihoi, was somewhere in this location, probably in the back, in November of 1980.

In February of 1990, Sam W. Feistner had his Feistner Land Surveying/Meeker County Land Surveyor office in the building along with Larry and another business called the White Insurance Agency. Feistner moved to Third Street West behind the Ed Olson Agency at some time. Karen McCarthy Accounting came here to a room sometime in the mid-nineties.

Larry's Barber Shop, owned by Ackerman, is still here today.

209 Sibley Avenue North. (28 Sibley in the early days.) The first building we come to south of Sederstrom's had more than one store occupying the building at a time, as did a lot of the buildings in town. The very first business I can find here was a book and notion store owned by W. W. Page in early 1872.

This building was torn down in March of 1954 and an addition to Whalberg's was erected. Whalberg's closed in December of 1974 after being at this location for fifty years. Dean Ohland bought the building and opened up a Ben Franklin store in March of 1975.

Dueber's for Variety, owned by Chuck Dueber, opened for business here in March of 2001.

Today it's been changed to Dueber's Department Store.

207 Sibley Avenue North. (26 Sibley in the early days and then 732 Sibley Avenue North in early the 1900s.) W. W. Page and Alex Cairncross had a general store sharing this next site with another building in mid-1872. Page sold out to Cairncross in October of 1872.

Older citizens remember Whalberg's V Store in this building. Whalberg's closed in December of 1974 after being at this location for fifty years. Dean Ohland bought the building and opened up a Ben Franklin store in March of 1975.

Anthonys Specialty Department Store came to this location in July of 1997. It was owned by a larger company and sold shoes and clothing. It closed in November of 1997 and was bought out by another chain called Stage. Carl Tooker owned the chain. It closed its doors in September of 1999.

Dueber's for Variety, owned by Chuck Dueber, opened for business here in March of 2001.

Today it's been changed to Dueber's Department Store.

205 Sibley Avenue North. (24 Sibley in the early days and then 734 Sibley Avenue in the early 1900s.) The lot in the next location, again heading south, had Robert F. Gordon and W. S. Knappen's National Billiard Hall in 1870. James Benjamin Atkinson, Jr. owned the twenty by sixty-four foot building on the lot. Postmaster/clothier Horace B. Johnson owned the lot in 1871. He also owned the corner lot next door.

For many years, a hardware store, specifically the Our Own Hardware store, was here.

In November of 1970, Duane Larson and Dale Harmon owned the store. They turned it into a Hardware Hank store.

Pat Meidal, who owned the Clothes Peddler down the street, had a store called The Shoe Peddler here starting in the summer of 1981.

Cynthia's Beauty Salon, owned by Cynthia Tongen was here starting in September of 1990. Cynthia sold out to Patty Schultz in July of 1999. She changed the name to Styles On Sibley.

Today Styles On Sibley is still at this location.

201 Sibley Avenue North. (22 Sibley Avenue North in the early days and then 738 Sibley Avenue in the early 1900s.) The last building on this block was originally Litchfield's first or second Post Office, depending on your way of thinking, and Postmaster Horace B. Johnson's clothing store in late 1869 or early 1870. The first Post Office was established on September 20, 1869 in John A. C. Waller's home. The newspaper tells us that Horace B. Johnson was the first postmaster, so Waller must not have been appointed, but he acted as a postmaster. So, Johnson's building, which was the second business building to go up in Litchfield, was the first "official" Post Office.

The west side of Sibley Avenue starting at Second Street and heading north in about 1880. The first building is Horace B. Johnson's clothing store and Post Office.

The most known occupant of this corner lot was the Northwestern National Bank of Litchfield.

> Call---
> **804**
> FOR A COMPLETE SERVICE
> **BANKING**
> **INSURANCE**
> • CHECK ACCOUNTS
> • LOANS
> • MORTGAGES
>
> *The Only National Bank in MEEKER County.*
>
> ***Northwestern*** **NATIONAL BANK OF LITCHFIELD**
> 201 N. SIBLEY

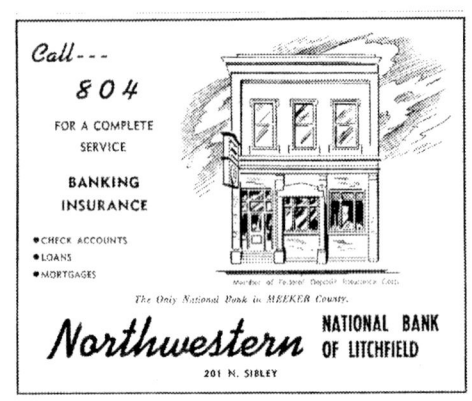

The bank's ad before the front was remodeled.

The bank moved out in the mid-sixties. In April of 1969, the Litchfield Centennial Headquarters was here.

Bill Falknor bought the building in September of 1970 and McGee Realty moved in from Depot Street. In September of 1972, Falknor's Electric Sales and Service Center moved into the building.

Falknor moved down the street to the north in the early eighties. The Shopper's Guide moved here from across the street at some time before the Berkes sold out to the *Independent Review* in November of 1982 and they retired. The West Central Community Services Center was here briefly starting in February of 1983. R & D Computer Services moved into the building in July of 1984 from another location. Then, in December of 1989, Arlen and Sally VanderPloeg brought in the Pizza Ranch restaurant. They sold it to John and Shonna Wichmann and Lois and Ted Salazar in September of 1995.

Today the Pizza Ranch still occupies this building with Work Connection in the building also.

Occasionally, I'll leave Sibley Avenue to go to some other interesting buildings. I'll head west on Second Street around the corner from the Northwestern Bank building. By the way, this first block heading west became one-way in June of 1976. Before the bank took up almost half the block, there was another small building behind Horace B. Johnson's clothing store building, just before the alley.

I'm vague about the different stores in the back part of the bank building except for a plumbing business in the fifties and sixties (Campbell's plumbing and heating business was sold to William "Bill" Harder in March of 1949 and later Harder moved down the block) The next occupant I can find of this part of the building was the Meeker County Emergency Food Shelf, which moved over here in

March of 1987. The Heartland Community Action Agency clothing center was here, sharing the building, in 1989.

The Food Shelf moved out in May of 1993. In February of 1994, this portion of the bank building was torn down.

West of the building was an alley.

24 Second Street West. (413 Second Street West in early 1900s.) In 1869, James Tinkham had a farm machinery business in the first building following the alley. It was Litchfield's first farm machinery business and Tinkham sold the McCormick brand.

For years Fred Maass' dentistry was in the front of the building and Bill Harder's Plumbing and Heating was in the rear in the early sixties. My second cousin, Dick Birkemeyer bought Harder's business in the late sixties. He called his business Birkemeyer Plumbing and Heating.

A store called Alley Boutique, owned by Claris Carlson, was in the rear in October of 1971. It sold "handcrafted artifacts". Dick Birkemeyer went into partnership with some other people in a business called J J & D Pumping Service, which headquartered here in the rear along with his plumbing business. Dick's wife, Doris, opened an antique store called The Porch out on west Highway 12 in November of 1972. In September of 1974, Dick took on a junior partner, Bob Groskreutz. They had the B & G Plumbing and Heating Company. Bob was a brother to another classmate of mine, Richard Groskreutz. Dick and Bob moved to a new building in July of 1976, vacating this one. Dick left the business in 1979 and Bob took on another partner named Rich Koll.

Litchfield Dental Laboratory was here in the late eighties and early nineties.

Today the Ed Olson Rental garages are at this location.

26-28 Second Street West. Next, heading west, was a pool hall. At one time, around the turn of the century, Olaf M. "Feed Ole" Olson had a feed store here. I don't know what was here before that. For most years, a saloon or pool hall was here.

Ray "Red" Oslund owned it in the late sixties and early seventies as Red's Pool Hall and Red & Joan's Pool Hall.

Then it was Smokey's, owned by "Smokey" Vick, in the mid-seventies.

Today there is a vacant lot here.

401

30 Second Street West. (403 Second Street West in the early 1900s.) Anderson Chemical and the old Fire Hall were the last two buildings on this block. Originally the David Gorman livery stable was here in one or both of the locations. The old fire hall was built in 1886.

Around late 1900, whatever building was at this location, probably the fire hall, became the town hall because the new Opera House had been built in the old town hall location.

The old Fire Hall in 1889.

A new fire hall was built at the southwest corner of Ramsey Avenue and Third Street in 1962, the rear of it being where the old paper shack was. Anderson Chemical bought the old fire hall site at this corner in December of 1963 and was still headquartered here in the early seventies and on into the year 2000.

The Anderson Chemical headquarters building was demolished in May of 2001.

Today the site is occupied by Curves.

100 Second Street West. E. M. Eastman had an office for his moving company and well digging business at the northwest corner across Ramsey Avenue to the west. Chris Mortenson had his Litchfield City Bakery, restaurant and boarding house at that corner, after erecting a building in June of 1886.

The site ended up being occupied by the freezer lockers for the turkey plant when a new building was erected here in July of 1958.

Today it is a vacant lot.

104 Second Street West. West of the corner building was a café named the Lunch Time Inn, which was owned by Kate Pierce. Kate sold the cafe to her son-in-law and daughter, Kenneth and Laura Mae Welsand, in January of 1949.

In October of 1971, Mary Ramthun bought Laura's Café here. Mary also had the Hide-A-Way Café around the corner on Ramsey Avenue.

Eventually the building was torn down and the lot is empty.

114-116 Second Street West. LeRoy "Roy" and Eldon Swanson moved into the building here following the alley in February of 1932.

The Automotive Machine shop was here for many years. Chet Olsen started the business in 1949 in a back room where Auto Parts was for years.

Chet sold the business to Gordon Savoie in February of 1991.

Today L S Customs is here.

122 Second Street West. (305 Second Street West in the early 1900s.) In about 1915, Dr. H. C. Peters had a veterinary business at this location. In the summer of 1919, the Johnson and Hanson auto repair business went into the building here.

Dave's Heating and Air Conditioning was here in the eighties and early nineties. Agnes Savoie, Gordon's wife from next door, brought in her collectibles, crafty items store in January of 1994. It was called Aggie's Kountry Keepsakes.

Kountry Keepsakes closed down in May of 2004.

124-126 Second Street West. Hans Christian Anderson's blacksmith shop had been here at the northeast corner of Miller Avenue and Second Street.

Dave's Heating and Air Conditioning was here in the eighties and early nineties. Agnes Savoie brought in her collectibles, crafty items store in January of 1994. It was called Aggie's Kountry Keepsakes.

Kountry Keepsakes closed down in May of 2004. Rich Koll took over B & G Plumbing after his partner Bob Groskreutz retired in the fall of 2004 and Koll moved the business to this location.

403

Anderson Chemical was across Second Street on the southeast corner lot and it later added on to the lot to the east of here.

In February of 1951, the Farm Home Administration moved their office to the Anderson Chemical building.

123 Second Street West. Noreen's Pavilion was to the east of that building. Originally, H. J. Kellman bought the lot in July of 1909. They built a fifty by eighty foot dance hall in the summer of 1909.

The building was converted over to the Anderson Chemical Company and the lot is vacant today.

121-119 Second Street West. (318 Second Street West in the early 1900s) The next lot, heading east, originally had the Litchfield Iron Works. H. J. Kellman owned it in the 1890s.

This location and the ones east of here became part of the produce complex. Jennie-O, the produce company, shut down in July of 1985.

The buildings were torn down in September of 1991, one month after my mother died. She had worked there for many years. The Produce had been in business under one of two owners, the Peifers who founded it or Earl B. Olson who bought it in 1957, for over seventy-nine years from 1906 to 1985.

Today the lots are still vacant.

117 Second Street West. (316-312 Second Street West in the early 1900s.) Herbert and James Atkinson built the Litchfield Automobile Company next to the previous wooden building in April of 1912. They sold out to the Vincent brothers, who sold out to W. Richard Berens in December of 1914.

Then the lot became part of the turkey processing plant. Jennie-O, the produce company, shut down in July of 1985.

The buildings were torn down in September of 1991.

Today the lot is vacant.

(325 Second Street in the old numbering system.) The southwest corner lot had H. J. Quigley's feed yard before the turn of the century. Lorenz C. Johnson had his confectionery near here, around the turn of the century.

This location also became part of the turkey processing plant complex or the Litchfield Produce Company. This particular building was where the turkeys were killed and eviscerated and where my mother worked on the line for many years. Jennie-O, the produce company, shut down in July of 1985.

The buildings were torn down in September of 1991.

The entire block is vacant today.

The Produce, with its office at the northwest corner of Ramsey Avenue and Depot Street, (325 Depot Street West was the address in the early 1900s), took up half of the 200 and all of the 300 numbered blocks of the west side of Ramsey Avenue North. The Peifer brothers, John C. and Frank A., and John's son Arthur E. moved the Produce here to that "office corner" in June of 1906 from Sibley Avenue across from the park. The Peifers, originally from Luxemburg, bought the brick Union House nine-room hotel at this corner location and converted it over.

Jennie-O, the produce company, suspended operations in Litchfield in July of 1985.

The buildings were torn down in September of 1991.

The entire block is empty today.

There was a grocery store run by Isaac Hines directly across the street from the hotel at the northeast corner of Ramsey Avenue and Depot Street in February of 1897. Today the Quality Craft factory is at this corner location facing south.

130 Ramsey Avenue North. North of it, mid-block towards the corner to the north, was a building that was the Israel Miller feed mill, which began operations in 1885. Miller came to Litchfield in 1884 to build and operate "LuLu" the steamboat on Lake Ripley.

Today Rainbow Body & Paint Shop, which came here in November of 1999, is still at this location. Brad Latham, who did repair, and Kelly Hedtke, who did reconditioning, owned it.

37-39 Second Street West/130 Ramsey Avenue North. The brick building that became Lund-Hydeen's angled the southwest corner of Ramsey Avenue and Second Street. Chris A. Bertelson may have had a blacksmith shop here or close by in May of 1883.

Lund-Hydeen Pontiac was here in the fifties and early sixties.

In the late sixties, the King Koin Launderette was moved here. The Bungalow Gift Shop was added to the Launderette also.

Gordon and Laura Bloomquist bought the Launderette in April of 1972.

The Answer, a clothing and handcrafted items store owned by Cheri and Mark Schmidt was here in February of 1983. Then, in September, two "businesses" came into the large building. They were the Meeker County Emergency Food Shelf and the Community Action Outreach and Clothing Center, a clothing distribution site, shortened to Community Action Agency. It was followed by the Litchfield Teen Center, also called Off Main, in September of 1987. It was run by an organization called C.H.A.T., which stood for Citizens Helping Active Teens.

The part of the building around the corner to the south became the Northland Car Care center jointly occupied by Dave Carlson's Northland Body and Paint shop and Greg Bent's Car Care business. They both came in December of 1989.

The Beauty Haven occupied the Second Street side of the building in October of 1990. It was a beauty salon owned by Norma Johnson Schlumpberger. The Teen Center shut down in May of 1993 because of apathy by the teens. Northland Body and Paint moved to 101 Miller Avenue North in February of 1997.

The building is now the home of Karen McCarthy's Tax Service.

27-29 Second Street West. Heading east on Second Street, back towards Sibley Avenue, the first location after the corner had a feed store owned by David Gorman before the turn of the century.

Auto Parts, owned by Bill Simmons, was here starting in 1952

The Youth For Christ/Campus Life came here in 1988, and it added a Christian Video free rental business. The director of the whole thing was Bryan Blomker. Bill Simmons brought his Auto Parts Co., Inc. store back here from next door and sold it to Michael Kopp in August of 1988. Kopp changed the name to The Parts Store On Second Street.

This is part of the previous vacant building today and also vacant.

23-25 Second Street West. Charles "Charley" Shaw, no relation to me, and Theodore Ehlers had a feed store here, the next location heading east, to go along with their mill a block away to the south on Depot Street. They moved out to another location in July of 1884.

Wilfred F. Baril's Paint and Wallpaper Store was here in the fifties and sixties.

His son Dick took over at some time and moved it to the old Super Valu location. Kent's Refrigeration was here in the early eighties and Video Cinema came here in May of 1984. Bill Simmons moved his Auto Parts store here at sometime and then to next door. Today's Concept, an exercise spa owned by Mary Susa, was here in early 1988. It must have moved in early 1989 because Video Attractions came here in March of 1989. Jerry Price owned it. Then it was Video Cinema.

Nan Greenhow's Prints Charming was also here in the late 1980's and early 1990's. It moved to the KLFD building on main street when Bob Greenhow brought back the radio station. Also in the building in 1990 was The Sound Doctor. I presume it was a repair shop for electronics.

This is another vacant building today.

135 Sibley Avenue North. (20 Sibley in the early days.) A. A. Brown owned the Sibley Avenue and Second Street southwest corner lot in 1871. Robert F. Gordon owned a building south of the tracks and he moved it here in May of 1871. I don't know what it was used for at that time, but the building had the Gottlieb C. Koerner and Joseph Roetzer meat market in it in 1874. For most of this corner's history, a bank was here.

A new bank building was built and it opened in June of 1963. It included the building next door to the south.

The public library moved in here in 1979 after the bank had moved, in May of 1978, to its new building at the corner of Third Street West and Ramsey Avenue North.

In September of 2000, the offices of Sparboe Farms or Sparboe Companies[87], owned by Bob Sparboe, moved into the building.

The building is still occupied by Sparboe Farms today. In 2004, Sparboe celebrated its 50th year of business.

131 Sibley Avenue North. (18 Sibley in the early days and then 806 Sibley Avenue in the early 1900s.) Butcher Jacob "Jake" Koerner, Sr. originally owned this next lot heading south on Sibley Avenue. Jake erected a small building here in 1870 and had a butcher shop here for a while. At some time in the early years, the building had the Litchfield Brewery bar, a saloon selling the local brew.

Wayne Rayppy's New Bakery came here in November of 1941. Rayppy had a fire here on April 12, 1954. The fire only shut Rayppy down for about ten days.

Rayppy had another fire on December 30, 1961 and it forced him to move down by Janousek's Café across from the park.

Eventually this building was demolished when the First State Bank next door expanded and built their new building in 1962.

129 Sibley Avenue North. (16 Sibley in the early days and then 808 Sibley Avenue in the early 1900s.) Pioneer shoemaker Nels B. Anderson had a shoe shop here in the next location heading south on Sibley Avenue after he bought the lot in 1873.

The Hagglund Furniture Store and undertaking business was here for decades.

Mrs. Dorothy Radunz had a store called Christine's here, which she sold to Harold and Eunice Harding in January of 1970. John Olmscheid bought the business in December of 1975.

A women's clothing store called CJ's came here in August of 1991. Carolyn Scully, Jan Vold, and Suzie Dalquist owned it. In September of 1998, Margie Polingo's Sunrise On Main, which started elsewhere in 1988 and closed here in 2002, was here.

---

[87] Bob Sparboe founded the Sparboe Chick Company in August of 1954. Over the years, Sparboe acquired or started many other businesses such as Agri-Tech, Center National Bank, Center Insurance Agency, Sparboe Farms and Sparboe Foods. The company is the nation's fifth largest egg producer with offices and plants in eleven different locations in three states.

Today Essence Of Flowers, owned by Tom and Sally Hulbert, is at the location. The business had begun on Sibley Avenue South in July of 1994.

The two right buildings are Butterwick's and Christine's.

127 Sibley Avenue North. (14 Sibley in the early days and then 810 Sibley Avenue in the early 1900s.) J. W. Glazier had the Litchfield Restaurant here in the early days of Litchfield.

Foster Butterwick bought the Lofstrom's business, which was here, in April of 1946. Foster took out the soda fountain and called his business Butterwick's Pharmacy. He kept it going for forty years, retiring in October of 1987.

The Meeker County Emergency Food Shelf moved to this location in July of 1993.

The Food Shelf is still here today.

An alley was next and the city closed it in July of 1972.

119 Sibley Avenue North. (12 Sibley in the early days and then 816 in the early 1900s.) In April of 1871, Clark L. Angell had his photographic gallery here at the next location heading south. He moved around town a lot and didn't stay here very long. In the summer of 1875, Phineas "Pat" Cary had his Cary's Store here, selling boots and shoes.

Tostenrud's Jewelry was here for decades starting in 1932.

In February of 1969, "Hub" Schiro bought the stock from the closed Becker Shoe Store and moved it here as Schiro's Shoe Store.

The Mt. Zion Bible & Book Store came here in February of 1972 when Schiro's moved to a basement location across from the park.

Vince's Video Attractions was here in the late eighties and early nineties. Litchfield Video was here in late 1998. DeAnn and "Jiggs" Rothstein, owners of DeAnn's Country Village Shoppe to the south, put a doorway connecting her store to this one and added Heritage Lace to her business.

The building houses Heritage Lace today and is still connected to the building to the south.

115 Sibley Avenue North. (8-10 Sibley in the early days and then 818 Sibley Avenue in the early 1900s.) The next building and the following one, heading south were once called the "old courthouse building". Reading Asher built the first building on this lot and he had his North Star Billiard Hall here in 1870.

Bernie Felling ran his Fairway here for quite a while until his new location around the corner on First Street (Depot Street) was remodeled from the old Minar Ford building in January of 1971.

Starting in December of 1970, the Litchfield Garment Company, a division of Butwin Sportswear Company of St. Paul, was here. It was moved to 412 Gilman Avenue South in the early spring of 1971. Then the Fabrific Fabric Center was here in the early seventies and John Forbe's Champion Auto Store followed it in March of 1975.

The location became the Christian Village Shoppe in April of 1980. Guy and Kay Anderson owned it. New Life, a shoe repair and upholstery shop run by Jim and Mattie Bunkers, came here in June of 1987. In December of 1989, the Bunkers added Christian books and changed the name of the business to New Life Christian Book Store.

DeAnn's Country Village Shoppe, owned by DeAnn Rothstein, came to the building in September of 1991. In April of 1995, she and her husband "Jiggs" expanded by obtaining the unoccupied building to the north and combining the two.

DeAnn still occupies the building and the one to the north of it.

113 Sibley Avenue North. (6 Sibley in the early days.) Nearing the corner, I come to a building with quite a history. In November of 1880, W. S. Wooley bought "the old courthouse" building here for $7500, but I don't believe he moved his folded hardware business here. The Litchfield Saturday Review was published here in September of 1884 for a short time.

The Northland Tot Shop, which became Boyd's, was here for decades starting elsewhere in 1952. Boyd Anderson had bought the old Litchfield Woolen Company store, which at that time was across the street from Central Park. He moved it here and changed it to a children's clothing store.

In October of 1994, Boyd retired and sold the business to his daughter Laurie Hall and his daughter-in-law Colleen Anderson.

This building still housed Boyd's Uptown Kids until the fall of 2004, when the store closed after fifty-one years of business.

109 Sibley Avenue North. (4 Sibley in the early days and then 824 Sibley Avenue in the early 1900s.) The next to last store location in this block had a "clothing store personality" over the years, but it started out differently. David Elmquist had his jewelry store here in 1883 in the south half of the building.

The most known occupant was the Viren-Johnson clothing store from June of 1908 until Jerry Tierney closed the doors for the last time in February of 1989. The store had been called Viren-Johnson under different owners for eighty-one years. None of the subsequent owners were related to either Viren or Johnson.

Nickelodeon Antiques, owned by Dick and Karen Heath, was at this location starting in March of 1989. Then a dance studio named Dance X-pressions came here in October of 1996. Lisa Jo Hicks-Ewald ran it. Litchfield Office Supply came next in October of 1998. Crystal and Craig Kallevig owned it.

That store moved and the building closed down and stood vacant for a long time until Very Vintage, an antique store owned by Susan Johnson, moved into the location in May of 2003.

103-105 Sibley Avenue North. (2 Sibley in the early days.) The corner location of this block had a building on it that is in almost every picture and postcard of downtown Litchfield, the Litchfield Hotel. Before the hotel was here, however, a small wooden building, which very little is known about, was here. I do know that Joseph Leaser had his furniture factory in it for a while in early 1871.

Of course the most known occupant of this corner lot was that Howard House/Lenhardt Hotel/Litchfield Hotel I referred to. Civil War veteran Colonel Jacob M. Howard built the hotel in the summer and fall of 1881 at a cost of $19,000 and called it the Howard House. The hotel had a coffee shop in the front right section called the Colonial Room, the Colonial Coffee Shop and the Colonial Café.

Jim Hannan leased the cafe in February of 1969 from Julie O'Keefe, who owned it at the time. She got it back after one year. The Greyhound[88] Bus service, which had used the Colonial as their Litchfield stop off for years, was moved to the Auto Fair gas station on Highway 12 East and then, in May of 1969, to the Cenex station, also on Highway 12 East. Later it was moved again to the Scotwood Motel. The hotel had been the Greyhound Bus Depot for many years. It was settled into the A&W Drive-In and Restaurant out on East Highway 12 in December of 1979.

J. B. Terry bought the cafe in February of 1972. Theodore T. Wold and Joe H. Herbranson had owned the hotel since April of 1951, but they sold it Dick Enstad in November of 1974. Enstad also bought the Colonial Café. He sold out to Gordon "Gordie" and Lois Anderson in September of 1976.

The Howard House in 1889.

The rising costs of upkeep, heating, and insurance, (there were no fire escapes), and the declining clientele in the hotel caused Gordie to make a painful but necessary decision in the fall of 1977. He pleaded with the city council to help him with his problem of trying to keep Litchfield's main landmark going. They couldn't help him without opening up a "can of worms" with a downtown of buildings

---

[88] Greyhound cut Litchfield from its route in August of 2004. From then on, people had to go to St. Cloud to catch a bus, just as they had been doing for years to catch a train.

all built around the same time before the turn of the century. (Most were built in 1885.)

On Christmas Eve in 1977, after serving the traditional noon dinner at the Colonial Café for the last time, Gordie and the staff cleaned up the café and locked the doors on it and the hotel at 2pm. The hotel had been open constantly for ninety-six years and two month.

In November of 1978, Bachman Construction Company of Hutchinson, Minnesota bought the vacant building and lot. An auction was held of all the furniture and fixtures. What wasn't sold, unfortunately, was thrown away, except for a few treasures my friend Pete Hughes had been given by one-time manager Nick Forte. Those treasures are on display at the Meeker County Historical Society (G.A.R. Hall).

On Sunday, December 18, 1978, the grand hotel was torn down. The construction company worked quickly and around the clock and by Monday morning there was nothing at the corner but a gaping hole.

Greenbriar Floral, owned by Dick and Karen Heath, occupied the site in a new building in April of 1981.

The floral business was sold to Pat and Duane Miller in September of 1998.

Today Jason Tibbits, a former student of mine in Glencoe, sells State Farm Insurance at this location.

I will turn the corner from the hotel and head west down Depot Street.

22-28 Depot Street West. (417 Depot Street West in the early 1900s.) J. H. Spelliscy had a machinery business in a building after the alley behind the hotel in May of 1898.

For many years, the Minar Motor Ford dealership was here. After Minar moved, the city bought the building and tore most of it down in March of 1967 to use the site as a parking lot. The Charmoll Manufacturing Company leased the remaining part in October of 1969 to make men's and boy's winter jackets and vests.

Charmoll didn't last long and Bernard "Bernie" Felling bought the building in July of 1970, remodeled it and moved his Bernie's Fairway here in January of 1971.

Bernie sold the business to his son Ken sometime in the eighties. Ken Felling closed the Fairway store down in March of 1994 and he and his wife Dollie remodeled the building to change it over to a telemarketing business called Quality Craft, Inc. It opened in January of 1995, selling signs, displays and award items.

Quality Craft, Inc. is still at this location today.

25 Depot Street West. Across Depot Street, by the railroad sidetrack, was the Roller Mill, which was built in 1872 by J. C. Braden, A. Adams, William S. Brill and John M. Waldron. In 1873, Adams and Brill sold out their interests to their partners.

Today the First District Ag Service/Cheese Store is at this site. They put up a new building here in the fall of 1979 and the Factory Outlet Cheese Store opened in March of 2001. Their address is actually 29 Depot Street West.

I'll leave the 100 block of Sibley and head south across the tracks to visit a few places. Right across the street to the south from the hotel was always the Railroad Park, a small piece of land the railroad had owned. For years, Col. Howard looked after it as a place for his hotel guests to go to relax. Eventually the land was given to the city, which looked after it. But in December of 1972 the City Council decided it would make a good parking lot for shoppers. Somehow the lot got sold and, in August of 1989, a Hardee's restaurant was built on the land and was given the address of 21 Depot Street West.

Hardee's closed in October of 1998 and Burger King moved into the building in February of 1999.

Today, the fast food restaurant here is still Burger King, complete with a model train inside in honor of the fact that just a few feet from the restaurant, on the other side of the railroad tracks, was Litchfield's beautiful depot.

The depot in the 1920s.

Litchfield's depot was built in August of 1901 and dedicated on January 9, 1902. Sadly, it was torn down starting in October of 1985. By December, it was completely gone. One of the reasons given for its demise was that the years of "trembling" by the roar of the passing trains had weakened the bricks and foundation.

Commercial Street was south of the depot. A lumberyard has always been across that street.

126 Sibley Avenue South/25 Commercial Street West. (918 Sibley Avenue in the early 1900s.) In the spring of 1870, Chauncey Butler had a lumberyard here. The lumberyard was sold to James H. Morris in September of 1873.

Most people will remember Economy Gas or the Fleet Wholesale Supply Company, the Fleet Distributing Supply Company or the Fleet Farm Supply, depending on the ad, being at this location.

The Ideal Lumber yard or Ideal True Valu Home Center took over the entire complex that this site became and it is still at this location today.

200-202 Sibley Avenue South. South of the lumberyard, across the street, was a house with a grocery store inside and gas station out in the front. In the early twenties, Mrs. R. Reynolds had the grocery there. She added the filling station out front in October of 1925.

Some people might still call this location Batterberry's, it's most know occupant.

Today this is a private residence.

415

201 Sibley Avenue South. Directly across Sibley Avenue South and kitty-corner from the lumberyard was the Carnegie Library. The library was built in 1904 with $10,000 donated by Andrew Carnegie. It was built on a site where Louis Larson had his house.

The Carnegie public library closed in late October of 1978 and it was moved into the old bank building on Sibley Avenue in December of 1978, but only opened for short periods during the day. So for a while, Litchfield was without a library until they officially opened up in January of 1979.

Rich Johnson bought the building here in June of 1980 for twice what it had been built for, $20,001. Initially, his idea was to convert it into low-income apartments. Then he thought an office building would be better. In the 1980s, a couple of different restaurants were here. Bill and Laura Harper's bought the building in September of 1982 and their Library Square Restaurant, originally called Library Restaurare, opened here in June of 1983. Also in the building were the New York Life Insurance agency and something called Hidden Manna. Gordon Peterson bought the restaurant in January of 1987 and then Bill Harper bought it back in February of 1989. Downstairs was Employment Plus and Secretarial, an employment agency, which began in December of 1989.

Wu's Chinese Restaurant took over the upstairs in November of 1992. It was owned and run by Kai Cheong Wu and his wife Chan. Steve Wadsworth bought the building in April of 1997 and did some major remodeling. Barberettes Salon & Rejuvenating Center, run by Paula Schlangen and Colleen Merkins (massage therapist), came to the basement in August of 1997. Shelly Krone either bought the salon in the late nineties or she was one of the owners from the start. An employment center named the Work Connection came here in July of 1998. Also at that time, a branch of the Green Lake State Bank opened here.

Today the building is still called the Library Square Building and the Barberettes Salon & Rejuvenating Center and Bohn Consulting Associates are a couple of the businesses located here. Lillith's Natural Health & Beauty and Heavenly Hands Massage was here until it moved in April of 2003.

(508 Darwin Street East in the early 1900s.) East of the library was a long tall white building called the Litchfield House. It was a hotel and was built by Charles J. Almquist and his brother Solomon M. "Sol" Almquist. The hotel opened for business in August of 1869.

Harold Lien bought the hotel in 1948 and it became the Lien Apartments and Rooms until 1979, when the business closed.

Today one of Ideal Lumber's buildings is on this site.

100-124 Commercial Street East. At the corner, heading east from the Litchfield House was Litchfield's very first lumberyard. John Esbjornsson and Charles Ellis Peterson started the lumberyard here in August of 1869.

The Litchfield Lumber Company, which began in 1955, is here today.

200 Commercial Street East. Across Holcombe, again heading east was an icehouse business. G. A. Neuman started an ice business in 1905. That small icehouse's location is unknown, but the ice business was moved into the larger icehouse at this location.

The icehouse here was built in 1910 by a group of stockholders consisting of John M. Learn, William Shoultz and A. W. Kron.

The icehouse building was torn down in May of 1962, after Consumer's Co-op Oil Company purchased the lot.

125 Sibley Avenue South. Heading back to the 100 block of Sibley Avenue from the library, I pass another lumberyard, which I remember as Weyerhauser. It originally was the J. F. Anderson Lumber Company, which became the Liberty Lumber Company and then Thompson Yards Inc. in February of 1916. But before all these lumberyards, there was an elevator here called the Minnesota & Dakota.

Thompson Yards became Weyerhauser Lumber in September of 1959 and today it's a warehouse for Ideal Lumber.

Still walking north on Sibley Avenue, I cross Depot Street/Highway 12 East and come to the east corner building, which is almost as famous as the hotel building.

100 Sibley Avenue North. (1 Sibley in the early days and then 831-833 Sibley Avenue in the early 1900s.) One of the first non-residential buildings to go up in Litchfield was at this corner of Sibley Avenue and Depot Street. The St. Paul and Pacific Railroad put the building up here for a land office in 1869. Hans Mattson was the land agent.

In 1870, another small building was added to the lot and it was used as county offices.

Most people will remember this corner as being "Greep's". Greep's, actually Greep-Trueblood, began in 1926. It was started by Pete Osdoba, O. F. Trueblood and I. Greep, and was run by the Osdoba family for forty-eight years after Pete bought out his partners in 1927. He decided to leave the name as it was. After Pete died, his daughters, Genevieve "Gen" Osdoba-Schelde and Virginia "Peg" Osdoba-Palmquist assumed ownership.

In the late sixties, the store's sign simply stated "Greep's". The top of the store's façade, the brick "parapet", was taken down in April of 1969.

In September of 1974, Greep's was sold to David and Pat Meidal and George Krawec. They kept the name as Greeps, Inc. In August of 1979, Greep's closed its doors. Falknor's Appliances moved into the building in September of that year.

Gordon Kable, who owned a furniture store in Hutchinson, owned the building in the mid to late eighties and he had Kable's Furniture and Appliance here. The Consignment Connection was here in 1986 and it was sold to Joyce Allen in December of 1986.

The name was changed to the Consignment Corner. Then Furniture Plus, owned by Delano Schultz, came here in June of 1990. Kable brought in an antique store and called the business Sibley Antiques. In April of 1992, Clarris Hedtke bought the business and then, in April of 1999, Doris and Bob Luhman bought it.

They sold the business to Mike Mihlbauer in January of 2000. Mike officially opened in March of 2001.

Mihlbauer's Sibley Antiques is still here today.

Greep's, prior to the "parapet" being taken off the top of the façade.

19 Depot Street East. Once again I will leave Sibley Avenue to walk east down Depot Street. The next building, after the Welch building (Greep's) on the corner was erected, was Litchfield's second telephone office. (The first telephone office was in back of the corner drugstore downtown.) Before that, someone sold McCormick machinery from a building on this lot.

I don't know what was here in the sixties and seventies.

The law office of Joseph P. Bluth was here in December of 1980. Lawyer Robert "Bob" Schaps joined Bluth in April of 1981 but he moved to 603 Sibley Avenue North in June of 1982. Jeff Olson joined Bluth here in August of 1982. W. R. Peterson Properties came to the building in the late eighties.

Today a body piercing and tattoo shop is here.

21-23 Depot Street East. (Today Depot Street is more often referred to as Highway 12 East.) The Litchfield Independent was printed at this site before 1881, heading east from Sibley Avenue.

For years a harness shop, a restaurant, or a furniture store were here.

The Red Door Thrift Store, owned by Don Anderson, was here in November of 1968.

Ralph Barrick had a Hi-Way Supply store here and he sold it in June of 1970 to Gerald Gartner and Jeff Benson. At some point, the name was changed to Highway Supply and then, in July of 1975, Bob Powell bought the business and moved it to a new building west of the new Farmer's Daughter on East Highway 12.

In January of 1981, the Willmar Travel Service put in an outlet, the Litchfield Travel Service, here. It was sold and moved in December of 1988. B. Lease and Sons, Inc followed it.

T-C Flooring's Remnants Plus, a carpet remnant shop owned by Bob Hedin, came here in July of 1991.

Today this building stands vacant.

25 Depot Street East. (Today Depot Street is more often referred to as Highway 12 East.) There were two buildings on this next lot to the east, so the information here may get confusing. The Chase and Dunn (R. W.) Pioneer Livery Stable was Litchfield's first livery and it was started here in the fall of 1869.

Charles O. Porter owned all the lots from this point to the corner at Marshall Avenue in 1874.

This building is gone today.

27 Depot Street East. (Today Depot Street is more often referred to as Highway 12 East.) Sam Brown had a harness shop in the next location heading east in the early 1900s. The building itself had been at the corner of Sibley Avenue and Depot Street and had been used as the courthouse and city government building for a while.

One of Litchfield's early bowling alleys was here. Art Krout and Warren Plath owned it in November of 1954. Art heard that a group from the cities was going to build a new bowling alley east of town on Highway 12 so he and Warren Plath quickly put up the Ripley Lanes[89] south of town by Lake Ripley on 22 in September of 1956. Of course, this bowling alley closed down.

---

[89] Art and Warren sold the Ripley Lanes to Martin Pedley in September of 1961 and Pedley sold it to Joe Nelson in September of 1971. An earlier bowling alley in town was where the King's Wok is now.

Jerry Beckman's Appliance store followed here in the late sixties and seventies. In September of 1968, Pat Joyce started his Litchfield Radio and TV in this building sharing it with Beckman.

America's Fitness Express, owned by Chad Kirchoff and Peter Taunton, opened here in August of 2001. It is still here today.

33 Depot Street East facing south, and 101 Marshall Avenue North facing east. (Today Depot Street is more often referred to as Highway 12 East.) Originally the Mitchell and Waller (John A. C.) Lumberyard was here at the corner of Marshall Avenue and Depot Street in 1870. The building was torn down in July of 1871 and the lot became vacant. It was used as an ice skating rink.

Litchfield Implement was here for decades and then a Sinclair gas station followed. It also was the site of Meeker County's first outdoor phone booth in late September of 1953.

In November of 1970, William S. "Mac" or "Bill" McGee, mayor of Litchfield in 1963, had a realty office in a building at this corner facing Marshall and, in May of 1973, the Benage Jewelry store, owned by Dexter and Gayle Benage, was in a building facing Marshall. I don't know if it was the same building or not but it stayed only months before moving to Sibley Avenue North. In September of 1973, my classmate John Ferguson had Ferguson's Used Cars here before moving out on east Highway 12 to the old Schwartzwald's Motors building for a new car dealership in October of 1976. Then Greenbriar Floral came here in November. Dick and Karen Heath owned that business.

The Dave Pierce Insurance Agency occupied the Marshall Street facing building in the seventies and moved next to Beckman's a few feet to the west in May of 1981 after Greenbriar Floral moved to the hotel corner in April.

Next to Pierce today are the Litchfield Therapeutic Massage and Exotic Specialty Travel/Lucky Mindy Adventures businesses.

There were many restaurants in Litchfield over the years. Most of them were downtown, but a couple had unique locations where Depot Street split into Highway 12 East on one side and First Street on the other.

The "triangle" with the Travelers' Inn at the point.

105 Depot Street East. In the next block heading west was Ole Larsen's Travelers' Inn in the forties and fifties at the point of this triangular block. The block, at the junction of Depot and First Streets, had Capt. Miller's feed mill in August of 1885.

Russ and Doris Peterson had the Inn next. They sold it to Donovan and Irene Blaha in January of 1966, bought it back in January of 1967, sold it to Ervin and Margaret Jensrud in the late sixties and got it back again in February of 1972.

Langmo Farms moved here at sometime and Tom Tranby brought his New York Life insurance business here to a room in August of 1988. Litchfield Distributing also came to the building at some time in the late eighties.

107 Depot Street East. (Today Depot Street is more often referred to as Highway 12 East.) East of the restaurant in 1879 was an old blacksmith and wood working shop building. Morris and Henry Neuman built it. Morris was the blacksmith.

Dale's 76 Service was here in the late sixties and early seventies.

Today Prints Charming is just east of the site of the Travelers' Inn, moving there in November of 2001.

215-225 Depot Street East. The Kopplins had a miniature golf course for a while east of the station where the Green Lantern was and the Super America station is today between Holcombe and Armstrong Avenues at 215 Depot Street East.

The Super America station came in the early sixties.

We'll head back to Sibley Avenue and the Greep's corner building where we'll head north, continuing our walk around town.

104-106 Sibley Avenue North. (3 Sibley in the early days and then 827 Sibley Avenue in the early 1900s.) Back on Sibley Avenue North, heading north from the Greep's corner, was Solomon M. "Sol" Almquist's saloon in 1870.

Most people will remember the Unique Theater being here at this location. The Unique and the Hollywood theaters were sold to Dean Lutz in April of 1978.

The Unique was torn down in May of 1996. The city had acquired it on tax forfeiture.

The location is just a vacant lot but a lot of great memories linger here today.

110 Sibley Avenue North. (5 Sibley in the early days and then 825 Sibley Avenue in the early 1900s.) M. Arthur Brown started out in Litchfield in a building next door to the north of the Unique in our city's early days. Brown sold hardware in a little shop and was a "turner" or lathe operator.

Then, for years a tailor shop was here until Roscoe Keller built a new building on this site in 1962.

Cynthia Tongen bought the Coiffure Beauty Salon here to the rear of Keller's building in August of 1970 and it became Cynthia's Wig & Beauty Salon. My classmate Sue Wisdorf Eisenbacher worked along side my ex-wife for Cynthia. Dr. M. L. Speckman practiced chiropractory and sold hearing aids from a room in the building in the early and late seventies. The Keller Barber Service was still here, although Roscoe's son David ran it. Roscoe had retired in the early seventies. He fell off the roof of his house in 1978 and never really recovered from his injuries. In the fall of 1979, the Diet Center went into a room in the building.

Bruce Kellogg bought the Keller building and the barber business in November of 1980. He called his business Kellogg's Barber Service. Dr. S. D. Curtis joined Dr. Steven Bachman here in the early eighties. Sometime in early 1985, Litchfield Speedy Print moved into a room here. Lee Hardy and Jan O'Keefe opened their JL Counseling Service in part of the building in July of 1985 and then moved it to another location in April of 1992.

Smokey's Card Shop, a sports trading card business owned by Joel Lutz and Warren Riele, came to a back room in the building in December of 1991. In May of 1992, Elam Pool and Patio moved into the room formerly occupied by JL Counseling. Wayne and Sue Elam owned that business. AFLAC insurance, run by Steve Koehn and Jack Heacock, came to an office here in November of 1992. In December of 1994, a regional office of the American Lung Association went into one of the offices in the building. H&R Block came into one of the offices here in the mid nineties, as did the Litchfield Dental Laboratory.

Today, the building still houses the Kellogg Barber Shop and H & R Block.

112 Sibley Avenue North. (7 Sibley in the early days and then 823 Sibley Avenue in the early 1900s.) In my day, a little store called Axel's Candy and Tobacco store or Axel's Place, owned by Axel Johnson, was the next store heading north. It was in half of the building where John E. Jorgenson Realty is now.

In 1875, however, the St. Paul and Pacific Railroad owned this lot and in the mid-1870s, a building housing the Rail Road Bonds and Real Estate Agency was here. In the summer of 1879, Per Ekstrom, August T. "Gus" Koerner and Company (Frank E. Viren) had a real estate office here.

Dr. Newell J. Vold's Optometry came in here in September of 1956 and his son Michael joined him in August of 1974.

In September of 1978, the Volds moved to a new building at 715 Sibley Avenue North and were joined by Dr. Gary P. Gross. At first the building there was called the Litchfield Professional Center but the name was soon changed to the Litchfield Optometric Center.

J L Counseling Service, Inc. was here in the late eighties and early nineties. John E. Jorgenson Realty moved into the building in February of 1997.

Today Jorgenson's Realty is still at the location of both Kate's and Axel's.

114 Sibley Avenue North. (7 Sibley in the early days and then 821 Sibley Avenue in the early 1900s.) Another tiny building followed Axel's. In 1875, the St. Paul and Pacific Railroad owned the lot here. In May of 1876, this site had the Independent Printing Office, which published the Litchfield Independent newspaper.

Today John E. Jorgenson's Realty is at the location of both Kate's Café, which was here and Axel's, which was next door.

An alley followed Kate's. As far as I can tell, there was always an alley or vacant lot there. The alley was closed down in July of 1972.

116 Sibley Avenue North. (9 Sibley in the early days and then 817 Sibley Avenue in the early 1900s.) The lot north of the alley had a couple of buildings on it; maybe one was straddling the eventual alley location. Andrew P. Nelson and Andrew Winger had a tailor shop here in 1876. In September of 1876, the Elmquist brothers, David and unknown, came from Minneapolis and started their Elmquist Brothers' jewelry store in one of the buildings here.

Dale's Rec was here in 1966, when Dale Lee bought the bar, which was already here.

In the late seventies, Ron's Palace occupied the building.

This is a vacant lot today.

118 Sibley Avenue North. (11 Sibley in the early days and then 815 Sibley Avenue in the early 1900s.) The first occupant of the next lot heading north was the Litchfield Exchange Hotel, built in 1870 by George Teigen, and sold to W. S. Knappen in early 1873.

The J. C. Penney Company built on this lot and the one to the north of it in 1958. The store opened up in January of 1959.

Penney's closed down in January of 1991 and the building housed Bob Hanson's Coast-To-Coast starting in June of 1991.

Today, True Valu hardware is here.

120-124 Sibley Avenue North. (13 Sibley in the early days and then 813 Sibley Avenue in the early 1900s.) Beginning in October of 1876, Samuel Hollingsworth's Uncle Tom's Cabin Saloon was in the building north of the last location.

Most people will remember this as the site of the Penney's store. After Penney's closed in January of 1991, the building became Bob Hanson's Coast To Coast starting in June of 1991.

It's the True Valu hardware store location today.

126 Sibley Avenue North. (15 Sibley in the early days and then 811 Sibley Avenue in the early 1900s.) The building north of the Penney's site sat on a lot originally owned by M. Arthur Brown and

Clark L. Angell. H. B. Brown had a lumberyard in town under the name of Brown and Brown and he erected a building here in September of 1878 after Angell had left the location. Samuel Hollingsworth moved his saloon and billiard hall here from next door in October of 1878. Cafes were on this lot for decades, the most well known being the Black Cat Cafe.

Starting in November of 1965, the building housed Thorp Loan and Thrift.

Finally Litchfield Chiropractic Center (Steven Bachman) moved into the building in the late eighties and it is still here today.

130 Sibley Avenue North. (17 Sibley in the early days and then 807 Sibley Avenue in the early 1900s.) There were a couple of small buildings on this lot north of the previous location. A Mr. Parker built one of them. D. E. Potter did his furniture construction in it for a short time before moving to one of his several other locations in town. Two gentlemen named C. B. Howell, a real estate agent, and Ortho Campbell eventually owned the little building and they sold it to George B. Lyon in March of 1871.

For decades, this lot was associated with the meat business. Koerner's and Sam's Meat Markets were the most well known.

In the early seventies, the Hub Fabric & Fashion store was here. Alan and Gayle Reff, who owned Something Special next door to the north, brought in the Village Yard Goods and Crafts store here in 1975 and then added the Village Frame Shop to it in the fall of 1976. The frame shop went down to the Reff-Askeroth Interiors store in the old Woolworth building and Village Yard Goods followed in the fall of 1979. Then Lorna's, Fashions, a ladies sportswear store owned by Lorna Menken, which had been north of the Hollywood Theater, came here in October of 1979.

SunRise Waterbeds, owned by George and Margie Polingo, moved here in February of 1983.

Brodin Studios, a bronze casting business owned by Neil Brodin and Danny (a woman) Rodgers came here in April of 2000.

The Brodin Studio is still here today.

132 Sibley Avenue North. (805 Sibley Avenue in the early 1900s.) Starting out as a vacant lot with a fence on it facing Sibley, this next location, still heading north, was owned by William S. Brill, who had a drugstore next door to the north.

Gale Plate's Toggery was here in the late 1960's.

After Plate's left in August of 1971, Something Special, a gift store owned by Askeroth's Interiors came here in November of 1972. It was sold to Alan and Gayle Reff in June of 1974. They joined forces with the Askeroths at the other end of town in the old Woolworth building in early 1978. Then Trademark Trends, a family clothing store owned by Pete and "Larry" Schlauderaff, came in June of 1979.

The Jeanery, owned by Dennis Hukriede, opened here in January of 1981. Doug and Jo Anne Patten bought into the business in March of 1982. The Fashion Boutique was the next store to come here in the mid-eighties. Donna Johanneck operated it. The Schlauderaffs still owned the building. I believe Dimensions, a store selling an unknown product owned by an unknown owner, was here in 1984. Then a fabric store was here. In late December of 1986, a fire gutted the building. It was torn down in March of 1987.

To lot stood vacant until Nicola's made it into the patio it is today.

134 Sibley Avenue North. (19 Sibley in the early days and then 801 Sibley Avenue in the early 1900s.) Drug stores, bakeries and shoe stores were the odd combinations and personalities of the corner store of this block. At first, there was a drugstore here. William S. Brill had the first drugstore in Meeker County down the street in 1869. He erected a new building here in September of 1870 and moved in.

For many years Sandgren's Shoes was here. Roy Lindeen bought the building and the lot in April of 1970. In July of 1976, John Sutterfield bought the business, keeping the Sandgren's name on the store.

Sutterfield eventually changed the name to John's Shoe Corner in the early eighties. Chester Saxby owned the building and lot in January of 1983 and Ron Tiffany bought it in November of 1983.

The business name was changed to Tiffany's Shoes in February of 1991. After the store closed, Paul and Pete Boushard bought this corner building in November of 1991 and brought in Music Plus in December. Music Plus sold guitars, strings, CDs, tapes and repaired instruments. Ron Nicholson bought the lot in August of 1995 and his son Mark, Shirley and Steve Neighbors and Ann and Mark Lien brought a bakery back to Litchfield in December of 1995. Coincidentally, this had been the location of Linne's bakery for many years and the first location of Wayne Rayppy's New Bakery. This newest bakery here was named Bakery...etcetera. Jim Majchrazak bought the business in May of 1998 and changed the name of it to Grandma's Gingerbread Haus in July of 1998.

After the Gingerbread Haus closed, Bob Greenhow and Steve Neighbors, who owned the building, convinced Matthew and Debra Olson to move here and try another bakery in March of 2000. They called their bakery Grandpa and Grandma's Bake Shoppe. Then Nicola's, owned by Nicole Johnson, came to the location in November of 2001. Mandy Nelson, Bob Greenhow's daughter, and her husband Steve started Sweet Promotions, a wholesale candy-making company in the rear part of Nicola's, where the actual bakery had been.

Nicola's is still at this location today.

It's time for another detour from Sibley Avenue. We'll turn the corner and head east on Second Street. By the way, this first block heading east became one-way in June of 1976.

18-24 Second Street East. (512 Second Street East in the early 1900s.) A couple of small wooden buildings had been here. The first of the two lots here had pioneer Clark L. Angell as its occupant. Clark L. Angell had his first photography business here in the next location just before the alley. At first Angell's gallery was a portable one. I assume that meant nothing more than a tent.

People will remember Askeroth's Paint Co. being here. Later Askeroth's became Askeroth's Interiors.

Then in January of 1978, Alan and Gayle Reff bought the business.

In the early eighties, Sleepy Hollow, a waterbed and furniture store was here. Then in May of 1982, George Polingo and Margie Strey bought the business and changed the name to SunRise Waterbeds. The owners eventually married. Natural Foods Co-op came here from the basement of Larry's Barber Shop in February of 1983 when the waterbed business moved elsewhere. The Co-op moved behind the Ed Olson Agency on Third Street West in the summer of 1984. In 1989, it became Smith's Appliances, owned by Gary Smith.

The appliance business moved to a Sibley Avenue location in August of 2000 and Litchfield Video, owned by Warren Riebe, moved into this location in September of that year.

The Litchfield Video store is still at this location today. At some time this location was combined with the next one to the east.

After the new brick building was built at the Askeroth location, a few businesses were upstairs. In July of 1938, Fred Maass came to town and opened his office up there.

In the mid-forties, the Hanson Studio photography business, owned by Kermit B. Hanson, was upstairs.

Lowell Wilson moved upstairs in 1950. James Anderson had an insurance office here also.

Walter C. Whitney opened up another optometry shop upstairs in April of 1962 and Frederick C. Brown had his dental office upstairs in the mid-sixties and early seventies.

The New Tattoo Studio, owned by Scott Clark, moved into a room upstairs in November of 1993.

26-30 Second Street East. (514 Second Street East in the early 1900s.) For many years, the large building after the alley was called the Snell Block because it initially had John Snell's furniture and undertaking business and was large enough to accommodate several other businesses. Snell started his business in 1877 at another location and built a new building here in May of 1879.

The Horseshoe Café was here for many years. The law office of Olson (Leland), Nelson (Wendell) & Nagel was here and Dr. Lennox Danielson had his office here in the seventies.

Steven Drange replaced Nagel at some point, probably in the early eighties. The law firm moved two doors to the east in February of 1984. In October of 1984, the Peterson – Bratland Real Estate Agency came here. The Edward D. Jones business came here in the late eighties, as did BOE John Land Surveyors.

Franklin Companies moved here in November of 1992. Representatives were Jeff Huston and Mark Lies. Meeker County Abstract was also in the building in the late nineties and on.

Today the Second Street Business Center is at this location. Dr. R. E. Patten has his chiropractic office here along with Franklin Companies Insurance, Minnesota Realty operated by John Chorzempa, and Jill Miller Insurance Agency.

32-34 Second Street East. (518 Second Street East in the early 1900s.) This location was actually the west part of a large building that ran to the east corner. F. Edward Scarp and Company's Litchfield Laundry was here initially in the late 1800s or early 1900s. Around the 1960s, an office building was built here.

The law firm of Olson, Nelson and Drange moved here from a couple of doors to the west in February of 1984. Mark P. Wood was added to the firm sometime in the eighties.

Jim and Jo McClure brought in R.P.V.S., Inc., an employment placement agency, in January of 1990. Lutheran Brotherhood was in the building in the early nineties as was the Meeker County Abstract Company. American Family Insurance, run by Steve and Jill Miller and Jilane Vinar, moved here in late 1998.

The Meeker County Abstract Company, American Family Insurance, Rebecca M. Rue's law office and Olson (deceased Leland), Nelson (deceased Wendell), Wood (Mark P.) and Berry (David G.) law offices share this location today.

40 Second Street East. (520-522 Second Street East in the early 1900s.) Eventually a large brick building that became Quinn Motors was at the southeast corner of the block, at Second Street and Marshall Avenue, but before that there was a small building on the lot that Chris Mortenson leased and moved his Litchfield City Bakery into in October of 1884.

For the longest time, Quinn Motors was at this corner location. When Quinn Motors closed in the late sixties, the L & P Selling Service, owned by Laura and Paul Clouse, moved in. They were related to a former girlfriend of mine, Patty. Steve Clouse joined them in the eighties and the name was changed to L & P Quality

Furniture briefly and then backs to Selling Service. Greg Halonen brought in his Realty World-Advantage business in March of 1987.

Dee's Family Hair Styling moved here in March of 1988 and is here today.

Turning the corner onto Marshall Avenue and heading north, there was a small building facing Marshall just to the south of the corner building, sharing this corner lot. It originally had J. W. Bartlett's Billiard Hall in it in 1875. He advertised that he sold no liquor.

This location eventually became the part of the Quinn Motors building that faced Second Street.

Burnett Realty moved into the building in October of 1994.

125 Marshall Avenue North. Heading south from the previous location, there was a building almost directly across from the city hall building, but not at the corner lot. It had Gottlieb C. Koerner's meat market in it. The market started in February of 1873.

In the late eighties and early nineties, the Soil Survey Office was here.

Raeann Rose Photography, owned by Raeann Carlson, came here in July of 1997, but soon she moved to Sibley Avenue in the old Sward-Kemp building.

Today Litchfield Office Supply is at this location.

115 Marshall Avenue North. Somewhere in the middle of the block, across from the hotel on Marshall Avenue, were lots owned by H. W. Simons. W. M. White had a farm machinery business on one of the lots here or near here in April of 1871. Also in April of 1871, A. H. Lofstrom built a small building here for his paint shop, before he moved to Sibley Avenue in 1874.

The Litchfield Welding and Machine Company was here for quite a long time, beginning before the turn of the century as a blacksmith shop and still going today as Litchfield Welding. Don Ellig had owned the business and in March of 1983 Dan Salzbrun bought it, changing the name to Dan's Welding and Repair. In March of 1984, Jim VanNurden bought it, changing the name back to Litchfield Welding and Machine Company. He was the stepson of Ellig.

101 Marshall Avenue North. A couple of buildings were just north of the western corner of Marshall Avenue and Depot Street. One was known as the Topping building because "Professor" Charles Griswold "Charley" Topping was one its most well known occupants. He began his business here in June of 1871. The businesses here today face Depot Street.

100 Marshall Avenue North/100 Depot Street West. At the eastern corner of Marshall Avenue and First Street, where the Wells Fargo Bank is today, was the Lake Ripley House hotel. William Gould & Co. built the hotel in 1870 on Gould's lot and it was leased to James Tinkham. He called it Tinkham House.
In 1967, the building here, which, over the years, had housed a car garage, a hatchery and a laundromat, was torn down and the Northwestern National Bank put up a new building in November of 1968.
It became Norwest at some time and then the Wells-Fargo Bank that it is today in July of 2000.

Next to that corner lot, heading north, was the building where Henry G. Rising published the Litchfield Republican newspaper starting in the January 24, 1871. He discontinued the paper in the following autumn.
At some time the building was torn down and the lot became vacant.

One door north of that lot was the Joseph Leaser furniture factory. It was a twenty-five foot square story and a half building that cost $500 to build in 1870. Mr. Leaser used it to make and sell furniture and coffins, which he started selling in the spring of 1871 on Sibley Avenue. He added a twenty by forty foot building for a sales room in February of 1873. I think Gottlieb "Jake" Keller and Jacob "Jake" Koerner had a meat market here for a short time before moving to Sibley Avenue.

114 Marshall Avenue North. In 1869, a house was moved from Forest City to the next lot, heading north. Adam Klass owned the house. It had been Klaas' saloon in Forest City and it became the same here, plus a boarding house. It eventually served as a unit of the Exchange Hotel, which was next door to the north.

Century Companies of America, an insurance business, had an office here in the mid-eighties. Kurt D. Werner ran it.

The original house was still at this location, but it was moved off the lot in May of 2004. One of its owners over the years, H. W. Simons, moved the Exchange, another one of Litchfield's hotels, from Sibley Avenue to the next site in June of 1879.

Next door to the north is a parking lot today, but when the old town hall was at the corner location, W. W. Rollins' saloon was here in 1870.

It is a parking lot today.

126 Marshall Avenue North. In the early days of Litchfield, a wooden City Hall building stood where the Community Building stands today at the corner of Marshall Avenue and Second Street. The "town hall" was built in the fall of 1874 by the city and the Masons to be used conjointly as a city meeting place and the Mason's Golden Fleece Lodge.

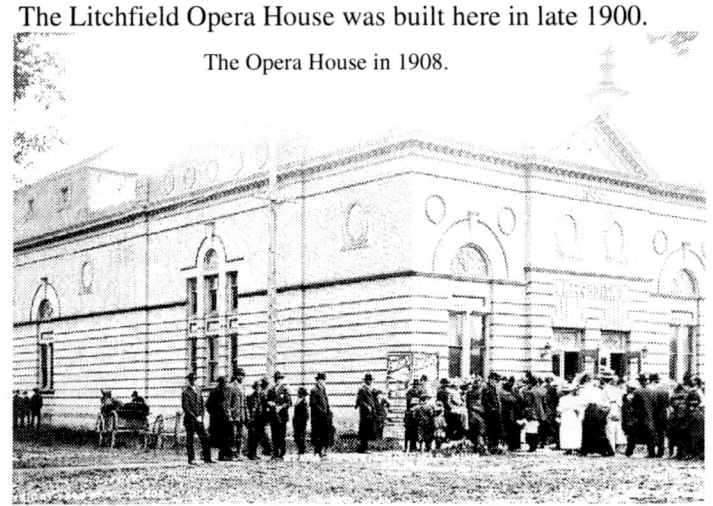

The Litchfield Opera House was built here in late 1900.

The Opera House in 1908.

The city offices were in the building for a long time but the building is vacant today because of mold problems.

In the spring of 2003, the Preservation Alliance of Minnesota named the Opera House building to its list of the Minnesota's ten most endangered historic properties.

202 Marshall Avenue North. Straight north of the Opera House at the corner is a residential home that was converted, for a period of

time, into a funeral home. This location was the site of the first residential building in Litchfield in 1869. It was an eight by ten foot shack owned by Truls Peterson, who conducted a tailoring business out of it, besides living there.

Erickson's Funeral Home was the most known occupant of this location. The funeral home was finally closed in October of 1967.

Today the house is back to being a regular home.

210 Marshall Avenue North. There was another residential house north of the funeral home, the fourth lot from the southeast corner of Marshall Avenue and Third Street.

An office building was eventually built here. Farm Credit Services of Minnesota Valley was here in the eighties, nineties and is still here today.

216 Marshall Avenue. The lot to the north of the last one had a building on it once that had been erected in 1874 by Nels Pearson, but I don't know what kind of business Pearson had. Litchfield's first Village Council President Jesse V. Branham, Jr. had owned the house.

Theodore W. "Ted" Kohlhoff built a new Super Valu store here in December of 1954.

In September of 1966, Ted sold his interest to his son Gene V. and retired. Ted had brought his Gene into the business as a partner several years before. Gene sold half of the business to his manager Bruce Cottington in November of 1968. Eventually Cottington owned the whole store and severed connections with Super Valu.

Bruce changed the name of the store to Cottington's Country Foods in March of 1977. He rented the building to Eric Vogt in March of 1979 and the store was called Vogt's Foods.

Jim Hobbin and Bob Terry bought business from Vogt in August of 1980 and changed the name of it to Miracle Mart. In December of 1981, Cottington sold the building to Richard "Dick" and Diane Baril who brought in his Ports of Scandinavia store in February of 1982. A few months later, Dick and Diane brought in Baril's Paint & Carpet.

In October of 1998, a partnership headed by Dennis Rutledge bought Baril's and changed the name to Litchfield Decorating Center.

The building stood vacant for a long time until Litchfield's new library was put into the remodeled building in 2003.

226 Marshall Avenue North. In 1870, Charles Forester, a carpenter/wheelwright, had a building here at this southeast corner of Marshall Avenue and Third Street.

The St. Cloud House hotel was here in the early 1880s and was still here into the early 1900s.

The Gold Bond Gift Stamp Redemption Center, owned by Kohlhoff's Super Valu, was here in January of 1969.

The Redemption Center was changed to the Golden Gift Center in April of 1973.

Something called Wet Pets, owned by John Cottington, came here briefly in June of 1986. He sold aquarium fish, I believe.

Today this is the parking lot for the new library.

30 Third Street East. Across the street, at the southwest corner of Marshall Avenue and Third Street, was F. G. Alvord's blacksmith shop in the early 1870s. For years, Nick Post's blacksmith shop was here.

In September of 1959, Dr. Lowell Wilson put up an office building here for his chiropractic business.

Lowell was here for almost twenty-one years before selling the practice to Dr. R. E. Patten in April of 1980.

26-28 Third Street East. West of Wilson's building on Third Street, where the McGowan house had been, another building was erected in the early sixties. It was called the Hugh Wegner building, so I assume that he put the building up for his insurance business. Dr. Roger A. Dahlseid moved his dentistry business into part of the building in October of 1966.

National Securities Underwriter was here in the early seventies along with State Farm Insurance and Doctor Donald Dille's office. In 1973, Lenny L. Henriksen had an accounting office in Dille's office after Donald was killed in a car accident.

Dee's Beauty Salon was here in the late seventies and mid-1980s. Henriksen moved to 702 Sibley Avenue North in May of 1984. Tom Tranby brought his New York Life insurance business here in June of 1987.

Edward D. Jones & Co., a stock broking business, came here in April of 1990. Bob and Kathy Cobb owned it until Ralph Couey got it in August of 1990. The Edward D. Jones & Co. business moved to 306 Ramsey Avenue North.

The Backyard, a tanning center, and the Litchfield Therapeutic Massage Center businesses owned by Darlene and Dave Meidal, moved here from its location at 317 East Highway 12 in January of 1994. Mary C. Root, an accountant, moved into an office here sometime in the mid-nineties. Tom Costigan had an insurance office here also before 2000.

The Backyard is still in this building today.

Wayne Rick put up a building to the west of the Wegner building for his Rick's Plumbing and Heating business in the late 1960s.

In June of 1978, the Plumbery Home Center for Plumbing and Heating was added to Rick's Plumbing. He is still at this location today.

We'll return to the Post Office location and head back up Second Street to Sibley Avenue.

35 Second Street East. (515 Second Street East in the early 1900s.) At the northwest corner of Marshall Avenue and Second Street is the Post Office. There was a livery at this corner for a long time.

In July of 1886, John Knights, from Canada, bought the corner lot here from the owner Nathaniel Frank Revell and started a livery in August.

Standard Oil built an oil station here in the late summer of 1919. It was Litchfield's first service station.

The present Post Office was built here in 1935 and it is still here today.

27-29 Second Street East. Heading back west on Second Street towards Sibley Avenue from the Post Office corner, the next location before the alley had an odd mixture of occupants. First there was a feed mill owned by John Knights, then a livery and my generation remembers Sando's being here.

Today a lawn for the Post Office site is at this location.

23 Second Street East. (513 Second Street East in the early 1900s.) Samuel Y. Gordon's old butcher shop was moved here in April of 1873 on the next lot heading west.

During my youth, Dick Baldwin's TV repair shop was here.

Likens Studio, a photography business, was here in 1971 and Jeannie's Place, an antique store owned by Mrs. Hugh Wegner, was here in May of 1973.

In June of 1982, the little building here was torn down.

Today there is a small parking lot here.

202 Sibley Avenue North. (23 Sibley Avenue North in the early days, and then 741 Sibley Avenue North.) Back on Sibley Avenue, M. Arthur Brown built the brick building which is here today in 1884. It was for his hardware and implements store. Prior to that, William "Billy" Patterson had a feed store in the front at this location. Billy sold the business to Chauncey F. Dart in March of 1874.

During my youth and beyond, Sward-Kemp Drug was here. Richard Moquist owned the drugstore in the seventies and early eighties.

The drugstore was sold to John and Marilyn Ringhold in February of 1984. They changed the name of it to Ringhold Drug.

Recently the building here had the Raeann Rose Photography business, owned by Raeann Carlson, in it and the jd Framing Store, owned by Joan Donnay, came here in April of 1996.

The framing store was sold to Paula Berg Rothstein in March of 2001. When the framing store closed in early 2003, Mary Moore opened up her Mutt's Bath and Bakery in March of 2003.

208 Sibley Avenue North. (25 Sibley Avenue North in the early days and then 737 Sibley Avenue in the early 1900s.) I head north again on Sibley Avenue, where the next building had mostly restaurants in it after a building was put on the vacant lot here. Before it became a vacant lot, grocer James M. Morris built a small building here in 1871. Most people will remember Fransein's Café being here for three decades starting in 1935.

The Shamrock Café, owned by Jan and Jerry O' Keefe was here in the early sixties.

The O'Keefes moved elsewhere in town after Don Burke bought the building in November of 1971. Burke and his son Bob moved their jewelry store here in February of 1972.

After having been a Sears Catalog Store in the eighties and early nineties, the building stood vacant until a business called S & R Everything Store was here for a short period.

In late 1998, Keepsake Ceramics 'N Craft Supply, owned by Pam Tacheny, moved into this building and the first version of

Nicola's Coffee & More, owned by Nicole Johnson, came to share the building.

Alex Morales brought in his Nexxlevel Auto Sports Inc. auto accessories and supply store in January of 2004.

210 Sibley Avenue North. (27 Sibley Avenue North in the early days and then 731 Sibley Avenue in the early 1900s.) It seems that the Hollywood Theater has been at the next site forever, but that's not true. In 1871, George B. Lyon owned the lot and in 1874, Joseph Roetzer, a brewer with Erhardt Lenhardt, owned it. McGee Realty was upstairs over the theater in the mid and late seventies.

The Hollywood Theater, built in 1936, was sold to Dean Lutz in April of 1978.

Peter Schoell bought the theater in April of 1994, expanded it to three screens in June of 1995.

The theater is still going today.

212-212½ Sibley Avenue North. (29 Sibley Avenue North in the early days and then 729-727 Sibley Avenue in the early 1900s.) The building north of the Hollywood had the same façade as the Hollywood. It was done on purpose when the Hollywood was built. At that time, the building also took on the same street number as the Hollywood for some reason. So we have a little confusion here, but not with the location of the businesses.

Originally several different stores in a couple of small wooden buildings had been in this location. In 1874, Joseph Roetzer owned the lot but I don't know if he did anything with it. He also owned the lot next door. Around 1876, all that was here was a vacant lot with a wooden fence facing the street.

After another building went up here, it became either a shoe store or a jewelry store over the years.

Burke Jewelers was here in January of 1967 when Don bought the business.

Burke moved next door in February of 1972. In February of 1972, Gerald F. Foote appropriately brought a shoe store here called Gerald's Shoes and Boots. He should have named it Foote Shoes, don't you think? Maurine's Fabrics, owned by Robert Pederson and Donna Duchene, came here in February of 1974. Frederick E. Schultz had an accounting office somewhere here in the early seventies. Lorna's, a ladies sportswear store owned by Lorna and Norman Menken came here in November of 1975.

Then, the building had the Dragon Shop, owned by Dirk Lutz, in the early eighties to early nineties.

Uptown Sports, owned by Marty and Ann Bush was here in October of 1993 and finally Jenni's Consignment was here. Steve Langness owned the craft consignment business and, in September of 2000, he had Nicole Anderson open a little coffee nook in a corner of the consignment store. She called her "nook" Nicola's Coffee & More. She later moved to the old Sandgren shoe store corner building where she still is today.

Today this building is vacant.

What this street looked like in 1800.

214 Sibley Avenue North. (31 Sibley Avenue North in the early days and then 725 Sibley Avenue in the early 1900s.) Originally I believe there were a couple of small buildings at this next location heading north. In 1869, the M. Arthur Brown Hardware was here (one of the first three businesses in town) and D. E. Potter had his furniture business (Litchfield's first) here also.

Deilke's Dry Cleaning and Dyers was here for decades starting in 1929.

The location became the Benage Jewelry store in 1973 and then Margaret Breitenbach's Clay Pot Floral and Gift Shop after the dry cleaners closed.

In May of 1985, David Piepgras and his aunt, Sharon Gaisbauer, bought the building and started the Pizza Factory.

Then it was Campus Life in the late eighties and mid-nineties and then the Crow River Area Youth For Christ moved in.

Youth For Christ is still in this building today.

218 Sibley Avenue North. (33 Sibley Avenue North in the early days and then 723 Sibley Avenue in the early 1900s.) Litchfield's first hardware store was at this location in the fall of 1869. Smith D. King and Vanderborck or Vanderhorck owned it.

Reed's Printing was here for years with the Legion Club upstairs.

When Reed downsized to half of the building, the Legion Club finally moved downstairs in November of 1972, with Reed's staying in this part.

The Legion Club took over Reed's part of the building in April of 1996.

The Legion is still at this location today.

Johns Hardware, where the present Legion building is today.

220-222 Sibley Avenue North. (33 Sibley Avenue North in the early days and then 721 Sibley Avenue in the early 1900s.) I believe more than one building occupied this lot in the early days. In September of 1873, W. S. Knappen and a Mr. Scott built a small building on this lot to be used as a hotel, billiard hall, saloon and restaurant. The hotel was actually a boarding house.

Most people remember Reed's Printing being here for years. KLFD radio moved upstairs in the early sixties.

In November of 1972, the Legion Club moved downstairs to this part of the double building, while Reed's remained in the south half of the large building.

The Legion expanded to include the south half in April of 1996. The Legion Club is still here today.

There was an alley next. The city closed it in July of 1972.

226 Sibley Avenue North. (35 Sibley Avenue North in the early days and then 719 Sibley Avenue North in early 1900s.) A lot that at first held two small wooden buildings in late 1869 followed the alley. Pioneer lawyer Charles Henry Strobeck owned both buildings. The very first occupant of part of the lot was William S. Brill, who came to Litchfield from Red Wing, Minnesota. He had the first drugstore in Meeker County here in 1869.

For many years this was the site of Cox's Market.

Andy Bienick started the first Farmer's Daughter restaurant here in February of 1970. He built the present Farmer's Daughter[90] out on

---

[90] Andy sold the east Highway 12 Farmer's Daughter to Tom Guggisberg and Marlin Torgerson in October of 1976. Pete Brynildson bought into the partnership in March of 1978. The restaurant closed down in the early eighties and then Luther Wright bought the building in April of 1988 and reopened the restaurant again in May. The name became the New Farmer's Daughter Restaurant and Lounge. Mike Dols bought the restaurant in February of 1989, changed the name to the Blue Heron's Daughter and put Paul and Pam Dols in charge. Then Steve and Lisa Schneider

east Highway 12 in late 1973, (it opened in February of 1974), and kept this one open for a year. People called it the "Downtown Café". It was Harold's Restaurant in September of 1975 when Harold Gendron bought it from Andy.

Ron Markovich bought the restaurant in January of 1989 and changed the name to the Main Street Café.

It is still the Main Street Café today.

East side of Sibley, about 1875: From the left: The Bank of Litchfield (Natural Food Co-op), Dowling's harness shop and Strobeck's law office (Main Street Cafe), alley, Forester's saloon (Legion Club), and Flynn Brothers (Legion Club)

228-230 Sibley Avenue North. (37 Sibley Avenue North in the early days and 717 Sibley Avenue North in early 1900s.) Continuing north on Sibley Avenue brings me to a lot with originally more than one building again. Justice of the Peace Fayette Kelley owned the lot in 1874 and he had an office in one of the buildings. Chauncey F. Dart's feed store was here in the early 1870s in the other.

Berquist's Electric, which was here for a long time, moved out and a store called Gibson's Discount Center was here in September of 1969 before Pamida moved in.

Janelle Johnson brought the Land Of Oz, a children's clothing store, here in the fall of 1983. Hairport was moved here in March of 1987.

---

bought the business in April of 1994 and changed the name back to the Farmer's Daughter.

Linda Alexander and Jerry and Jan O'Keefe moved their JL Counseling Service here in April of 1992. Litchfield Oak & Things, managed by Julie Swanson, moved into the building in November of 1994. She sold craft items and futon furniture. Natural Food Co-Op moved to this building in July of 1995.

Natural Food Co-Op or Natural Foods Market is here today.

232-234 Sibley Avenue North. (39-41 Sibley Avenue in the early days and then 711 Sibley Avenue in the early 1900s.) Elizabeth Rust owned the next lot to the north in 1871. She had the Mrs. E. Rust Millinery here in May of 1871.

The Gamble's store was here in the fifties.

Gambles had a bad fire in December of 1970. It pretty much gutted the inside of the building. In March of 1971, it reopened.

Gamble's added Alden's Catalog Sales in the early seventies. Bill and Mary Olson bought Gamble's in September of 1976.

In the early eighties, Falknor's Appliance and Electronics moved in here, but it closed down in February of 1989. Then Steve and Shirley Neighbors had the Top Notch Men's Wear store here in November of 1989.

In July of 1991, Bob Greenhow and Steve Neighbors, under their company Mid-Minnesota Broadcasting, came to the building to bring KLFD back to Litchfield. They expected to be on the air in September but legalities held them back until December. At some time Nan Greenhow brought Prints Charming into the building, sharing it with KLFD. Randy Quitney purchased the business in July of 1997. He still worked at KLFD as its Sports Director. Jim and Barb Johnson, who also owned the Clip Clop trolley service, bought it from Quitney in August of 1999. In November of 2001, it moved out on East Highway 12, east of where Travelers' Inn had been.

Today the building still houses the KLFD radio studios and Bright Star Cleaning Company.

236 Sibley Avenue North. (2 Sibley Avenue North in the very beginnings of the town, 43 Sibley Avenue North in the early days and then 709 Sibley Avenue in the early 1900s.) Litchfield's first Village Council President Jesse V. Branham, Jr. owned this next lot in 1871. Mrs. C. M. (Fayette) Kelley's Millinery was here in a small wooden building in 1873 before she moved across to the west side of Sibley Avenue.

A women's clothing store and then a real estate office were here. Then the Shopper's Guide, owned by Fred and Norma Berke, was here in the late sixties and early seventies, sharing the building with the Rooney Real Estate office and Tri-County Conditioning.

American Family Insurance, with agent Robert E. "Bob" Gauer, was here sharing with the Shopper's Guide in the mid-seventies.

Shopper's Guide and Gambles in 1969.

The Berkes sold the Shopper's Guide to the *Independent Review* in November of 1982 and the operation was moved out of the building. West Central Community Services came here in February of 1983. The Heritage Bake and Coffee Shop or Heritage Café and Bake Shop, run by baker Clarence Nelson's daughter Sandy and her husband was here next in May of 1984. Then the Beauty Haven, owned and run by Norma Johnson was here. It was sold to Bonnie Thompson in August of 1988 and the name was changed to Bonnie's Beauty Salon.

Oscar Trelstad brought in his Litchfield Shoes store here in June of 1992. The attorneys' offices of Robert Schaps and Brad A. Kluver came into the building in the late nineties.

Today Schaps and Kluver are still at this location.

240 Sibley Avenue North. (45 Sibley Avenue North in the early days and then 705 Sibley Avenue in the early 1900s.) In 1869 Wait H. Dart had a dry goods store on the next lot heading north. He sold the store to W. D. Stanton in 1870.

Most people remember a dry cleaning business being here. Harding's was the most well known of the occupants.

H. Robert "Bob" Wannow bought the cleaning business in March of 1968.

Then it became the Litchfield Cleaners dry cleaning business and it is called Litchfield Dry Cleaners today.

I finally arrive at the corner building on this block, my walk around Litchfield nearly completed. The building at the corner has been called the Masonic Building for years.

242-244 Sibley Avenue North   (1 Sibley Avenue North in the very beginning of the village, then 47 Sibley Avenue North in the early days of the town, and then 701-703 Sibley Avenue in the early 1900s.) The first general store in Litchfield was here on this corner lot. But it wasn't the first store. That was across the street. Wait H. Dart owned the general store in 1869. The Masonic Hall was over the store that followed Dart's. The local chapter was called the "Golden Fleece Lodge No. 89". A new brick building was built in 1885 and the Masonic Building Association bought the building in April of 1927. The entrance to their upstairs lodge hall was on the side facing the park at 18 Third Street East. The downstairs was leased out to the J. C. Penney Company.

For years, Penney's and then Woolworth's were here. Woolworth's closed their doors in January of 1978 and Reff-Askeroth's Interiors went into the building that spring.   The

445

Askeroths and Alan and Gayle Reff owned it. Their Village Frame Shop was soon added to the store.

In April of 1983, Lyle and Judy Hames brought Hardware Hank back to Litchfield, opening up their store here.

The store was sold to the partnership of Jim and Cindy Theis and Larry and Deb Valiant in July of 1998. They changed the name of the business to Partners Hardware Hank.

Partners Hardware Hank is still at this location today.

Orphans

Orphans are businesses that I came across in my research but was unable to find their locations. The orphans from this book are:

Crow River Sporting Goods – George W. "Bud" Freelander '82
Litchfield Greenhouse – Paul Minton '82
D & F Electric – Dick Farmer '82
Ted Becker shoe repair – '84
Litchfield TV Service – 9/86 Owned by David Luoto and Mark Stoner
Framemakers – late eighties.
Merrill Lynch – Ann Nonweiler – 1989
American Family Insurance – 6/90, Mike Johnson, North Ramsey
Hometown Kitchen – early 1990's.
Autopac U.S.A. – 7/91, Jim Williams
Medication Works – 10/94 – Mary Jo Smith, counseling
First Priority Mortgage – 8/2000 – Art Quade

Acknowledgements

For this, my second book in print, I again relied heavily on the information I dug out of the old newspapers at the G.A.R. Hall (the Meeker County Historical Society) in Litchfield. Once again the ladies there gave me a lot of help and let me use the many pictures of early Litchfield, which have been entrusted to them. Thanks Cheryl Almgren and Cheryl Bulau.

Peter Hughes' widow, Darlene, gave me permission to write about Peter, as painful as it must have been, and let me use the Litchfield poster he had commissioned as this book's back cover. Thank you, Dar.

Once again, the Litchfield Area Oral History Project tapes, made by Joe Paddock several years ago, were helpful with my stories. Your work did not go unnoticed, Joe. Many people wrote me emails, which helped me write more stories. I thank Herbert Schuermann, Guy Shoultz, Dick Whalen, and Maynard Watkins. I interviewed many people, such as Patty Aaker, and I wish to thank all of them and especially Patty.

My oldest brother, Dennis, whom I can't keep from calling Dennie, which is what our mother called him, again contributed a great story to this book just as he had done with *Terry Tales*. Once again, the big brother helps the little brother. Thank you Lamar Gene Gumbuddy. (Inside joke.)

My daughter Andrea helped me by proofreading this book and I thank her once again. The student teaches the teacher.

Finally, the motivation for writing my first book was the birth of Ethan Ryan Peterson, my first grandson. Since that book was published, Ethan has acquired a little sister, Karra Bree Peterson. She and her big brother continue to motivate me to write down these tales in hopes that they will someday read Grandpa's two books and enjoy my memories of the things I did as a youngster in my wonderful hometown of Litchfield, Minnesota.

Last, but not least, as the saying goes, I want to thank my wonderful wife Lois for her continued support, patience, tolerance and monetary commitment to my work. Louie, you make my life a joy.

About the Author

Terry R. Shaw was born in Mankato, Minnesota in April of 1945 but he grew up in Litchfield starting in 1947. He has a Bachelor of Arts from the Minneapolis College of Art and Design and a Bachelor of Science from St. Cloud State University. He taught art in Glencoe, Minnesota for twenty-five years and was a full-time substitute teacher in the Willmar, Minnesota school district for six years before retiring.

Terry played drums in various rock and roll bands steadily since 1963, except for his two-year stint in the Army, until he retired from rock drumming in the summer of 2003. Two of those bands were with his brother Mick and the most famous was a band called Shaw-Allen-Shaw. Terry still drums in church every Sunday and plays guitar and sings almost every day of the week in local nursing homes and senior citizen centers.

Besides *Terry Tales* and *Terry Tales 2*, Terry has written over eighty songs and three other books, one about the Beatles, one about Buddy Holly, and one about Elvis, which are on the Internet. They can be found online at the addresses given.

The Beatles*: Every Little Thing We Said Today*
http://homepage.ntlworld.com/p.moorcroft/
Buddy Holly: *The Buddy Holly Recordings*
http://www.pmoorcroft.freeserve.co.uk/tshaw1.htm
Elvis Presley*: Elvis Sessions*
http://homepage.ntlworld.com/p.moorcroft/elvisite/Homepage.html

Terry Shaw and his wife Lois.

Index

NAME	PAGE
	(Photographs or illustrations are in italics.)

A

Aaker
Amy Anne, Andrea
   Allison, Annette
      Alise & Neal   318
  Anthony Allen "Tony"   302, 318, 332
  Bernie   296, 299, 301, 302, 317-333, *319, 321, 322, 326, 330, 331*
  Patricia Christel "Patty"   320, *321,* 322-333, 449
  Suzanne   332

Ackerman
  Baldy & Francis   123
  Larry   397

Ackerson
  Ethel   156

Achterhoff
  Cindy   273

Adams
  A.   414

Alexander
  Linda   443

Alheim
  Marv   391

Allen
  Andy, Archie, Arnold, & Blanche   46
  Cathy Osdoba   See Osdoba
  Jim   245, 247, 249-254, *250, 251, 264,* 296, 301, 317, 361, 388, 392, 393
  John Algot, Mr./Mrs.   46, 68
  Joyce   418
  Lloyd   46
  Myrtle   68
  Raynold Algot   46, 68
  Richard, Werner, Wilhelmina "Minnie & Willard"   46

Almgren
  Cheryl   214, 373, 449

Almquist
  Charles J.   416
  Solomon M. "Sol"   416, 423

Alvord
  F. G.   102, 435

Anderson
  Alfred   106
  Andrew L. "Andy"   383
  Boyd   411
  Bruce   106, 107
  Charlie   122
  Colleen   411
  Don   420
  Eugene "Skeeter"   50, 172
  Frank   389
  George, Mrs.   387
  Glenn A.   393
  Gordon "Gordie"   412
  Guy   410
  Hans Christian   383, 403
  Helen   200
  James   429
  J. F.   417
  Kay   410
  Kern   88
  Lil   211
  Lois   412
  Nels B.   408
  Nicole   439
  Paul E., Sheriff   45, 97, 99
  Ralph   303

Andreen
  Ludwig, Jr.   217-227, *218*

Angell
  Clark L.   62, 120, 409, 426, 428
  Hiram S.   120

Archibald
   Kenneth   268
Arness
   James   137
Ashby
   Turner, General   38
Asher
   Reading   410
Askeroth
   Andrew O.   201
   Clarence M. "Skip"   201, 202, 213
   Jerry, Olaf O. & Vernon   201
   Todd   202
Atkinson
   Herbert   404
   James Benjamin "Ben", Jr.   387, 397, 398, 404
Autry
   Gene   140
Aveldson
   Ernie   168
Axel
   (Clelland Card)   134

B

Bachman
   Steven "Steve", Dr.   423, 426
Baden
   Joe   385
Bailey
   Harvey   79, *80*, 90
Baker
   Ann   11
   Howard   11, 12
Baldwin
   Dick   13, 231, 436
Baril
   Diane   307, 434
   Richard "Dick"   307, 308, 434
   Wilfred F.   407
Barnes
   George   78

Barnstad
   Ole   87
Barnum
   P. T.   145, 146
Barrick
   Ralph   420
Barry
   Jack   *171*, 172
Barth
   Joseph "Joe"   385
Bartlett
   J. W.   431
Bartos
   David   308
Bates
   Danny   238, 239
Bauer
   Francis, George & Jerry   190
Baylor
   Don   51
Beach
   George H.   42
Beach Boys   250
Becker
   Ted   447
Beckman
   Elaine   See Bock
   Jerry   421
Beckstrand
   Mrs. and Mrs. Melvin   268, 269
Bedney
   L.   84
Belfoy
   Frank   390, 393
Benage
   Dexter & Gayle   421
Benjamin
   Hugh   67
   John, Dr.   26
Bennet
   Bill   229
Benny
   Jack   169
Benson
   Ed   62
   Jeff   420

John	329
Bent	
Greg	406
Berens	
W. Richard	404
Berg	
Otto	205
William	81
Berke	
Fred	444
Norma	117, 294, 444
Bernatson	
Emil & Emma	152
Harry & Henning	149-158
Berry	
Chuck	230, 243
David G.	430
Bertelson	
Chris A.	405
Berube	
Amy & Joseph	394
Bienick	
Andy	441
Bierman	
Bernie & William F.	201
Binsfeld	
David	385
Birkemeyer	
Dick & Doris	401
Bissell	
Frank E., Dr.	67
Bjorkland	
Al, Reverend	332
Blaha	
Donovan & Irene	422
Blesener	
Charlie	328
Blomker	
Bryan	406
Blonigan	
Dick	233, *234, 235, 245, 262,* 283
Bloomquist	
Gordon & Laura	406
Blosser	
Albert & Ed	48
Bluth	
Joseph P.	419
Bock	
Elaine Beckman	186
Boettcher	
Hal	293, 299
Bokander	
Bugs	134
Bolden	
Lionel & Shannon	273
Booth	
Marlin	205
Borg	
George & Torre	181
Boushard	
Paul & Pete	427
Bowen	
C.	121, 388
Boyd	
Belle	*37*, 38
Braatz	
Mariann	184
Braden	
J. C.	414
Brady	
Pat	145
Brandt	
Bill	123
Branham	
Delaney Ezra "Abe"	62, 92
Hiram S.	20, 58-62, 91, 92, 386
Jesse V., Jr.	19, 20, 59, 92, 386, 434, 443
Jesse V., Sr.	16, 17, 19
William	23
Branner	
Nellie	35
Braunhut, von	
Harold aka Harold N. Braunhut	145, 146
Breitenbach	
Bob	287
Margaret	388, 439

Brill
  William S.   414, 426, 427, 441
Brodin
  Neil   426
Brogren
  Einar   78
Brokaw
  Vernon   176
Brown
  A. A.   407
  Frederick C.   429
  H. B.   426
  M. Arthur   423, 425, 437, 439
  Sam   420
Brunkin
  Paul   152
Brynildson
  Pete   441
Bryntenson
  Art   217
Bulau
  Cheryl   449
Bunker
  Archie & Edith   227
Bunkers
  Jim & Mattie   410
Burke
  Bob   437
  Don   437, 438
Burns
  Ruthie   134
Burress
  Orville   150
Bush
  Ann & Marty   439
Buska
  Howard   184
Butler
  Chauncey   415
Butterwick
  Foster   409

C

Cairncross
  Alex   398

Campbell
  Arthur   176
  Edward A.   386
  Ernest   176
  Ortho H.   62, 426
Capone
  Al   80
Carlson
  Claris   401
  Dave   406
  Raeann   431, 437
Cary
  Mrs.   380
  Phineas "Pat"   396, 409
Casey
  Florence   338
  Patrick Joseph, Sr.   9, 27, 67
  Patrick Joseph "P. J." III   27, 311, 338
Cash
  T. I.   64-66
Cassady
  Wes   106
Cassidy
  Hopalong   140, *141*
Cetanwakuwa   14
Chase
  Geraldine   184
Chinnock
  R.   120
Christensen
  Jack H.   299
Christenson
  Mr.   154
Chubb
  E. C., Mrs.   397
Clark
  Scott   429
Clausen
  Herman   266-269
  Lenora   266-269, *267*
  Rudolph   268
Clouse
  Laura, Paul, Patty & Steve   430

Cochran
  Eddie   237
Colberg
  John   167
Coleman
  Frank   79, 82, 90
  T. E.   97
Collins
  John   242, *243*, 247, *263*
Colman
  Alma   2, 159
Colvin
  A. H.   81
Connor
  Dennis   368
  Mabel Shaw   146
Conrad
  William   137
Corbin
  Alderman   84
Chorzempa
  John   430
Costigan
  Tom   299, 301, 323, 436
Cottington
  Bruce   434
  John   435
Crawford
  Larry   299
Crockett
  Davy   137, 141, 142
Crow
  Little, Chief   14, *15*, 23-27
Current
  Dennis   217
Curtis
  Dale   191
  Harvey   194
  Judy   184
  S. D., Dr.   423
Cut Nose
  Chief   9, *10*, 24

D

Dahl
  Larry   329
  M. Raleigh   385
Dahlseid
  Roger A., Dr.   435
Dale
  Hazle   89
  Lymon & Sue   395, 396
Dalquist
  Suzie   388, 408
Danforth
  E. L.   60, 62
Daniels
  Eva   64-66
Danielson
  Lennox, Dr.   429
  Nels   9, 10, 12, 24
Dart
  Chauncey F.   437, 442
  Mrs. Charles H.   380
  Wait H.   444, 445
Dayley
  Ken   52
Dean
  John   254
Dedrickson
  Hubert   *184*
De Rosier
  David & Vera   395
Dickson
  Dr. William   62
Dille
  Donald, Dr.   9, 435
  Steve, Senator   9, 131
Dillinger
  John   78, 80
Dillon
  Matt   137
Dodge
  A. W.   385
Doebler
  C. W.   295
Doering
  Ray   394

Doffing
  Esther   397
Dollerschell
  Harper   390
Dols
  Mike, Pam & Paul   441
Domstrand
  Randy   303
Donnay
  Joan   437
Donnelly
  Dick   127
Doran
  Myrtle   96
Dorman
  Benjamin   9
Doubleday
  Abner   120
Drange
  Steven   429
Duchene
  Donna   438
Dueber
  Chuck   398
Duininck
  Holly Tostenrud   186
Dunn
  R. W.   420
Dylan
  Bob   243

E
Eastman
  E. M.   402
Eckberg
  Alvin   107
Ehlers
  Theodore   406
Eidenshink
  Kenneth   299, 322, 323
Eisenbacher
  Sue Wisdorf   423
Ekbom
  Louis   395
Ekstrom
  Per   424

Elam
  Sue & Wayne   424
Elj
  Nate & Ralph   68, 69
Ellig
  Don   431
Elmquist
  David   411, 425
Elofson
  Gladys (Rayppy)   See Rayppy
  Nels   13, 14, 43
Endersbee
  Danny "Parker"   296, 298
  Frank   294, 295
  Greg   294
Engelson
  Doug   *186*
Enstad
  Dick   412
Ericson
  Eldor   229
  Grandma   2
Erickson
  Willard   135
Esbjornsson
  Ericka   47
  Hugo   47, 49, 209
  John   47, 417
Evans
  Dale   145
  Sam   77, *85*, 88
Everly Brothers   250, *251*, 263

F
Falknor
  Bill   391, 400
Farley
  Tom   209
Farmer
  Dick   447
Farnquist
  Patricia   184

Farrish
  Robert "Bob"　　49, 50, 290
Favreau
  Lee　　294
Feistner
  Sam W.　　392, 397
Felling
  Bernard "Bernie"　　323, 410, 413
  Dollie　　414
  Ken　　413
Felt
  Howard "Howie"　　135, 202, 271, 296
Fenner
  George　　50, 100, 144, 296
  Jim　　296
Fenton
  Hugh　　293
Ferguson
  John　　394, 421
Fischer
  John　　182
  Red　　127
Fitterer
  Eugene　　158
Fladeboe
  June (Anderson)　　78, 83
Fleur
  Marcia　　325
Floyd
  Charles Arthur "Pretty Boy"　　80
Flynn
  Errol　　320
Foley
  Father　　188
  Michael　　36
Foote
  Gerald F.　　438
Forbe
  John　　410
Forester
  Charles　　435

Forsberg
  Frank　　388
Forsch
  Bob　　51, 52
Forte
  Nick　　413
Foss
  Claire　　183
  Marty　　299
Fransein
  Frank L.　　84, 202
  Wally　　84
Frasier
  S. W.　　121
Freed
  John　　96
Freelander
  George W. "Bud"　　447
Fritsche
  Fezz　　232
Fuller
  Jewell　　176
Fuhrman
  Cheryl "Cherie" Olson & Bill　　*197*

G
Gable
  Clark　　317, 323
Gaetti
  Gary　　53
Gagne
  Greg　　51
Gainer
  Art　　210
Gaisbauer
  Sharon　　440
Gardner
  Elmer　　84
Gartner
  Gerald　　420
Gauer
  Robert E. "Bob"　　389, 444
Gendron
  Harold　　442

Gerretson
 C. E., Dr. 77, 88
Gervais
 Paul 395
Gibney
 James 36
Gildea
 Donna *87, 90*
 Thomas 87
Gilman
 Donald 89
Glazier
 J. W. 409
Gleek
 Edward 18, 19
Glieden
 Mike 242, 254
Godfrey
 Arthur 167
Goran
 Conductor 40
Gordhammer
 Eleanor 78
Gordon
 Robert F. 398, 407
 Samuel Y. 436
Gorman
 David 402, 406
Gould
 William 432
Graphenteen
 LeRoy 274, 276, 277
Graf
 Larry 235
Grant
 Amy 358
Graves
 Abner 120
Greenhow
 Bob 300, 301, *302*. 407, 428, 443
 Nan 301, 407, 443
Greenleaf
 Charles A. 58, 61, 62

 William Henry 58, 394
Greep
 I. 418
Gribbel
 Edwin 6
Grono
 A. Fred 385
 William 389
Groskreutz
 Bob 401, 403
 Richard 401
Gross
 Emil C. "E. C." 208
 Gary P., Dr. 424
 Herb 302, 323
Grossnickle
 Danny *251*
Guggisberg
 Tom 441
Gunter
 Jim 196

H

Hackbarth
 Emil 95
Hagen
 Bill, Dr. 363
Haggart
 Vi 247
Hale
 Evelyn C. 322
Hall
 Laurie 411
Halonen
 Greg 431
Hames
 Judy & Lyle 446
Hankey
 Fred 42
Hanley
 William "Bill" 386
Hannan
 Bill 305
 Charlene 305-309
 Jim 123, 125-*128, 126*, 305-*309,* 412
 Joe 122

Larry	309
Hannula	
J. A.	93
Hanson	
Bob	425
Jack C.	393
Kermit B.	429
Peter E.	64, 67, 293
Nels	14
Happ	
Joseph "Joe" A.	385
Harder	
David, Dr.	*186*
Jim	271
William "Bill"	400, 401
Harding	
Eunice & Harold	408
Hardy	
Eldon	50, 268, 269
Lee	423
Harper	
Bill & Laura	416
Harmon	
Dale	399
John M.	292, 396
Harris	
Alice & Jack	189
B. E.	120
Virgil Homer, Judge	34, 383, 392, 397
Harrison	
Jim "Jimbo"	294-296
Hartmann	
Donna & Kevin	389
Hatch	
Charles	123
Hawk	
Charging	14
Hawkins	
Dale	237
Hayford	
Dick, John & M. T.	34
Heacock	
John	424
Heard	
Samuel A.	391, 392
Heath	
Dick & Karen	411, 413, 421
Hecksel	
Jeff & Kelly	395
Hedin	
Bob	420
Hedtke	
Clarris	418
Kelly	405
Heitmann	
Alice (Hipp)	83
Henriksen	
Lenny L.	435
Hensley	
Darryl "Mad Hatter"	*300*
Henslin	
Steve	241
Herbranson	
Joe H.	412
Herman	
Doug	*240*
Herr	
John	127, 128
Herzog	
Whitey	51
Heston	
Charleton	317
Hicks-Ewald	
Lisa Jo	411
Hines	
H.	121
Isaac	405
Hirman	
Mike	69
Hoar	
David	21
Hobbin	
Jim	434
Hokanson	
Don	68
Holden	
Thomas	*79*, 90

Hollaar	
Garritt "Garry" & Lee	287, 288, 293
Hollingsworth	
Samuel "Sam"	425, 426
Holly	
Buddy	250, 300, 449
Holmes	
Thomas G.	20
Holmgren	
Joanne	387
Julie	392
Holtz	
Karen	197
Hong	
Howard	85
Hoopes	
W. T.	62
Hooser	
Jim, Marshall	34
Howard	
Guy Garfield	72
Jacob M., Col.	*70*-75, 411, 414
Jacob M., Sr.	70
Emma Pennoyer	*70*-75
Howell	
C. B.	426
Hrbek	
Kent	51, *52*
Hughes	
Bridget & Tony	377
Darlene "Dar"	377, 449
Mary	9
Peter Allen "Pete"	*373*-377, 413
Hulbert	
Sally & Tom	409
Hukriede	
Dennis	427
Hultgren	
Johnny	88
Huberty	
David	314
Humphrey	
Hubert	362
Hunter	
Jack A.	45
Huston	
Jeff	430

I

Inselman	
Len T. "Buck Buck"	42, 43, 133, 149

J

Jackman	
Maureen	397
J. C.	67
"Stonewall"	38
Jacks	
J. C.	67
Jacobsen	
Ed	290
James	
Jesse	77, 91
Joseph	394
Sonny	231, 237, 263
Janousek	
Henry	388
Paul	388, 389
Jensen	
Hans	9
Mary	2, 159
Jensrud	
Ervin & Margaret	422
Jerabek	
J. H.	95
Jessup	
Terry	253
Johanneck	
Dick	302
Donna	427
Johnson	
Abe	106, 109-111
Albin	292
Arthur	88
Axel	135, 424
Barb	443

Bill	196
Bob	50
Bull	34
Doris	298
Emil, Mrs.	*87*, 90
George	109-113
Horace B.	398-400
Ida	196
James M. "Jim"	109, 111
Janelle	442
Jim	443
J. R.	109, 111
J. R., Mrs.	71
Keith	324, 325, 328
Linnet	*349*
Lois (Shaw)	*349, 355,* 449, *451*
Lorenz C.	404
Louis "Louie"	110
Marvin	269
Maurie	49
Mike	447
Nathan	17
Nicole	428, 438
Norma	444
Paul	109, 111
Ray	220, 394
Rich	416
Robert "Bob"	111
Rodney & Mrs.	*186*
Rosalind & Walter D.	109-111
Susan	411
Walter Jr.	110, 111
Van	*253,* 354

Jones

Casey	171
Edward D.	386, 387, 430, 435
Norman "Red"	302
Robinson	10, 11

Jorgenson

John E.	424, 425

Joubert

W. D.	31, 33, 120, 121, 390

Joyce

Pat	421

Juul

Carl	81

K

Kable

Gordon	418

Kahl

Rennae	391

Kaihoi

Bruce	397

Kalkbrenner

Kim	386

Kallevig

Craig & Crystal	411

Keating

Francis "Jimmy"	*79*, 90

Keller

David	423
Gottlieb "Jake"	432
Roscoe	3, 146, 286, 423

Kelley

C. M. (Fayette), Mrs.	443
Fayette	442

Kellman

H. J.	404

Kellogg

Bruce	423

Kelly

Gene	127, 128
George R. "Machine Gun"	78, *79*, 82, 90
Tom	51

Kent

Jon	298, 299

King

Smith D.	440

Kinsel

Bob	127

Kinsella

Bob	393

Kirchoff

Chad	421

Kjelland
  Irv & James   295
Klass
  Adam   432
Klitzke
  Herman   308
Klose
  Gary & Monica   *186*
Klug
  John   203
Kluver
  Brad A.   444
Knappen
  W. S.   398, 425, 440
Knights
  John   436
Knox
  Buddy   237
Koehn
  Jerry   193
  Steve   424
Koenig
  Phyllis   135, 294
Koerner
  August T. "Gus"   75, 424
  Butch   123
  Gottlieb C.   407, 431
  Gottlieb, Mrs.   97, 123, 380,
  Jacob "Jake", Sr.   397, 408, 432
  Karl   106
Kohlhoff
  Gene V. & Theodore W. "Ted"   434
  Jerry   217
  Terry   238
Koll
  Rich   401, 403
Kopp
  Michael   406
Kopplin
  Dorothea Simons   115-118, *117,*
  Edwin H. "Ed"   116-118

  Edwin, Jr.   115, 117
  Fred A. Jr. & Fred A. Sr.   117
  Rosemary   116
Kraehling
  Bud   136
Kragenbring
  Ron   299, 302
Krause
  Bob "Bobby"   *253,* 254, 354
Krawec
  George   418
Kreun
  Darrel   274, 276, 277
Kron
  A. W.   417
Krone
  Shelley   416
Krout
  Art   123, 182, 205-209, 211-215, *215,* 420
  Jacob   205
  Myrtle   214
Krueger
  Bill   149
Kuckler
  Jim   186
Kuhn
  Keri   386

L
LaBrie
  Fred   98
Lamson
  Birney   *26*
  Chauncey & Nathan   25, *26*
Langness
  Steve   439
LaRue
  Jean   18, 19
  Suzanne   19
Larsen
  Ole   422
Larson
  Alva "Al"   397

Dewey	251		**Lindberg**	
Don	17		Pete	229
Duane	399		Vernon	103
Louis	416		**Lindeen**	
Peggy	214		Roy	427
Latham			**Linderholm**	
Brad	405		Harry	191
Lawson			**Lobdell**	
Larry	293, 298		Lucy Ann "La-Roi"	
Leach			"Rev. Joseph"	6-8
Cecil, Dr.	330, 331		**Lockwood**	
Leaf			G. H.	380, 381
Randy "Uppercut"	393		**Lofstrom**	
Leaming			A. H.	431
Jeremiah	21		**Lohr**	
Learn			Sylvester "Spotty"	238
John M.	417		**Lombardozzi**	
Lease			Steve	53
B.	420		**Lounsbury**	
Leaser			Dwight B.	45
Joseph	411, 432		**Luhman**	
Leavett			Bob & Doris	418
Silas Wright	33, 389		**Lund**	
Lee			Levi	98
Dale	425		Peter J.	12, 13, 16, 23
Gypsy Rose	283			
Pinky	133		Sarah	13
Lenhardt			**Lunderby**	
Edmund	193		Stanley	*288*
Erhardt	193, 438		**Luoto**	
Irene	212		David	447
Rose	17		**Lutz**	
Lenz			Dean	423, 438
Chris	302		Dirk	439
Lewis			Joel	424
Jerry	356		**Lyon**	
Jerry Lee	230, 240, 243, 245, 250		George B.	426, 438

M

Lien			**Maass**	
Ann & Mark	389		Fred	401, 429
Harold	417		**Maccabe**	
Lies			Paul	78
Mark	430		**Macklin**	
Lincoln			Dr.	107
Abraham	24, 70		**Madden**	
			Jim	128

Madson
   Vernon "Vern"   324, 396
Majchrazak
   Jim   428
Manion
   Frank   205, 208
Mankovich
   Debra   395
March
   Charles Hoyt   75, 121, 293
   Nelson D.   121
Markovich
   Ron   442
Markus
   W. T.   64
Marshall
   Carol Schneider & George   186
Marstad
   Pedar J. "Pete"   229
Martin
   Dean   356
   Reuben   308
Matsen
   J. E.   93
Matthews
   William   92
Mattsfield
   Ann & John   397
Mattson
   Hans   417
Mayo
   Charles Horace & William James   10
   William Worral   *10*, 24
McCamy
   Curt   202
McCann
   John   36
McCarger
   A.   121
McCarthy
   A. M., Dr. "Doc" & Eugene   362
   Karen   397, 406

Mary Beth   See Yarrow, Mary
McClure
   Jim & Jo   430
   T. F.   67
McCormick
   Pat, Mrs.   2
McCune
   Charles & Mrs.   21, 22
McCurdy
   Elmer   55, *56*, 57
McEwen
   Cyrus   18
McGannon
   James A.   25
McGee
   Dan   303
   William S. "Mac" "Bill"   421
McGowan
   Elizabeth "Lizzie" & Sadie   394
   Father   280
   James   36
McHugh
   Gene   122
McKenzie
   Mike   *236*, 239, *240*
McLane
   R. H.   231
McQuay
   Warren   60
Meidal
   Darlene & Dave   436
   Dave   418
   Pat   393, 399, 418
Meis
   Julie   339
   Mr.   162
Menken
   Lorna   426
   Norman   438
Merkins
   Colleen   416

Merriam
  George   392, 393
Mickelson
  John   89
Mihlbauer
  Mike   418
Miller
  Capt.   422
  Dorothy   75
  Duane & Pat   413
  Israel   59, 66, 405
  Jill & Steve   430
  Johnny   122
  Keith   *248*
  Mike   302
  Mrs.   33
  Robert   299
  Vern   123
  Vernon "Verne"   79, *80*, 90
Mills
  Joseph   396
Minton
  Paul   447
Monson
  Mr.   13
Moore
  Dave   136
  Mary   437
Morales
  Alex   438
Morris
  James H.   415
  James M.   437
  Unknown   422
Morrison
  James   79, 90
Mortenson
  Chris   402, 430
Moquist
  Richard   437
Mullen
  John T.   62
Myers
  Charley & William H.   121
  Deputy   33, 34

N
Nash
  Frank   80
Neighbors
  Shirley   427, 443
  Steve   301, *302*, 427, 428, 443
Nelson
  Andrew P.   396, 425
  B. P.   396
  Charles   206
  Clarence   388, 444
  Frank T.   45, 97
  Henry M.   110
  Joe   213
  Mandy & Steve   428
  Ray   49
  Sandy   444
  Sigfrid W.   385
  Swan   13
  Wendell   429, 430
Ness
  Ole Halvorson   13
Neuman
  G. A.   417
  Henry   422
Newman
  Dick   235, *236*, 238, 241, 242
Nicholson
  Mark & Ron   427
Nixon
  Richard   362
Nolen
  Mary & William, Dr. "Bill"   325
Nonweiler
  Ann   447
Norbloom
  John   49
Nordlie
  Dick   217
  O. G.   293
  Polly   294

Nordstrom
  A. H. "Obbie"   78, *84*
  Laila   78
  Vance   84
Nygaard
  Dennis   108

O
Oberg
  C. A.   87
O'Brien
  Jerry   125
Ohland
  Dean   398
O'Keefe
  Jan   423, 434
  Jerry   434
  Julie   412
Okinajin
  Marpiya   9
Oliver
  Darlene   234
  Jeanette   4, 53, 197, 234, 299
Olmscheid
  John   408
Olmstead
  Connie   *230, 232, 236,* 238, 239, *262*
Olsen
  Chet   403
Olson
  Andreas or Anders   12
  Aslog   23
  Bill & Mary   443
  C. F.   78, 86
  Cheryl "Cherie"   See Fuhrman
  Debra & Matthew   428
  Earl B.   404
  Ed   62, 120, 387, 392, 394, 397, 401, 429
  Gregory, Dr.   127
  Jacob "Ollie" & Ray   213
  Jeff   419
  Jerry   239

  Leland   429, 430
  Nels   12
  Olaf M. "Feed Ole"   401
  Ole A. "Music Ole"   389
  Ole   43
  Paige & Steve   386
  Rich   274, 275
O'Neil
  William   88
Orbison
  Roy   250
Osbeck
  Charles   104
Osdoba
  Cathy   245, 296, 301, 317, 388, 392
  Nan   See Greenhow
  Pete   418
Osdoba-Palmquist
  Virginia "Peg"   418
Osdoba-Schelde
  Genevieve "Gen"   418
Oslund
  Joan & Ray "Red"   401
Osmunds
  Henry   89

P
Paffrath
  Rudy S.   77, *85,* 87, 90
Page
  W. W.   398
Palmquist
  Andrew O.   65
  O. M.   92, 93
Parker
  Danny   See Endersbee
  Fess   *142*
  Mr.   426
Patten
  Doug & Jo Anne   427
  John   397
  R. E., Dr.   430, 435

Patterson
  William "Billy"   437
Payne
  Josiah   385
Pearson
  "Jolly"   88
  Nels   434
Pederson
  Robert   438
Pedley
  Martin   213, 420
Peifer
  Arthur E., Frank A.
        & John C.   405
  Bob, Jr.   *233,* 234, 236, *262*
Peltier
  Bill   329
Peipus
  Roy   133, 278
Pena
  Tony   52
Pennertz
  Howard   122
Perry
  B. L.   394
  Marina   8
Person
  Ernest   83
Peters
  H. C., Dr.   403
Peterson
  Andrea Shaw   *147,* 163, 341, 342, 350, 353, 356, 357-*359*
  Charles Ellis   417
  Christ   66
  Doris & Russ   422
  Earl A.   84
  Ethan Ryan   *27,* 367, 449
  Gordon   416
  Karra Bree   359, *360,* 367, 368, 449
  Ryan   *357,* 359, 367
  Truls   434
  W. R.   419
Phelps
  G. B.   59
Piepgras
  David   440
Pierce
  Dave   421
  Kate   2, 403
Piepenburg
  Willard   52, 53
Pikal
  Wally   327
Ping
  Zheng Qiu   388
Pixley
  B. F., C.   394
  Mary L., Mrs.   121, 394
Plate
  Gale   426
Plath
  Warren   213, 420
Poirer
  Wayne   388
Polingo
  George   426, 429
  Margie Strey   408, 426, 429
Pope
  Orville "Orv"   106, 107
  Ray   106
Porter
  Charles O.   420
  Mary   41
Post
  Ann, Catheryn, Dan,
    Gertrude & Mathilda   102
  John & Lloyd   103
  Nick   102-104
Potter
  Bob   387
  D. E.   426, 439
Powell
  Bob   420
  Frank   27

Price
  Jerry 407
  Jim 247, *248*
Puckett
  Kirby 51
Putzier
  Don 209

Q
Quade
  Art 447
Quigley
  H. J. 404
Quinn
  Cora 380
  Harlan 187, 189, 190
  Tom 385
Quitney
  Randy 303, 443

R
Radunz
  Dorothy 408
  Ernie 166
  Ervin 268
  Harry 213
Ramsey
  Governor 20
Ramthun
  Mary 403
Rangeloff
  Evan "Dingo" 122, 133, 151
  Helen 158
  Virgil "Bud" 151, 155, *156,* 158
Rasmussen
  Claude 86
Rayppy
  Gary 235
  Gladys 13
  Sandy *186*
  Wayne 13, 43, 132, 286, 408, 427
Reff
  Alan & Gayle 426, 427, 429, 446
Regenscheid
  Renee 394
Reinke
  Arvid 213
Reitz
  Fred 385
Revell
  A. J. 62
  Nathaniel Frank 436
Revere
  Paul 19
Reynolds
  Burt 146
  R., Mrs. 415
Rheaume
  Grandma (Rose Anne Connor) 199, 344
  Grandpa (Louis) 68, 181, 199
  Helen 368 and See Young
  Robert 232
Richards
  William 6
Richetti
  Adam 80
Rick
  Wayne 436
Riebe
  Warren 429
Riele
  Warren 424
Ringhold
  John & Marilyn 437
Rising
  Henry G. 432
Robb
  Sherman *233, 234,* 236, *262*
Robbins
  George M. 84-88, 90
Robeck
  Caroline & Clinton 199
  Guy 199, 200

Robertson
  James W., Dr.   60
Rodgers
  Danny   426
Roehn
  Herb & Laura   395
Roeser
  Stan   205, 211, 215, 396
Roetzer
  Joseph   407, 438
Rogers
  John   50, 391
  Roy   140, 145
Rollins
  W. W.   433
Roman
  Axel   229
Root
  Mary C.   436
Rosenow
  Larry   127, 128
Ross
  Phil   325
Rothstein
  DeAnn & "Jiggs"   410
  Paula Berg   437
Rue
  Rebecca M.   430
Ruotsinoja
  Lowell   392
Rusick
  Mike   79, 82, 84, 86, 90
Rust
  Mrs. E. (Elizabeth)   443
Rutledge
  Dennis   434
Ryan
  Dik   301
  Jean   150
  Michael   36

S

Sabatke
  Don   299
Salazar
  Lois & Ted   400
Salzbrun
  Dan   431
Sandberg
  Ben   104
Sandstede
  Bob   388
Sandstrom
  Stina Greta   16
Savoie
  Agnes & Gordon   403
Saxby
  Chester   427
Scarp
  F. Edward   430
Schaber
  Jerry   128
Schaefer
  Cliff   44, 393
Schaps
  Robert "Bob"   419, 444
Scharmer
  Rolly   135
Schiro
  "Hub"   387, 409
Schlangen
  Paula   416
Schlauderaff
  "Larry" & Pete   427
Schlumpberger
  Norma Johnson   406
Schmidt
  Avis   144
  Cheri & Mark   406
  Clara   108
  Harold "Smokey"   108, 144
Schoell
  Peter   438
Schoultz
  George   190
Schranz
  Walt   213
Schreifels
  Andy "Monk"   189, 281, *288*

Donald "Pokey" 281
Schuermann
 Brigitte & Ellen *180*, 182
 Herbert *180*, 181, 183-186, *184*, *185*, 449
Schultz
 Bing 149, 176, 177
 Dean 159
 Delano 418
 Erlin 393
 Frederick E. 438
 Howie 127
 Patty 399
Schwartzwald
 Oscar 213
Schwenzfeier
 Rosalie Krussow 186
Scotch
 J. B. 300
Scott
 Bartles 89
 Hal 136
 Mr. 440
Scully
 Carolyn 408
Sederstrom
 Noel 301
 Vern 67
Selin
 John 89
Selvig
 Ed 78
Settergren
 Blanche 212
 Esther 132
 Gustav 117
Setzaphant
 Alvin "Bud" 247
Shaughnessey
 Michael 35, 36
Shaw
 Adrian 29, 357, *358*
 Alissa (Aleesa) 391
 Andrea See Peterson
 Bill 144, 260
 Catherine 70
 Charles "Charley" 406
 Christine 312-*316*, *315*
 Dean 143
 Dennis "Dennie" 2, *3*, 68, 143, 144, 160, *168*, 170, 173, 179, 213, 216, *217*, 219, *222*, *230*, 231, *232*, *233*, *234*, *235*, *236*,237-239, 245, 251, 254, 258, 259, 261, *262*, 263-265, 294, 295, 298, 299, 334, *335*, 339-341, 371, 372, 449
 Florian *260*, 368
 Karen 37
 Lois See Johnson
 Mabel See Connor
 Michael "Mick" *3*, 37, 46, 193, 213, 237-240, *240*, 241-243, *243*, 245-250, *250*, 253, 254, 259, *263*, *264*, 265, 299, 301, *335*, 361, 451
 Patrick "Pat" 2, *3*, 4, 37, 51, 53, 63, 122, 140, 141, 143, 144, 146, 149, *159*, 160-162, 164, *168*, 172, 175, 176, 187, 188, 191, 192, 194, 237, 239, 259, 264, 276, 280, 281, 283, 298, 299, 311, *335*, 336, 342
 Shirley 31

Terrance "Terry"	Too numerous to list. Pictures at *3, 159, 168, 175, 233, 243, 248, 250, 251, 253, 255, 259, 263, 264, 335, 355, 359, 360, 451*

Sheardown
Dr.	24

Shelley
James or Joe	125
Sharon	*230*

Shosten
Elsie	98

Shoultz
David "Mickey"	193
Guy	193, 197, 296, 449
William	193, 417
Sharon	296

Siebert
Dick	125, *126*, 128

Silverman
Harry	See Stein

Simmons
Bill	406, 407
Dick	183
Frank G.	73

Simons
H. W.	431. 433

Slater
Henry aka George Washington	7

Sletten
E. T.	83

Slinden
Bernice	197

Smith
Gary	394, 429
Mary Jo	447
Vern	384

Schneider
Lisa & Steve	441

Snell
Charles & Finley	36
John	429

Sparboe
Bob	384, 408

Spartz
Doug "Tamba"	239, *240*

Spaulding
A. G.	120

Speckman
M. L., Dr.	423

Spelliscy
J. H.	413

Spence
Albert or Allison "Van"	64, 122
Van Artis	122

Sperry
Albert H.	20

Stanton
W. D.	444

Steen
Mac E.	393

Stein
Sammy aka Harry Silverman	79, 90

Stenson
Henry	88

Stevens
Hamlet	59

Stewart
David & William	36
Marvin "Bill"	245, 396
Marvin "Marv", Jr.	245

Stoner
Mark	447

Stookey
Noel Paul	*361*, 364, 365

Strey
Margie	See Polingo

Strobeck
Charles Henry	34, 441, 442

Strout
Captain	20

Struxness
  Albert — 78, 86
Stuart
  Rick — 300
Stubeda
  Wally — 135
Sunburg
  Adeline — 78
Susa
  Mary — 393, 407
Sutterfield
  John — 427
Sutton
  Willie "The Actor" — 91
Swanson
  Eldon & LeRoy "Roy" — 403
  Emma & Esther — 102
  Hugo — See Esbjornsson
  John — 100
  Julie — 443
  Mrs. — 47
Swenson
  Arthur J. — 83, 84
  John — 84
  Larry — 393, 397

T

Tacheny
  Joe — 153
  Pam — 437
Tallakson
  Norman H. — 82
Taunton
  Peter — 421
Taylor
  Charles — 121
Tayoyateduta — 14
Teigen
  George — 425
Terry
  Bob — 434
  J. B. — 412
Teske
  Brad & Linda — 394
Theis
  Cindy & Jim — 446

Thompson
  Bonnie — 444
  Dave — *234*
Thorne
  Kathryn — 78
Thurston
  S. E. — 92
Tibbits
  Jason — 413
Tiemens
  Diane — 184
Tierney
  Jerry — 17, 411
Tiffany
  Ron — 427
Tileston
  C. M. — 384
Tinkham
  James — 401, 432
Tollakson
  Gary — 100
Tommeraasen
  Agnes — 78
  E. L. — 78
Tongen
  Cynthia — 399, 423
  Dean — 303
Tooker
  Carl — 398
Topping
  Charles Griswold — 432
  Oren Wilbert "Bert" — 384
Torgerson
  Marlin — 441
Tostenrud
  Arthur L. "Art" — 17
Tranby
  Tom — 422, 435
Travers
  Mary — *361*
Trelstad
  Oscar — 444
Troland
  Maynard — 299
Trueblood
  O. F. — 418

Tursso
  Wayne — 301

U
Urdahl
  Dean & Jerry — 298
Utz
  Dr. — 331

V
Valen
  Janet — 388
Valens
  Ritchie — 300
Valiant
  Deb & Larry — 446
Van Brunt
  Reid — 395
VanderPloeg
  Arlen & Sally — 400
VanNurden
  David — 184
  Jim — 431
  Kathryn — 122
Veenhof
  Dean — *273*, 274-277
Verby
  Dr. John "Jack" — 127, 128
Vick
  Dick — 313
  Sandy — *230*
  "Smokey" — 401
Vilhauer
  Russ — *248*
Vinar
  Jilane — 430
Vincent
  Gene — 230, 231
Viola
  Frank — 53
Viren
  Frank E. — 16, 17, 424
  Hedvig & Josephine — 16
  Nils Axel (Werin) — 16, 17
  Rose (Lenhardt) — 17

Vogt
  Eric — 434
Vold
  Jan — 408
  Michael — 424
  Newell J., Dr. — 424
Vorys
  Percy — 64

W
Wacker
  Marie — 84, 87, 90
Wadsworth
  Steve — 416
Wagoner
  Don — 68
Wakefield
  Leander L. — 39
Wakeman
  Thomas — See Wawinapa
Waldron
  John M., Judge — 387, 388, 414
Waller
  John A. C. — 66, 399, 421
Walstad
  Loren "Wally" — 241, *243*, *263*
Walters
  Hazle — 132
Wannow
  H. Robert "Bob" — 445
Ward
  C. D. — 391
Warta
  Floyd — *134*, 324, 328
Watkins
  Alvin "Alvie" — *238*, 270, 299
  Arnold "Ray", Donald, Emery, Harold & Marvin "Muck" — 270
  Maynard — 270, 271, 449

Wawinapa
　(One Who Appears or
　　Thomas Wakeman)　27
Weber
　Clarence　132, 213
Webster
　Viranus　11
　Mrs.　11, 12
Wegner
　Joe　106
　Hugh　435
　Mrs. Hugh　435
Weinman
　Jay　303
Welch
　Thomas　36
Welsand
　Kenneth & Laura Mae　403
Werner
　A. N.　32
　Curt D.　433
Wheeler
　Don "Donnie", Floyd
　　　& Yvonne　54
　Jerry　54, 183,
　　　229, *230,* 238, *239,*
　　　241, *242,* 245, 294
　Ray　54, 393
Whelan
　Dick "Dickey"　187-192,
　　　　190
　Fran "Frannie"　*190*
　Mrs.　189
Whitaker
　Edna　183
Whitcomb
　George C.　20
Whitney
　Walter C.　429
White
　George E.　121
　W. M.　131, 431
Wichmann
　John & Shonna　400
Wiley
　John　393

Williams
　Barbara　85, 86
　Esther　50
　Freddie　133
　Jim　447
　John　41
Wilmot
　Cecil, Dr.　49
　Harold, Dr.　156
Wilson
　Clara Davis　11
　Jacob H.　85
　Lowell, Dr.　104, 429,
　　　　435
　Myrtle　77, 85
Wimmer
　Brendan "Jopey"　271, 280
　Dougy　189, 192,
　　　　271, 276, 280
　Jerry　132, 189,
　　　　192, 270, *271,*
　　　　274-*277,* 280
　Kevin　271
Winger
　Andrew　425
Wisdorf
　Helen & Lawrence　67
Witthus
　Dennis & Wendy　387
Wogenson
　Walter　384
Wold
　Theodore T.　412
Wood
　Mark P.　430
Woods
　Clement "Dig"　36
　Pat　385
Wright
　Luther　441
Wu
　Chan & Kai Cheong　416
X
Y
Yarrow
　Mary Beth McCarthy　362-364

Peter	*361, 362,* 363
Young	
Floyd	108, 173, 196, 338, 340, *343,* 345
Helen	3, 108, 340, *341, 343, 335,* 368
John & Tina	386
Val	340
Younger Brothers	77, 78
York	
Bob	254

Z
Zhi
Zheng Ting	388